Rethinking State Theory

In the last two decades, objects of analysis such as 'the state' have increasingly been seen as uncertain and contested theoretical concepts. The very idea of the state as a recognizable object of analysis has been questioned. In this important work, Mark J. Smith presents the argument that existing theories of the state can be taken seriously as a way of addressing the present problems of understanding governance.

The book raises important questions to highlight how existing theoretical approaches can provide useful tools for understanding contemporary political developments. For example:

- Has governance deserted 'the state' as traditionally understood?
- Was the state always the primary focus of attention in state theory?

Against this background, Smith explores three well-known approaches in contemporary political and social theory: neo-pluralism, neo-liberalism and neo-Marxism, and explores the work of thinkers such as Dahl, Hayek and Jessop.

This work acts as a lively and accessible introduction to the way in which state theorists see society and the state. Furthermore, by exploring the connections between substantive claims about the relationship between state and society, and the assumptions and values at work in state theories, this book makes a vital contribution to our understanding of both political theory and political 'reality'.

Mark J. Smith is Lecturer in Social Sciences at the Open University and Visiting Professor in Philosophy and Methodology of the Social Sciences at the University of Oslo. He has been Visiting Lecturer in Social Theory at Queen's University (Canada) and in Critical and Cultural Theory at the University of Brighton. His recent works include *Social Science in Question* (1998), *Thinking Through the Environment* (1999) and *Culture: Reinventing the Social Sciences* (2000).

Routledge innovations in political theory

1 **A Radical Green Political Theory**
   Alan Carter

2 **Rational Woman**
   A feminist critique of dualism
   Raia Prokhovnik

3 **Rethinking State Theory**
   Mark J. Smith

4 **Gramsci and Contemporary Politics**
   Beyond pessimism of the intellect
   Anne Showstack Sassoon

Rethinking State Theory

Mark J. Smith

London and New York

First published 2000
by Routledge
11 New Fetter Lane, London EC4P 4EE

Simultaneously published in the USA and Canada
by Routledge
29 West 35th Street, New York, NY 10001

Routledge is an imprint of the Taylor & Francis Group

@ 2000 Mark J. Smith

Typeset in Garamond by Curran Publishing Services Ltd
Printed and bound in Great Britain by
St Edmundsbury Press, Bury St Edmunds, Suffolk

All rights reserved. No part of this book may be reprinted or
reproduced or utilised in any form or by any electronic,
mechanical, or other means, now known or hereafter invented,
including photocopying and recording, or in any information
storage or retrieval system, without permission in writing from the
publishers.

British Library Cataloguing in Publication Data
A Catalogue record for this book is available from the British
Library.

Library of Congress Cataloging-in-Publication Data
Smith, Mark J., 1962–
  Rethinking State Theory/Mark J. Smith.
  296 pp. 156 x 23.4 cm.
  Includes bibliographical references and index.
  1. State, The. I. Title
  JC11.S57 2000   99-053000
  320.P01--dc21

ISBN 0-415-20892-0 (alk.paper)

For Jane

Contents

List of figures   ix
List of tables   x
Acknowledgements   xi

Introduction   xii

1 Situating state theory:
  metatheorizing and critical exegesis   1

2 Empiricism, idealism, realism   13

   Introduction 13
   Empiricism 14
   Challenging empiricism 18
   Idealism 20
   Challenging idealism 37
   Realism 39
   Some metatheoretical reflections on state theory 51

3 Polyarchic civility and the state   54

   Introduction: two Dahls or one? 54
   *Behaviourist foundations: empiricist epistemology meets
      empirical realist ontology 55*
   The conundrums of power 66
   *Acknowledging complexity: towards a deontology of
      the future 72*
   Pluralism goes normative 85
   Imagining polyarchy I: facing the dilemmas 93
   Imagining polyarchy II: fulfilling the third wave 95
   Imagining polyarchy III: civic reorientation and equality 100
   Conclusion 107

4 The horizon of catallactic possibilities — 110

Introduction 110
Time and subjectivity: from praxeology to phenomenology 111
Knowing the social as mutual exchange:
  one principle and two postulates 119
Hayek and the use of knowledge:
  competition as a discovery procedure 126
The phenomenological constitution of liberty:
  rationality, democracy and equality 130
Rule of law as a political ideal: the two functions of the state 141
The model constitution and the dangers of discretion 147
Conclusion 156

5 Capitalism, the state and societalization — 158

Introduction 158
Exchange, power and institutionalization:
  the idealist foundations in Jessop's early work 161
Towards a theory of the capitalist state I:
  economy and polity 174
Towards a theory of the capitalist state II:
  ideology and polity 183
From corporatism to Thatcherism:
  characterizing the conjuncture 192
Towards the state as strategy 200
Autopoiesis and relative autonomy 204
The new synthesis: state theory, regulation theory
  and discourse analysis 209
Whither state theory? 217

6 Metatheorizing the state: preliminary conclusions — 222

Introduction 222
Dahl and realism? 223
Hayek and realism? 225
Jessop and realism? 233
Problems in realism 237
Some preliminary comments on
  further research in state theory 240

Notes — 246
Bibliography — 260
Index — 274

Figures

1.1	The conditions of possibility of the state	6
2.1	The covering-law model of scientific explanation	16
2.2	Bhaskar's analogical grammar of empirical realism	19
2.3	Rickert's four-fold definition of science	27
2.4	Kuhn's theory of scientific revolution	33
2.5	The logic of discovery	41
2.6	The empirical, the actual and the real	41
2.7	The recognition of transitive and intransitive domains	42
2.8	Causal laws and empirical regularities	43
2.9	Bhaskar's transformational model of social activity	47
2.10	Realist causal explanations	48
3.1	Dahl's conceptual terms of reference	59
3.2	Dahl's account of political beliefs	81
4.1	Hayek's conceptual terms of reference	137
5.1	Willer's representation of Dahrendorf's conception of interests	168
6.1	Empirical realism	237
6.2	Transcendental realism	237
6.3	Triangular formation 1: from abstract-simplicity to concrete-complexity	243
6.4	Triangular formation 2: a multidimensional framework for social-scientific research	243

Tables

2.1	Closed and open systems	40
2.2	Theoretical and practical analysis	50
5.1	Jessop's synthesis of functionalist, conflict and exchange theories	163
5.2	Blau's constitution of the social 1	165
5.3	Blau's constitution of the social 2	165
5.4	A brief outline of Parliamentarism and Corporatism	193

Acknowledgements

This study and the broader project of which it is an important part are the products of some years' work exploring the underbelly of philosophy of social science and social and political theory. I have incurred many debts in this labour and those I have not acknowledged here by name will, I hope, forgive me. Of particular importance in the formation of these arguments were the dialogues I had with William Outhwaite, Andrew Sayer, Luke Martell, Bob Jessop, Darrow Schecter, Peter Dickens, Mark Neocleous, John O'Neill, Jennifer Platt and especially the late Mary Farmer who pushed me in the direction of writers such as Hayek and Buchanan. Without the companionship and conviviality of friends such as Phil Larkin, Claire Donovan, Jules Morton, Annabel Tomas, Alan Buckingham, Andreas Hess and Zdenek Kavan, this project would never have been sustained in its early stages. I must also thank all the students who attended the MA in 'Cultural and critical theory' and the 'Concepts, methods and values' experience for letting me try out different approaches and for responding critically (as well as positively when things worked).

As the project unfolded I began to acknowledge the complexities of representation in my recent research on knowledge construction, which added an extra dimension to the arguments developed here. For this, I owe a great deal to colleagues at the Open University, namely Simeon Yates, John Blunden, David Humphreys, Lynne Slocombe, Stuart Hall, Kath Woodward, Jessica Evans, Vivienne Brown and Martin Le Voi. Chris Meeks also provided invaluable and ingenious secretarial support in helping me to juggle this and four other writing projects. I must also thank Craig Fowlie, Liz Brown, Joe Whiting and Simon Whitmore at Routledge publications, and especially Susan Curran at Curran Publishing Services, for their patient support and careful editing in the development of this project. Most of all, this text could only have been completed with the love and support of Jane, Harold and George.

Mark J. Smith

Introduction

Objects of analysis are not what they used to be. Despite enormous argument and considerable dispute about the proper focus and character of social scientific inquiry, there have been strong continuities in academic practices over time and across fields of knowledge as diverse as economics, psychology, sociology, geography and, our main concern here, political studies. We have experienced two centuries of disciplinarity where the study of the social has presumed that 'objects of analysis' are concrete things with a definite structure, or alternatively that they are constituted by a set of components accessible to some procedure of knowing. Whether we consider the constitution of the 'economy' as a *sui generis* object in the definition of economics, or the emergence of 'society', the 'mind' and the 'polity', in each case we can find an attempt to legitimize and promote a specific brand of inquiry. The emergence of disciplinary fields of knowledge is tied to the emergence of particular forms of governmentality in the institutions of the academy, yet each has been destabilized over the last two decades. Objects of analysis are increasingly seen as complex, uncertain and contested spaces. This is not the place to conduct an inquiry into knowledge transformation (see Smith 1998b, 2000a, 2000b) but it is possible to explore some of its implications for understanding theories of the state.

For the study of political institutions, then, this is a crucial juncture; a period of enormous transition and change where the very ideas of 'the state' as a recognizable object of analysis, and even 'the good polity' as a normative ideal, are now in question. Political studies is not the only area of social scientific knowledge to experience the cumulative dislocating effects of problematizing its own foundations. Do we discard decades of useful research on political institutions because the loci of decision making and agenda formation have moved to informal networks and co-ordinating mechanisms above, below and alongside the national state? In this study, I present an argument for taking existing theories of the state seriously as a way of working towards the present problems of understanding governance. Indeed, as the story unfolds, it will be demonstrated that many existing state theories have been preoccupied with the close relationship between political institutions and cultural conditions.

Each of the substantive bodies of political theory selected for this study indicates the need to look closely at the interconnections between the processes and relations which social scientists have placed under the disciplinary spheres of politics, economy, culture and society. Indeed, this text is the first step in a four-volume investigation into political institutions and cultural politics. In *Rethinking State Theory* I am concerned to investigate the connections between substantive claims about the relationship between the state and society, and the assumptions and values at work in state theories. This demands that we should pay close attention to the approaches to knowledge construction deployed and combined in theoretical accounts of the state. The subsequent three volumes will consider theories of governance (with attention to the substantive relations between political, economic and cultural dimensions of societalization), social policy, welfare and citizenship (considering the development of policy regimes through political participation), and finally, the ethical and cultural conditions of political discourse.

As you work through *Rethinking State Theory*, you will find that a number of questions are raised in order to highlight how existing theoretical approaches can provide useful tools for understanding contemporary developments in political institutions. Has governance deserted 'the state' as traditionally understood? Was the state always the primary focus of attention in state theory? Can we think of the state without acknowledging the sociality of politics (that all political institutions have cultural conditions)? To provide an answer for the first question (which is in large part the focus of the second volume in this investigation), this text focuses on the second and third questions. Throughout *Rethinking State Theory*, you will find that the approaches considered have been concerned with political culture and, as such, offer preliminary tools for constructing an appropriate conceptual vocabulary for understanding governance above, alongside, below and through the state.

This text considers how state theories can be understood more effectively when it is seen how they are situated with respect to both existing traditions of knowledge construction, and the social context which provided the institutional conditions and textual reference points of meaning production. To show this, I have adopted an approach which can also be seen in *Social Science in Question* (Smith 1998b) and *Ecologism: Towards Ecological Citizenship* (Smith 1998a). In fact, the research in this study was conducted alongside the writing of these two texts. The key to situating a specific approach is the identification of the assumptions and values in the knowledge-construction process, and in particular, the ontological and epistemological presumptions through which the character of objects of analysis takes shape, and the rules of conduct which govern how we can know about them. However, the point is not to pigeon-hole the approaches under consideration: theories are human products and are therefore usually too complex for this to be accurate or useful.

State theories, as human products, are complex, open to change, at times contradictory, and they tend to synthesize and articulate various ideas and arguments (or uses of evidence). Even when social scientists endorse a particular approach to knowledge construction or a tradition in social theory, we should tread carefully. Labels such as positivism, empiricism, idealism, conventionalism and realism are often deceptive; they are used differently by different people and approaches, and they are hardly ever applied in the way intended by philosophers concerned with scientific knowledge. In the studies within this volume, I hope you will come away with the feeling that we should never take such things for granted, and should always expect theoretical construction in the social sciences to be a complex business. My purpose however is not just to tell cautionary tales, but to indicate that a more flexible approach to knowledge construction can reap benefits in the concept formation needed to resolve new problems. In short, this study attempts to work towards a more adequate account of the state, political institutions and their cultural conditions. It is in this sense that this study is a metatheoretical one.

1 Situating state theory
Metatheorizing and critical exegesis

Why metatheory rather than theory? Many books have been written about *'the state'*; this is not one of them. The concern here is with the ideas, assumptions and values through which social scientists have imagined the state and its role in social relations. The idea of metatheory (literally beyond-theory) has a wide range of connotations, although it usually refers to the principles and assumptions which organize a particular domain of inquiry. In this case, since the domain is state theory, we are concerned with the assumptions behind the theories of the state. Another feature often attributed to metatheorizing is the implication that somehow we are one step removed from the research practices of gathering empirical evidence about actual states. To accept this criticism would imply not only that somehow theoretical concerns and empirical research are distinct activities marked by a clear boundary, but that descriptive accounts of actual states are not connected to our ideal vision of a good polity. As I have argued in *Social Science in Question* (Smith 1998b), nothing could be further off the mark. A useful and necessary corrective against such assumptions is the commentary by Charles Lemert in the opening passages of the anthology *Social Theory: The Multicultural and Classic Readings* (1993):

> Social Theory is a basic survival skill. This may surprise those who believe it to be a special activity of experts of a certain kind. True, there are professional social theorists, usually academics. But this fact does not exclude my belief that social theory is something done necessarily and often well by people with no professional credential. When it is done well, by whomever, it can be a source of uncommon pleasure.
> (Lemert 1993: 1)

For Lemert, theory has both uses and pleasure. Theory involves a wide range of metaphorical and metonymic devices, and metatheory no less so. If theory is the academic equivalent of a Swiss army knife, serving to uncork, chop into pieces, cut through, prise out, and occasionally lance the odd blister, in creating and organizing empirical evidence in the social sciences, then where does this leave metatheory? In this example, the metatheorist is engaged in the study of the design of theory, just as Swiss army knives are the product of design processes. A successful design is the product of past design successes and many design failures, or at least inadequacies. An effective metatheorist is therefore a reflexive agent responding to the application of ideas to concrete situations. However, while we may applaud such sentiments, this does no more than restate the tendency to divide the empirical, theoretical and metatheoretical into separate, if complementary, levels. The purpose of this study of state theory is to demonstrate the possibility of complex relations between these levels, so that the relations appear as interconnected dimensions, and the notion of separated levels no longer holds substantive weight.

Metatheorizing can take a range of forms, from the investigation of the influences of intellectual sources to the identification of metaphorical associations. Of the range of approaches which can be used to trace intellectual influence, a small number have had a significant role in defining the dimensions of this study, yet each in turn is limited by its rejection of other factors. One such approach, drawing upon the ideas of Quentin Skinner (1969), focuses upon authorial intention alongside the historical and social context of the author, as the basis for establishing the meanings located within intellectual work (Winch 1996a; Burrow 1981; Collini 1991). For J. W. Burrow, this is tantamount to 'eavesdropping on the conversations of the past' (Burrow 1987, cited in Winch 1996a: 28) and Donald Winch has commented upon the need to maintain an 'acuteness of hearing and sensitivities to tones of voice' (ibid.) within a body of texts. This form of evidence is certainly used within this study, particularly in Chapter Four, as demonstrated by the identification of Viennese intellectual circles as having an important role in the formation of Hayek's intellectual project.

An alternative empirical research method which can be used to identify intellectual influence has been developed in the field of the history of sociological research methods by Jennifer Platt, most recently in her account of *A History of Sociological Research Methods in America 1920–1960* (1996). Where Winch sought out competing voices in the original works of an author in order to reconstruct that author's attitudes and values, Platt searches for much more tangible empirical evidence of intellectual connections through citations, acknowledgements, archives, personal documents, correlative trends in research methods and interviews with sociologists from the period in question. This work provides a useful corrective to the tendency of sociological theorists to construct family trees of intellectual links on flimsy and in some cases inaccurate evidence, by tracing the origins of a particular perspective from the point of view of the present. These 'invented traditions' or 'origin myths' are, she argues, the product of a range of contingent factors such as the way in which a particular source casts light upon a tricky contemporary issue, or the use of a particular set of sources within those textbooks which claim to demonstrate an authoritative account of sociological classics. However, the author's intent, the context of the writing and the empirical evidence of intellectual influence do not, in themselves, provide an adequate basis for explaining or understanding the unacknowledged conditions, tacit motivations, and unintended consequences of intellectual debt in the work of particular contributors or of others in their field.

From the perspective of discourse analysis, Vivienne Brown adds another important dimension which is ignored when focusing on the meaning of a text solely in terms of 'authorial intent plus historical context'. She argues that the focus on the 'author' as the sole authoritative voice serves as a means of creating a canon (Brown 1994). This means that the production of meaning is a more complex affair than is often suggested within intellectual history. Brown's approach draws upon the contrast between 'dialogism' and 'monologism' developed by Mikhail Bakhtin (1981). A dialogic text carries an interplay of voices drawing upon a range of positions, while a monologic text has one voice which always seeks to have the 'last word'. By drawing upon Brown's analysis, as well using the techniques of literary criticism to identify their stylistic, figurative and rhetorical forms (in the senses developed by Derrida, Foucault and Rorty), we can begin to consider the complex play of meanings involved in theoretical work. These techniques provide a means of identifying the metaphoric strands which can highlight developing story lines in the works considered. Metaphoric strands can be identified in the accounts of 'polyarchic civility' in Dahl's work (Chapter Three), 'streams and pathways' in Hayek's account of time and the emergence of social order (Chapter Four) and , finally, 'society effects' in Jessop's account of the role of the state (Chapter Five). In each case, we will be able to identify the interplay of voices at work in the development of a convincing and plausible narrative.

Beyond intellectual history, we can also identify explicit attempts to develop metatheories in the social sciences. In sociology, George Ritzer (1992) provides a useful guide to the role of metatheory as a way of establishing reflexivity and maturity in a discipline. It is clearly the case that, as a discipline begins to feel comfortable and institutionally secure, the emergence of acceptable assumptions and values (which serve as the object of analysis for the metatheorist) can hasten the process of generating confidence, and stability through which knowledge comes to be taken on trust. In this way, it is possible to identify when a field of human knowledge has achieved a degree of legitimacy: when the 'official history' of a discipline becomes widely dispersed among the members of the discipline and, in turn, becomes part of their identity. In time, the body of theoretical references can grow to an immense size, and the major contributors come increasingly to be engaged in the metatheoretical identification and discussion of antecedents and sources. At this stage, the disciplines in question respond to these debates by linking contemporary contributors to the established corpus of beliefs. In addition, Ritzer adds that there are certain contingent factors which have led to the development of metatheoretical work within sociology. These include the emergence of a crisis in the way theoretical work has been done; the periodic effect of generational transition (when a cohort of sociologists dies and has to be replaced); and the emergence of a distinctly new approach which challenges the foundations upon which the discipline is based (such as the succession of structuralism by post-structuralism). He also argues that metatheorizing has emerged in response to the enormous growth of theoretical production, and the need to readdress the often implicit metatheoretical aspects in the classic texts within a particular discipline. Metatheorizing can be usefully, if in a simplistic way, divided into three forms.

- *First-order metatheory* involves the production of theoretical works which are themselves the creative synthesis of a range of approaches and sources.
- *Second-order metatheory* involves reinterpretations and narrative explorations of a range of existing bodies of thought.
- *Third-order metatheory* utilizes the existing body of knowledge in order to transcend a particular problem or dualism within the corpus of knowledge, such as the dualisms between necessity and contingency, structure and action, and macro and micro-orientations (see Ritzer 1992, ch. 1).

This metatheoretical investigation into state theory is primarily concerned with second order metatheorizing, although at specific points in the text there are clearly first-order and third-order concerns as well. In this study, I will concentrate on identifying and situating three state theorists by locating their foundational assumptions. It is important to note the changes in these foundational assumptions, particularly their epistemological and ontological terms of reference. Identifying these changes can help make it clear how and why theories of the state themselves change. This study is therefore a work of clarification and exegesis designed to serve as an under-labourer for the substantive reappraisal of contemporary state theory. At the close of Chapter Six, I will begin to suggest how a metatheoretical approach can help in understanding the state itself. However, to achieve this, it is necessary first to address the existing body of state theory.

Metatheories have also been developed through the application of the Kuhnian concept of paradigm, such as with Ritzer's own work within sociology. In this case, the concept of paradigm has been applied loosely, as a set of social practices which provide a distinct perspective for a community of intellectuals with common goals. To date, the metatheoretical techniques developed in the social sciences have presumed the use of one account of knowledge construction. It is often assumed that the adoption of a singular perspective from the philosophy of social science or the sociology of knowledge can serve as a conceptual tool (a 'one size fits all' strategy) regardless of the character of the object of analysis under investigation, or the adequacy of the research methods in play. However, this study breaks with the tendency to apply one perspective from the philosophy of science.

Instead, it seeks to establish the range of the epistemological and ontological principles and assumptions upon which a political theory can be based, and particularly to identify clearly the range of positions upon which existing state theories are based. To facilitate this, the second chapter is divided into three sections, devoted to empiricism, idealism and realism, with particular attention being given to a range of idealist approaches which are relevant to the case studies in the following chapters. In addition, these approaches have been outlined to demonstrate how it is possible to use a range of approaches in order both to clearly situate a particular form of state theory, and still to retain a basis for critical assessment. Of course, this does not exhaust the range of approaches to knowledge construction which exist in social scientific practice (see Smith 1998b for a wider survey). Their status is more heuristic than conclusive. As indicated earlier, this study also draws upon recent theories of language, discourse and culture to explore the role of narratives and the importance of telling plausible stories to specific audiences (ibid., chs. 6 and 7). One of the key themes I have addressed elsewhere is the inadequacy of the fact/value distinction and its role in maintaining the arbitrary description between descriptive and normative social inquiry (Smith 1998a, 1998b, 2000a; and to be addressed in 2001a, 2001b).

In social and political theory, a convention has emerged whereby we must consider normative theories about what makes a 'good polity' as clearly separate from studies which focus on the conditions, activities and consequences of actual states. This split of political studies into normative accounts of politics and substantive empirical work is a common one which derives from the empiricist distinction between scientific studies of facts and the ethical consideration of values. However, this convention misrepresents what theorists or researchers into politics and society actually do.

This study advocates two responses to the problem. First, in each of the three examples of contemporary state theory considered here, it is clear that ideas about what makes a 'good polity' are the product of detailed work on the operation of actual political systems and the social context in which states are constructed. Turning this around, it is shown in the following chapters how the study of actual states is never theoretically neutral or innocent, but is produced by drawing upon complex values and political orientations. So even at a basic level, whenever political researchers categorize states as 'authoritarian', 'democratic' or 'liberal', they are already involved in quite complex judgements grounded upon tacit systems of classification. Just as it is impossible to think about what a 'good' or ideal political system will be without investigating the politics of actual states, so too normative considerations are relevant every step of the way in the study of these actual states. All judgements are made within specific frameworks of knowledge which are already historically and culturally situated. As a consequence, the first response I wish to make is to argue that the distinction between theories of actual states and theories of the 'good polity' is unhelpful for understanding how the state has been understood within the social sciences. Instead, a practically adequate approach to political institutions needs to recognize the interconnections between them.

In the second response, the idea that political research should address actual states and/or theories of a 'good polity' also draws an artificial line between politics and the social and cultural conditions of existence of states. This is a function of the tendency to make a ritual distinction between 'the political' and 'society' in much of political science and social and political theory. Indeed, the following chapters will focus upon how state theories only make sense when it is explicitly considered how they are related to definite cultural practices. Later it will be argued that understanding the state depends on having a clear sense of the cultural conditions of possibility of both actual and imagined political institutions. This study argues that a more effective understanding of state theory can only be secured by thinking through the complex relations between the empirical and the normative concerns involved in research practice, and between the states and their cultural preconditions.

Putting these two responses together in Figure 1.1 gives an indication why state theorists have been misunderstood in the past. In the examples of the state theorists explored in the later chapters, it is possible to identify how they all work through their approach towards the state, both from a concern with actual social relations, and by thinking about the characteristics that would serve as appropriate cultural conditions for a 'good polity'. Of course, state theorists work through the relationship between the actual and the ideal in very different ways, because of their personal knowledge systems, cultural values and political orientations. As a social-scientific practice, research on the state is likely to discover considerable complexity and uncertainty. This study provides a useful indicator of how awareness of the assumptions and values can lead to a more effective and reflexive understanding of the knowledge produced.

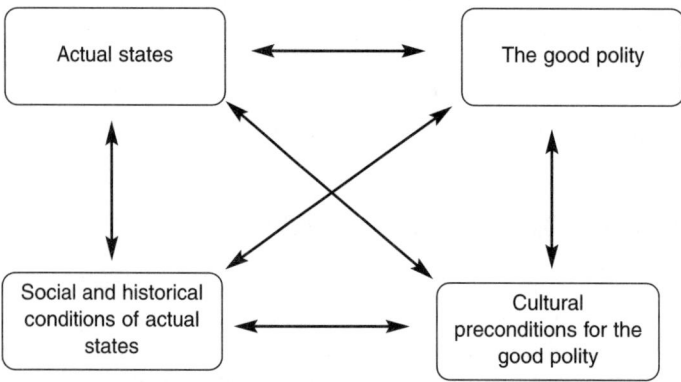

Figure 1.1 The conditions of possibility of the state

The remainder of this introduction concerns the task at the heart of this study, to identify how it is possible to understand the way in which state theories have been constructed. Three accounts of politics and the state have been selected and explored in some detail. This study establishes the contours of argument and the shifting epistemological and ontological foundations of the neo-pluralist theorist Robert Dahl, the neo-liberal theorist Friedrich Hayek and the neo-Marxist theorist Bob Jessop. Each belongs to a different generation of political theorists, with Hayek establishing his reputation as an economist in the inter-war years, Dahl as a political scientist in the post-war years, and Jessop as a political sociologist in the 1970s and 1980s. In the event, the positions they develop have a great deal of pertinence in the context of the various crises in the West since the 1960s. Dahl, following his work on the pluralist model of democracy in America in the 1950s, became a strong advocate of participatory democracy in order to remedy the faults of corporate capitalism in the late twentieth century. Hayek was consigned to the political wilderness for his anti-statist views during the Keynesian consensus of 1950s and early 1960s, but achieved prominence because of his association with Reaganomics in the USA and Thatcherism in the UK in the 1970s and 1980s. Jessop provides an example of a consistent neo-Marxist position (when many have deserted this cause), yet his approach remains sensitive to the need to reconcile Marxist theories with the actual historical and social conditions of advanced capitalism. In order to achieve this, Jessop turns to a variety of accounts of 'the social' and the relationships between the economy, ideology and the polity.

Despite these different contexts, political motivations and affiliations, the theorists selected highlight certain common features in the construction of state theories. There is a strong normative content running throughout the work of all three. This guides their investigations into actual political systems and directs their focus towards political power and the generation of consent in contemporary society. In addition, in each approach, there is a recognition that significant conceptual innovation is necessary if each is to deliver his respective intellectual goals. In particular, it is possible to identify how each theorist's treatment of social relations has a significant impact on his conception of the polity. All these approaches consider the state as a horizon or limit on social relations, although these social relations are understood and defined in different ways. Each of the state theories considered in fact advances an account of the 'sociality of politics': in the form of 'polyarchic civility' in Dahl's studies, 'intersubjective catallaxy' in Hayek's writings, and through the relationship between 'societalization' and the state in Jessop's accounts.

As you work through this study of the relationship between knowledge construction and social scientific practice, you will discover that biography meets hermeneutics, intellectual history meets contemporary social and political theory, situated theory meets abstraction, and exegesis meets critique. As a result, both in the senses of epistemological and ontological clarification, and in terms of the substantive political theory of those under

8 *Rethinking state theory*

consideration, this approach can be labelled one of a *critical exegesis* of state theory. Before highlighting the contents of the following chapters, I will consider this distinctive mode of inquiry in more detail. There is a tendency in all areas of research to look for simple answers to complex problems. In many ways, the approach adopted here is a response to the difficulties encountered in seeking simple, immediate and direct causes to explain complex phenomena in uncertain conditions. Certainly, establishing the intellectual influences at work in any form of theoretical work presents its own difficulties. Theories are social products, and the production of meaning involved in any theoretical intervention (including the relationship between the writer and the existing literature, the cultural conditions of the writer, the relationship between the writer and reader and so on) is characterized by considerable complexity. Assumptions are often left implicit and the practical and intellectual conditions of theoretical construction are often left unacknowledged.

Theoretical construction involves the production of meaning and, as such, raises four main concerns for any metatheoretical analysis. First, and perhaps the most immediate concern, theories attempt to represent the character and effects of a substantive object of analysis, in this case, the state. Even at the most basic level, how we define 'the state' will be shaped by how we negotiate the relationship between the actual and the ideal. This involves the recognition that all theories carry normative messages, that is, they all seek ethically to evaluate politics. Second, as part of the complex practices involved in representation, theories involve the construction of stories and narratives which, if the theory is to have any plausibility, resonate with, and make sense to, a specific audience. Third, these theoretical approaches are grounded upon definite assumptions about the construction of authoritative knowledge (the epistemological issues). Fourth, all these levels are grounded upon a more or less explicit understanding of 'reality' (the ontological issues). In each of these four levels there is considerable variety, although it is possible to trace ways in which, for instance, particular epistemologies appear to have coherence when combined with particular ontologies.

This study does not attempt a fully-fledged account of these concerns, but simply points to their importance when considering the way in which state theories are constructed. In short, if we are to understand state theorists, then we have to anticipate complexity in the theoretical systems they devise and elaborate during the course of their research. In summary, a critical exegesis of any body of theory should attempt to understand the following six dimensions.

- Identification of intellectual projects devised by state theorists: *the normative dimension*.
- Exploration of the narratives and story lines in state theory: to establish the role of analogy and metaphor within the work of a writer or group of writers (or a school of thought).
- The situation of state theorists in definite historical, cultural and

intellectual locations in order to identify sources and parallels with other texts or systems of thought which may have had some impact.
- A consideration of the ways in which state theorists study the institutional practices of actual states (their conditions, organization and effect).
- A consideration of the representation of the object of analysis in theory, in this case, the way in which the state is represented with reference to the established texts of social and political theory.
- An identification and elaboration of the foundational assumptions of the state theory in question, in both epistemological and ontological terms.

In effect, critical exegesis involves an exploration and a reinterpretation of the narratives of existing theories (which is, in Ritzer's terminology, a second order metatheoretical analysis) in order to identify how theories synthesize a range of ideas, assumptions and values from existing bodies of knowledge (that is, first-order metatheory). As a consequence, a critical exegesis of state theory serves as an under-labourer for any attempt to resolve the dilemmas and problems produced through theorizing the state, which pose a barrier to understanding (that is, third-order metatheorizing).

In order to identify the complexities involved in the intellectual positions explored, Chapter Two provides a map of much of the contested terrain of the philosophy of the social sciences. This takes the form of an account of empiricist, idealist and realist approaches to knowledge construction. The use of these divisions is necessary for the purpose of epistemological and ontological clarification in state theory. Indeed, it will be demonstrated that Dahl, Hayek and Jessop bridge these distinctions in both synchronic and diachronic ways. At times the state theorists in question synthesize different approaches to knowledge construction, and the mix of ideas within their work clearly changes over time. By drawing upon the distinctive conceptions of causality (the status of causal laws in relation to 'constant conjunctions of events' or empirical regularities), the awareness of social complexity, and the various relationships posed between experience, knowledge and being in different accounts of natural and social science, it is possible clearly to identify elements of continuity and moments of rupture in these accounts of the state and politics. This will not, therefore, involve a crude reductionist attempt to fit these state theories into a set of preconceived pigeon-holes. However, this study does contend that it is possible to follow the development, and establish the synthetic qualities, of a particular approach by identifying the processes of concept formation involved.

In this study, the use of critical exegesis has enabled the identification of aspects of intellectual formation in the work of Dahl, Hayek and Jessop which have been overlooked by contemporary social and political theory and intellectual history. In particular, it has been possible to identify substantial evidence of continuity in the works considered, which raises doubts about attempts to periodize these approaches in the form of a series of breaks and definite stages. In addition, this raises the prospect of viewing such work as examples of the synthetic combination of ideas and evidence, rather than placing them within simplistic oppositions between predetermined approaches to politics, society and knowledge. In particular, it suggests that it is misleading to consider the processes of intellectual formation in terms of an identification with well-defined political projects, without engaging in a sensitive treatment of the epistemological and ontological assumptions involved in each body of theory. The range of approaches from the philosophy of social sciences raised in Chapter Two is by no means comprehensive, and the choice of empiricism, idealism and realism is a reflection of what is relevant to the discussions of the following chapters. In particular, a much greater amount of attention has been given to idealist compared with empiricist approaches, in order to provide a more useful means of mapping the shifts and syntheses of assumptions in the writings of Dahl, Hayek and Jessop. This is an area often neglected in recent debates in the philosophy of social science (where contrasts are often made between empiricism and realism).

In Chapter Three, the focus is on the evolving pluralist position of Robert Dahl on the state, democracy and civility. Attention is given to the epistemological shifts in Dahl's account of polyarchal democracy, and how this account moves in parallel with the movement from an apparently descriptive to an explicitly normative stance, as he develops a case for the democratization of economic enterprises. This politicization of pluralism is often characterized as a move from classical pluralism to neo-pluralism. However, it is possible to demonstrate both ontological continuity in Dahl's work, and an ongoing commitment to the construction of an account of politics grounded upon certain assumptions of civility. This establishes a strong theme within the works considered in the following chapters, that state theories are as much about the sociality of politics (if not exclusively so) as about the state itself.

Chapter Four turns to the interdisciplinary work of Friedrich Hayek, and his associations with the intellectual circles which provided a unique dynamic core to his critique of 'scientistic' assumptions in social science. Unlike Dahl's approach, Hayek's work is explicitly normative throughout his intellectual development. This provides an important basis of continuity running throughout his interventions in economics, psychology, social scientific methodology and, the main concern here, the conceptual clarification of state theory and political philosophy. However, an investigation of the epistemological and ontological foundations of Hayek's thought reveals that his position is unlike (if not hostile to) that of rational choice theory and other rationalist accounts of markets and states. While other neo-liberal thinkers shared his emphasis upon the role of individualism and subjectivism in their analysis of social processes, Hayek went much further in questioning the assumptions of both empiricist and rationalist social science. (The role of phenomenological assumptions within Hayek's political philosophy is outlined here but considered in detail in Smith 2000b.)

It is the contention of this chapter that Hayek shared with other notable

Austrian refugees a conception of social life grounded in a particular branch of phenomenology. This was most influentially articulated by Alfred Schütz. Hayek's identification of the temporal, communicative and meaningful dimensions of markets prompted him to reconceptualize the market as catallaxy and exchange relations as mechanisms of mutual discovery. This goes against the tendency of market theorists to treat markets as composed of autonomous and atomised individuals. The shift of focus towards political philosophy in Hayek's work from the 1950s also reveals affinities with Schütz's account of concept formation. In this account, discussion of the specific character of political institutions is subordinated to Hayek's preoccupation with the social and political conditions for enabling the emergence of the spontaneous order. As a result, the state becomes the 'horizon' or limit on catallactic possibilities rather than an object of analysis in its own right.

Chapter Five considers the more recent work of Bob Jessop on the state over the last thirty years. In the intellectual formation of Jessop's work we can identify the emergence of an initially-submerged normative stance, and the development of a sophisticated neo-Marxism. Jessop attributes enormous significance to the capitalist economy in state theory, but he also attempts to develop a non-essentialist account of politics and other cultural and social spheres. To break through some of the logjams in neo-Marxist state theory, Jessop utilizes a range of tools drawn from approaches which can identified as both idealist and realist. The synthetic mix of concepts and theoretical assumptions creates a complex epistemological and ontological framework upon which to construct a theory of the state. Nevertheless, the emphasis upon state formation in relation to economic processes, and the treatment of the state as the horizon of the capitalist economy and social relations, raise interesting comparisons with both Dahl's and Hayek's accounts of the sociality of politics, and beg the question whether any of these approaches really do offer a state theory.

The final chapter addresses these questions within the context of recent claims about the realist character of the work of Dahl, Hayek and Jessop. In the case of Dahl and Hayek, the claims of realist insights have been made by others. Jeffrey Isaac has identified what he claims to be realist assumptions in Dahl's account of the preconditions of pluralist democracy. Tony Lawson is representative of recent attempts to appropriate Hayek's account of knowledge for the realist approach. Jessop, however, explicitly situates himself within the realist camp, despite drawing extensively upon concepts developed in idealist and discursive intellectual approaches. Another important dimension is the association of realist thought on science with political projects for transformation and emancipation. Clearly, in the case of Dahl's advocacy of participatory democracy, Hayek's calls for the frontiers of the state to be rolled back, and Jessop's affiliation with political projects for socialist emancipation, there are grounds for reassessing this relationship.

The purpose of this final chapter is to assess the accuracy of these claims and identify what it means to be 'realist' in the light of them. In particular, the realist account of the ontological and epistemological basis of idealist approaches is reassessed. The point of this study is to problematize rather than challenge the status of epistemological and ontological assumptions; to raise questions about the willingness of some social scientists to draw battle lines between different approaches to knowledge construction. There remains a tendency to treat philosophies of social science as an authoritative benchmark, as a last resort in authenticating arguments. If we acknowledge the complexities of social scientific practice, then since knowledge construction is also a social activity, we should take care with epistemological and ontological claims.

2 Empiricism, idealism, realism

Introduction

This chapter seeks to demonstrate a range of relevant positions in the philosophy of the natural and social sciences in order to provide a heuristic framework for identifying the often subtle shifts that can take place in social scientific practice (in this case social and political theory). The point of the chapter is not just to provide a literature review of the approaches to knowledge construction which are relevant to state theory (approaches which I have grouped together as empiricism, idealism and realism), but also to use these approaches to situate the three kinds of state theory considered in the following chapters. The point of the technique of critical exegesis, however, is not just to situate social and political theories, but to offer an epistemological and ontological assessment of their assumptions. This enables us to identify the tasks which should be addressed in the development of an adequate account of the state in contemporary societies. Inevitably, a number of positions receive a sharper focus than other alternatives, for the size and scope of this chapter is dictated by the concerns of the substantive social and political theories to follow.

The threefold division adopted here of the approaches from the philosophy of the social sciences into empiricism, idealism and realism is designed to highlight the three different conceptions of causal laws which feature in different approaches to knowledge construction. By focusing on different conceptions of causality, it is possible to identify how each approach deals with the problems of specifying the relationships between theory and observation, facts and values, and explanation and prediction. These differences provide valuable tools for tracing the development of a particular intellectual project (in state theory or in other fields of knowledge), and for conducting an examination of theoretical syntheses in these projects where the central assumptions are drawn from more than one of these approaches. Whenever attempts are made to identify the epistemological and ontological assumptions of a body of intellectual work, there is a tendency to drop the work in question into a preconceived pigeon-hole. It is useful to remember Pierre Bourdieu's advice on the uses of classification systems, that they tell us more about the classifier than the classified (Bourdieu 1986).

14 *Rethinking state theory*

In this study, I have attempted to demonstrate how intellectual projects are often eclectic and synthetic. Therefore, it would be more accurate and effective to work from the premise that an explanatory account of an aspect of social life may draw from a range of sources, use various analytical devices, and bring together a range of epistemological and ontological assumptions. Theoretical synthesis is usually a response to the inadequacies of an existing body of knowledge when dealing with new sets of problems or the anomalies contained within the knowledge system in question. However, such innovations often generate their own contradictions and tensions. In Chapters Three, Four and Five, I demonstrate how state theory can be read epistemologically and ontologically. This makes it possible to identify the different ways in which ideas and assumptions are strung together, as well as demonstrate how they can change in response to new problems and the emergence of new ways of defining objects of analysis.

Each of the state theorists selected address the central problems in his field of work and, as such, serves as an exemplar of his tradition. Each also offers us an opportunity to explore some of the practical issues involved in identifying the complex combinations of epistemological and ontological assumptions which can take place.

- When an intellectual project undergoes a reorientation of epistemological and ontological assumptions (as in the shift from empiricism to idealism in Dahl's work).
- A synthesis of positions within a broad epistemological and ontological approach (as in Hayek's synthesis of elements from different idealist approaches).
- A synthesis of different epistemological and ontological approaches (such as Jessop's use of elements of both idealist and realist approaches to knowledge construction).

In short, to metatheorize state theories is to situate them in epistemological and ontological terms. This chapter, then, provides a review of these approaches to knowledge construction drawn from the philosophy of natural and social sciences (with particular attention to the conceptions of causality in empiricism, idealism and realism) in order to make the subsequent analysis of state theory itself possible.

Empiricism

Empiricism has been so deeply rooted within the social sciences that it has often formed the taken-for-granted common sense assumption upon which much social scientific practice is based. Following the eighteenth-century divorce of science from the concerns of philosophy, epistemology and critical thought, a very solid idea of what constitutes science came into existence. This served as a point of departure both for those who wish to transpose the logic and methods of natural science to the social sciences (naturalism) and for those who oppose this approach to studying 'the social' (anti-naturalism). Either way, the scientific method was conventionally portrayed as the most rational and objective approach towards the real world (natural or otherwise) and the source of a cumulative body of knowledge through which the mysteries of life would be resolved. Anti-naturalists merely disagreed whether such an approach was applicable to meaningful and unpredictable social life. However, given the often messy and discontinuous nature of the development of science, a huge gulf exists between the practice and ideology of science. Indeed, as Peter Manicas states, 'the very idea of science is contestable' (Manicas 1987: 3). Therefore it should not be surprising that empiricism has been subject to a series of increasingly effective challenges.

These challenges to empiricism have been made on the grounds of its inadequacies in dealing both with the role of interpretation and agency within scientific practice, and with the complex nature of causality in natural and social relations. Manicas draws a useful analogy between empiricism (characterized as 'naive' realism) and a 'house of cards'. He suggests that the whole edifice of empiricism, which is composed of various elements, is supported by a 'pair of cards' (that is, two responses to problems) which would collapse if these two cards were withdrawn. First is the response to the metaphysical problem of the 'external world', whereby empiricism adopts the neutral route of establishing the objects of analysis through 'sense-data', in terms of experience. Second is the problem of causality, which is resolved in the Humean way. This involves the generation of general statements based upon regular relationships between clearly identifiable, and thus measurable, variables. This establishes a clear cause and effect relationship which appears to be plausible within the existing body of knowledge on such matters (Manicas 1987: 244). Within the empiricist approach, the truth of such statements cannot be known by a priori means but only through the accumulation of empirical evidence from experimentation and/or observation, with all else conceived as fictitious accounts based upon mere speculation or 'objectionable metaphysics'. For the empiricist tradition, these procedures simultaneously produce explanatory and predictive knowledge of the external world (Keat and Urry 1982: 4–5). As Jeffrey Isaac usefully expressed it:

> Laws are understood as conditional empirical statements whereby given a general law and a statement of appropriate initial conditions, events can be deduced from the law. It thus follows that on this view, explanation and prediction are seen as 'symmetrical'; to be able to predict an event is to have explained it by bringing it under a covering law; and to be able to explain an event is simply to employ 'retrospective prediction'.
> (Isaac 1987a: 20)

Within this approach, scientific explanation becomes simply a form of logical argument, in order to establish the necessary and sufficient conditions for a given object of analysis (along the lines of Carl Hempel's covering law model (Hempel 1965)). This is represented in Figure 2.1. Such a formal logical explanation can assume a variety of forms, although they can generally be identified as following either an 'inductive' or a 'deductive' model of scientific enquiry. The former involves a process through which it is assumed that a scientist gathers evidence in order to infer general laws. Hence, the 'truth' of a statement is confirmed through the accumulation of evidence, or verification. This approach has been widely, and quite rightly, criticized for treating the mind as a passive receiver of sense-data: in Popper's terminology, a bucket theory of mind. In the case of deduction, the process through which valid conclusions are deduced from valid premises, one proceeds from general law statements (within specified antecedent conditions) to explain and predict particular cases (Keat and Urry 1982: 12–13; Hacking 1983: 2–6).

The most widely respected, and hence influential, version of the deductive model is Karl Popper's 'hypothetico-deductive method', generally known as 'falsificationism'. This is an 'idealized reconstruction' of the process through which scientists construct their theories and weigh up their hypotheses against the empirical evidence. For Popper, scientific advance can only come about through the testing and attempted falsification of hypotheses which, if necessary, are replaced by modified or new hypotheses. These in turn are subject to the continual process of conjecture and refutation, a sort of trial and error methodology. Statements which cannot be empirically tested are simply designated non-scientific or tautological, and theories composed of such statements are dismissed as 'pseudo-sciences'. Popper specifically identifies psychoanalysis and Marxism (alongside astrology) as such approaches. Taking the latter case, Popper suggests that Marx made categorical rather than conditional claims about the nature of capitalism. For instance, he argues that Marx believed that the interests of capital always overcome the interests of the workers within the capitalist system. He also argued that Marx made a series of predictions which have not been borne out by experience, regarding the laws of motion of capitalism and the historical inevitability of revolution in advanced capitalist societies. So according to Popper's criteria, Marxism falls far short of the scientific method on a number of counts (Popper 1957, 1959, 1963).

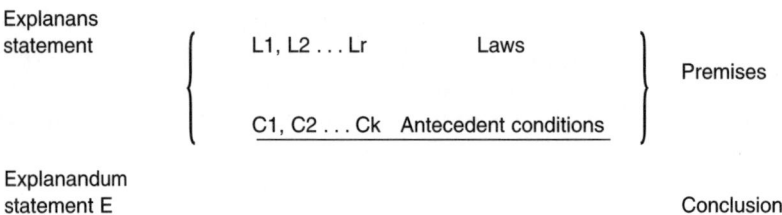

Figure 2.1 The covering-law model of scientific explanation
Source: Keat and Urry 1982: 10

In response to earlier positivist approaches, Popper claimed to have solved the problem of induction. He argued that without an original conjecture one would not know where to start or which knowledge to seek, that there is no way of arriving at a theory simply from experiment and/or observation. Hence, falsification rather than verification becomes the criterion of science and science itself becomes simply a *method*, a set of logical procedures for the construction or testing of hypotheses, a process of 'trial-and-error', rather than the search for some universal or objective truth. This approach is the only one compatible with Popper's liberal assumptions about what should constitute an 'open society', whereby each possible explanation of events is scrutinized in an open-minded and sensible way within an atmosphere of tolerance. Conjectures or hypotheses which survive attempts at refutation, while they are not seen by Popper's approach as true, are nevertheless seen as 'corroborated' (Popper 1963, 1969, 1972).[1]

Despite such wide differences regarding the relationship between theory and observation, the inductive and deductive programmes share a great deal in common, especially over the fundamental issues of causality and rationality. This battlefield, rather than being strewn with dead bodies and mortally wounded scientists, is reminiscent of a ritual mock battle by the English Civil War Society, with a great deal of smoke but very little real conflict. Hacking provides a neat summation of the superficial differences between Popper and Rudolf Carnap (a verificationist):

> Carnap thought that 'meanings' and a theory of 'language' matter to the philosophy of science. Popper despised them as scholastic. Carnap tried to explicate good reason in terms of a theory of 'confirmation'. Popper held that rationality consists in 'method'. Carnap thought that knowledge has foundations; Popper urged that there are no foundations and that all our knowledge is 'fallible'. Carnap believed in 'induction'; Popper held that there is no logic except 'deduction' . . . whenever we find two philosophers who line up exactly opposite on a series of half a dozen points we know that in fact they agree about almost everything. They share an image of science.
>
> (Hacking 1983:4–5)

At the end of the day, in terms of what scientists actually do, there is not a great deal of difference between 'corroboration' and 'confirmation' except in terms of which formal logic such scientists adopt as their background frame of reference and mode of presentation. Even so, they still agree upon the 'pretty sharp distinction between observation and theory', that 'the growth of knowledge is cumulative', that 'science has a tight deductive structure', that 'scientific terminology is or ought to be precise' and that there should be a 'unity of science', that all sciences should utilize the same logic and methods (Hacking 1983: 5). On the big issues it is impossible to slip a cigarette paper between them.

Challenging empiricism

To understand the differences between empiricism, idealism and realism, this chapter focuses on the idea of 'causality' and what it means to different approaches to knowledge construction. To do this, I have drawn upon the arguments developed in Roy Bhaskar's *A Realist Theory of Science* (1978). This account of the conditions of possibility of science provides us with a useful interpretive framework for identifying the weaknesses of 'classical empiricism' (hereafter labelled empiricism) and idealist and realist responses to these weaknesses. In particular, it indicates how the facade of value freedom associated with empiricist accounts of social science conceals many unacknowledged normative implications in supposedly factual accounts. Empiricism is attractive for its claim to be able to deliver law-like predictive generalizations about behaviour (subject to the rules of verification or falsification) with the ultimate object of analysis being atomistic events and their conjunctions (Bhaskar 1978: 24). For empiricists, this means that any talk of underlying causes and natural necessities can be dismissed as metaphysical nonsense. This relationship between knowledge and reality can be described as one of 'isomorphic correspondence', which is in turn tied to the distinction between theory and observation identified earlier. For empiricism, theory can be taken to represent universal statements or laws, while observations involve the creation of particular statements. Theoretical statements do not involve an ontological commitment to the unobservable, but only to that which can be established through experience. Theory (the non-observational) and observation (the non-theoretical) are to be taken as mutually exclusive, and thus the truth or falsity of a statement can only be verified or falsified by reference to the observed natural world (Keat and Urry 1982: 17–22).

The terms of reference of the empiricist approach specifically exclude any discussion of the relationship between the 'transitive dimension' of scientific activity, the philosophical conventions which fashion knowledge at a given time and place, and the 'intransitive dimension' of real causal mechanisms existing, operating and enduring quite independently of discourse (Bhaskar 1978: 26). For Bhaskar, empiricism involves a double mistake for it only recognizes causal laws by reference to actual events (ibid.: 34–5). This latter point presupposes the ubiquity of closed systems, whereby both the intrinsic state of the object of analysis and the external forces of a given situation remain constant, as in the field of experimental science. This simply assumes that, within a closed system, an event of type A is invariably accompanied by an event of type B ('whenever this, then that') with the concept of cause defined by a total set of conditions that regularly precede and accompany an event. Such 'regularity determinism', according to Bhaskar, unnecessarily restricts both the ontological presuppositions and the methodological responses which can legitimately be classified as scientific (ibid.: 69–71; Smith 1998b, chs. 2–3).

Use of the realist approach developed by Bhaskar helps us to pinpoint the close connections between epistemological and ontological assumptions in the empiricist approach. Bhaskar identifies how empiricism, as a procedure for knowing, is founded upon the broader position of *empirical realism* (indicating what can be known) which he describes as being more than an implicit ontology based upon the category of experience. For Bhaskar, empirical realism also involves an implicit sociology based upon the *model of man* which conceives men (sic) as passive 'sensors of given facts and recorders of their constant conjunctions: passive spectators of a given world rather than active agents in a complex one' (Bhaskar 1978: 198). This in turn generates an ontological atomism and, in common with the bulk of empiricists (excepting the positivist organicist approach such as that developed by Auguste Comte), a predisposition towards epistemological, methodological and political individualism. If the world were not constituted of perfectly simple and atomistic items independent of each other then, within this approach, its constitution would be susceptible to analysis and hence demand justification (ibid.: 241–4). Empirical realism can be seen as deriving from three sources, which can best be represented in the form of a complementary triangle (see Figure 2.2). Together they form an 'analogical grammar' or scientific substance which lends plausibility to empirical realism's metaphysics and gives credence to its philosophical form (ibid.: 198).

Celestial closure in this account refers to the particular closed systems of stars and planets (referred to by astronomy and Newtonian science) where constant conjunctions of events prevail, and which is founded on the constancy of intrinsic states and external forces, making possible the observation of invariable regularities between events (Bhaskar 1978: 68). The classical paradigm of action works on twin pivots composed of the 'corpuscularian view of matter' (where the motion of corpuscles accounts for aggregate observed behaviour) and a 'mechanical view of matter' (whereby action consists of the impression of external forces upon these corpuscles). According to Bhaskar, the essential features of the classical 'corpuscularian–mechanical' world-view are:

(i) the externality of causation;
(ii) the passivity of matter and the immediacy of effects;
(iii) the atomicity of fundamental entities (whether corpuscles, events or sense-data;

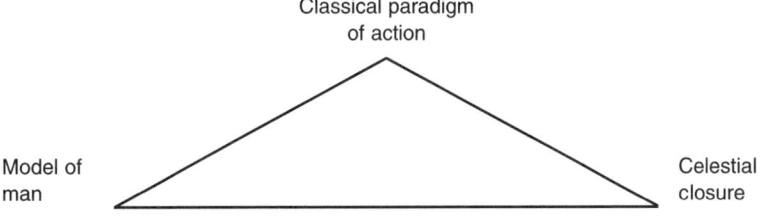

Figure 2.2 Bhaskar's analogical grammar of empirical realism

(iv) the absence of internal structure and complexity;
(v) the absence of preformation and of material continuity;
(vi) the subjectivity of transformation and of apparent variety in nature.

(Bhaskar 1978: 83)

From the standpoint of Bhaskar's realist approach, this leads us inevitably into a series of objections to empiricism based upon its ontologically restrictive conception of science. Not only can empirical realism *not* sustain the intelligibility of perception and experimental activity; it also, in positing a correspondence between sense experiences of constant conjunctions and causal laws, makes scientific change and the explanation of things existing and operating in open systems (where no constant conjunctions of events prevail) impossible (Bhaskar 1978: 241). Consequently, empirical realism has operated as a conservative ideology for science by providing an inadequate basis for theorizing the existence of the 'transitive dimension' (recognizing that so-called 'facts', experiences and constant conjunctions are socially produced) and the 'intransitive dimension' (where the objects of analysis are structures and generative mechanisms, existing and acting independently even when no empirical regularities prevail).

Idealism

Before turning to the realist account of scientific activity, which recognizes both these dimensions, I will deal at greater length with the idealist approaches, which I shall divide into four areas: Kantian, neo-Kantian, phenomenological approaches, and conventionalist views of science. All these approaches seek to go beyond (to transcend) empiricism, by acknowledging the role of the 'transitive dimension' in the production of meaning, although they reconcile the relationship between knowledge and experiences in different ways. Such differences in the analysis of science are not startlingly original and, in fact, often dress up old debates in new theoretical clothes.

This section of the chapter demonstrates a range of approaches which can be labelled idealist, for they all recognize that mental constructs play an independent role in the conceptual organization of the experience of sensations, impressions and perceptions. Nevertheless, they can be distinguished in terms of how they consider the role of theory in relation to observation and lived experience. First I consider Kant's contribution to understanding the way that mental constructs shape and organize our perceptions.

Kantianism and the conceptual organization of experience

Both empiricist and Kantian positions emerged as a response to the inadequacies of Cartesian and Leibnizian metaphysics. Their responses to these problems have shaped the main areas of discord between these positions. For Hume, metaphysical concerns about substance, mind and matter are sophistry or illusions which contaminate scientific thinking and should be eradicated. Hence, since mental and material substances (and thus the mind–body problem) are unintelligible in terms of sensory experience (they cannot be touched, seen, heard, smelt or tasted), they cannot be ascertained as either true or false by any scientific criterion. For the empiricist position, only trifling conceptual truths can be known a priori, that is, grasped through reason alone rather than through human experience. Such 'analytic' statements are logically true by virtue of the meanings of the words within the statement, that the predicate is already contained within the subject. Examples are 'A short man is a man' or '5 + 7 = 12' or a more interesting one (drawn from Locke's conception of natural rights) 'where there is no property, there is no injustice'. All other statements are 'synthetic' in that they express in ideas the textures, colours, sounds, odours, tastes and motions of the objects of our experiences. No causal relationships themselves can be observed; that is to say, we cannot tell from experience whether or not specific events are necessarily produced by others, therefore we can only recognize constant conjunctions of events.

A full discussion of Kant's contribution to knowledge construction is beyond the scope of this inquiry. I will limit myself to considering a small part of his work which is relevant for understanding idealist approaches to social-scientific knowledge. Kant sought the answer to a very different question by critically analysing metaphysics as a discipline worthy of investigation. Kant established a 'critical philosophy' based upon transcendental inquiries into the conditions of possibility of knowledge and, for that matter, the limits of reason. This synthesis of rationalist and empiricist concerns recognizes the mind as an active agency in the production of knowledge, but nevertheless does not seek to go beyond the boundaries of our senses into metaphysical speculation. Initially under the influence of Hume, Kant accepted that a priori truth existed in mathematics, geometry and physics, but in the *Critique of Pure Reason* (Kant 1987) he questions the distinction between analytic and synthetic statements. To use his stock example of '7 + 5 = 12', by asking the question 'how is mathematics possible?', he discovers that this contains information which is neither solely of a logical nature nor the product of experiment and observation. This elementary proposition presumes that one must be aware of the infinitesimal combinations of numbers which produce the sum of 12. He concludes that mathematical truths can be simultaneously a priori and synthetic. Similarly, in geometry, within the statement that 'a straight line is the shortest line between two points' the subject does not contain the full meaning of the predicate (for the idea of 'straight line' does not contain the idea of 'shortest'). For that matter in physics, we can also see the problems in assuming that 'every event has a cause' is a universal and necessarily true statement. In this way, Kant reformulated the problem of understanding experience as one where we should try to identify under what conditions synthetic a priori judgements would be possible (Kant 1987: 32–4).

For Kant, the phenomenal world of appearances is the product of both our experiences of the objects of analysis (which, as 'things-in-themselves' or 'noumena', are beyond cognitive faculties and are essentially unknowable, such as God or the immortality of the soul) and the a priori conditions within the mind which give shape and a logical form to this experiential content. The sense data flows from the object itself, while human nature, it is argued, supplies the 'forms of intuition' whereby sense data is arranged in 'space' and 'time', and through which we 'compare' and consider one piece of sense data as the 'cause' of another (Russell 1912, ch. 8). Since experience can only be conceived in spatial, temporal and causal terms, this means that our sensory experiences of objects already have an a priori basis. For Kant, the establishment of objective knowledge involves the recognition of two levels of a priori explanation: 'forms of intuition', identified above, and 'categories', twelve forms of thought through which human beings construct or build our knowledge of the world, grouped together under four headings: quantity, quality, relations and modality. Knowledge cannot transcend these fundamental concepts or 'categories' which allow us to think about our experiences. Hence, from the Kantian perspective, the task of philosophy becomes the study of the necessary conditions of knowing anything (Kant 1987: 70–85; Dancy 1985, ch. 14).[2] It is this conception of the subject as a creative, purposive and rational agent, as a source of an organizational framework through which empirical science is able to comprehend the world, to which I will return when examining the social and political theory of Friedrich Hayek and Robert Dahl.

Kant's concern to explore the conditions of possibility and limits to human knowledge has been a source of inspiration to a variety of approaches from those who advocate both a naturalist and an anti-naturalist standpoint. Idealist critics of positivism and empiricism have used Kant's theory of knowledge to construct alternative epistemological accounts of scientific activity within the disciplines of the social sciences. Two aspects of Kant's approach can be highlighted in this respect. The first is the active role of the knowing subject in the constitution of knowledge. The second is the distinction between *phenomena* and *noumena* which, following the assumption that it is impossible to know 'things-in-themselves', opens the way for a relativistic conception of knowledge of phenomena. These conceptions of knowledge are combined with the position of anti-naturalism, that the objects of analysis within the natural and the social sciences can be seen as fundamentally different, and that the concepts which act as the foundation for social science are at the same time the concepts through which human beings construct the social world.

Neo-Kantian variations: from the methods debate to the value judgement debate

In the mid-nineteenth century, a movement emerged which explicitly attempted to utilize Kant's ideas in order to study social relations and historical change. This movement has been labelled neo-Kantianism, although there was considerable variation within it. The concerns of this movement were focused upon two debates which highlighted the key issues at stake: first, the *Methodenstreit* (the battle over methods); second, the *Werturteilstreit* (the battle over value judgements). The *Methodenstreit* in the late nineteenth century was focused primarily on certain problems in the study of history and economics. Rather than being a debate on research methods, it was a dispute about which key organizing principles should act as a foundation for economic research. In the study of the economy in Germany, it had become widely established that it was appropriate to consider an object of analysis in terms of the historical conditions in which it existed. This tendency to construct general laws on the basis of particular empirical conditions was developed by Wilhelm Roscher, Bruno Hildebrand and Karl Knies, and came to be labelled *historicism*. Even though their successors, such as Gustav Schmoller, disagreed on the scope and purpose of economic laws, they remained committed to the study of social institutions in national economies rather than a consideration of the economy as a concept. The focus of the German Historical School was thus historical and empirical, even if the object was, for Roscher, the entire social organism or, for Schmoller, the short-run empirical regularities in sequences of definite variables. This empirical approach dominated in Germany until 1900 because of the substance it lent to the social and economic policies of Bismarck in his attempts to stabilize the social order through state intervention and welfare reforms. For Schmoller and others in this movement, the social-scientific knowledge they produced would deliver human progress and the social improvement of the condition of the working classes through the state.

In response to Schmoller, Carl Menger, in *Untersuchungen über die Methode der Socialwissenschaften und der politischen Ökonomie insbesondere* (Investigations into the Method of the Social Sciences with Particular Reference to Political Economy) translated as *Problems of Economics and Sociology* (Menger 1963), attempted to demonstrate that it was possible to develop an abstract conceptualization of the object of the discipline and avoid the dangers of 'economics without thinking'. He argued that it was possible to view economic history as one of a number of branches of economics, alongside those of economic theory and of economic policy and public finance, with each branch having its own distinctive form of theory and method. Menger was particularly concerned to develop a theoretical account of the general relations of the economic phenomena, rather than to describe social collectivities and their typical economic relations in a particular time and place. For Menger, the appropriate method involved the identification of a 'defining quality' (or essence) in an individual phenomenon which could be treated as representative of a 'type' of economic relation. In this approach, relations were seen as particular connections between economic variables.

Menger sought to break down phenomena into their smallest elements and use these in order to deduce the development of more complex social phenomena. In this way, he anticipated the development of conceptual causal systems which corresponded to the real world. For Menger, there were no exceptions to the law-like regularities established through this 'exact method', for they were a function of the definite individual actions which produced them. This approach was to become known as methodological individualism. Menger was to establish a line of argument which rejected the aggregate concepts of macroeconomics in favour of microeconomics. The emphasis he placed upon economic theory (as akin to natural science mechanics), with economic history as subsidiary, caused considerable offence. The debate was unresolved, and is important primarily in terms of establishing the framework of discussions on the methodology of the social sciences, and in immediately stimulating a wider philosophical debate in Germany about the relationship and differences between the assumptions and methods of the natural sciences, and the social and cultural sciences and history.

The neo-Kantian milieu within which these debates took place was in many respects the scene of carnage left by the intellectual battles over the *Methodenstreit*. This was stimulated by, among others, Dilthey's critique of positivism. The resistance of specific historical and social sciences to 'naturalistic optimism or empiricist pessimism' (Arato 1974: 115) would have been dissipated if hermeneutics had not been used as the foundation for the human sciences (*Geisteswissenschaften*). This coincided with Menger's critique of the German Historical School for failing to distinguish consistently between the precepts of theoretical as opposed to practical economics and, in particular, for suggesting that economic laws could be established through the examination of the formation of actual economic systems (*Nationalökonomie*).

The neo-Kantian approach was initiated through the work of Herman Lotze, who returned to the Kantian transcendental question, 'what are the conditions of possibility of knowledge of the objects of experience?' This led to an exploration of the grounds for establishing the validity of propositions of the objects of experience. Lotze established a framework for discussion by attempting to resolve the dilemmas created in accommodating both objective truth and subjective values within the same approach. Where, for Kant, truth had been the agreement of knowledge with its object, for Lotze, truth was defined through judgements about relationships between ideas. This broke the relationship between knowledge and experience and, given that validity and value are defined independently of real existence, maintained validity of concepts such as truth by interpreting them as values. This is a position which Kant, in his argument that judgements must be arrived at in part through experience, had seen as rationalist.

Two responses emerged to the problems posed by Lotze. First, the Marburg School (notably Hermann Cohen, Paul Natorp and Ernst Cassirer), who followed in his footsteps, focused upon the validity of logical propositions. Second, the Baden or Heidelberg School (notably Wilhelm Windelband and Heinrich Rickert) chose to dwell instead upon the thorny question of cultural values and their relationship to the generation of historical knowledge. To keep the discussion focused upon social scientific knowledge, I will focus upon the Baden School in this chapter. Windelband, in 'History and Natural Science' (1894), a critique of positivist approaches, regarded both the natural sciences and the human sciences as the study of empirical reality but distinguished between them in terms of the interest of the scientist in the objects of analysis, and the ways in which scientists constitute them. In the natural sciences the objects remain constant, allowing for a science of laws (*Gesetze*), while in the social sciences the object involves unique configurations of events (*Gestalten*). Thus, for Windelband, there was a difference in method between two forms of scientific thought: *nomothetic*, involving the construction of generalizing models and the identification of general laws, and *idiographic*, the individualizing method of the cultural sciences concerned with the detailed depiction of particular circumstances.

This allowed Windelband to distinguish sharply between the study of natural objects in establishing objective knowledge and the important role played by the values and interests of the researcher in the study of social objects. In this latter kind of investigation, the objects of analysis are other knowing subjects, that is thinking, creative and communicative beings. However, Windelband did not differentiate between these respective objects of analysis in the cultural sciences and the natural sciences, but rather distinguished between their modes of analysis. The cultural sciences, such as history, were seen as deploying the individualizing or 'idiographic' method, while the natural sciences using the 'nomothetic' method aimed to produce general laws. Within this framework values, as the product of an evaluative procedure, can only be conceptualized as subjective and individualized, not as the objective basis for a general logic of knowledge. Yet if values are subjective, how can we make a judgement about them; do we give different values the same status as in relativist solutions? This did not, of course, resolve the problem, but shifted the value dilemma sideways towards consideration of the grounds for making judgements. In relation to values, Windelband avoided the spectre of relativism by appealing to the metaphysical escape route of 'normal consciousness'. This served as a repository for 'absolute values', securing the valuation of values at a metatheoretical level.

This recognition of subjectivity was developed further by Heinrich Rickert, in his account of value relevance in *The Limits of Natural Scientific Concept Formation in Natural Science* (1986, first published 1902). This initiated the second debate, the *Werturteilstreit*, on the role of value judgement in social science. Rickert, a student of Windelband, faced the same dilemma when he attempted to establish a foundation for valid theoretical values. Rickert argued that values have objective validity but not existence, unlike actual historical subjects which do exist in the real empirical world. Nevertheless, Rickert was forced to ground such valid or 'transhistorical' values, not in the transcendental 'normal consciousness' of Windelband, but in the empirical world or reality which becomes the 'bearer' of values (Parsons 1990: 303). Again the attempt to avoid the charges of relativism and historicism leads Rickert clearly to separate questions of validity (thought) from questions of existence (experience). It was in this context that Max Weber's interventions were to become crucial.

The value judgement debate is, of course, most often associated with Weber. However, greater stress will be placed upon the wider context, from which Weber himself drew and to which he responded. The contribution by Rickert on the relationship between values and social science is the key starting point. Rickert distinguished between the logical methods of the natural and the cultural sciences in much the same way as Windelband; however, he was also concerned with the material differences between the sciences. For Rickert, it was possible to distinguish, within both the natural and social sciences, the ways in which the objects of the sciences have a relationship to the values of those engaged in research, and are meaningful within our culture. Physics in this framework is formally nomothetic, concerned with general laws, and the objects are unrelated to values, while phylogenetic biology is formally idiographic in attempting to establish the unique characteristics of earthbound species even though it has the same relationship to its object as physics. In the social sciences, where the objects are value-laden and culturally meaningful, economics concentrates upon developing general laws from the identification of recurrent patterns of events, while history is concerned with unique and specific events.

For Rickert, this reformulation of the task of the social sciences raised its own problems, and these became the substance of the value judgement debate. Neither the nomothetic method nor the idiographic method provide us with a clear criterion for deciding what we should actually study. For Rickert, this is resolved in the nomothetic method by the abstraction of general characteristics from the object under investigation, thus generating objective knowledge. In the idiographic method, the subjective nature of choosing an object of analysis leaves it open to the accusation that the approach is not scientific. Rickert suggests that it is possible to define objects, and form concepts about them, by following the criterion of value relevance. Thus, the objects raised by a social scientist using the idiographic method would already relate to the cultural values of the society in question, and hold some meaning for the members of that culture. Social-scientific concepts would relate the object in question to the values of a given community and, in addition, to the general standards of morality considered to be universal within that community. The principle of value relevance means that concept formation should be relevant to the problems of a particular society at a particular time, and that value judgements are the concern of philosophers in that time and place. (See Figure 2.3.)

While Weber drew a great deal from Rickert, he was concerned not to demarcate the different forms of scientific method, but to bring them together in a coherent and unified approach to knowledge. For Weber, this unified approach would provide a bridge between the interpretive understanding of

Empiricism, idealism, realism 27

		Formal difference	
		Generalizing *(natural)*	*Individualizing* *(historical)*
Material difference	unrelated to values (nature)	Physics	Phylogenetic biology
	related to values (nature)	Economics	History

Figure 2.3 Rickert's four-fold definition of science
Source: adapted from Bryant 1985: 71

human action and the scientific explanation of the causes and consequences of a particular relationship. To do this, he used a device which had been developed in Menger's economic theory, the *ideal type*. The notion of an ideal type is a theoretical device for facilitating generalization while at the same time acknowledging the complexity of social relations. Ideal types are deliberate simplifications, categories which exaggerate an aspect of social life, but which act as a yardstick against which it is possible to compare and contrast empirical evidence. There is an important difference between Weber's and Menger's uses of ideal types. Menger constructed ideal types in the study of economics, where he treated the economy as an abstract composite of equally abstract simple relations. Weber, however, only saw ideal types as useful in relation to explaining and understanding concrete empirical reality. In this way, Weber's work drew the *Werturteilstreit* to a close, even if many issues remained unresolved.

Hermeneutics and phenomenology

Dilthey's '*Introduction to the Human Sciences*' (1883) marked a widening of debate about the character of the social scientific method. For Dilthey, the main concern was to identify a distinctly human science which did not treat the study of society and history as the automatic play of objective forms and processes. The natural sciences presented an inappropriate analogue for social science, because natural objects were fixed and hence meaningless. The study of human beings and the social relationships they constructed was meaningful and, therefore, the study of society and history involved very different ground rules. This implicitly accepted that human values, ideas, concepts, purposes and desires were an inescapable part in understanding (*verstehen*) social life. Within this approach, human beings acted *upon* the natural environment but also *within* the social environment. The social and cultural forms, taken as the objects of analysis in the social sciences, were expressions of the mind rather than external to the mind. While Dilthey focused upon consciousness as the source of human understanding, he differed from Kant in rejecting the possibility of a 'knowing subject' or transcendental position independent of the social and historical conditions in which that consciousness was located. Dilthey developed these arguments into a 'descriptive psychology', which treated the lived experiences of individuals as the source of understanding, in contrast to the tendency of analytical psychology to search for mental laws along the lines of physics and chemistry. Dilthey identified the problem of the *hermeneutic circle*:

> The whole of a work must be understood from individual words and their combination but full understanding of an individual part presupposes understanding of the whole. This circle is repeated in the relation of an individual work to the mentality and development of its author, and it recurs again in the relation of such an individual work to its literary genre.
> (Dilthey, *The Development of Hermeneutics* (1896), cited in Bryant 1985: 66–7)

A common metaphor for explaining this idea is the 'sentence analogue', whereby the meaning of a word is identified by reference to its place in a sentence, and the meaning of the sentence is established through the meanings of the individual words in particular combinations and sequences.

While Dilthey rejected metaphysics, he did not turn to empiricism for inspiration. Instead, he focused upon the lived experience of human beings in their social and historical context. Hence, Dilthey argued that descriptive psychology was the key to the human sciences, at the same time as Wundt and the experimental psychologists were attempting to apply the methods and assumptions of natural science to the study of the human mind. In this 'life-philosophy' approach, the task of the human sciences is to reconstruct the fragmented parts of a shared system of meaning. In this task, Dilthey built on Kant's approach by providing a critique of historical reason as a complement to Kant's critiques of epistemology, ethics and aesthetics. This is a Kantian critique in the sense that it attempts to identify the conditions of possibility of, and limitations to, this branch of reason. However, he was also keen to stress that he disagreed with the application of the *Critique of Pure Reason* to knowledge of the natural and social worlds. This approach undermined Kant's claims to have established universal categories of thought. For Dilthey, all mental constructions were historically and socially specific, and hence prone to change as part of the web of cultural forms (see Outhwaite 1975).

In the writings of Edmund Husserl (e.g. Husserl 1931, 1960, 1970), the life-philosophy approach was developed into a more rigorous phenomenological account of knowledge. Husserl attempted to demonstrate the naive fallacies and prejudices which he regarded as an inherent part of objective detached rational science, and to transcend the separation of subjectivity (the ego) from the objective world (corporeality). The treatment of subjectivity and objectivity as distinct had led to the conclusion that the subjective dimension was of little or no importance, or merely a pale reflection of some deeper or more authentic state of affairs. Instead, Husserl starts from the Cartesian position of the '*ego–cogito*' principle (that 'I think, therefore I exist') whereby Descartes attempted to demonstrate the existence of conscious reasoning as the means of approaching the external world. He also recognized that this attempt to secure an absolute foundation for knowledge starts from the premise (or prejudice) that it is possible to do so. Husserl extends this approach by introducing the conception of *intentionality*, reaching the logical conclusion of '*ego–cogito–cogitatum*' (I think something). For Husserl, this overcame the Cartesian dualisms between mind and body, inner and outer, consciousness and matter, and private (experience) and public (objects). Husserl attempted to develop an approach which avoided presuppositions and was grounded in pure consciousness as a means of reaching the truth.

For phenomenologists, the concept of intentionality indicates the active involvement of the ego in the constitution of the (thing) world, as well as its operation as a tacit process. The creation of the phenomena of experience enlarges the intentional act of description of experience in such a way as to create the object of analysis and the distinction between surface appearances and an underlying reality. To do this, Husserl developed the theoretical device of the *transcendental epoche*, or bracketing of the objective. This demands that we should suspend our belief in the existence of the objective world and abstain from making judgements about whether the world does or does not exist as an object. It involves bracketing other egos and cultural contexts as well as things, in order to comprehend experience. This process of eliminating all but conscious reflection is labelled the phenomenological reduction, and is characterized as the peeling away of the layers of cultural presuppositions in order to reclaim the original or pre-scientific forms of experience of the *lebenswelt* (life-world). In this way, Husserl established that 'I alone, am the pure ego'. This enables Husserl to dispense with Kant's distinction between phenomena and noumena, for the 'things in themselves' were created through acts of consciousness.

In Husserl's account of pure consciousness, the existence of other egos poses a problem, for the approach cannot accept the validity of the presence of other conscious beings. Alfred Schütz argued that this presented a misleading picture of human experiences, and developed a form of phenomenology where the existence of others within everyday experience is taken for granted. For Schütz, it is the condition of intersubjectivity through which the individual actors involved are able to grasp each other's consciousness and construct their life world. This was developed in *The Phenomenology of the Social World* (Schütz 1967, originally published in 1932), which Husserl regarded as one of the few attempts successfully to penetrate to the core of his philosophical work. Schütz attempted to draw together insights from

Weber and Husserl as well as Henri Bergson, in order to construct a more adequate account of social phenomena which could accommodate intersubjectivity. While he draws upon the emphasis placed on 'meaning' in Weber's work, he remains dissatisfied with Weber's attachment to the ideal types deployed by objective scientists. Schütz draws upon the ideas of Husserl and Bergson, who clearly identified the subjective meanings of human actors as the source of understanding, that only in the 'stream of consciousness' of experience is to be found the source of meaning (*Sinn*) and understanding (*Verstehen*).

Schütz brings together Bergson's idea of the 'simultaneity of experience', the sharing of time and space by two individual actors involved in communication, and Husserl's concept of intersubjectivity, so that the process of understanding the other person involves grasping what is going on in the other person's mind (Schütz 1967: 112–13). In the 1940s, as a refugee in the USA, he encountered pragmatism and incorporated the ideas of John Dewey and William James on the simultaneous coexistence of the *alter ego* with one's own 'stream of consciousness'. This provided Schütz with the basis for developing a sociological account of the social world constituted by typifications and recipe-knowledge of everyday common sense. While Weber had developed the use of ideal types as theoretical tools against which empirical evidence could be compared, he nevertheless treated the evidence as factual, even though it was open to various interpretations. For Schütz, there are no hard facts and the typifications are the taken-for-granted organizing devices of all human beings. By treating facts as intersubjectively constructed, Schütz sought to establish connections between the second-order constructs of social science and the first-order constructs of everyday life (Schütz 1953).

Conventionalism: knowledge as a social product

Conventionalism does not represent the views of a unified group of philosophers or sociologists of science, nor does it provide a homogeneous view of what constitutes science. What unites conventionalist accounts of science is simply their recognition of the part played by human agency and, in particular, the role of interpretive understanding within scientific activity. It has increasingly been acknowledged that science takes place within a language community, and that the criteria for assessing good scientific practice are established normatively within the boundaries of a shared core of conventions. Hence, not only is sense-data influenced by the theoretical beliefs and values of the scientist, but the very meanings of observational terms are dependent upon the scientific theories and methods already laid down as acceptable and proper. This leads us to the inevitable conclusion that theory (interpretation) and observation (of sense-data) are inseparable (Keat and Urry 1982: 50–4; Hanson 1958, 1969). This approach has significantly undermined the credibility of empiricism in particular, and has initiated a 'crisis of rationality' more generally. Conventionalism has challenged the orthodoxies of empiricism by suggesting that observations alone cannot determine whether a theory is true or false (or whether it can be corroborated or falsified) and that there are no universal criteria for the rational evaluation of competing theoretical models. Hence, the adoption of a particular theory or model is simply a matter of convention.

Falsification does not provide an absolute guarantee against the effects of the conventionalist argument for, as Willard Van Orman Quine states, it is always possible to avoid falsification and rescue a theory simply by adding further assumptions which enable the theory to correspond to the evidence in a plausible way. Quine's contention (in *From a Logical Point of View*, 1961) is that scientific hypotheses cannot be tested in isolation from other theories. However, it is also impossible to draw the line between what is relevant knowledge and what is not. Consequently, the whole of human scientific knowledge is in the frame and conclusive falsification becomes impossible. Ultimately, he claims, 'Any statement can be held to be true come what may, if we make drastic enough adjustments elsewhere in the system' (Quine 1961: 43).

Rather than conceptualizing scientific progress as a gradual accumulation of discrete facts and pieces of data, and by stressing the accidental and messy way in which scientists have actually behaved, conventionalism challenges this notion of a smooth methodical progress from which science has traditionally drawn its legitimacy.[3] This position is best represented by reference to the work of Thomas Kuhn who denies all that empiricism stands for. According to Ian Hacking, for Kuhn:

> There is no sharp distinction between observation and theory.
> Science is not cumulative.
> A live science does not have a tight deductive structure.
> Living scientific concepts are not particularly precise.
> Methodological unity of science is false: there are lots of disconnected tools used for various forms of inquiry.
> The sciences themselves are disunified. They are composed of a large number of only loosely overlapping little disciplines many of which in the course of time cannot comprehend each other . . .
> The context of justification cannot be separated from the context of discovery.
> Science is in time and is essentially historical.
> (Hacking 1983: 6)

This directs our attention to the significant differences between empiricism and conventionalism. However, unlike Quine, Kuhn was concerned with more than the theoretical frameworks through which statements make sense. Kuhn focuses on the organized scientific communities and belief systems in which statements and theoretical frameworks are considered to be plausible. To understand why some theories are plausible and others not, he argued that we have to consider the role of paradigms. Kuhn developed the concept of 'paradigm' to characterize scientific change and 'the standards governing permissible problems, concepts and explanations' (Kuhn 1970: 106) within the context of a historical and sociological approach. The meaning of the concept of paradigm is a matter of much dispute; however it can be taken in this context to mean the 'universally recognized scientific achievements that . . . provide model problems and solutions to a community of practitioners' (ibid.: viii) and therefore comprises the implicit taken-for-granted common sense assumptions of a scientific community. Kuhn also provided an outline of the turnover of authoritative knowledge. His historical account of scientific knowledge starts with the pre-scientific stage, where a range of approaches competed for dominance but were unable to achieve it. The natural sciences, he argued, achieved dominance with the development of Newtonian physics, closely followed by chemistry and biology. He argued that the social sciences remained in the pre-paradigmatic state and had not, as yet, achieved the maturity which followed from the broad acceptance of one dominant set of rules.

Kuhn adopted a conventional story-telling device common in historical narratives, that of periods of stability broken by sudden revolutionary change and rupture. During the tranquillity of periods of 'normal science', foundational assumptions and the theoretical frameworks based upon them go unquestioned; so that problems are subject to the accepted procedures of puzzle-solving whereby established theories are modified to maintain consistency with the evidence. Gradually, Kuhn suggests, anomalies within a paradigm build up to the point of generating a crisis which precipitates a scientific revolution or paradigm shift. As a result, a new paradigm emerges through a form of conversion experience or 'Gestalt-switch' (analogous to a religious conversion), rather than by any rational logic. However, many scientists are left behind in this process, unable to cope with the trauma of such a transformation, for 'A new scientific truth does not triumph by convincing its opponents and making them see the light but rather because its opponents eventually die and a new generation grows up that is familiar with it' (Kuhn 1970: 151).

A great deal of attention has been devoted to Kuhn's account of scientific revolution. However, this neglects his concern with the stable periods when the dominance of one paradigm prevails (a period of normal science characterized by the aforementioned puzzle solving). For instance, Isaac Newton's mechanics provided physics with a set of principles (rules of experimental inquiry and scientific laws of motion) for the development of further scientific laws and the identification of facts. However, by the mid-nineteenth century, a series of problems or anomalies emerged in the application of Newton's laws to astronomical objects which could not adequately be explained. By the 1890s, these anomalies had accumulated to the point where physics was in a state of crisis. With the emergence of an alternative set of principles, physics experienced a scientific revolution as a new paradigm emerged to replace the old. Kuhn argued that this revolution involved a 'Gestalt shift', for the scientists involved had to go through a conversion experience in order to move from the old paradigm to the new one. In this case, Newton's mechanistic laws were challenged by Albert Einstein's theory of relativity.

For Kuhn these paradigms were mutually exclusive, and the members of these scientific communities in their separate paradigms interpreted their experiences so differently that they can be said to have occupied different worlds. In practice, the shift takes place over a generation, for few of those who have worked their way up the academic career ladder are likely to question the theories upon which their research and careers are based. By the middle of the twentieth century, Einstein's and subsequent theories provided the underlying rules for physics in the new period of normal science, in much the same way as Newton's had in the previous paradigm. To suggest that members of different paradigms experience different worlds had further implications for understanding the process of knowledge construction. Kuhn argued that each paradigm has its own way of demarcating science from non-science. Consequently, it was inappropriate to use the criteria of one paradigm to judge the truthfulness of the theories of another paradigm. In practice, this means that there is no true knowledge, and also that paradigms do not progress, they merely change.

While positivist and falsificationist accounts had both been committed to progress, even though Popper had given up on the search for unquestionable truth, Kuhn's approach suggested that it was not even possible to identify a progression in knowledge. Instead, through a careful study of the ways in which natural science had developed and changed, Kuhn suggested (as indicated in Figure 2.4) that scientific knowledge went through long phases of stability and transformation. So instead of establishing a universal standard against which it was possible to compare statements about the world, Kuhn argued that knowledge was a social product and, as such, changed as society changed. He described each period of stability as a paradigm, in which the rules of scientific method are well established and the role of scientists is to solve problems and puzzles without questioning the rules within which they work. These rules involve widely accepted 'demarcation criteria' on what forms of knowledge are scientific or not scientific. In the case of logical positivism, if something could not be reduced to a simple observation statement and the theories could not be empirically verified (and the statement was not

Paradigm A → anomalies → crisis → scientific → Paradigm B
(Normal   revolution   (Normal
Science)   science)

Figure 2.4 Kuhn's theory of scientific revolution

analytically true) then the statement had metaphysical components and was meaningless. Such rules become part of the institutional life in which scientists work, and their work is judged according to how closely they operate by the accepted principles of their disciplines.

Even though paradigms are more than bodies of theories or even theoretical frameworks – they are scientific communities through which knowledge is produced and understood – there is considerable ambiguity in Kuhn's writings. Kuhn has also been criticized for conceptual imprecision, most startlingly by Margaret Masterman's identification of twenty-one (possibly twenty-two) uses of the concept of paradigm (Masterman 1970). Kuhn responded to this, in the second edition of *The Structure of Scientific Revolutions* (1970), with a sharper definition of paradigm as a disciplinary matrix consisting of a strong network of theoretical, instrumental and methodological commitments. This suggests that because the standards of assessment are internal to each paradigm, scientific revolutions involve a shift in the standards which govern legitimate explanations. Competing paradigms are seen as incommensurable (involving mutually exclusive assumptions) for the differences in the theoretical and observational vocabularies of each paradigm mean that the scientists in each case inhabit 'different worlds'. Despite this, Kuhn did later provide five, imprecise, characteristics of good scientific theory: 'accuracy' within its domain; 'consistency' with existing theory and internally; a 'broad scope' explaining more than it set out to explain; 'simplicity'; and, finally, 'fruitfulness' in disclosing new phenomena or previously unnoticed relationships between such phenomena (Kuhn 1977: 320–9; Hacking 1983: 13).

Other conventionalist responses, such as the approach of Paul Feyerabend, tend to place less emphasis upon clear periods of stability and change. In *Against Method* (1975), Feyerabend argued that the main characteristic of scientific knowledge is its messy, accidental and discontinuous nature. This was directed partly against Kuhn's concept of paradigms as periods of normal science, and partly against positivist and empiricist accounts of the scientific method. Like Kuhn, Feyerabend challenged the assumptions that science involves a theory-neutral observational language and that universal standards can be applied. Unlike Kuhn, he developed a standpoint which suggested that science was not rational, that no rules had operated effectively and that scientific knowledge could be oppressive rather than an instrument of progress. For Feyerabend, to treat science as if it had been a rational and objective enterprise was to construct a myth. In addition, he argued that the pursuit of scientific explanations, from the positivists through to Popper, was undesirable, for it substituted the accumulation of knowledge for the preferred goal of emancipating human beings.

For Feyerabend, there was only one principle that could be defended in all circumstances and at all stages of human development: the principle of 'anything goes'. Within Feyerabend's anarchistic 'humanitarian attitude' which laid stress upon the 'free man', any talk of rationality as an objective process indicated an external constraint upon the free will of the individual. Hence

Feyerabend's solution for the construction of knowledge was the principle of 'anything goes'. This allowed the wishes, tastes and values of the individual scientist to rise to the fore. He rejected Kuhn's 'puzzle-solving normality' in favour of the 'principle of proliferation' (Feyerabend 1975). This earned him the title of 'epistemological anarchist', although he is more accurately described as an advocate of methodological pluralism. The anarchistic vision Feyerabend held was a positive one, for he hoped that it would be possible to live in a situation where all views could be taken seriously. Feyerabend did not consider himself to be a political anarchist, and actually preferred the label 'Dadaist', after the avant-garde artistic movement of the early twentieth century, whose adherents took every opportunity to question and parody all the truths and established artistic conventions they encountered.

Feyerabend questioned the key principles of science when it was reeling from the impact of Kuhn's work, and he advocated the principle of proliferation as the alternative strategy to the imposition of one view (methodological monism). Sympathisers with this critique in the social sciences have embraced the idea of methodological pluralism while critics, such as the social anthropologist Ernest Gellner, have warned against the relativism that this view implies (Gellner 1979: 182–98). For critics like Gellner, this leaves social science in a position where it cannot support or condemn any position with certainty; it merely stands on the sidelines and is unable to offer judgements on important issues. Such criticism condemns Feyerabend for leaving us in a position where it is impossible to condemn events such as the holocaust. Feyerabend responded by arguing that his approach was not relativistic in that sense, and in *Science in a Free Society* (1978) he advocated that all knowledge should contribute to human freedom and not oppression.

While the studies of scientific knowledge by Kuhn, Feyerabend and others contributed towards, and perhaps provoked, a crisis of rationality, they also undermined the more positivistically inclined approaches. However, the sceptical treatment of truth by Popper and Imre Lakatos ensured that the supporters of naturalism in sociology could still draw upon a versatile approach which could accommodate some of the criticisms raised against empiricism. Lakatos provided some useful qualifications to the Popperian approach, and tried to draw some lessons from the work of the conventionalists. He drew upon the historical evidence produced by Thomas Kuhn on the ways in which knowledge is organized in communities of scientists, and on how academic and scientific organizations are as important as methods. However, he also remained committed to the principle that knowledge should deliver progress.

In 'Falsification and the Methodology of Scientific Research Programmes' (1970), Lakatos argued that philosophers of science were faced with three alternatives: induction, conventionalism and falsificationism. He ruled out induction on the grounds that it could not adequately account for the construction and use of theory, and criticized conventionalism for giving up on the accumulation of knowledge and progress. Regarding the last approach, he argued that it was important to distinguish various forms of falsificationist approaches. Those who had interpreted Popper in too simplistic a way, and who had immediately discarded and disregarded any hypotheses which had been refuted, he labelled *dogmatic falsificationists*. This position was to be distinguished from Popper's approach, which accepted that a refuted hypothesis may still be useful as a predictive statement in a different context and should simply be shelved unless it has been more comprehensively falsified. This was in part a recognition of the problems involved in conclusively falsifying a statement. However, because Popper's position was still focused upon individual laws, theories and hypotheses rather than accepting the relationship of a theory to the body of theories and evidence on a particular problem, Lakatos labelled Popper's approach as *naive methodological falsificationism*. In fact, according to Lakatos, Popper and Feyerabend had much in common in their focus upon individual theories and the importance of protecting individual freedom (Lakatos 1970: 91–196).

In recognizing that theories do not exist in isolation, Lakatos drew upon the contributions of Kuhn on the way in which knowledge was historically and socially located. However, unlike Kuhn, he argued that a viable methodology had to be both descriptively accurate and prescriptively useful. In the development of *sophisticated methodological falsificationism*, Lakatos felt that he could account for the institutional life of scientists and still offer a guide for progress in scientific research. Lakatos distinguished between the 'hard core', the key foundational assumptions of a 'scientific research programme' (his alternative to the concept of paradigm) and the 'protective belt' of auxiliary hypotheses which could be tested and falsified at any point in time. In addition, he suggested that a scientific research programme is governed by two sets of methodological rules. First is the 'negative heuristic' which indicates the research pathways which should not be studied. This protects the 'hard core' from criticism. Anyone who violates the negative heuristic is often treated as a heretic or is viewed as dangerous to the programme, finding that research funds dry up and that their work is marginalized. Defence mechanisms like this are a common feature of social-scientific practice. Second, the 'positive heuristic' indicates the research pathways which are legitimate and worthwhile. It is the combined operation of both negative and positive heuristics that ensures the solidarity of the research programme. For example, behaviourist approaches in the social sciences which focus upon human actions as a series of effects from various stimuli, such as pluralism in political sociology, could not accept the existence of human beings as creative and reflective beings. In the case of pluralism, the positive heuristic led political scientists to follow the legitimate research pathways and study those decision-making situations which could be observed, measured and explained (predicted). On the negative side, both behaviourists and pluralists reject the purported existence of inner selves and intentions as speculative constructs beyond the concerns of science. These kinds of assumptions regulate what can and cannot be done and what is meaningful within a research programme (Lakatos 1970).

For Lakatos, even if a set of theories and the core assumptions have been falsified, so long as they continue to offer useful predictions, then it is worth hanging on to them. In addition, in the absence of a more adequate alternative, it is also better to hang on to a bad theory than to have no theory at all. Thus scientific research programmes, even if inadequate, can be identified as progressive (contributing genuinely new knowledge) or degenerating in the long term. While this retains an attachment to the idea of progress through the accumulation of knowledge, it is a considerable way from Popper's falsificationism. By treating scientific knowledge as a social product, and the rules by which we judge knowledge to be scientific to be merely conventions, critics of conventionalism such as Popper and Imre Lakatos have argued that such approaches offer little hope for humanity. For instance, Lakatos suggested that by giving up on the possibility of progress, Kuhn's account was equivalent to a 'mob psychology' of scientific knowledge (Lakatos 1970).

Attempts to rescue the falsificationist approach, such as sophisticated methodological falsificationism, shift the criterion for theory abandonment from refutation to the clear identification of a better alternative theory. However, this simply concedes more ground to the conventionalist position. For if 'it is reasonable to abandon T if and only if there is an alternative theory which explains everything that T explains, and generates predictions not derivable from T, some of which have been confirmed by empirical testing' (Keat and Urry 1982: 49), this means that the criterion for evaluating theories refers no longer to the empirical evidence, but primarily to alternative theories (though it retains some element of empirical testing). Since knowledge is a social product, the standards of inquiry are generated through the ongoing practice of theoretical research (ibid.: ch. 3). The neo-Kantian, phenomenological and conventionalist approaches to knowledge construction differ in their emphasis on the role of subjective values, the extent of detachment and involvement in the investigation of objects of analysis, and their response to the question of whether truth and objectivity is possible and desirable. Yet they all emphasize the way in which experiences are a complex synthesis of observation, and the use of mental constructs, theories and models. (For more detail and more variety in these approaches, including praxeology, see Smith 1998b, chs. 4 and 5.)

Challenging idealism

In the same way as realism offers a useful critical vantage point on empiricism, so too can such idealist currents be interrogated through a consideration of their approach to causality. For this reason, Bhaskar attributes the distinctive character of the conventionalist position to its adoption of the transcendental idealist philosophy of science (explicitly identifying its neo-Kantian origins). According to the realist approach, idealism takes the epistemological standpoint that objects of knowledge are models or artificial constructs. Such mental constructs, although independent of particular human beings, are not independent of human activity in general. For transcendental idealism, 'knowledge is given structure by a sequence of models rather than by a fixed set of a priori rules' (Bhaskar 1978: 27). By accepting that there can be no knowledge without social activity, this contradicts the empiricist account of science, where valid content is exhausted by atomistic facts and their constant conjunctions. Nevertheless, transcendental idealism as a procedure for knowing retains a commitment to empirical realism, because of its tacit acceptance of the empiricist account of being (the concept of the empirical world). Therefore, by this realist argument, both idealism and empiricism share a common ontology which prevents their recognition of the independent existence of the causal structures and generative mechanisms which lie behind events. So while idealism accepts that a constant conjunction of events (an empirical regularity) is necessary for the attribution of a causal law, it argues that this is in itself insufficient. This involves a different account of causality from empiricism, for idealism adopts 'intelligibility determinism'. This assumes that the causes of events are simply those which render an event intelligible to the human mind. According to Bhaskar, this creates a dilemma for empirical realism.

> Either theoretical entities refer ultimately to experience, in which case they can be eliminated or theoretical entities constitute experience (in whole or in part) in which case they cannot be eliminated, but must, given the equation of empirical realism, constitute the world (in whole or in part).
> (Bhaskar 1978: 163)

Since the objects of analysis (as mental constructs) are not taken to exist independently of human activity, idealism is not able to sustain a conception of the 'intransitive dimension'. Therefore it is argued that idealism cannot bridge the differences between the 'real' and the 'empirical', but merely reflects the different attitudes of human beings towards them. Consequently, idealism cannot sustain the 'rationality' of the transitive process of science for it fails to explain the conditions under which science is possible (Bhaskar 1978: 24–30). From the standpoint of a realist, the practices of science presuppose a 'real world' which is 'structured, differentiated and changing'. Realists argue that idealism and the derivative forms of conventionalism are simply not equipped to comprehend, never mind make sense of the existence of the 'real world', conceived in this way.. This is not to say that we should adopt a correspondence theory of truth by confusing what we know with what exists. According to Bhaskar, transcendental idealism adopts a 'false dichotomy', that:

> either knowledge must conform to objects [of analysis] or objects conform to knowledge: that either how we speak must be a function of things or that things must be a function of how we speak. . . . Science is an activity, a process in thought and nature which attempts to express in thought the natures and constitutions of and ways of acting of things that exist independently of thought. Thought has a reality not to be confused or identified

with the reality of its objects: knowledge may change without objects and objects change without knowledge. There is no correspondence, no conformity, no similarity between objects and thoughts. . . . Things exist and act independently of our descriptions. . . . Descriptions belong to the world of society and of man; objects belong to the world of nature.

(Bhaskar 1978: 249–50)

If science is to comprehend the structures and mechanisms which exist and operate independently of our knowledge of them, and thus recognize the 'structured', 'complex' and 'changing' nature of the (natural and/or social) world, it must take care not to fall into the trap of the 'epistemic fallacy': of 'confusing the ontological order with the epistemic order, priority in being with priority in deciding claims to being' (Bhaskar 1978: 250). It is precisely this fallacy which Kuhn commits when constructing his conventionalist account of the history of science. When paradigms break down and a scientific revolution ensues, this is not simply a revolution of the 'transitive domain' whereby we come to view the same world with different conceptual spectacles. For Kuhn, the new and old paradigms can represent two completely different and incommensurable worlds, suggesting a transformation in what a transcendental or critical realist would identify as the 'intransitive domain'. Such a conflation of 'being' with our 'knowledge of existence' is particularly common in the social sciences, although according to Bhaskar it often takes the form of the 'linguistic fallacy', the reduction of existence to language or discourse. (For a discussion of recent linguistic, semiotic and discursive approaches to social science, see Smith 1998b, ch. 6.)

Realism

So what is the alternative that Roy Bhaskar presents? In the place of empiricist and idealist approaches, he constructs an extensive and sophisticated account of science, derived from one 'transcendental' question: 'what are the conditions of possibility for science?' He found that:

> the intelligibility of experimental activity presupposes the categorical independence of the causal law discovered from the pattern of events produced. . . . [Thus] in an experiment we produce a pattern of events to identify a causal law but we do not produce the causal law identified.
>
> (Bhaskar 1978: 34)

Such 'transfactual' causal laws operate in open systems, where no constant conjunctions (regular sequences) of events prevail. Indeed, closed systems take place when conditions are artificially or (in some instances, as in the spontaneous closure of the solar system) naturally controlled, allowing for the rigorous observation and measurement of predetermined variables in isolation from the distorting influences of extraneous variables. Hence, given that 'the intelligibility of experimental activity presupposes the intransitive and structured character of the objects of scientific knowledge' (Bhaskar 1978: 35), transcendental realism regards the proper focus of science as both the 'structures' and 'mechanisms' that generate phenomena and the knowledge produced through the social activity of science. Consequently, the objects are not 'phenomena', as empiricism presupposed, nor are they 'social constructs' as is suggested by the idealist approach. Instead, they are seen as 'real entities' which endure and operate independently of our knowledge, experiences and the conditions which allow access to them (ibid.: 25–6). (See Table 2.1.)

Bhaskar's 'immanent critique' of the traditions within the philosophy of science, identified earlier, allows him to identify three steps in order to develop an adequate rationale for the use of laws to explain phenomena in open systems. This involves working through the ontological and epistemological assumptions of a particular approach in order to establish its conditions of possibility, and in so doing, identifying its limitations and attempting to overcome them. It must be emphasized at this stage, to avoid possible misunderstandings, that the term 'law' is defined in this context as a 'transfactually efficacious causal mechanism' rather than in the sense of empirical regularity between two or more variables. These three steps are represented in Figure 2.5. Before I address the realist analysis of the social, the following passages demonstrate how realism responds to and evaluates empiricist and idealist approaches to knowledge construction.

Table 2.1 Closed and open systems

		Closed systems	*Open systems*
1	Simplicity and complexity	A limited number of measurable variables to increase the possibility of identifying and predicting clear relationships.	A state of complexity is acknowledged as the condition of one's objects of analysis and the relations between them.
2	External boundary	Exclusion clauses ensure that the confusing mass of possible influences are screened out (such as the *ceteris paribus* clause, that holding all other things constant x will lead to y).	No external boundary is assumed to exist, so each object can be part of multiple causal relations and one cannot predict an outcome with any degree of certainty.
3	Intrinsic properties	All objects of analysis are taken at face value, so the intrinsic properties of an object are not considered.	Recognition that all objects have intrinsic properties and structures which affect their performance in different conditions.

Empiricism, idealism, realism 41

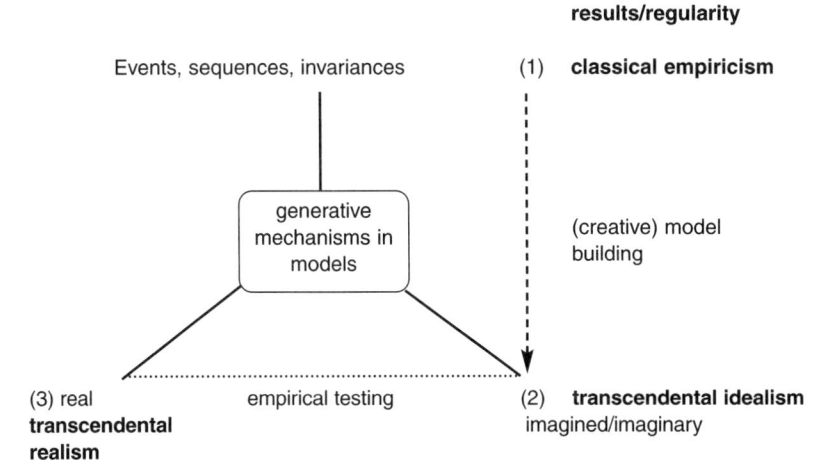

```
                                              results/regularity
     Events, sequences, invariances    (1)  classical empiricism

              ┌─────────────┐
              │ generative  │
              │mechanisms in│              (creative) model
              │   models    │              building
              └─────────────┘

(3) real            empirical testing    (2)  transcendental idealism
transcendental                                imagined/imaginary
realism
```

Figure 2.5 The logic of discovery
Source: Bhaskar 1978: 15

Against empiricism

From the realist standpoint, the objects of knowledge are structures and not simply events. Realism is founded upon the irreducibility of structures to events. This is represented in Figure 2.6. Bhaskar specifies a minimum of three progressively abstract and inclusive domains. First is the empirical domain, composed of experiences and hence involving partial representations of the actual and the real. To suggest that experiences are in some sense erroneous would lead us into the trap of the 'epistemic fallacy'

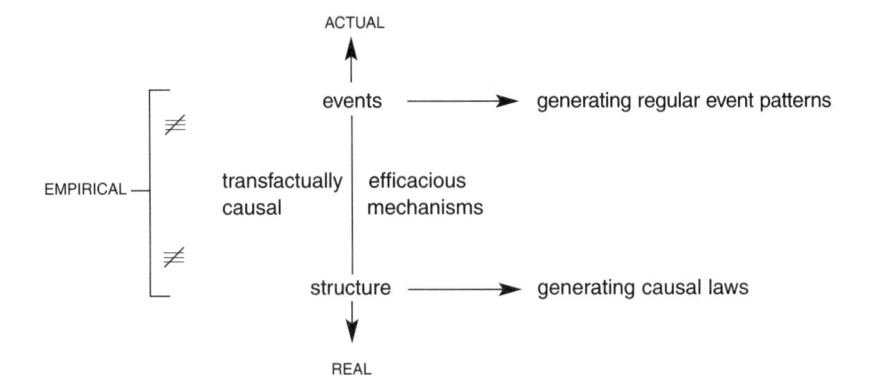

```
                         ACTUAL
                           ↑
                         events  ──────→ generating regular event patterns
        ⎡ ≢
EMPIRICAL ⎢     transfactually │ efficacious
        ⎢     causal          │ mechanisms
        ⎣ ≢
                         structure ─────→ generating causal laws
                           ↓
                         REAL
```

Figure 2.6 The empirical, the actual and the real
Note
While we may 'experience' aspects of the actual and the real domains, the empirical is in no way 'equivalent' to them.

identified earlier. Indeed elements of the real will inevitably be present in our experiences. Second is the actual domain, made up of events and constituting the surface phenomena upon which natural and social scientists focus their gaze. Third is the real domain, made up of the structures and generative mechanisms which produce events. The empirical and the actual are not equivalent, for not all events are experienced, whereas the real includes the actual and the empirical. However, causal mechanisms can neutralize each other's effects with the net product that no event takes place. For instance, if two equally matched 'hypothetical' tug-of-war teams were pulling on a rope and neither side were willing to give way (leaving the rope stationary, a state of equilibrium), this does not mean that considerable 'causal powers' are not being put into operation, despite the fact that no physical changes can be observed and an event (victory for one side in the contest) does not take place.

Against idealism

For the realist, objects of knowledge are 'intransitive' and not simply the 'transitive' artificial objects fashioned into items of knowledge through the scientific and philosophical conventions of the day. Transitive objects are constituted in and by knowledge (theories, methodologies, models, paradigms and so on). Intransitive objects, on the other hand, are the real causal structures and mechanisms which exist, operate and endure quite independently of knowledge. In the natural sciences, this latter point is unproblematic. However, in the social sciences intransitive objects are concept-dependent and thus include the transitive, which in turn suggests that there are certain ontological limits to naturalism, a point which will be explored later. The relationships between the philosophies of science considered and the distinction between the transitive and intransitive domains are represented in Figure 2.7.

Within the realist conception of science, a constant conjunction of events is neither a necessary nor a sufficient condition for the attribution of a causal law. Contrary to the 'regularity determinism' that characterizes empiricism and the 'intelligibility determinism' of idealism, according to Bhaskar, realism adopts a radically different conception of causality, that of 'ubiquity determinism'.

	Classical empiricism	Transcendental idealism	Transcendental realism
Transitive	x	√	√
Intransitive	x	x	√

Figure 2.7 The recognition of transitive and intransitive domains

This asserts that while every event has a real underlying cause or set of causes, nevertheless there is 'no presumption that the real cause of an event will also be intelligible to men [sic]' (Bhaskar 1978: 71). Within open systems, involving multiple causal mechanisms, our experiences are usually out of step with the real entities and causal laws to which experience (however imperfectly) gives us access. The relationship between the philosophies of science and conceptions of causality is shown in Figure 2.8.

For realism, it is the way the world is that makes science possible. The distinctions between structures and events, and between open and closed systems, are respectively and closely tied to the recognition of the 'stratification' and 'differentiation' of the real world. The stratification of the world involves the recognition of 'ontological depth' and the need to use the conceptual tool of abstraction, while the differentiation of the world recognizes the complexity of causal relationships within the open systems identified earlier. Bhaskar provides us with a useful way for conceptualizing this 'ontological depth' in developing a threefold conception of 'necessity':

Real essences   This kind of natural necessity is implicit in the concept of a thing's real properties or 'powers', without which it would not be the thing it is. Knowledge of natural necessity at this level is expressed in real definitions of natural kinds, whereby an intrinsic structure is discovered (by empirical and/or theoretical means), constituting the natural tendencies or 'causal powers' of an object. Questions of contingency are only relevant to whether things of a given kind exist.

Structure   This kind of natural necessity is implicit in the concept of a causal law, in the activity of a generative mechanism or in the existence of a thing's

The status of a constant conjunction of events is . . .	NECESSARY	SUFFICIENT	for a law statement
Empiricism	√	√	regularity determinism
Idealism	√	x	intelligibility determinism
Realism	x	x	ubiquity determinism

Figure 2.8 Causal laws and empirical regularities
Note
Both empiricism and idealism are ontologically committed to the position of empirical realism, and hence to the concept of the empirical world. This involves a series of related mistakes. First, 'the use of the category of "experience" to define the world . . . giving . . . a particular epistemological concept, a general ontological function'. Second, that an 'essential property of the world' is its susceptibility to experience, when this in in fact 'an accidental property of some things'. Third, 'the neglect of the (socially produced) circumstances under which experience is . . . epistemically significant in science' (Bhaskar 1978: 28).

tendencies (regardless of their realization). Knowledge of natural necessity at this level is expressed in terms of causal laws. In relation to a social object of analysis, it is contingent that an object has the structure it has but, once that particular structure is in place, it is necessary that it behaves in such a manner.

Events The kind of necessity which holds between events is the connection made by a generative mechanism (hence this is derived from the second form of necessity) and is dependent upon the contingent operation of the conditions within which behaviour takes place. Knowledge of natural necessity at this level is expressed in statements of relations between events, whereby a pattern is identified and an invariance is produced. According to realists, it is at this ontological level that empirical realism resides (Bhaskar 1978: 170–4).

Throughout this chapter, I have tended to present the realist approach to science as if the concerns of the natural and social sciences were one and the same, taking the 'possibility of naturalism' largely for granted. However, it should be noted that a number of ontological limits to naturalism exist. These stem directly from the distinctive character of the objects of analysis within the social sciences, compared with those of the natural sciences (although the latter are by no means uniform themselves).

(i) Social structures do not exist independently of the activities they govern;
(ii) social structures do not exist independently of the agents' conceptions of what they are doing in their activity;
(iii) social structures may be relatively enduring (highly space-time specific);
(iv) social structures are reproduced-transformed in agency, in turn dependent upon the articulation of structure and praxis.
(Bhaskar 1978: 38; 1986: 131; 1989a: 175)

Indeed, because of the activity-dependence, concept-dependence, time–space-dependence, and social relation-dependence of social structures, it seems appropriate to move away from 'experimentalist' science (whereby physics is taken as the best exemplar of natural science research techniques) and consider alternative sources of natural science analogues for the social sciences. Attempts have been made in meteorology, seismology, astronomy and palaeontology to establish determinations without falling into the difficulties of determinism (for an example see Gould 1977: 251–9; 1989 *passim*).

Realist analyses of social life emphasize the way in which social structure is ultimately related to the concrete practices of members of society (through social agency). They argue that many widely-accepted contemporary approaches inadequately theorize this relationship, and that they often fall into the trap of treating structure or agency as the residual category of the

Empiricism, idealism, realism 45

other. This leads to what Bhaskar has labelled the ontological errors of 'reification' and 'voluntarism'. First, reification (and the corresponding epistemological error of determinism) takes place through an over-concentration on the unacknowledged conditions or unintended consequences of agency. In this situation, agency is reduced to the position of a 'passive subject' or 'träger' (carrier) of social roles and thus tends to neglect the need to understand purposeful and meaningful action. Second, voluntarism (and the corresponding epistemological error of methodological individualism) takes place through an over-concentration on actions and individual capability to secure 'ends' against the will of others. This exclusive focus upon intentions and purposes neglects the unacknowledged conditions and the unintended consequences of action. Both approaches offer a partial account of the structure–agency relationship.

A number of attempts have been made to overcome the one-sided nature of these reified or voluntaristic approaches, the most influential and comprehensive of which is structuration theory, developed by Anthony Giddens. This approach assumes that neither structure nor agency have logical primacy, that 'each is constituted in and through recurrent practices' (Giddens 1982: 8–11). Giddens attempts to overcome the view that social structure and the actions of agents are two different things, seeing them instead as two sides of the same coin. To understand human action in a way compatible with a consideration of the structural components of social relations, one must focus upon the duality of structure and agency (in Bhaskar's terminology, agency is termed 'praxis'). Giddens attempts to avoid the structure–agency dualism by viewing the structural properties of social systems as both enabling and constraining for human action. This means that structure is seen as both the medium and the outcome of knowledgeably sustained and capably exercised social practices.

To illustrate the relationship between structure as a medium and as an outcome, Giddens utilizes the 'language-analogue'. First, language structure as a 'medium' for 'communication' (speaking) must generally conform to the rules of the linguistic game (through the possession and the exercise of a range of skills) so that it can be understood. Second, language structure is simultaneously the 'outcome', for the practice of communication reproduces-transforms language, just as voting and political group activity reproduces-transforms the political system, being employed as wage-labour reproduces-transforms capitalism, and domestic servitude reproduces-transforms patriarchal family life. These examples illustrate the way in which the practical knowledge and capabilities necessary for everyday life are preconditions for social structure (Giddens 1976; 1979: 69–79; 1984) and they also highlight their attractiveness to modes of thinking concerned with human emancipation. Hence, while social structure facilitates, is continually reconstituted by, and is only perceptually observable through, human agency, at the same time the resources which agents deploy in using their 'causal powers' derive from that very structure. However, Giddens still links power to agency in a logical relationship, and thus does not escape the dualism that he seeks to escape. As a result, his concept of power treats the structural conditions for agency as ephemeral to the concept of power. From a realist viewpoint, power is more adequately conceptualized in the sense of 'causal powers' as the 'structured capacity of real entities' which exist whether or not they are operationalized at a given moment.

When considering the part played by agency in relation to structure, Bhaskar provides a similar approach to Giddens but prefers to talk of 'reproduction-transformation' rather than 'structuration'. The differences are not purely semantic, for Bhaskar gives structure a stronger ontological grounding and places greater emphasis upon the 'pre-existence of social forms' as a basis for the 'empirically controlled theoretical analysis of historical possibilities' (Bhaskar 1983: 85). He presents these issues in terms of two dualities:

- The *duality of structure* as the ever-present condition (material cause) and continually reproduced-transformed outcome of agency. Structural forms have a necessary pre-existence which can condition the possible responses made by agents, in that they may operate as constraints for certain agents while offering opportunities for others by facilitating a strategic advantage. For instance, in feminist appropriations of realist arguments, the structural forms of 'patriarchy' can facilitate opportunities for men in some situations but present constraints, obstacles and 'glass-ceilings' for women.
- The *duality of praxis*, involving the conscious production of social life (through work, organization and signification) and the – possibly – unintended and/or unconscious reproduction-transformation of structure (the future conditions of production). This capacity for reproduction-transformation depends, in turn, upon the structural location, the capacities and the mobilization of the agents concerned within certain (as yet to be specified) conditions (Bhaskar 1979: 34–44).

Indeed, as Bhaskar argued, as well as being subject to 'exogenous sources' of social change (the activities of other agents), structures may contain within them 'endogenous sources' of social change (Bhaskar 1989a: 175). Such 'auto-subversive' properties within structural forms themselves partially account for the generation of 'crises' and disruption which, in turn, allow for previously unrecognized causal mechanisms. This complex relationship can be more clearly represented in Figure 2.9.

In this approach, real situations are seen as constituted through complex multiple determinations which are themselves comprised of analytically-distinct relations. Therefore, social scientists must take care to adopt appropriate abstractions which can accommodate the simultaneous co-presence of structure and agency. In addition, realism considers causality as the actualization of the properties of real entities which possess both 'causal powers' (capacities to do certain things) and 'causal liabilities' (susceptibilities of certain kinds). These causal powers and liabilities are given a specific form by virtue of

Empiricism, idealism, realism 47

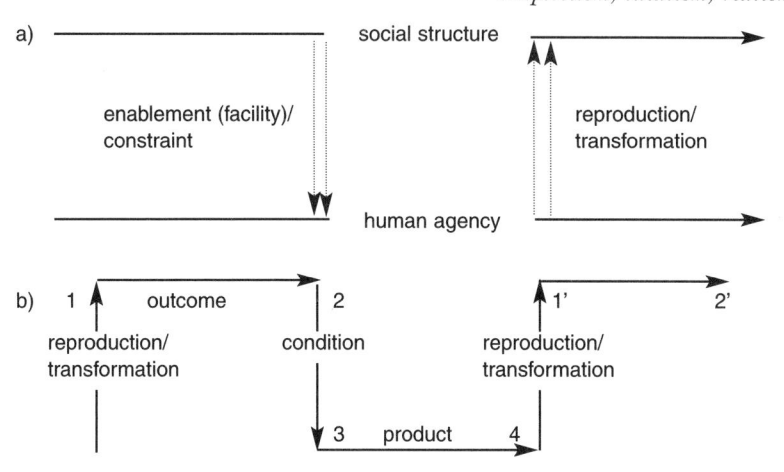

Figure 2.9 Bhaskar's transformational model of social activity

Notes
1, 1' – unintended consequences
2 – unacknowledged conditions
3 – unconscious motivation
4 – tacit skills (properties of agents

  1 and 2 place limits upon the individual's understanding of social life, while 3 and 4 place limits upon one's understanding of oneself

Source: Bhaskar 1986: 126.

the internal and necessary relations of the object in question, such as those between husband and wife, parent and child, landlord and tenant, teachers and student, tyrant and subject and capitalist employer and wage-labourer. In each case, one cannot exist except in terms of the existence of the other. Bhaskar sums up this situation by saying, 'A relation R_{AB} may be defined as internal if and only if A would not be what it essentially is unless B is related to it in the way it is' (Bhaskar 1979: 42).

In the social sciences, such internally and necessarily related objects and practices are subject to two forms of contingency. First, the forces at work within one (set of) structure(s) may simultaneously be involved with other (sets of) structures. For instance, class relations between wage-labour and capital are contingently related to gender, racial and status relations. Second, the constitutive elements of social structure are subject to the transformative capacity of human agency. Hence, it is contingent whether any given structure retains the same form through time and across space (that is, structures are socially and historically specific).

Since social structures are part of the tacit web of relations that constitute social relations, it is often difficult to reconstruct the ways in which social structures operate. This involves the combination of two theoretical tools, abstraction and causal explanation. Abstraction is a 'synchronic' theoretical tool, a static idealization which can be used to generate comparisons with similar static representations (in a comparative-historical sense). This must be combined with causal explanation, a 'diachronic' theoretical tool, if it is to establish an adequate understanding of social process and change. Causal explanation can only be rendered intelligible through the analysis of the structure's possession of powers that can generate change within the context of certain conditions. For instance, in a somewhat gruesome example, fire has the capacity (or causal power) to burn human beings. This is because fire involves the production of heat, and the biochemical constitution of human beings includes the liability to combust when subject to intense heat. However, whether one is burned or not is a contingent matter: for example, one will not burn if one wears an asbestos suit (see Isaac 1987a: 47). Causal relations can be represented as shown in Figure 2.10.

To summarize, the realist approach avoids both a reified conception of power, as structural constraint, and a voluntarist conception of power, which tends to regard the conduct of agents as 'arbitrary, rationalistic and willed' (Gramsci 1971: 367–7). Since events are conceptualized as complex causal outcomes, this means that causal law statements should take the form of an exposition of structured capacity and dispositional properties, if they are to be compatible with the realist account of scientific practice. Peter Manicas suggests that this provides a basis for 'determination without determinism'; although this is still subject to three guidelines.

- Knowledge of dispositional properties is 'a posteriori', involving a movement from establishing effects to establishing causes.
- There is no requirement that such properties are either universal or eternal (hence avoiding essentialism).
- We should accept the metaphysical assumption that there are things which exist independently of us and that they can be theorized.

Given the existence of a 'radical asymmetry between explanation and prediction' (Manicas 1987: 256), no matter how well grounded our knowledge

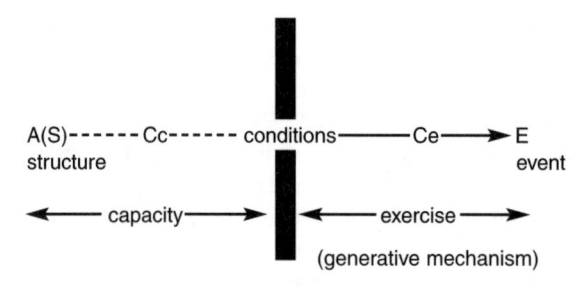

A(S)------Cc------ conditions ———— Ce ———▶ E
structure   event

◀——— capacity ———▶   ◀——— exercise ———▶
                    (generative mechanism)

Figure 2.10 Realist causal explanations

Notes
Under certain conditions, A tends to produce E by virtue of its structure S.
(Cc – conditions which activate mechanisms; Ce – conditions which mediate or block certain effects)

appears to be, an indefinite number of things could happen for 'the future is never exactly like the past' (ibid.: 257). Reality constantly involves change, therefore theorizing about that reality will never offer a complete or totalized conception of everything for all time. Grand theory is impossible in this approach.

So where does the realist approach lead us? One recommendation is that the focus of scientific theory, conceived as the search for (relatively) enduring mechanisms, should be directed towards the causal powers of the objects in question. In addition, these causal powers should be expressed (given the contingencies identified) in the form of 'normic' laws, as law-like tendencies. Two lessons can be drawn from the preceding discussions of empiricism and various forms of idealism. On the one hand, given the existence of open systems which characterize objects of analysis, it should be remembered that 'no science can demand more precision than its objects allow . . . [and it] can never get away from the flesh and blood reality of social practice and historical process' (Isaac 1987a: 12). On the other hand, there is no unmediated means of achieving access to the truth: in a Popperian moment, realists argue that all knowledge is fallible. They argue that it is through the transitive process of science that we come to know higher-order entities. These entities or objects are portrayed as 'real' in the stronger ontological sense, that they exist independently of the knower, rather than the weaker epistemological sense of what we know to be real at any given time. Realism argues that through our rational capacities for constructing knowledge, we can attempt to establish the real structures and mechanisms which, in their complex ways, are responsible for the social phenomena that we experience.

What epistemological considerations are raised by these ontological concerns? Using realist arguments, three epistemological steps can be identified in social-scientific practice.

- The identification and description of regularities or significant effects: Andrew Sayer refers to relations of (dis-)similarity (Sayer 1985, 1992).
- The construction of theoretical models which include hypothetical causal mechanisms (the 'conditions of possibility') which, if realized, would account for the regularity or significant effect.
- The empirical testing of the authenticity of the models or the hypothetical causal mechanisms to demonstrate their (in-) adequacy and eliminate counter-hypotheses.

Hence, realism seeks to transcend the sterile separation of 'empirical research' and 'theoretical construction' by seeking to integrate them in a commensurable way. Outhwaite has suggested that this approach, based upon a non-empiricist epistemology, must allow for complex reconceptualization as and when necessary (Outhwaite 1987, ch. 2). This can be achieved through two basic models of explanation which I shall label as 'retroduction', and 'retrodiction', and which Bhaskar describes as the DREI scheme (theoretical analysis) and the RRRE scheme (practical analysis). (See Table 2.2.)

Table 2.2 Theoretical and practical analysis

Theoretical analysis	Practical analysis
The analogical-retroductive movement from manifest phenomena to generative structures (the identification of the abstract from the concrete)	The decompository-retrodictive movement from resolved components to antecedent causes (the recovery of the concrete from the abstract)
Description of law-like behaviour (regularities, patterns and such like)	*Resolution* of a complex event into its components (causal analysis)
Retroduction by exploiting analogies with already known phenomena, to explanations of behaviour	*Redescription* of their components in theoretically significant terms
Elaboration and elimination of alternative explanations	*Retrodiction* through independently validated normic or tendency statements to possible antecedents of these components
Identification of the causal mechanisms in an empirically controlled way.	*Elimination* of alternative possible causes.

Retroduction assumes that antecedently available cognitive resources are used to construct plausible models of the unknown structures and mechanisms which generate identifiable patterns of phenomena. Retrodiction assumes that validated knowledge is transfactually applied through the reconstruction of the diverse determinations which constitute events. Both are subject to the constraints of empirical adequacy, consistency, coherence, and relevance (Bhaskar 1979: 129; 1986: 68). While Kant asked the question 'what are the conditions of possibility of experience?', the realist approach asks 'what are the conditions of possibility for science?' To conclude, let me draw upon Jeffrey Isaac, who identifies two grounds on which critical realism stands:

- The *historical grounds* that philosophy is necessarily practical and practically conditioned by extra-discursive philosophical interests and standpoints. For Isaac there are good reasons (though not indisputable grounds) for the belief that scientific rationality provides us with a warranted knowledge of the structure of the real world.
- The *epistemological grounds* upon which critical realism carries out an 'immanent critique' of both the empiricist and idealist approaches to knowledge construction through the construction of a 'transcendental' account (a second-order inquiry) of the pre-existing accounts of science in order to pull the rug from underneath their feet (Isaac 1990: 9–11).

An adequate conception of science must recognize the existence of 'open systems', the distinction between the transitive and the intransitive domains, the complex relationship between structures, mechanisms, events and experience, and the distinctive view of 'causality' as the dispositional property of an object (the capacity or propensity to do something). In the social sciences this is complicated further by the identity of subject and object, and by the need to take account of the simultaneous coexistence of structure and agency as mutual preconditions.

Some metatheoretical reflections on state theory

In order to demonstrate the differences between these approaches, I have focused upon the different conceptions of causality within empiricism, idealism and realism, and the role they play in the construction of social-scientific knowledge. By drawing upon the relationships between regularity determinism and empiricism, intelligibility determinism and idealism and ubiquity determinism and realism, it is possible to examine the differences between explanatory accounts of the state, or any other social scientific object. Empiricist approaches to the state and politics overwhelmingly focus upon the observable instances of political decision making, within the terms of reference of existing political institutions. The empiricist approach assumes that closed systems can be constructed whereby it is feasible to identify simple causal relationships and ignore the complexity of both of the empirical world and the intrinsic properties or structure of the objects in question. Theories are considered relevant in that they are treated as pictures of a state of affairs, or in so far as they can repeatedly be tested against observational evidence drawn from the context in question. The separation of facts and values in empiricism is an indicator of the tendency of such approaches to present descriptive (or concealed normative) accounts of political events and states of affairs. This can be seen within the broadly pluralist political science of the 1950s and 1960s.

In the idealist approach, the adoption of the position of intelligibility determinism in respect to the status of causal laws plays a significant role in distinguishing it from the empiricist approach. The idealist approach can accommodate the prior existence and imaginative uses of mental constructs in relation to the observable evidence. Thus, it can identify the distinctive role of human interpretation in the conceptual organization of experience, as distinct from the passive account of the knowing subject in relation to sensations, perceptions and impressions within empiricism. By accepting that constant conjunctions of events are not sufficient in themselves for generating causal laws (by acknowledging that theories cannot replicate the complexity of social life), the idealist approach clearly breaches the conception of the closed system at the heart of empiricism. In particular, idealism breaks with the empiricist assumption of symmetry between explanation and prediction. Idealists suggest that, since theories are not mimetic reflections of reality, it is only possible to predict patterns rather than specific outcomes. However, in common with empiricism, idealism does not specify the intrinsic states and properties of the objects in question (which is the distinctive feature of realist approaches).

Idealist approaches in political theory are often explicitly normative in their identification of political relations and their explanation of political events. In posing a distinction between the actual state of affairs and the ideal situation, they also pose the possibility of a transformation around some principle of human realization. However, they differ in terms of their respective characterizations of how this human realization can be understood and achieved. The forms of human realization explored in Chapters Three and Four are located in terms of the relationship between the state and society. In the case of Dahl, it is founded upon a conception of citizenship, and in the case of Hayek upon the intersubjective relations of the catallaxy. Each, in its own way, attempts to establish the conditions of possibility of the social and political order which are considered to be desirable. In short, Dahl and Hayek apply the transcendental mode of reasoning to the political domain. Rather than taking the existing state of affairs for granted, they specify the conditions of possibility within which human subjects can exercise full autonomy, whether this refers to the political conditions within which they can directly participate in the decisions which affect their lives (as in Dahl's account) or to the conditions within which economic actors can engage in the realization of their plans and motives in the market economy (as in Hayek's approach).

The realist approach incorporates the insights of the idealist approach (particularly, the recognition of the transitive dimension). However, in posing a different transcendental question, 'what are the conditions of possibility of (social) science?', it also attempts to identify the properties and structures of the real world (the intransitive dimension), which can be seen as existing independently of our knowledge of them. By focusing upon the unobservable structures and mechanisms which generate events, this approach redefines the basis for constructing a causal law, a position identified earlier as ubiquity determinism. The distinction between the concrete-in-thought and the real-concrete, developed within the neo-Marxist approach towards political economy, provides a good illustration of the use of the transitive/intransitive distinction. Neo-Marxist state theory draws upon the realist assumptions of Marx's method within his studies of the capitalist economy in order to construct an account of the superstructure and the role of the state within capitalism.

The focus upon the state theory of Bob Jessop in Chapter Five provides us with an account which is remarkable for its epistemological and ontological self-awareness, as well as his consistent defence of the Marxist position. Jessop's work is also useful in another way. In attempting to resolve some of the important dilemmas within neo-Marxist political economy, he draws quite heavily from a range of sources which would otherwise be identified as idealist. Jessop's defence, that the insertion of concepts from non-Marxist accounts within a Marxist problematic transforms their meaning, is a common one in Marxist theorizing. In response, Chapter Five explores the precise character of Jessop's use of idealist concepts and assumptions in relation to developing a neo-Marxist account of capitalism, the state and the societalization process. This exploration provides an opportunity to think through some of the problems and issues involved in constructing a realist theory of the state and politics. William Outhwaite suggests that realism combines ontology and epistemology in a way that is both 'ontologically bold and epistemologically cautious' (Outhwaite 1987: 34). If a realist account of the state and its conditions is to be achieved, then we also have to think through what it means to be ontologically bold in developing state theory. We will return to the prospects for such a state theory in the concluding chapter.

In the following chapters, I will attempt to clarify the relationship between empiricist, idealist and realist approaches within the field of state theory, not as theoretical pigeon-holes but as complex sets of assumptions which can be combined in interesting and perhaps contradictory ways in the actual practice of social-scientific research. This chapter has demonstrated how the realist approach and its critique of empiricist and idealist positions provide us with vital clues for situating social-scientific knowledge. In addition, this approach helps us to identify where the significant shifts can take place. Of particular importance are the theory of causality and the differing terms of reference within which a causal law can be established. This matters not just for state theory but also for gaining a better understanding of the generation of all forms of social-scientific knowledge.

3 Polyarchic civility and the state

Introduction: two Dahls or one?

The work of Robert A. Dahl on politics, power and democracy has rarely been considered systematically, and he is often caricatured as a pseudo-systems theorist, a hard-nosed political scientist and an apologist for political apathy. More considered responses to Dahl's contribution to political sociology, on the concept of power and the organization of political communities, will be considered in the section on the conundrums of power. The purpose of this intervention is to demonstrate how Dahl's work responded to such criticisms and, in particular, how he shifted his epistemological standpoint to accommodate this refocusing of theoretical and empirical concerns.

The Dahl most often cited in reviews of the literature is the 'behaviourist Dahl', fixated upon actual decision making in observable concrete situations. The texts which dwell upon his later work raise the possibility of a fundamental reorientation of his position as he began to adopt an explicitly normative stance regarding the possibility and the desirability of participatory democracy. Others have portrayed this as a technical shift in focus in Dahl's research, from a concern with political inputs into the state towards a greater attention to policy outputs (notably Dunleavy and O'Leary 1987: 13–71, 271–349). This tendency to divide his work into two phases, which we can label Dahl I and Dahl II, obscures the important strands of continuity which need to be recognized if we are to appreciate the distinctive qualities of his work on the state, democracy and civility.

While it is fair to argue that few people's work stands still, it remains crucial to engage in the activity of a critical exegesis of contemporary social and political theorists, such as Dahl, in order to help us understand such interventions on democratic theory and the state. While the epistemological shifts involved in his work are significant, as demonstrated later, there is remarkable ontological continuity, even as he problematizes his earlier position. The most important strand of substantive continuity throughout his work is the consistent utilization of a particular conception of *polyarchic civility*, which he developed to construct his account of democracy. Indeed, the main thrust of this line of inquiry is to establish Dahl as a leading contributor on the *sociality of politics* and the cultural conditions of democracy, rather than as a state theorist.

Behaviourist foundations: empiricist epistemology meets empirical realist ontology

Throughout the development of his work, Dahl's pluralist account of the state and power can be seen as a consistent attempt to develop a particular metaphor of causality. This metaphor is ultimately derived from Hobbes, Locke and Hume, and is sustained throughout his use of the work of Madison, Montesquieu and Tocqueville. The political imagery upon which Dahl draws speaks volumes in this respect. The concept of political community is taken to be a sovereign subject constructing the rules of the political game in order to regulate individual behaviour. In a similar way, Dahl's basic units of analysis are individuals (or groups as their organized aggregation) operating within the context of the liberal distinction of the state and civil society, who are 'subjects constituted as individuals with clear preference orders [and as such] are sovereign' (Clegg 1989: 39).

Pluralism, in its early phases, concentrated upon the operation of participatory politics and how this impacted upon the process of public policy making. In the terminology of David Easton, this can be expressed as an analytical focus upon *input* politics as opposed to policy outputs or consequences (Easton 1965, 1967; Dunleavy and O'Leary 1987: 23–41). This focus upon voting, political parties and interest groups followed Arthur Bentley's emphasis upon the collection and analysis of quantitative empirical data. It also included the treatment of collective agents as having no specificity beyond the individuals which constitute them (Bentley 1967). In Bhaskar's terms of reference, this position involves the ontological error of voluntarism compounded by the corresponding epistemological error of methodological individualism (see Chapter Two; Bhaskar 1979: 28–32).

The lines of development in Dahl's work can be seen in his first substantial treatise on political philosophy, *A Preface to Democratic Theory* (1956), where he establishes the range of available possibilities in developing a theory of democracy. This involves a contrast between 'maximizing theory' and 'descriptive theory'. Maximizing theory involves the specification of the 'end' of some state of affairs and the identification of the conditions in which such a state could be realized. Descriptive theory examines a given set of institutions and organizations, establishes their common features and seeks to establish what conditions are necessary and sufficient for their existence (Dahl 1956: 2). Dahl distinguishes Madisonian democracy, with its focus on minimizing the danger of the tyranny of the majority, from populist democracy, with its emphasis on popular sovereignty and egalitarian ends. Both of these, he suggests, are illustrations of the maximizing type which tell us little or nothing about 'the real world' (that which can be studied empirically). Dahl develops his ideas on democracy and the state by interrogating representatives from the two distinctive liberal traditions, which have been identified by John Hall as critical (Anglo-American) and egoistic (continental European) liberalism (Hall 1987: 9–24).

In his early work, Dahl addresses the critical liberal tradition directly. His initial focus upon James Madison's contribution to the Federalist Papers is clearly an attempt to make his advocacy of the model of polyarchic democracy intelligible to an American audience who are already receptive to ideas of civic responsibility. In addition, Dahl engages in the perilous activity of reading between the lines of Madison's account of the nature of *the republic* (the concept of democracy associated with direct democracy among Madison's contemporaries). Madison's position emphasized the need for external constraints on individuals and groups in order to prevent tyranny: that is tyranny by majorities (the legislative) over minorities (the executive) and vice versa. In addition, he argued that these 'external checks' are susceptible to being undermined by the 'accumulation of powers' in the same hands, infringing the principle of the separation of executive, legislative and judicial powers. For Dahl, the implicit premises behind Madison's position involve the assumption that the external checks can be conceptualized as 'rewards' and 'penalties' enforced for (in-)appropriate behaviour. In addition, it is assumed that the state of 'tyranny' involves the infringement (as Dahl puts it, 'severe deprivation') of natural rights. While these are now taken to be life, limb and property (in the Lockean sense), there was no definite agreement about what constituted natural rights. Nor was there any clear idea of when infringements went beyond 'consent' in the period in question and, for that matter, in Madison's own writings (Dahl 1956: 6–10).

Madison's concerns, in accepting that frequent elections were not sufficient for guarding against such infringements, were more directed towards the practical needs of limiting the length of terms of office and limiting the development of factions, as well as ensuring that the various powers of government should be in different hands. Dahl, however, is keen to extend the analysis of power beyond the institutional context of the constitutional safeguards of separate constituencies, the division of responsibility between the institutions of the state, federalism, judicial review and a range of other checks and balances. This has some basis in Madison's account of the need to control majority factions through the creation of a large and diverse republic, as well as with pre-revolutionary concerns with the moral virtue of the populace. Dahl draws upon Machiavelli to identify the necessary constraints on leadership by the attitudes, networks and habitual relations of society, as well as to identify a potentially fruitful area of research.

> Family structure, belief systems, myths, heroes, legitimate types of behavior in primary groups, prevailing or modal personality types, these and other similar factors would be crucial in determining probable responses of leaders and non-leaders and hence the probability of tyranny or non-tyranny.
>
> (Dahl 1956: 18)

Finally, Dahl turns his attention to the logical status of the key concepts adumbrated by Madison, such as tyranny and faction. In the absence of a clear specification of natural rights, the objective of a non-tyrannical society has consequences clearly at odds with Madison's intent, for even the punishment of criminal actions would be a violation. However, a return to a justification based upon majority consent would have undermined his stance against the tyranny of the majority. The existence of factions is also difficult to square with Madison's approach. He defined factions as a group of citizens who unify around a passion and/or interest adverse to the rights of other citizens. In the absence of any conception of what those rights are, we are left with no way of distinguishing a faction from 'other citizens'. If these central concepts are meaningless, then the contention that majorities can vote down factional minorities and that majority factions can be avoided through enlarging the scale and diversity of the republic are also untestable. Indeed, Dahl suggests that it is feasible to envisage a minority using its veto over majority decisions, in order to abolish deprivations of freedom such as child labour or the absence of welfare support (Dahl 1956: 22–33).

When examining the principle of the absolute sovereignty of the majority, associated with *populist democracy* (a label for the egotistic tradition in liberalism borrowed from Edward Shils), Dahl again attempts to reconstruct the implicit assumptions within this approach. Briefly, in popular democracy, policy making must be compatible with the conditions of popular sovereignty and political equality, and must assume that, as a procedural rule, a majority is in favour of one policy over and above alternative policies (Dahl 1956: 37–8). Dahl proceeds to establish which of the many objections to such a stance hold water. The technical objections – that some will not express a preference – do not constitute an obstacle for Dahl, for only explicit preferences for and against enter the political domain. However, the problems raised by an evenly balanced and divided populace with contrary (possibly irreconcilable) policy preferences deserve greater attention, especially given the consequences of deadlock in a political system. This is further complicated if the policy differences are between a policy already in operation and any alternative policy. In such situations, deadlock ensures that the existing state of affairs is perpetuated. Finally, there is the technical difficulty of establishing the most appropriate voting system both to represent the views of the electorate and to meet the practical requirements of that society, a choice which may affect the outcome of any policy negotiations. One way around this would be to use referenda with a clear choice between two alternatives, but these pose other practical limitations (Dahl 1956: 38–44).

The majoritarian principle also creates objections on ethical grounds. Dahl contrasts the Madisonian position, in which a majority ought to be necessary but not sufficient for establishing a policy, to the populist position, for which a majority is both necessary and sufficient. The commitment to popular sovereignty and equality in the absence of a convincing transcendental ethic is difficult to sustain. This leads Dahl to speculate how it would be possible 'rationally' to compare the condition of popular sovereignty with a limited amount of popular sovereignty. Consequently, the populist democratic approach fails to address the 'real world', in much the same way as Madison's approach. One instance would be the recognition of the intensity of feeling of a small minority. In some cases, a generally opposed majority with a low level of commitment may acquiesce to such a strongly-held minority preference. Empirical research, Dahl argues, reveals a wider range of political goals than popular sovereignty and equality, which have historically been taken as a cover for rule by minority elites in the name of the many. In a revealing passage, Dahl contends:

> Most of us are marginalists. Generally we experience diminishing marginal utility the more we attain any one goal; or in the language of contemporary psychology, goal attainment reduces the drive value of the stimulus. Political equality and popular sovereignty are not absolute goals; we must ask ourselves how much leisure, privacy, consensus, stability, income, security, progress, status, and probably many other goals we are prepared to forego for an additional increment of political equality. It is an observable fact that almost no one regards political equality and popular sovereignty as worth an unlimited sacrifice of these other goals.
>
> (Dahl 1956: 51)

As a result, Dahl proposes polyarchal democracy as an antidote to the 'exercises in axiomatics' so far discussed. He starts from the problem of dealing with the intensity of preferences, that we must either incorporate this into an account of democracy, with all its attendant problems, or assume that all preferences are equally weighted. Clearly, the possibility of the existence of one actor able to deploy his or her preference on either side of a political conflict with a decisive impact is likely to upset any resolution in favour of the first option. In any case, in order to avoid being overwhelmed by social complexity, Dahl assumes that each preference is identical and that all preferences are interchangeable. In addition, this begs the question of what exactly constitutes a preference. A range of indices are available, such as voting or statements of opinion. Two stages are relevant to Dahl as he builds an account of the social prerequisites of polyarchic democracy, focusing on the election stage and the inter-election stage. The election stage is divided into pre-voting, voting and post-voting periods. In effect, Dahl constructs a closed system model of political influence, establishing relationships where many of the most important variables are held constant. Five initial conditions are specified.

1 Equally weighted preferences.
2 Preferences are expressed as voting.
3 The alternative preference with a simple majority wins.
4 The possibility of citizens inserting alternative preferences in the ballot.
5 Participants have identical information about the alternatives on offer.

Polyarchic civility and the state 59

The fourth condition is inserted to distinguish democratic voting from authoritarian plebiscites, and the fifth condition to ensure the avoidance of the problem of the manipulation of information in the model (an anticipation of critical points on agenda formation raised below). To ensure the implementation of election promises, three further conditions were added:

6 Majority alternatives replace the minority alternatives.
7 The orders of officials are carried out; inter-election decisions are controlled by election results.
8 New inter-election decisions are governed by the aforementioned seven conditions.

Dahl is realistic about the inaccuracy of the assumptions made in this programme, particularly on the fourth and fifth conditions, and sees it merely as an exploratory device in order to construct a means of classifying political systems and distinguishing polyarchies from autocratic and oligarchic systems. In effect, Dahl is attempting to find a way of reconciling the maximizing method with the descriptive method. Thus, the question he seeks to address, given that the eight conditions are now interpreted as continua or scales rather than as an unobtainable limit, is, 'What are the necessary and sufficient conditions in the real world for the existence of these eight conditions, to at least the minimum degree we have agreed to call polyarchy?' (Dahl 1956: 75).

To express this in Kantian terms, the question can be rephrased as 'what are the conditions of possibility of polyarchic democracy?' However, rather than accepting social openness, Dahl opts for a closed-system analytical framework. Polyarchic democracy becomes a means of settling disputes between contending interests. If the social institutions have successfully ensured that these conditions have been translated into norms through the training of individuals, then the operation of these eight conditions or norms (polyarchy) depends upon the degree of agreement over both political and non-political goals. He expresses this relationship in the form of a continuum, alongside that of autonomy and control (see Figure 3.1).

In the case of the second continuum, autonomy is defined as the degree to which a group's policies are not controlled by external individuals or groups. For Madison, the most effective limitation on the capacity of a majority to control government policy is a situation where a high degree of autonomy is

Agreement ⟷ Disagreement

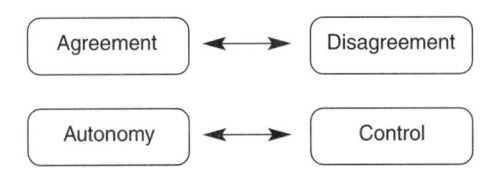

Autonomy ⟷ Control

Figure 3.1 Dahl's conceptual terms of reference

combined with a high level of disagreement. Yet, for Dahl, complete autonomy renders a group beyond any possible governmental relationship with another group, thus 'they cannot be members of the same polyarchy' (Dahl 1956: 80). This can in fact save polyarchic political systems, for contentious and potentially dangerous policy issues tend to become non-political, such as on moral issues like religious tolerance. If groups are less than autonomous, that is there is some degree of control. In conditions where given policy issues provoke extensive disagreement, the eight norms underpinning polyarchy are undermined. The extent and character of disagreement does have consequences: 'Beyond some point, the sharper the disagreement over policies within a social organization, and the larger the proportion of individuals involved in the disagreement, the greater the amount of social autonomy required for polyarchy to exist at any given level' (ibid.),

This, he suggests, cannot be separated from consideration of the political activity of members of an organization (their capacity to vote, campaign and disseminate information) which are related to social cleavages. Dahl points to evidence which contradicts Madison's fear of the 'tyranny of the masses', such as the activism of higher income earners, the well-educated and the well-endowed in financial and organizational terms, compared to the few resources, low levels of interest and general passivity of the uneducated strata of American society. Polyarchy, then, can be defined as a combination of higher levels of autonomy where disagreement is more intense and widespread, *and/or* higher levels of control on issues where agreement is more manifest. Consequently, in opposition to the Madisonian fixation with constitutional constraints, Dahl concludes that the theory of polyarchy redirects our attention towards 'social checks and balances' and the 'social separation of powers', that is, the social prerequisites for a healthy democratic order. In Dahl's words, 'Whether we are concerned with tyranny by a minority or tyranny by a majority, the theory of polyarchy suggests that the first and crucial variables to which political scientists must direct their attention are social and not constitutional' (Dahl 1956: 83).

Dahl clearly pins his democratic hopes upon the 'ethos of society', rather than the 'sovereignty of the majority'. He suggests that while the forms of polyarchy vary, the constitutional frameworks are much the same. He presents two explanations for this. First, the prerequisites of polyarchy (on any scale) 'impose a definite limitation on constitutional types' (Dahl 1956: 136). Second, an efficient large-scale society presupposes an increasingly specialized division of labour at all levels, and the emergence of a correspondingly specialized administrative or bureaucratic structure. Such emergent vested interests in the various parts of the administration, which are in competition with one another, generate their own checks and balances. Thus, even in the administrative, executive, legislative and judicial institutional structures, the primary guarantee of democratic processes is delivered through non-constitutional rules. Where constitutional rules remain important, Dahl argues, is in the allocation of 'advantages' and 'handicaps' to

Polyarchic civility and the state 61

particular groups. It is here, in the contestation of such rules, that we can find the source of the greater part of conflict in the USA.[1] The uneven political weight and resources of politically mobilized groups are considered to be facts of life in a society premised upon voluntary association, and in relation to which the polyarchal system for facilitating negotiation, bargaining and compromise is most appropriate (ibid.: 124–151).

At this point, Dahl clearly argues that political science should take the social preconditions of democratic political systems much more seriously. This focus upon political participation and the social checks and balances reinforced criticisms that pluralism has an inadequate conception of the state (in Easton's terms, as a sort of 'black box'). As the following chapters also indicate, it is worthwhile considering theories of the state as grounded upon particular conceptions of the social domain. Having identified the eight social prerequisites of polyarchy, Dahl then proceeds to outline the possibilities of measuring polyarchy quantitatively, bearing in mind the impossibility of measuring the intensities of actions (Dahl 1956: 118). Each of the conditions is translated into a measurable frequency of actions to be determined empirically (on a scale of probabilities of 0 to 1), acknowledging that the most amenable data available is that associated with voting, and the difficulties in identifying useful data for the other conditions. This enables him to construct a classification system for polyarchies:

1   Polyarchies are defined as: organizations in which all eight conditions are scaled at values equal to or greater than 0.5.
1.1   Egalitarian polyarchies are defined as: polyarchies in which all eight conditions are scaled at values equal to or greater than 0.75.
1.2   Non-egalitarian polyarchies are defined as all other polyarchies.
2   Hierarchies are defined as: organizations in which all eight conditions are scaled at values less than 0.5.
2.1   Oligarchies are defined as: Hierarchies in which some conditions are scaled at values equal to or greater than 0.25.
2.2   Dictatorships are defined as: hierarchies in which no conditions are scaled at values equal to or greater than 0.25.
3   Mixed polities are defined as: the residual, i.e. organizations in which at least one condition is scaled at a value greater than or equal to 0.5, and at least one at a value less than 0.5.

(Dahl 1956: 87)

In constructing this closed system of measurable variables and a cross-cutting typology of political systems, Dahl's position offers the best possible shell for retaining the Hobbesian prioritization of causality. However, in its rejection of natural necessity, the precise conceptualization of cause and effect is Humean. This is also mediated through the behaviourist approach to American political science which predominated in the 1950s. The causal relationship in Dahl's work is a spatio-temporal one, existing between discrete and separate objects (whether these are taken to be events and/or individuals). At one and the same time, the causal relationships between these entities are conceived to be contingent (possessing their own *sui generis* specificity) and the entities themselves are understood to be 'ontologically autarkic' (Ball 1978b: 102; also see Ball 1975, 1978a, 1988). This conforms to the ontological assumptions of empirical realism, identified in Chapter Two.

Another interesting feature, or rather absence, is the failure to address power clearly as an intentional phenomenon, in the sense of Russell, Berlin and Hayek. This is a direct consequence of Dahl's early fascination with behaviourism and its potential in political science. The behavioural tradition originated in psychology, and spread to the other social sciences as they sought to establish their legitimacy in the mid-twentieth century. In particular, it is important to establish the influence of J. N. Watson's 'methodological individualism'. As a rationale for political and social analysis, this Humean ontology has profound implications when adopted in conjunction with an empiricist epistemology. It involves 'the belief that the social world is nothing more than a series of behavioural regularities' (Isaac 1987: 7). The empiricist approach underpinned the tradition of political science during much of the post-war period, and the field of public administration before that. As a consequence, when discussing the concept of power, political scientists have tended to focus on *power over*, the production of effects expressed in a relationship between two independent entities. In this case the irreducible unit of analysis is, predictably, the individual. However, the role of the intentional or purposeful actor is absent, given the behaviourist rejection of the 'autonomous man'.[2] Political scientists, such as Dahl and Polsby, explicitly adopted the behavioural approach towards social-scientific research, when constructing the pluralist model of the state and politics. For Dahl the pluralist model is 'Based upon the study of individuals in political situations, this approach calls for the examination of the political relationships of men . . . with the object of formulating and testing hypotheses concerning uniformities of behaviour' (Dahl 1961a: 764).

The concept of power is reduced to an empirical regularity whereby the behaviour of one agent causes the behaviour of another, so that the latter does things he or she would not otherwise do (to use Clegg's terminology this is a decisionist or episodic conception of power). Dahl states that his 'intuitive idea of power' can be characterized as, 'A has the power over B to the extent that he can get B to do something that B would not otherwise do' (Dahl 1957: 203–4).[3] This approach limits research on power to research into actual decision-making behaviour and active choices within situations of identifiable (presumably observed) conflict. Lukes neatly summarizes the essentials of this position when he writes that the one-dimensional view of power involves 'a focus upon behaviour in the making of decisions on issues over which there is an observable conflict of (subjective) interests, seen as express policy preferences revealed by political participation' (Lukes 1974: 15).

By focusing on the specific outcomes of observable behaviour, researchers using the pluralist approach are able to gather reliable data (that is, data which can be retested and which produce the same or similar results). Pluralist assumptions dictate that we can only understand causal analysis in terms of the data gathered through experience, preferably in the form of quantitative data and in order to facilitate correlative analysis (Dahl 1984: 140–1). In a defining passage, originally published in 1968, Dahl clearly links power relations to causality.

> The closest equivalent to the power relation is the causal relation, for the assertion 'C has power over R', one can substitute the assertion 'C's behavior causes R's behavior. . . . [Thus] power is merely a term for a causal relation involving human beings. . . . [P]roperties used to distinguish causation also serve to define power relations: co-variation, temporal sequence and asymmetry, for example.
> (Dahl 1986b: 46–7)

While viewing power relations as a sub-category of causal relations, Dahl seems well aware of the dangers involved in transferring the methods and assumptions of the philosophy of the natural sciences on to the analysis of power. Notwithstanding his acknowledgement of the definition of causality in terms of the necessary and sufficient conditions of existence, he recognizes that the study of human beings entails the acceptance of greater degrees of complexity than those which are taken to exist in natural scientific experimentation. He raises the difficulty in distinguishing true from spurious causation, and the problems which are raised by the coexistence of a number of competing models which all plausibly fit the 'inescapably crude and limited evidence'. Consequently, Dahl opts for a model of causal inference drawn from the work of Hubert Blalock (1964). This concerns the inadequacy of causal models, or at least, it can provide a basis for eliminating models which fail to live up to certain predictive criteria and achieve a surrogate closure. Dahl does not take this opportunity to reconsider the appropriateness of 'regularity determinism' and make a shift towards 'intelligibility determinism'. To do so, he would have to accept that a constant conjunction of events is necessary but not sufficient for establishing a causal law (the transcendental idealist resolution of the problems of causality). Thus, at this stage in his work, Dahl remains committed to the empiricist account of causality.

If we examine Dahl's position at this stage, we can see that power is defined in a decisionist way as episodic agency. Individuals are taken as the basic unit of analysis from which he then moves to examine personalities, groups, roles, offices, governments, nation-states, and other human aggregates. Interests are understood as subjectively constituted, and identified as express policy preferences within concrete decision-making situations. This excludes any conception of interests as unobserved and unarticulated in the political process (for these would be rejected as metaphysical speculation along Popperian lines). Dahl's comments on the Marxist tradition are instructive here. He argues that the prime movers of the capitalist mode of production, the bourgeois and proletarian classes, cannot be said to exist if no empirical evidence substantiates the supposed 'irreconcilable antagonisms' between such collective actors.

> According to Marxist theory, in capitalist societies the capitalist class unilaterally rules over the society. In this sense class as a whole might be considered to be the prime mover. But the unilateral dominance of the capitalist class is more a theoretical postulate or hypothesis than a well verified description of contemporary non-socialist nation-states with democratic governments.
>
> (Dahl 1984: 34)

Indeed, the impetus for Dahl's interventions appears to have been the impact of such speculative metaphysics in political research on elite politics in the USA, notably that of Floyd Hunter (1953), based upon the 'reputational method', and, more polemically, C. Wright Mills (1956).[4] It was what Dahl considered to be the inadequate methods in such accounts that led to his 1955–9 investigation of political decision making in New Haven as a typical American city hall (with Nelson Polsby and Richard Wolfinger as research assistants). This was finally published as the classic pluralist text *Who Governs?* (Dahl 1961b). In this study, Dahl examined the observable concrete decision making involved in the expression of policy preferences, initiation of proposals, casting of votes for or vetoes against formally sanctioned decisions. The key policy issues identified as objects for research were urban development, public education and nominations for political office. Dahl's conclusion that no one group dominated in all policy areas, all of the time, enabled him to argue that New Haven, while not an ideal democracy, was considerably more polyarchic than oligarchic. In addition, he claimed that the resources which contributed to power were so dispersed and fragmented that direct political influence was limited (with most having only indirect influence, through the vote).

In the closing sections of *Who Governs?*, Dahl addresses the reasons for stability in New Haven and, by implication, polyarchies in general. He considers the conventional explanation of the degree of civic knowledge and agreement on what constitutes a democratic polity, 'the basic rights, duties, and procedures that serve to distinguish democratic from non democratic systems' (Dahl 1961b: 311), by drawing upon Alexis de Tocqueville. Of the three causes of democracy developed in Tocqueville's *Democracy in America* (1968), Dahl places a particular stress on the importance of custom as 'the whole moral and intellectual condition of the people', alongside laws and the physical, social and economic condition of the people. Noting the underdeveloped nature of this contribution, which in Tocqueville's work largely focused on the 'small platoons' of civil society, Dahl proceeds to examine the flaws in explanations of stability achieved through the acceptance of the political rules of the game. First, widespread agreement on the principle of democracy conceals disagreements on their application. Second, widely-held views can be contrary to the actual rules of the game. Third, the level of agreement is more heavily distributed in the 'political stratum', that is, in those who are politically active. Finally, even the level of agreement in the political stratum does not account for the stability of the political system (Dahl 1961b: 312). Dahl argues that the degree of consensus achieved in any political system is transitory and fragile. When consensus is achieved, it is through the *reciprocal process of interchange* between and among 'political professionals', the political stratum and the general populace. Consensus is portrayed as a dynamic process rather than the static quality of a society and its political system (ibid.: 315–16).

The prevailing belief in democracy, and the general acceptance of flaws in the American polity because it is a fairly effective and reasonably fair working political system, is strongly sustained through a 'variety of powerful social processes', with formal schooling singled out as the most important institution, reinforced by the activities of the mass media. At this stage in Dahl's development, the consideration of the social retains a behavioural quality in which individuals are conditioned to accept a set of principles, and the construction of social relations is downplayed. When examining the general populace, citizens are characterized as manifesting low levels of sophistication, and the democratic creed is flexibly interpreted. A higher and consistent commitment to democratic norms is identified in the political stratum and, within their fold, political professionals; a reflection of their investment in political life. When disagreement does take place among the political stratum, this rarely generates anxiety among citizens and it is resolved through institutions beyond party conflict (such as through judicial review).

For Dahl, much depends upon how the political stratum handles the issues. He treats public involvement in the political decision-making process as an exception to the normal condition (raising the example of how Senator McCarthy bypassed the political professionals by appealing directly to public opinion). Even when explicitly consulted by the 'legitimators' and 'dissenters' normally operating in the political stratum, ordinary citizens have a tendency either to consult local political sources of political leadership (the leaders of the 'small platoons' such as churches or unions) or to retreat even further from the political gaze. *Who Governs?* has been criticized for a series of methodological flaws, which relate to the choice of 'key' issues and an assessment of their relevance for potential oligarchic groups (who resided outside New Haven). However, this does not refute the approach to knowledge construction which underpins Dahl's work at this time. To make this kind of assessment, we must address the ontological and epistemological bases of this form of social inquiry.

In the next section, I consider the debate on the concept of power in the 1960s and 1970s, and explore its relationship to knowledge construction. Dahl's approach to the concept of power is open to criticism on two important counts, both of which stem from his attachment to the Humean conception of causality and the consequent regularity determinism. At this stage (to use Kant's vocabulary), he neglects the conditions of possibility of knowledge in his understanding of the role of mental constructs in the activity of political science. First, Dahl only accepts observational evidence, and regards the posing of social structure or hidden interests as dangerous and unwarranted. This reveals his empiricist rejection of methodological essentialism (the search for inner essences) in favour of methodological nominalism (the description of objects in various circumstances). For students of politics this is a profoundly limiting approach, given that the object of analysis, *the state*, is characterized by the existence of backroom political deals and institutional secrecy. Dahl's position is something of an over-reaction to the perceived excesses of the conspiracy theory explanations characteristic of some of the elite theories developed in the period. In addition, there are difficulties in the assumption of symmetry between explanation and prediction at the heart of the empiricist approach to causality. As was shown in Chapter Two, the alternative realist conception of causality, conceived as ubiquity determinism, rejects the view that a constant conjunction of events is either necessary or sufficient in establishing causal laws, making this assumption superfluous. The history of politics as a discipline is littered with problems generated by this obsession with prediction as the sole criterion of success.

The conundrums of power

The account of power developed by Dahl and Polsby is often taken as an apologia for the political status quo. The reformist critique of this position was initiated by Peter Bachrach and Morton Baratz (1962, 1963, 1970). Bachrach and Baratz's approach was anti-behaviourist in intent, but nevertheless retained many of the assumptions of the pluralist approach. Bachrach and Baratz specifically address two problems with Dahl's conception of power. First is the fact that the scope of decision making is limited to safe issues, for it 'unduly emphasizes the importance of initiating deciding and vetoing' (Bachrach and Baratz 1970: 6). To go beyond the pluralist position, they developed the concept of 'non-decision making'. This enabled them to account for how issues on which decisions are made are organized into and out of politics (or the public domain) so that observable conflicts do not arise. Such conflicts of interest, which cannot be observed within the terms of reference established by Dahl and Polsby, are labelled 'latent conflicts' by Bachrach and Baratz. Hence, rather than 'A having *power over* B', 'A devotes his energies to creating and reinforcing social and political values and institutional practices that limit the scope of the political process to public consideration of only those issues which are comparatively innocuous to it' (Bachrach and Baratz 1962: 950).

Second, Bachrach and Baratz address the absence of an objective criterion in Dahl's work for distinguishing between key and unimportant issues. They conclude that a 'key issue' is one which, in fact, challenges the rules of the game. For Bachrach and Baratz, these rules of the game are defined as 'the dominant values and the political myths, rituals and institutions which tend to favour the vested interests of one or more groups, relative to others' (Bachrach and Baratz 1962: 950).

Hence, Bachrach and Baratz raise the problems of accounting for the less articulate and organized groups, and the part played by anticipated reactions and the mobilization of bias in a political system. The *law of anticipated reactions* is drawn from C. J. Friedrich's conceptualization of power, authority and rationality. On the one hand, public officials will avoid raising issues likely to provoke a 'strenuous reaction' by deciding not to decide (Bachrach and Baratz 1962: 952). This is not strictly non-decision making but a negative form of decision making. On the other hand, citizens will in most cases choose compliance to defiance in situations involving power (Bachrach and Baratz 1963: 638–9). Bachrach and Baratz drew upon the way in which E. E. Schattschneider used the term '*the mobilization of bias*', to illustrate how agenda formation is as important to policy outcomes as the observable making of decisions. Non-decisions can thus be identified by establishing the existence of covert grievances. In their later, more qualified, critique of Dahl, they redefined key issues as 'a genuine challenge to the resources of power or authority of those who currently dominate the process by which policy outputs in the system are determined' (Bachrach and Baratz 1970: 47–8).

Steven Lukes provides a useful and vivid summary of this second dimension of power as involving the 'consideration of the ways in which *decisions* are prevented from being taken as *potential issues* over which there is an observable *conflict* of (subjective) *interests*, seen as embodied in express policy preferences and sub-political grievances' (Lukes 1974: 20).

This approach has been demonstrated empirically by Matthew Crenson's *The Un-Politics of Air Pollution* (1971), in a comparative study of two steel towns, East Chicago and Gary, which experienced a thirteen-year discrepancy in implementing air pollution control legislation (in 1949 and 1962 respectively). In the case of Gary, a single industry town, there was an absence of organized opposition to legislative inactivity on clean air. This can be explained by the widespread acceptance that the imposition of such controls could lead (as an anticipated reaction) to industrial relocation and a consequent decline in the local economy. In East Chicago, the fragmented nature of the industry and the alternative opportunities for employment created the context for overt conflicts of interest, amenable to the limited tools available to pluralists. Andrew Blowers developed a similar case study of the responses to the pollution caused by the London Brick Company, although the comparative method utilized is diachronic rather than synchronic. In this account, Blowers identifies separate phases of non-decision making, respectively phases of negotiation, confrontation and finally resolution (Blowers 1983).

For the pluralist approach, however, the analysis of anticipated reactions presents only practical difficulties in operationalizing the research programme. For pluralists, ultimately, non-decisions remain a form of decision (Polsby 1963: 205). In addition to being simply an ordinary organizing device to ensure a degree of predictability in human life, non-decisions are seen as unspecifiable and are not amenable to research (Wolfinger 1971: 1065–72). The onus is thus shifted back on to the supporters of the non-decision approach to demonstrate empirically when a group would clearly have acted in a different way had the mobilization of bias not effectively operated to prevent political conflict (ibid.; Frey 1971). For these reasons the Crenson study is particularly effective, since the issues revolve around the potential health risks in maintaining the status quo, and the conflicting interests of local employment opportunities and of avoiding the concentration of dangerous pollutants. For Steven Lukes, however, Bachrach and Baratz's account can be criticized on three further counts. First, their qualified critique of behaviourism does not go far enough for:

> the bias of the system is not sustained simply by a series of individually chosen acts, but also, most importantly, by the socially structured and culturally patterned behaviour of groups, and practices of institutions, which may indeed be manifested by individuals' inaction.
> (Lukes 1974: 21–2)

This entails the adoption of a 'methodologically individualist' approach to power (Lukes 1974: 22), in which the Weberian understanding of power as the 'realization of will against resistance' comes to the fore.

Second, Bachrach and Baratz associate power only with actual observable conflict which ignores the exercise of power 'by influencing, shaping or determining his very wants. . . that the most effective and insidious use of power is to prevent such conflict from arising in the first place' (Lukes 1974: 23).

Third and finally, their insistence that non-decision making only exists where grievances are denied entry into the political process in the form of 'issues' still invokes the assumption that the absence of grievances is equivalent to a genuine consensus. Therefore, this approach cannot adequately recognize and conceptualize the existence of a *manipulated consensus*, where grievances are neither articulated nor perceived. A manipulated consensus is the product of the ways in which 'perceptions, cognitions and preferences' imply the acceptance of the prevailing ways in which things are organized and alternatives are not even ventured, never mind discussed. This draws out points made by Dahl on the limitations of his method, especially when faced with authoritarian governments which attempt, sometimes successfully, to shape preferences (Dahl 1958: 468; 1961b). However, both Dahl and Polsby retain their commitment to limiting political analysis to the study of express preferences. Unlike Lukes, they avoid conceptions of 'real interests', those interests which are regarded as existing independently of whether they generate observable preferences. Hence, in his account of the 'most effective and insidious' dimension of power, the third dimension, Steven Lukes radicalizes Bachrach and Baratz's approach. Lukes concentrates upon how the emergence of visible conflict is pre-empted.

> In summary, the three dimensional view of power involves a *thoroughgoing critique* of the *behavioural focus* of the first two views as too individualistic and allows for consideration of the many ways in which *potential issues* are kept out of politics whether through the operation of social forces and institutional practices or through individual's decisions. This, moreover, can occur in the absence of actual observable conflict which may have been successfully averted – though there remains an implicit reference to potential conflict. This potential may never be fully actualized. What we may have is a *latent conflict* which consists in a contradiction between the interests of those exercising power and the *real interests* of those they exclude.
> (Lukes 1974: 24–5)

The defining characteristic of this approach is the consideration of the concept of real interests as being 'ineradicably evaluative'. This enables Lukes to identify the role of social institutions in shaping values and hence preferences, potentially preventing groups from having a clear sense of their real interests. For Lukes, conceptions of real interests vary according to one's value position (with the position of Dahl and Polsby being liberal, Bachrach and Baratz reformist and Lukes explicitly marking himself off as a radical). For Clegg, the moral choices within these positions are fixed 'a priori, but also beyond the bounds of analytical explanation' (Clegg 1989: 87). However, it is important not to misunderstand the purpose of the evaluative critique developed by Lukes, as one which sets clear blue water between himself and those approaches he is considering. For Lukes, the three dimensions are inclusive, not mutually exclusive, domains: involving a progressive inclusion of the first by the second and both by the third dimension.

When this scheme has been operationalized, however, the conception of real interests has hindered rather than facilitated clarity. The cases where the approach is easiest to demonstrate are those institutional situations where a strongly-held ethos of the purpose of the institution predominates. For instance, Chris Ham identifies the dominant value system in the provision of health care which operates in such a way as to maintain the existing power relations between doctors and other professional groups in relation to patients (Ham 1985). However, such situations are exceptional rather than the norm. In the case studies of J. A. Whitt (1979, 1982), interests are located in structure, while with John Gaventa (1980), we can see the construction of a three-dimensional model without using the concept of 'real interests'. These studies demonstrate the need both to move beyond the level of surface appearances and clearly to adopt a cautious attitude about what we attempt to conceptualize at this level. This also avoids the dangers of falling back upon tautologous explanations, based on a conception of false consciousness with which explanations based on 'real interests' are associated. Whitt's investigation of the political lobbying involved in Californian public transportation policy, through a comparison of pluralist, elitist and neo-Marxist models, can be interpreted as revealing some utility in each of the three dimensions of power, and also demonstrates the inclusive nature of Lukes' approach.

John Gaventa's *Power and Powerlessness: Quiescence and Rebellion in an Appalachian Valley* (1980) also applies the three-dimensional model, in this case to the mining community of Clear Fork Valley on the boundaries of the American states of Kentucky and Tennessee. This study reinforces the arguments of the critics of pluralism, who stressed the importance of participation in the formation of the consciousness of actors, and the tendency of apathy to generate further inertia. In addition, Gaventa overcomes some of the difficulties involved in identifying the processes of legitimation, myths and ideology by grounding them in a historical case study. For Gaventa, the identification of the mechanisms of power at work in the third dimension involves:

> specifying the means through which power influences, shapes or determines conceptions of the necessities, possibilities, and strategies of challenge in situations of latent conflict. This may include the study of social myths, language, and symbols, and how they are shaped or manipulated in power processes . . . the means by which the social legitimations are developed around the dominant, and instilled as beliefs or roles in the dominated.
>
> (Gaventa 1980: 15).

Gaventa focuses upon the interests of the people involved in terms of the actual distribution of wealth and the consequences of mining on local communities (especially health consequences), then seeks to demonstrate how this has not produced an 'effective rebellion' in such conditions. In Gaventa's study, it is clearly demonstrated that power mechanisms are related to the quiescence of a community even when the conditions would generate considerable conflict elsewhere.

Ted Benton raises the problem of 'the paradox of emancipation' as being common to both Lukes' radical and the Marxist conception of 'collective self emancipation' (although one could also add the radical feminist analysis of patriarchy, and perspectives representing oppressed ethnic minorities). This refers to the issue of how it is possible to define what the real interests of a social object can be, as well as how they can be identified independently of the perceived interests of the group in question. In other words, how is it possible to reconcile 'collective self emancipation with a critique of the established order which holds that the conscious preferences of those from whom collective self emancipation is to be expected is systematically manipulated, distorted and falsified by essential features of that order' (Benton 1981a: 162).

The paradox for Lukes is such that, if he is to establish criteria on which he can determine interests, he must make explicit his own position of moral absolutism and consider the issue of ideology. Alternatively, he could opt for moral relativism and abandon the concept of 'real interests' upon which his approach is based. This latter choice would indeed be more consistent with Lukes' own commitment to 'responsible individualism', and it remains in line with his conceptualization of power as agency, that 'choice entails responsibility' (Clegg 1989: 99). In addition, Derek Layder has pointed out that in conceptualizing power in this way, Lukes does not clearly identify 'where structural determinism ends and structural constraint begins' (Layder 1985: 139). Consequently Lukes' bottom line is voluntarist, and he conceptualizes structure as a constraint rather than as facilitative. This is most clearly expressed in one short passage by Lukes when he argues that power:

> presupposes human agency. To use the vocabulary of power . . . in application to social relationships, is to speak of human agents, separately or together, in groups or organizations, through actions or inaction significantly affecting the thoughts or actions of others. In speaking thus, one assumes that although agents operate within structurally determined limits, they nonetheless have a relative autonomy and could have acted differently.
> (Lukes 1977: 6–7)

Stewart Clegg suggests that Lukes' position represents an uneasy mixture of conventionalism (along the lines of Kuhn and Feyerabend) and realism (along Bhaskarian lines). This combination is founded upon a central tension 'between his evaluative theorization of the interests implicit in action and the absence of any coherent theoretical framework by which these interests might be evaluated' (Clegg 1989: 118). Thus it can safely be assumed that the studies of Bachrach and Baratz and of Steven Lukes extend Dahl's approach to include structural concerns, with Lukes also contributing the concept of real interests. However, consistently with pluralism, they all conceptualize these in terms of an agency (or in Clegg's terminology, an 'episodic') concept of power which prevents the conceptualization of structure as an independent reality. Clegg argues that this approach leaves us in a limbo between objective and subjective interests, and could be more adequately theorized and characterized through a dispositional concept of power which 'is distinguished by reference to a notion of the differentiated capacities for power which agencies have irrespective of whether or not they exercise this power' (Clegg 1989: 84).

While Lukes appears to ask the most pertinent questions, his approach

72 *Rethinking state theory*

lacks the theoretical tools for resolving the issues these questions generate, particularly for explaining the emergence of causal powers. In the next section, I examine Dahl's response to this barrage of commentaries and criticism, and identify the epistemological shifts involved in the emergence of neo-pluralism. In Dahl's later work, it is possible to identify how Dahl attempts to address the concerns raised by such critiques.

Acknowledging complexity: towards a deontology of the future

Dahl's research and writings in the 1950s and early 1960s remained steadfastly empiricist. However, as the problems in Western liberal democracies mounted throughout the 1960s, a clear shift in Dahl's work can be identified. Although Dahl had a sense of the complexity of his chosen object of analysis, he remained, in his early work, committed to a descriptive approach on political community rather than to constructing a deontology. This attempt to maintain a non-normative stance (or rather leave his norms implicit) could be expressed as a *deontology of the present*. The shift in Dahl's work could thus be characterized as a move towards embracing a *deontology of the future* (a new system of rules for conduct). Dahl attempted to identify the conditions of possibility which need to be in place in order to ensure that polyarchy actually comes into being. This apparently simple and unproblematic shift, from describing polyarchal democracies towards adopting the position of promoting polyarchy as a normative ideal, required a fundamental epistemological reorientation from empiricism to transcendental idealism. What remained unchanged was the ontological commitment towards empirical realism. In terms of his substantive political sociology, Dahl also had to shift his concerns towards public policy outputs as he became more concerned with the consequences of political processes as well as the preconditions of polyarchal democracy.

What does an ideal polyarchal situation look like? It is clear, from the start, that Dahl envisages a very important feature of the preconditions of polyarchy to be the guardianship role of the agencies of civility, the whistle blowers of the media, parties and interested groups and, most importantly, a lively and active citizenry. This certainly contradicts the prevailing view that pluralism considers apathy to be indicative of public satisfaction. In the context of Dahl's approach, it would be an issue of concern that governments appeared to be beyond public scrutiny. In this sense, Dahl's concerns emerge in much the same way as a developing theme within the work of Jürgen Habermas, specifically his preoccupation with the discursive conditions for effective 'debating publics'. Habermas states that:

> The rational quality of political legislation does not only depend on how elected majorities and protected minorities work within parliaments. It also depends on the level of participation and school education, the degree

of information and the precision with which controversial issues are articulated — in short, on the discursive character of non-institutionalized opinion formation in the political public sphere.

(Habermas 1992: 570)

This theme, initially developed in his work in the sixties (Habermas 1989), seems to have re-emerged particularly strongly in Habermas' recent work, *Between Facts and Norms* (Habermas 1992; see Outhwaite 1994: 137–51). The relationship between Dahl's position and Kantian assumptions will be developed further in Chapter Six. Patrick Dunleavy and Brendan O'Leary provide an excellent statement of the effective importance of the *sociality of politics*, in terms of both the analytical framework of pluralism and its underlying normative intent:

> In a polyarchic culture citizens insist on participation in decisions affecting them. They are willing to question governmental decisions and to appraise them by independent standards and criteria. Undeferential citizens are characteristic of the culture. They believe in their capacities to make informed decisions, to turn out of office a government which ignores public opinion or breaches established democratic practices, and to secure redress for grievances against public officials' mistakes or wrongdoings. Citizens are prepared to organize collectively to advance aims, and are confident that organized groups will secure media coverage and government attention. A fundamental safeguard of democratic liberties is the cultural dispositions of a politically aware citizenry, competent to organize themselves.
>
> (Dunleavy and O'Leary 1987: 25–6)

This shift emerges clearly in Dahl's *Polyarchy: Participation and Opposition* (1971) where he considers the ways in which different regimes engage in democratization. In *Polyarchy* he argues for explicit consideration of the positive consequences involved in moving from a hegemonic to a more competitive regime and ultimately to polyarchy. In particular, he elaborates two theoretical dimensions in the democratization process, the extent of liberalization or *public contestation* and the extent of participation or *inclusiveness* (the entitlement to participate in elections and in the offices of the state). This enables Dahl to construct a fourfold typology of regimes:

1 *Closed hegemonies* with low levels of participation and contestation.
2 *Competitive oligarchies* with high levels of contestation combined with low levels of participation or inclusiveness.
3 *Inclusive hegemonies* which facilitate participation without allowing for greater contestation.
4 *Polyarchies* which are characterized as having high levels of contestation and participation, and are said to have experienced the processes of both liberalization and popularization (Dahl 1971: 6–7).

This model represents a substantial simplification of the process of democratization (within which polyarchies are conceived as relatively democratized), and attempts to construct a simplified analytical system in order to examine a limited number of variables. In practice, Dahl accepts that the vast bulk of regimes will fall into the grey areas between such clearly-defined types, and thus develops a fifth category of 'nearly regimes' (including both near-hegemonic regimes and near-polyarchies). These dimensions are given further complexity by the recognition that such processes may operate in different ways at the national level and in subnational organizations (such as trade unions, businesses and their associations, local government bodies, non-governmental organizations, churches and universities). Finally, he introduces a form of utilitarian or opportunity-cost calculus in order to establish the degree to which governments undergoing processes of liberalization and/or popularization are able to tolerate an opposition. This leads him to conclude that government tolerance increases as the costs of opposition fall and/or the costs of suppression increase, so that if suppression is more costly than toleration, then there are net benefits in allowing a competitive regime to exist (Dahl 1971: 8–16).

The consequences of polyarchy in political systems are marked by greater liberal freedoms, such as those of expression, association, assembly and the secret ballot. In addition, they are evident in the composition of the political leadership, since polyarchies are more open to the inclusion of representatives of previously marginalized groups or strata. Consequently, in polyarchies, political leaders and political parties are driven to consult and penetrate the constituent groups of the society. They have to articulate the concerns of citizens and their interests in order to mobilize sufficient support and achieve power (so ending one-party hegemony). Dahl argues that this facilitates the proliferation of preferences and interests in numerical terms as well as in variety, giving the emergence of polyarchy both qualitative and quantitative dimensions. Throughout his justifications of polyarchy, Dahl makes significant references to the complexity of the objects in question and the crude nature of his classification system in the face of this difficulty. This is a clear admission that constant conjunctions of events, while necessary and useful, are in no way sufficient for establishing a causal law. Dahl's typologies are thus attempts to model complex political systems, and he clearly recognizes that it is difficult to ascertain the consequences of lower thresholds for participation and contestation for government policies at the national level, or in terms of different regimes. This consideration of complexity is a function of the recognition throughout the study that there is a reciprocal relationship between the regime types and their social context, of 'beliefs, attitudes, culture and personalities' (Dahl 1971: 30).

At this point, Dahl provides only general recommendations for 'political innovators' who are seeking to shift the regimes they inhabit towards greater public contestation and inclusivity. In particular, he tells cautionary tales by warning against optimism and by raising the existence of limits on the possibilities for change inherent in the conditions of each society. The explicit recognition of social complexity serves as a basis for constructing a model, underpinned by *intelligibility determinism* (see Chapter Two), which can identify seven sets of interdependent conditions facilitating or constraining the emergence of polyarchy (Dahl 1971: 202–7).

The *historical sequences* most favourable to polyarchy have been identified above, with the most favourable circumstance being that of competition preceding inclusivity (and inclusivity preceding competition constituting the least favourable circumstance). By examining the periodization and variable courses of democratization, *Polyarchy* contains the seeds of Dahl's later work on participatory democracy. He suggests that the democratization process can be divided into three phases.

1 The transformation of closed hegemonies and competitive oligarchies into near-polyarchies in the West in the late-nineteenth century (civil liberties or civil citizenship).
2 The transformation of near polyarchies into full polyarchies in the early twentieth century (political citizenship).
3 The democratization of full polyarchies in two phases:
    • The emergence of the welfare state in the mid-twentieth century (social citizenship).
    • A renewal of the process in the 1960s, driven by the young, as demands emerged for a wider democratization of social institutions (Dahl 1971: 10–11).

Dahl suggests that in the road to democratization in England and Sweden (both of which followed the most common route) the process of liberalization preceded inclusiveness, while in the German case, prior to the Nazi regime, inclusiveness preceded liberalization. More dramatically, the French Revolution is characterized as a 'short cut' or 'abrupt transformation', with a simultaneous shift towards both inclusiveness and liberalization. Dahl considers one pathway to be responsible for the most stable polyarchal regimes. This involves the gradual establishment of the rules of the political game by allowing contestation in elites, then, when civility and trust are ensured, expansion of the franchise to create a more inclusive political system. In the other cases, legitimation is weaker and conflict resolution is less likely to be successful. This reinforces Dahl's emphasis upon the importance of the cultural preconditions of polyarchic democracy, especially in establishing the mutual guarantees upon which stability is grounded.

On a more sceptical note, he also registers the point that since most non-polyarchal regimes are already inclusive without revealing significant contestation, we cannot expect democratization processes to be unproblematic. The lessons drawn from previous transformations into polyarchy suggest that in the cases of closed hegemonies, the most auspicious circumstances depend on the initiation of competition and the encouragement of evolutionary rather than revolutionary change. Military conquests seem to have ensured the necessary stability, although the most successful regimes were those already in the form of competitive oligarchies, as with the evolution of the English Parliamentary system. In addition, he suggests that the colonial context is no longer a relevant variable. Significantly, Dahl stresses the unpredictability of such processes, and the way in which it is feasible only to ascertain patterns of change and not to predict specific outcomes (Dahl 1971: 35–47). This is an important clue in identifying the epistemological shift in Dahl's work.

Beyond the recommendation of gradual change and the construction of mutual trust and institutional guarantees, most non-polyarchies appear to be heading for a bleak time. Certainly, Dahl is keen to explode the 'boundless optimism' which appears to characterize a considerable amount of political theory and philosophy on democracy in the USA, and which had built up following the successful (re-)establishment of polyarchal democracy in Western and Southern Europe in the aftermath of the Second World War. In addition, Dahl points to the dangers and failures in American foreign policy in seeking externally to facilitate the emergence of (presumably sympathetic) polyarchal regimes within its sphere of influence, by invasion and occupation, supporting revolutionary movements, or shoring up existing regimes with aid and armaments while applying pressure for internal liberalization. In the place of such unreliable strategies, he proposes the judicious use of foreign aid (especially where signs of near-polyarchy are manifest), in order both to eradicate misery and to facilitate socio-economic development. Interestingly, he suggests that this should happen regardless of the nature of the regime. Dahl's case for aid is clearly made upon the grounds of 'morality and compassion' and 'rational self-interest', rather than in the vain hope that such policies would be a means of levering such regimes to initiate programmes of liberalization. He argues that it is trends in socio-economic development that matter for the emergence of polyarchy, as demonstrated in the next two sets of conditions for polyarchy.

The second condition is the *type of socio-economic order*. Dahl is concerned with the extent of access to 'violent means of coercion, persuasion and inducement', access to socio-economic sanctions (non-violent control of economic resources, communications and the processes of socialization) and whether the society in question is agrarian or commercial/industrial. The crucial variant here is whether the sanctions or organization of agrarian and industrial practices are decentralized or monopolized. When considering the use of sanctions, Dahl takes a bottom line for the existence of polyarchy to be a depoliticized military. Beyond the conditions of hegemony and polyarchy, the most likely combination of elements is a quasi-pluralistic social order with repressive violence (such as Franco's Spain or Peronist Argentina). In the case of agrarian societies (drawing from Tocqueville's emphasis upon equality of land holdings), free farmers rather than peasants (and in industrial societies, market competition rather than public or private monopolies) are more conducive to fostering polyarchy. Thus Dahl's empirical illustrations establish a strong association between the free use of private property and the stability of polyarchal democracy, although the former is not seen as either necessary or sufficient for the latter. For Dahl, in contravention of the orthodox liberal view in this period, it is the existence of a high degree of centralization, regardless of (socialist or capitalist) ownership, which is the crucial determinant in facilitating the emergence or sustenance of a hegemonic regime (Dahl 1971: 48–61).

The third condition is the *level of socio-economic development*. This is expressed in terms of national income measures (as closely correlated with other indices ranging from urbanization and literacy rates to the level of material possessions). Dahl established that a clear relationship exists between the level of national income and the extent of political competition and inclusivity. However, while polyarchal democracy is strongly associated with societies experiencing mass consumption, there is considerable variation in the emergence of polyarchy in relation to the levels of per capita GNP. Clearly, other mediations are significant in contemporary and historical terms. Significantly, Tocqueville's study of *Democracy in America* (1968) revealed extensive polyarchy with relatively low levels of income (much like contemporary India, if we ignore the higher levels of inequality). The part played by *intelligibility determinism* is much clearer in Dahl's discussion of these causal factors. He seeks to establish the empirical regularities (or constant conjunctions of events) between levels of socio-economic development, and the distinctive features of the emergence of polyarchal democracy, without viewing these as sufficient in terms of generating a causal law. Indeed, he is keen to establish the unique and complex social conditions which distinguish the pre-industrial polyarchy of the United States from the equally complex social conditions of contemporary post-colonial societies. Again, the crucial set of conditions (see condition seven below) is the existence of competition between the 'politically relevant' groups or strata, alongside the social preconditions of literacy, education, communication and the absence of 'extreme inequalities', which had preceded the emergence of industry in America.

The relationship between the economy and the polity is conceptualized as a 'loose fit' which appears to be somewhat tighter at low levels and high levels of development. Dahl states categorically that an advanced industry needs workers with elementary literacy, skilled workers with advanced literacy and numeracy, and a range of professional groups who also aid the constitution of a 'pluralistic social order'. Such a social order demands consensus building between voluntary groups and institutions, rather than the hierarchical and monopolistic exercise of sanctions. Prophetically, he suggests that societies with higher levels of development, yet which retain hegemonic social orders (such as the Soviet Union), will find it difficult to withstand the pressures of increasingly complex social forces, against which coercive responses by political leaders are increasingly costly. Similarly, he warns that economic crisis and failure can generate pressures for a hegemonic regime, with telling consequences for societies which have mass participation without stable and effective competition, *inclusive hegemonies* (Dahl 1971: 62–80).[5]

The fourth condition is the *extent of equalities and inequalities*. These are divided into two forms. First is the *distribution of political resources and skills* which, for Dahl, denotes the allocation of 'key values' (such as wealth, income, education, status, knowledge, popularity and organization). Such resources can then be used by some actors to influence others. It is the utilization of these resources in a particular way, to serve purposes, that makes them political. For instance, actors who, by virtue of their existing resources, occupy positions in the institutions of the state, can reallocate political resources to benefit themselves further (such as through taxation redistribution) or by creating new political resources (for example by expanding the franchise). Political resources therefore tend to be cumulative, although the degree to which inequalities are accentuated by such uses also depends upon the social relations in which these resources are situated. Dahl uses the example of the contrast between peasants and free farmers to show how the equal distribution of property, and hence political resources, can lead to a very different outcome from the 'extreme inequalities' which characterize traditional peasant societies. Notwithstanding this recognition of different outcomes, Dahl does link the industrialization process in more general terms to the fostering of widespread aspirations in the populace and the spread of socio-economic resources, and hence indirectly to the dispersal of political resources (Dahl 1971: 81–8). Interestingly, Dahl does not emphasize the dependence of such processes of accumulation and dispersal on the very feature of the social order that makes them political, their uses in relations of power.

Second, the creation of resentments and frustrations which follows from the existence of inequalities tends to reflect the degree of dispersal or accumulation of inequalities of values (wealth, income, education and so on). This is, in part, dependent upon government policies on fiscal matters and social welfare. The tendencies towards *social rights* (defined in terms of T. H. Marshall's (1950) conception of social citizenship, that is, security, education and welfare) are causally attributed to the inclusivity of the polyarchies. Social rights serve as a means of ameliorating the states of affairs within which pressures emerge, and help to avoid the conditions which can lead to social and political instability. Again, the complexity of the relationship between inequality and the type of regime is emphasized. While it assumed that polyarchic societies (as a function of their inclusivity) are more likely to be responsive to the needs of disadvantaged groups, and that political resources (as a function of competition) are likely to more dispersed, so limiting coercion, in reality more contradictory yet sustainable dual situations can emerge. For example, in what Dahl describes as 'repressive violence within a quasi-pluralistic social order' (Dahl 1971: 93), the American South was both competitive and inclusive with respect to the white population while the formerly enslaved groups experienced a hegemonic regime (even though, in the states of South Carolina and Mississippi in 1860, they constituted a majority of the population). Dahl concludes that the maintenance of the processes which inflict relative deprivation upon a group require a hegemonic polity and social order, and cites the evidence of the dismantling of the mechanisms of repression in these states in the 1960s.

In his account of why deprivation is relative (drawing from Runciman's (1966) analysis of subjective perceptions of poverty and Cantril's (1965) empirical attitudinal research), Dahl also implicitly recognizes agenda formation and anticipated reactions. The extent and form of opposition is attributed to the reflexive characteristics of the members of the groups in question, their perceptions of disadvantage, their evaluations of the legitimacy of such relations (acknowledging the role of socialization), the intensity of frustration and anger, and a conscious decision to organize and mobilize. All of these inevitably involve calculating what sort of responses are likely to follow from the existing authorities (Dahl 1971: 95–104). Indeed, the anticipation of reactions played a substantial part in the formulation of desegregationist strategies by the NAACP in the 1950s and 1960s. While polyarchy is portrayed as the best possible shell for ameliorating inequalities, it is also recognized that polyarchies can exist with substantial inequities, and even fall prey to their destabilizing effects (a clear acknowledgement of the role of inequalities raised by earlier critics of Dahl's work in the 1950s and early 1960s).

The fifth condition is the *extent of subcultural pluralism*. By this, Dahl is referring to the measurement and comparison of the sectoral cleavages (in terms of class, religion, race, ethnicity, region and language) which exist in different societies. In defining these group affiliations, he does not deviate from the conventional Weberian conceptions of the economic (market) position, status and organizational power of groups of individuals. It is plausible to use such conceptual frameworks in both conservative and radical-leaning projects (see Parkin 1972). What is distinctive about Dahl's approach is his strong emphasis on the lifestyles, identifications, loyalties, social structures and other subcultural forms which exist alongside class location. Dahl is particularly concerned with the capacity of subcultural polarization to undermine the relations of trust, tolerance and mutual guarantees necessary for the successful operation of a polyarchic democracy. Subcultural polarities are a distinctive feature of a number of artificially constructed postcolonial regimes, and in some cases this explains the consequent civil discord and secession. Dahl notes the existence of reinforcing factors associated with such situations, such as low levels of socio-economic development.

For polyarchic democracy to be viable in such societies, three things should hold. First, it is crucial that no groups are permanently excluded from participation, and that groups clearly understand both that co-operation is necessary at least some of the time, and that participation in a governing majority is underwritten by such co-operation. Dahl's strongest illustration is the 'panoply of subcultures' constituting India which 'compels the leaders of every group to learn and practice the arts of conciliation and coalition building and prevents any single unified group from even approaching a monopoly of political resources' (Dahl 1971: 117–18).

Second is the existence of a 'set of understandings and engagements' contributing to mutual security, beyond the formal political rules of the game. These act as a series of guarantees for ensuring the continuous investment of the subcultures in the society. Dahl raises the importance of the translation of minority support into accurate representation in political institutions. Also significant is the extent to which such groups can sustain local autonomy, in terms of social policy and educational provision, the legal system, religious affiliation, independent political parties and economic representation, and in the operation of mass media. However, it is not clear whether Dahl has in mind devolution or decentralization, merely that some mechanism for maintaining local autonomy should be established.

Third and finally is the general prevalence of the belief (at least in political activists if not the general populace) that a polyarchic democracy actually fulfils their expectations and demands in an effective way. Here, Dahl seems to be expressing a desire for civic idealism which was very much at odds with the experiences of Western societies at the time he was writing this text. Indeed, as the 1970s progressed many pluralists were shortly to be seen as endorsing the 'ungovernability thesis' (King 1975), and developing dramatic accounts of 'pluralist stagnation' combined with pleas for the restoration of civic culture (Beer 1982).

Where does this lead us? Dahl's work poses a dilemma for governments in the unfortunate circumstances of attempting to reconcile such pressures. He suggests three choices are open to them: to provide mutual guarantees at the cost of resolving internal problems, to resolve internal problems by coercing a minority subculture, or to divide the country (territorial partition). As Dahl succinctly states 'Thus the price of polyarchy may be a breakup of the country. And the price of territorial unity may be a hegemonic regime' (Dahl 1971: 121).

When Dahl's characterization of polyarchal democracy is analysed in terms of the features of competition and inclusivity, such subcultural pluralism is treated as both a condition and a consequence of polyarchy. This undermines Dahl's earlier stated project to produce a causal account of polyarchal emergence, even within the terms of reference of his conception of causality. It is hard not to conclude that Dahl is unaware of the full implications of attempting to acknowledge social complexity, and the epistemological shift from regularity to intelligibility determinism (that is, from empiricism to idealism) which this requires.

The sixth condition is the *form and degree of domination by an external power*. Dahl belatedly attempts to address the global situation of all nation states, and how this effects conditions for polyarchy. He limits his brief analysis to a consideration of the 'international environment', defined as 'multinational' political and economic factors such as trade links or debt obligations, which hinder or foster hegemonic and polyarchic regimes. The consequences of the Second World War and the cold war furnish him with a range of examples of (the threat of) direct military intervention, although the impact of each intervention on polyarchal emergence has been contradictory. When considering the effect of decolonization, Dahl highlights the emergence of polyarchal tendencies in a number of cases (such as India, the Lebanon, and the Philippines) prior to the departure of colonial administrations. Yet in a wide range of cases (such as Israel and Chile), he suggests that post-colonial polyarchies arose outside the context of foreign intervention. In terms of the comparative and historical evidence, Dahl again acknowledges the complexity of the empirical situation and identifies the possibility that 'overt foreign intervention is not necessarily fatal to an existing polyarchy and may actually strengthen it in some respects . . . [and] frequently produces a boomerang effect' (Dahl 1971: 197–8).

Finally, the seventh condition is the *beliefs of political activists*. These are crucial in establishing a degree of legitimacy and trust upon which polyarchal civility is founded. For Dahl, this is the 'key' aspect of the processes analysed earlier, acting as both the intellectual cement of his work and the social cement of the empirical processes identified as polyarchal. The initial assumptions are behavioural in form, as he specifies the causal links under discussion, but he then proceeds to problematize the whole framework, as shown in Figure 3.2.

While Figure 3.2 suggests a deterministic relationship, Dahl wanted to establish how it is only possible to move beyond this analysis by working through its problems and limitations. Dahl's critique raises the complexities which problematize the behaviourist application of closed-system analysis (see Table 2.1). Here, beliefs are considered both as intimately related to actions and as a form of contested knowledge (raising the issue of the social distribution of knowledge, to which I return in Chapter Four). This can immediately be identified as a shift away from Dahl's earlier behavioural focus on beliefs as express preferences. It also indicates that he questioned the sharp line drawn by behaviourist analysis between motives and intentions, and the consequences of acts.

The social location of belief systems is incorporated into the framework in two ways. Dahl recognizes that the beliefs of some strategically-located actors will have a greater sway over outcomes than those of other actors. In common with many other political analysts, he suggests that some individuals (largely political activists) hold 'rich and complex' beliefs which are more likely to guide their political actions, while most belief systems are rudimentary and an indication of political inactivity, and are only significant in so far as they (de-)legitimize polyarchy. In this respect, the two dimensions of polyarchy (public contestation and inclusivity) are raised to demonstrate how it is

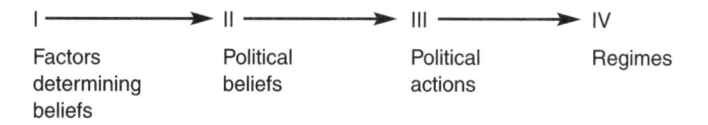

I ⟶ II ⟶ III ⟶ IV

| Factors determining beliefs | Political beliefs | Political actions | Regimes |

Figure 3.2 Dahl's account of political beliefs
Source: Dahl 1971: 124

possible to have widespread legitimacy for competition without inclusivity (the eighteenth-century British Whig oligarchy). Alternatively, it is possible to identify inclusivity without competition (the Peronist regime in Argentina). In particular, a strong emphasis is placed upon the ways in which the beliefs of political activists are a vital element of polyarchy. As a consequence of this, polyarchy can emerge irrespective of socio-economic development, as Dahl demonstrates through a case study on the emergence of polyarchic democratic tendencies in Argentina. In this instance, the emergence of polyarchy from 1853 to 1930, a case where competition preceded inclusivity, is compared favourably to developments in Western Europe. In 1930 the regime suffered a military coup, and polyarchal developments have been intermittent and fragile since. From the evidence on socio-economic development, Argentina clearly has a great deal of potential for the emergence of polyarchy, yet it has not witnessed an enduring belief in the legitimacy of its social and political institutions. For Dahl, this is a function of a failure to install fair election practices (with competition conducted in other ways, including the forceful overturning of election results), and the exclusion of a significant proportion of the population from participation. In Europe, a prolonged period of franchise expansion gradually introduced a larger part of the population to the rules of participation and competition, until universal suffrage was finally achieved. The exclusion from citizenship of large numbers of immigrants to Argentina further destabilized the regime. Hence, on both of the dimensions of polyarchy, the legitimation of existing social and political institutions has been weak in Argentina (Dahl 1971: 124–40).

Further support for the importance of legitimation processes in this approach is evident in Dahl's citation of Harry Eckstein's studies of unilateral authority relations. The identification of Norway as uniquely located at one end of a spectrum of authoritative legitimacy (at least in terms of respect for functional expertise) provides Dahl with a useful yardstick for the measurement of commitment towards existing institutional frameworks as a means of resolving conflicts and grievances. Similarly, expectations about the effectiveness of governments and the degree of trust in political leaders are more often deeply lodged in political culture and socialization, rather than as a response to individual issues. However, the performance of governments can lead to the reorientation of these legitimizing beliefs. Dahl highlights the part played by intellectuals in the (re-)formation of beliefs, specifically in providing plausible frameworks for considering alternatives, both real and imagined. The degree and extent of trust is partly related to the question whether co-operation is possible and desirable. We should also consider how mutual trust can serve as the basis for co-operation, alliances, competition and peaceful conflict. Cultural traditions and established ways of working through problems, through which trust is established, have a vital role to play. For Dahl, polyarchy is more likely where there are ground rules for establishing relations of both competition and co-operation. Rather than seeking to establish perfect harmony or unleashing conflicts without institutional constraints, this strategy seeks to find pragmatic pathways towards democratization. Dahl is thus more concerned to provide the institutional means for resolving conflicting ends, rather than to specify ends as good in themselves.

Thus, the vital component which makes a polyarchal democracy work is the extent to which a political culture is supportive of the existing social and political institutions. In this way, legitimizing beliefs are effectively transmitted through these institutions to the members of the political community (apparently, at differing levels of complexity, and when the individuals are most receptive or impressionable). Consequently, a deeply-felt civil bond is established between the people and the governing institutions (Dahl 1971: 140–75). Indeed, at one point Dahl suggests (subject to the proviso that new beliefs are accepted in terms of their consistency with one's existing beliefs and experiences) that the 1960s generation in the USA has been exposed to a wider range of beliefs and experiences than previous generations, undermining their commitment to American polyarchy. Specifically, this generation engaged in a 'confrontation with inequity' and experienced the domestic consequences of the Vietnam conflict. This radical counter culture, Dahl suggests, both in *Polyarchy* and, a year earlier, in *After the Revolution* (1970), was consistent with a strong attachment to the belief in the principle of equality in American political culture. In Dahl's words:

> once a social or political principle becomes firmly embedded in the political culture, it can serve quite literally as an axiom from which new unanticipated, and seemingly inescapable conclusions can be drawn. The 'functions' originally fulfilled by a principle, the 'interests' initially served by it, can no longer control or dominate the conclusions to be drawn from it.
>
> (Dahl 1971: 176)

The identification of political culture as a significant factor in explaining democratization leads Dahl to propose a new paradigm for political studies. This new paradigm would find a way of mediating between the blanket attribution of the 'spirit of an age' explanation to the acquisition of beliefs, characteristic of the history of ideas, and the dangers of 'naive psychological reductionism'. The latter dominated political science in this period 'as if one tried to explain the collective behavior of the players in a game of football by attributing it mainly to each player's toilet training in infancy' (Dahl 1971: 182).

Dahl's new paradigm for political studies is based upon three concerns: first, that all the above conditions of polyarchy take place through the influence of beliefs; second, that these conditions affect the receptivity, crystallization and stability of the form and content of beliefs (which retain their own specificity in sense of being ideologies; and third, that the acquisition of power and beliefs is accidental and uncertain. This recognition of the complexity of objects of analysis in political studies is consistent with the epistemological shift towards transcendental idealism identified in

Chapter Two. This can be seen in the modification of Dahl's stance towards the epistemological status of a causal law (in relation to the identification of a constant conjunction of events). There are some useful clues in his writings at this time:

> When we say that an event is an 'accident' we do not necessarily imply that it is without a cause. It does mean, however, that the theory with which we operate does not enable us to predict or explain such events. Our theory can only take them into account after they occur: it cannot subsume them under some more general law, hypothesis or conjecture. To be sure, some kinds of accidents are subject to fairly accurate statistical prediction; they are, in this sense, 'lawful'. But many accidents are not: assassinations, for example. But even where statistical predictions are reasonably accurate, they may furnish little or no help to a theory that seeks to account for certain kinds of historical happenings in which 'accident' plays a salient role.
>
> (Dahl 1971: 187)

Dahl comes to the uncomfortable position that existing and foreseeable explanatory accounts are simply incapable of answering the question of the causes and consequences of political beliefs. This recognition of complexities and uncertainty, he acknowledges, goes against the current of received opinion in social scientific research. However, it is a clear indication of a transcendental idealist response to the problems involved in assuming the existence of closed systems when examining empirical evidence. For Dahl, empirical regularities and the link between explanation and prediction are recognized as useful in a limited number of clearly-determined circumstances, yet they are insufficient when faced with empirical complexity. As such, Dahl's position attempts to establish in what circumstances nomothetic and idiographic explanatory frameworks are most suitable. To achieve this he develops an account which can confidently be identified as intelligibility determinism (to restate, that empirical regularities are necessary and useful but certainly not sufficient for establishing a causal law).

At this point in his work, Dahl identifies grounds for cautious optimism about the emergence of polyarchy. At best, he suggests that small steps towards participation and contestation can improve the prospects for democracy in the long term, and he stresses the slow layering process which is involved in the emergence of polyarchy. This is described as a liberalization process, a trust-building exercise whereby inter-group tolerance can be generated through the construction of mutual guarantees, so reducing the fear of hostility. Such searches for mutual guarantees are, Dahl argues, historically and socially specific. As such, their form can be implicit, as in homogenous cultures, or explicit, as in divided or plural societies. In some societies, the very process of liberalization itself could lead to the emergence of previously latent cleavages. It is in these situations that Dahl justifies the considerable scope for independent executive authority, characteristic of politics in the twentieth century, in order to avoid or overcome the dangers of division, deadlock and immobilism.

The central state is resurrected as a crucial means of ensuring that the party system does not fragment to such an extent that it nullifies the benefits of emergent polyarchy (increasing the costs of toleration). Rather than viewing the party system as a 'mirror' of social divisions, he suggests that considerable and persuasive evidence exists of the management of electoral and party systems at both national and local levels. Evidence of such management of the coalitions of support for political parties can be seen in the size and composition of electoral constituencies, and the processes through which voting blocks can be translated into disproportionate representation in national legislative assemblies. The final piece in the jigsaw of polyarchal emergence is the role of sub-national representative institutions in facilitating and fostering the arts of conflict resolution in opposition movements (Dahl 1971: 208–27). Dahl's account of political leadership in heterogeneous societies could be construed as contrary to the aspirations of participatory democracy. Nevertheless, in analytical terms, it is not satisfactory simply to point out that the only auspicious conditions which exist for the production of stable polyarchal democracies are those which have produced that very consequence, certainly not without a serious attempt to specify the structures and mechanisms which facilitate the formation of democratic societies and polities. This points to a need to reassess the limitations of Dahl's empirical realist ontological assumptions, and the fixation with empirical regularities between discrete variables which characterizes his use of the comparative historical method.

While Dahl deliberately focuses on processes which were already complete in the West, there are some clear instances of the normative dimension of his work emerging when he considers the exclusion of black people in the regimes of the southern states of the USA. He argues that 'I do not believe that polyarchies are more considerate than other regimes toward people who are effectively excluded from the rights of citizens' (Dahl 1971: 29). It is with this in mind that I turn in the next section to Dahl's *third wave* of democratization, and his proposals for participatory democracy in transforming existing polyarchies into fully democratized polyarchies.

Pluralism goes normative

So far, I have explored how Dahl unravelled the pluralist approach and challenged its descriptivist tendencies. In this section I address how it is possible to overcome the limitations of the *fact/value distinction* in pluralist political studies. By the 1980s, Dahl's work reveals a strong and explicit concern with the negative consequences of existing polyarchies. He is especially concerned with how these relate to the underlying principles identified in his theorization of the conditions of emergence of polyarchic democracy. Dahl conceptualized this as a dilemma, that the emergence of autonomous organizations (precipitated by democratization processes) invites the very same groups to inflict harm and injustice upon other groups. Inevitably, this raises the possibility that democratization can generate instability in the social and political order. The problem of 'democratic pluralism', then, is how to manage the relationship between two complementary imperatives in a democratic order – autonomy and control – each of which is vital to the stability of polyarchy. The relationship between them is portrayed as analogous to that established by Isaiah Berlin between negative and positive liberty. This is subject to Dahl's proviso that freedom involves the exercise of both autonomy and control; that in no cases should control or autonomy exist in a pure form (Berlin 1969: 118–72; Dahl 1982: 19–20).

Dahl initiates his analysis through an exercise of clarification of his conceptual framework, a reflexive activity which allows for an assessment of his movement from earlier statements of his methodological position. In this exercise, autonomy is defined as independence from the control of others. Control is granted the status of a causal relationship whereby 'the actions of one actor are interpreted as having been brought about, or caused by, the preferences of other actors' (Dahl 1982: 16–17). Control is also taken to be distinct from benefits, such as income, wealth and status (for control is a process not a consequence). Control is more inclusive than intentions (it acknowledges that control can be unintentional) but less inclusive than influence (which has a broader causal status including forms of indirect influence). In addition, Dahl introduces the analysis of social structures into his account, described as both restraining and providing opportunities for actors (although this is undermined by his treatment of structures as if they are social actors). While he deliberately avoids attributing desires and motivations to such regulative structures as the economic order, his empirical realist attachment towards causal explanations (in terms of constant conjunctions of events) leads him into the inevitable position of postulating causal chains between actors, structures and other actors as discrete entities. He is also forced to address the paradoxes this creates within his own analysis, by distinguishing between organizational autonomy and social autonomy (in order to avoid a conflation of control and social regulation). In another startling moment of reflexivity, Dahl problematizes his earlier conceptualizations of causal relationships:

> As everyone knows, the idea of causation is jam packed with difficulties, which are compounded when causal explanation extends to human actions. Nonetheless, causal thinking enables us not only to orient ourselves toward the world but also to act in and upon the world, to seize hold of certain levers in order to achieve our purposes. By understanding causes sometimes we can bring about effects. Even though freedom and causality are irreducible antinomies, I do not see how we could act freely without understanding causes.
>
> (Dahl 1982: 20)

Autonomy thus only becomes intelligible in the context of actual practices. Dahl is visibly shifting from his earlier inclination to generate nomothetic explanations about the political community, towards situating his approach in an idiographic recognition of historically specific conditions within which political relations emerge. There is no evidence of ontological depth in this development, and he remains committed to empirical regularities as analytical devices in the face of social complexity. Dahl's position is thus almost exactly that of neo-Kantian idealism, which one would have expected of someone often interpreted as a follower of Max Weber. This interpretation is reinforced when we consider his response to the issue of how to replicate, in theoretical terms, the 'magnitude' of control or influence, a context in which quantitative measures are best interpreted as 'metaphors'. He makes an explicit comparison between his own approach and that of fellow pluralist Ralf Dahrendorf's (1959) tendency to conceptualize power in absolute terms 'as if it could be described by only two quantities: all or none' (Dahl 1982: 22). The arbitrary treatment of power and control as 'all or nothing' means that domination and subjection are difficult to disentangle. The difference between the theoretical reconstruction of a scale of magnitudes of autonomy and control and its concrete specification is, Dahl argues, an indication of the limits of his analysis in the face of complexity. However, it is also an insight into the role of political scientist as imaginative interpreter in constructing an intelligible account of political relationships (ibid.: 23–4). This concern with the a priori judgements of researchers is then connected to prevailing collective experiences (such as the Vietnam war), civic orientations (beliefs about capitalism, democracy, socialism and racism) and social structures (the market, the governmental constitution and so on) which are themselves constituted through the historical experiences of American society. This awareness of the narrow confines of closed systems is best illustrated in a passage from *Dilemmas of Pluralist Democracy*:

> the boundaries around an account of why Beta does x are not rigidly fixed by some palpable phenomenon revealed by our senses, like a chain-wire fence around a factory. Instead the boundaries are creations of the human mind – more like the boundaries the ancients drew around the constellations they saw in the heavens on clear nights. Where one decides to draw boundaries around a causal system that is intended to explain human actions seems to depend in a significant way on many factors, including one's curiosities, purposes, and prior judgements as to the usefulness of a particular bit of additional knowledge. In order to answer the persistent Why? one may be challenged to move from one region of explanation to another. Where one stops in the search for conclusive answers will depend on contestable judgements as to what one thinks it is crucial to explain, and how far outward in time and social space one wants to explore in search of a satisfactory account. To be sure, one may

finally arrive at a boundary where the causal system is closed, in the sense that no further factors need to be taken into account in order wholly to explain the outcome. But when significant human actions are to be accounted for, complete closure is sure to require a vast system.

(Dahl 1982: 25)

Nowhere else in Dahl's work is there such a clear statement of both his epistemological position, a transcendental idealist account of the status of causal laws, and his ontological commitment to empirical realism, indicated by his reluctance to dispense with explanatory accounts of the concrete empirical relations in terms of constant conjunctions of events within closed systems.

In much the same way as in his earlier work, Dahl is concerned to limit the scope of his inquiry, by focusing upon only democratic regimes, on organization rather than individuals, and by recognizing that real solutions to such dilemmas can only be established in historically and socially specific conditions. This is a work at the interface of the theory and practice of 'democratic pluralism', explicitly recognizing that conceptual categories can be 'out of joint with reality' (Dahl 1982: 3). Dahl's work has now entered a specifically normative phase, and the concerns of constructing a democratic praxis are consistently deployed throughout. He starts by contrasting 'democracy as an ideal' with 'actually existing democratic regimes'. Ideal democracy involves equally weighted voting in collectively binding decisions, effective participation in agenda formation as well as expressing preferences within debate, an *enlightened understanding* of the issues and likely outcomes, that the citizenry should have the final say in the agenda itself, and that all adults are included in the demos (ibid.: 1–7). Such an idealized model remains just that, a model, and only offers a heuristic framework for the analysis of concrete democratic processes and institutions.

Democracies in actuality, he argues, are distinguishable partly by reference to their size, and also in terms of their ideals and practices. Relatively democratized city states are clearly distinct from relatively democratized nation states (the first being the United States in the nineteenth century) which are in fact closer to Dahl's understanding of polyarchy. The small scale and exclusivity of classical city states and, in addition, the inadequate tension management arrangements of medieval Italian city states, emphasize the inadequacy of such institutional forms for the resolution of social and political issues in the twentieth century. Dahl identifies seven distinct institutional features of the democratic regimes (which are closely related to his earlier closed-system model) which have come into existence since the nineteenth century: the election of officials; fair and frequent elections; inclusive voting practices; inclusive practices for the nomination of candidates; freedom of expression, in particular, to criticize the existing government, socio-economic order, ideology and so on; the existence of, and widely understood entitlement to utilize, alternative information sources; and freedom of association, facilitating public competition between groups and parties (Dahl

1982: 10–11). Thus we can see fleshed out in more specific detail the institutional processes Dahl had earlier identified as constitutive of polyarchic democracy. Dahl does not offer any guidance as to whether these are the preconditions or the consequences of the emergence of public contestation and inclusivity. Nevertheless, by virtue of how they are defined, they are taken to be responsible for the negation of closed hegemonies. Dahl clearly addresses the relationship between the ideal and the actual when he states 'Democracy in the ideal sense is a necessary condition for the best political order. It is not a sufficient condition' (ibid.: 4).

Size, he suggests, inhibits the 'participatory ideal' in the context of a large-scale political community, and hence raises the possibility of seeing smaller democratic units or societies within a given nation state as desirable. Dahl rejects the argument that democracy is desirable only on a small scale, on the grounds that in order to resolve transnational issues (energy, pollution, defence, nuclear weapons and so on), some form of national political representation is necessary; and by implication, this will preferably be democratic in character. He raises the potentiality of applying the same argument to small-scale democracies, to be utilized for the democratization of the transnational environment (subject to the problems of identifying a constitutive demos). These arguments parallel developments initiated by David Held in his account of the potential for, and limitations on, cosmopolitan democracy (Held 1993; Archibugi and Held 1995). In Dahl's words, the difficulties in dispensing with the national level of analysis can be expressed thus, 'no unit smaller than a country can provide the conditions necessary for a good life, while no unit larger than a country is likely to be as democratically governed as a modern polyarchy' (Dahl 1982: 16).

Dahl returns to the part played by political culture in democratic systems by considering the role of associations (drawing from Tocqueville and also from Rousseau on particular or partial societies) to identify the subsystems necessary for democracy, equality, liberty and civilization. In particular, he suggests that the intimacy and autonomy of kinship and educational, religious and cultural associations are an ineradicable component of the condition of democracy. In terms of political autonomy, Dahl places a strong emphasis on the way in which organizational pluralism occurs in the field of political representation (political parties, interest groups and particularly business and trades unions) and in the internal organizational dynamics within governments (such as the institutional autonomy of the powers of central and local government). He highlights the important contributions of earlier pluralists (including Émile Durkheim), on the ways in which associations fulfil 'basic human needs for sociability, intimacy, affection, friendship, love, trust and faith; for individual growth, personal integrity, and socialization into community norms; for the preservation and transmission of culture; for the human qualities of human beings' (Dahl 1982: 31).

Cultural variety and specificity have to be accommodated in institutional terms, acknowledging the existence of variations in constitutional systems, such as the differences between a fusion and a separation of powers, and between unitary and federal constitutions. He argues that, while some institutional solutions offer more favourable conditions for polyarchal democracy, the existence of some degree of relative organizational autonomy is common to all. Political regimes struggle to balance autonomy and control regardless of whether they are socialist or capitalist. This also corresponds with his earlier arguments that extensive state control inhibits polyarchic democracy in all societies. So, in response to what he considers the simplicities and inadequacies of Marxist and elitist accounts of society, political culture and the state, Dahl develops what can be effectively described as the *iron law of polyarchy*:

> Throughout history, relatively autonomous organizations have developed around certain universal human situations that generate common experiences, identifications, and values: we and they, insider and outsider, friend and enemy, sacred and profane, true believer and infidel, civilized man and barbarian. Kinship, language, birthplace, residence, religion, occupation, everywhere stimulate a thrust toward organization and independence. Alongside Michel's famous iron law of oligarchy – 'Whoever says organization says oligarchy' – stands another: Every organization develops an impulse toward its own independence. The two universal tendencies are alloyed; and in the alloy, the law of oligarchy bends more easily than iron.
> (Dahl 1982: 33)

Reinforcing his earlier comments on democracy as not being, in itself, necessarily pluralist, Dahl also raises the existence of organizational pluralism beyond situations characterized by democratic practices (Dahl 1982: 27–30). However, he is more categorical on large-scale democracies, where organizational pluralism is seen both a precondition and an inevitable consequence of democratic institutions (ibid.: 36–40). He identifies five structural conditions which can be taken to account for the 'constellations of pluralism'. Two of these are common to all democratic societies, that they are polyarchic by definition and capitalist in terms of historical and empirical evidence. The variations in the 'constellations of pluralism' are seen to be the product of distinctive patterns of conflict and cleavage, the nature of concrete political institutions, and the degree to which organizations are inclusive (in terms of membership) and concentrated (in 'peak associations') (ibid.: 55–80). By developing cross-cutting typologies in terms of bipolar and multipolar adversarial conflicts, reinforcing and cross-cutting cleavages, and by including a measure of the intensity of antagonisms between groups, Dahl attempts to simplify what would otherwise be 'patterns of such bewildering variety as to defy concise summary' (ibid.: 56). Thus, Dahl develops an account of pattern prediction not unlike that which can be identified in Hayek's accounts of causal explanations and pattern predictions in economics and psychology (see Chapter Four).

Polyarchic civility and the state 91

In these comments, the definition of the economy solely as a market is assumed to be unquestionable, and the existence of the relative autonomy of economic associations within the economic sphere is, in part, constitutive of polyarchy. Clearly, Dahl defines socialism and capitalism as ideological frameworks rather than in terms of economic relations. For Dahl, the independence, plurality and mutual control of organized groups are an important part in the mechanisms which check the tendencies towards hierarchies and domination by certain groups who would otherwise tend to capture the governing institutions in pursuit of their own interests. In an extension of earlier arguments in *Polyarchy* (1971) on the costs of domination, he suggests that rational subjects choose to act in ways which increase the expected costs of domination. Consequently, a rational government opts for policies which maximize their expected benefits and enhance the further development of organizational pluralism, which increases the anticipated costs of domination still further. He suggests that this is illustrated by the emergence of religious tolerance in Europe following the intense conflicts of the Reformation and Counter-Reformation, when the costs of conflict exceeded the costs of toleration (Dahl 1982: 33–6). An introductory citation from Tocqueville, linking Dahl's programme for the democratization of the polity to the conceptions of the sociality of politics in his early work, is particularly instructive:

> Amongst the laws which rule human societies there is one which seems to be more precise and clear than all the others. If men are to remain civilized, or to become so, the art of associating together must grow and improve, in the same ratio in which the equality of condition is increased.
> (Tocqueville, *Democracy in America*, vol. 1, 2nd book, ch. 5, 1840; cited in Dahl 1982: vii)

The emergence of associational forms, initially the product of the 'slightest diversity', develops its own momentum as these groups become aware of the advantageous consequences of effective organization and mobilization, a feature which Dahl describes as characteristic of modernity. Dahl argues that organizational pluralism flourishes within the operation of democratic societies, where the barriers to organization and participation do not serve as a block upon their development. As an example, he cites the examples of post-war democratization and liberalization in Germany, Italy and Japan alongside the sometimes brief flourishes of pluralism in the context of the Warsaw Pact and Comecon. Reconsidering an example of constitutionalism from his earlier work, Dahl draws upon the illustration of the collapse of Chilean democracy and the emergence of military dictatorship as the process in reverse (Dahl 1982: 36–40). Dahl is also much more explicit in highlighting the defects of pluralist democracy, preparing the way for his advocacy for participatory democracy within the subsystems of society. In particular, he highlights four defects:

1 The coincidence of organizational pluralism with 'extensive inequalities' tends to stabilize inequities and injustices (especially if those excluded from such benefits are disorganized). If such inequalities become institutionalized in a corporatist system of mutual accommodation between established organized groups, they can become a obstacle to newly emergent pressures for change.
2 Although it is often assumed that a plurality of associations coincides with a plurality of interests, the effective practices of groups depend on a focused orientation toward certain interests and the blurring of internal conflicts. They also depend on the emphasis of conflict with non-members which, by reinforcing internal solidarity and cohesion and external discord and division, can lead to the deformation of civic consciousness.
3 Some groups can have an 'unequal influence' upon the range and form of alternative issues taken seriously, and the policies considered, leading to the distortion of the public agenda. In part this is a product of the unequal resources at the heart of the first defect, and the distrust fostered by the processes in the second defect.
4 The necessary existence of an administrative executive, and the relative advantages of decentralization (or relative disadvantages of centralization), can combine with opportunities for institutional capture by specific subsystems (with sufficient resources to resist and inflict large costs on a government). This raises the issue of whether contemporary democracies violate the principle that the demos should have final control over the agenda within a complex social and political environment (a feature of Dahl's earlier work).

These accommodations with critical responses to his earlier work are, in part, also a response to the contributions of Charles Lindblom on the 'privileged position' of business (Dahl 1982: 40–54). Dahl's choice of citation from Lindblom's work is instructive, in identifying 'whatever businessmen need as a condition for performing the tasks that fall to them in the market system: income and wealth, deference, prestige, influence, power, and authority, among others' (Lindblom 1977: 174; cited in Dahl 1982: 51).

Dahl is clearly aware of the limits imposed on the redistributive policies pursued by governments in their attempts to sustain the market economy in its present, privately owned form. He draws out the importance of the interaction between polyarchy and capitalism in shaping the operation of incentives in the marketplace, and suggests that once that limit upon redistribution has been achieved, structural changes in ownership and control are inevitable (Dahl 1982: 76). By drawing attention to the flaws in polyarchy, Dahl attempts to address the next steps in the process, imagining polyarchy itself. In the next section we will turn to the way in which Dahl leads us 'to imagine a country where all the familiar obstacles to voting equality, effective participation, and enlightenment are no longer significant, where the demos is fully inclusive and where it exercises final control over the agenda of decisions' (ibid.: 82).

Imagining polyarchy I: facing the dilemmas

The role of the imagination within idealist accounts of social-scientific practice is a central part of constructing models. In this case, the models represent political relationships. The ability to formulate utopias, in the positive sense of the term, through which the inadequacies of the present state of affairs are hypothetically resolved via creative and imaginative theoretical constructions, is a key element in any radical project. Dahl's post-1960s advocacy of participatory democracy is just such a radical project. This does not reflect any disillusionment with democracy or pluralism as political ideals, only with actually existing polyarchies. As Dahl argues:

> If polyarchies were more fully democratized, one might argue, majorities would govern more effectively; because policies would express majority preferences and interests rather than the mere tugging and hauling among a variety of narrow interest groups ...the defects in democratic pluralism are caused not so much by pluralism or by democracy as by the failure of existing polyarchies to achieve a high level of democracy. In a truly democratic country, the defects of pluralism would tend to disappear.
> (Dahl 1982: 81)

For Dahl the choice is clear-cut, self-government is a superior state of affairs, and his later work reinforces the need to establish this as a guiding principle in establishing the social and economic foundations for a *new democratic order*. Dahl seeks to address two questions: can political equality between individuals and organizational inequalities be reconciled; and, given that the demos controls the agenda of public affairs, how do we define both the demos and public affairs? These questions raise the importance of establishing clearly the relationship between the procedural and substantive characters of the democratic process. In response to the first question, Dahl returns to an earlier consideration of this issue in his collaboration with Charles Lindblom, in *Politics, Economics and Welfare* (1953). Dahl and Lindblom had attempted to demonstrate that, given the unequal access to organizations with varying resource levels and different levels in skills, if the principle of voting equality applies to individuals it cannot be applied to organizations. On the second question, whether the final control over an agenda or one issue by one demos invalidates the controls by another demos, the possibility of conflict over jurisdiction between different representative bodies should be anticipated. Dahl considers two grounds for conflict resolution, on 'substantive grounds' (as matters of rights and/or utility) or, if no substantive resolution is forthcoming, on 'procedural grounds' (such as the majority principle). However, even here, the question of 'which demos is most appropriate' can produce further difficulties, as can a jurisdictional conflict over an issue that involves fundamental rights such as the right to self-government.

To clarify his position, in *Dilemmas of Pluralist Democracy* (1982) Dahl imagines different outcomes from the combination of a majoritarian system of democracy with different patterns of social cleavage and degrees of conflict. In a few cases the prevailing consensus will ensure that the majority of citizens are satisfied with democratic outcomes. However, with the more common outcome of large dissatisfied minorities there is a danger of the majority rule leading to conflict, even if the same group is not permanently excluded (the case of complete polarization). Yet the modification of the majority rule undermines the argument that democracies presuppose such a rule. The other way to resolve the problem is to provide a political framework for greater political autonomy for the excluded minority. However, in this case, it is assumed that the newly-autonomous minority also signs up to the majority principle, since 'an increase in the organizational autonomy for some persons may adversely affect the rights, freedom, or welfare of others' (Dahl 1982: 93). Dahl is effectively outlining the moral maze of liberal values by focusing upon the political framework within which democratic regimes exist, and within which a full polyarchal democracy will have to live as well.

Dahl identifies six dilemmas within which the limits and possibilities of polyarchy are defined. In the first three dilemmas posed, he reiterates his painstaking analysis of the political framework for a polyarchal democracy. The first dilemma involves the issue of whether *rights* (which are inviolable independently of any other considerations) or *utility* (the consequences of actions in terms of their contribution to collective welfare) should govern democratic decisions. Dahl expresses the relationship between rights and utility as such:

> Given certain fundamental rights as given, then within the limits set by such fundamental rights, utilitarian judgements can apply: provided only that fundamental rights are maintained, then let the policy prevail that provides the greatest benefit for the greatest number.
> (Dahl 1982: 86)

The second dilemma involves the scope of the demos: as Dahl expresses it, the *inclusivity or exclusivity of the demos*. In the absence of a global demos, all are exclusive, although disputes over jurisdiction can be complicated by the degrees of inclusivity in each demos. Third, there is the tension between *equality among individuals* and *equality among organizations* which, as demonstrated above, means that 'votes count, but organizational resources decide'.

In the last three dilemmas he develops his earlier arguments on autonomy and control. The fourth dilemma, between *uniformity and diversity*, demonstrates that Dahl is not merely advocating diversity (of culture, tradition, language, religion, place and so on) as an end in itself. While he recognizes that diversity can be defended on utilitarian grounds as well as in terms of a 'right to be different', he also recognizes that political equality can conflict with diversity. The uniformity of fundamental rights of citizenship, such as the right to be treated equally with respect to a fair trial, is an important barrier against discriminatory practices and injustice. Uniformity presupposes a degree of *centralization*, while diversity presupposes a degree of *decentralization*, the fifth dilemma. The centralization of a political community involves an increase in control by the political centre and a decrease of autonomy of the subsystems, while decentralization produces the reverse effect. This should be qualified by adding that (de)centralization varies across different issues, and that decentralization of resources from the centre does not guarantee that these resources are used democratically and may, in fact, result in local domination. This brings us to the final dilemma, the *concentration or dispersion of power and political resources*. For Dahl, the main limit on the development of the full potentialities of polyarchy is the existence of wide inequalities in political resources. In conclusion, Dahl develop two triads, each of which is a limiting case. On the one hand, there is the combination of uniformity, centralization and concentration of power and political resources associated with totalitarian regimes. On the other hand, there is the combination of diversity, decentralization and dispersion of power and political resources characteristic of classical liberalism, 'a movement away from the uniformity imposed by means of power imposed in the crown' (Dahl 1982: 105). In each case, Dahl appears to be using these categories as ideal types (one-sided exaggerations) in order to compare and contrast empirical evidence. He argues that in a polyarchal democracy there will need to be a balance struck between each set of limits, but that the dilemmas are real none the less. Within the imaginary political order he has constructed, assuming that some definition of fundamental rights is accepted, he develops a utilitarian resolution of these difficulties: 'Human problems have better or worse solutions . . . even the better solutions will usually have disadvantages, sometimes grave ones. But to say that a solution has disadvantages is never a good reason for preferring the worse to the better' (Dahl 1982: 107).

Imagining polyarchy II: fulfilling the third wave

With these concerns in place, Dahl moves on to consider the operation of these dilemmas within the contemporary socio-economic conditions of corporate capitalism, centrally controlled economies and 'actually existing' decentralized democratic socialist economies. In particular, he contrasts the ideals established within the emergence of decentralized agrarian capitalism in the USA up to the late nineteenth century with corporate capitalism in the twentieth century. In a powerful citation from John Blum, Dahl demonstrates the peculiarities of this shift in American capitalism: 'Man became economic man, democracy was identified with capitalism, liberty with property and the use of it, equality of opportunity for gain, and progress with economic change and the accumulation of capital' (Blum, *The National Experience* (1963): 432; cited in Dahl 1985: 72).

For Dahl, 'The giant corporation thus became, *de facto*, if not yet *de jure*, both a public enterprise and a political system' (Dahl 1982: 110). He focuses upon the theoretical confusions over ownership and control of the means of production, suggesting that the variation in capitalist and socialist societies provides grounds for reconsidering the issues. Thus, the 'enormous number of possible (and existing) combinations of private and public ownership, and mixtures of governmental, market, consumer and enterprise control over decisions' (ibid.: 111) constitutes sufficient evidence to treat control as 'theoretically prior' to ownership. He is particularly concerned to establish the basis for fostering organizational pluralism in both capitalist and socialist orders. Therefore, the extent to which decisions are decentralized is paramount. Here again, it is the *control* of resources (and its inverse, *autonomy*) rather than ownership which is the key determinant; as the following extract indicates:

> A shift from private to social ownership then need not *necessarily* reduce the amount of organizational pluralism in a country. It is altogether possible that in some conditions (the United States might be one) where important decisions are strongly influenced by giant corporations hierarchically dominated by their managers, the inauguration of a decentralized socialist economy – in which, for example, economic enterprises were democratically governed by a demos consisting of all person employed by the firm – would result in an increase, not a decrease, in the number and autonomy of economic organizations.
>
> (Dahl 1982: 111–12)

The decentralized economic order which Dahl appears to have in mind is one where the central authority takes a few key strategic decisions, but most decisions occur in autonomous subsystems (families, associations, state and local authorities, and firms). The strategically important decisions would include identifying the permissible range of inequalities and securing this through the distribution of income and wealth. However, he is concerned to avoid the problems of state intervention in the twentieth century, which combined 'unselective and excessive centralization and unselective and insufficient decentralization' (Dahl 1982: 116). In the attempts to deal with the arbitrary and unmerited nature of present distributions of resources, he argues that the strategy of dealing with the consequences rather than the causes of inequality has simply produced an extensive state regulatory apparatus of welfare intervention and subsidization. While he recognizes that a decentralized order would have its own costs, he contends that the benefits of diversity, decentralization and dispersion would outweigh them. Dahl thus makes a plea for *selective centralization* which, in the American context where redistribution is viewed as an illegitimate expropriation, would require a major shift in civic orientation about the relationship between property rights and the right to self government.

In the case of socialist societies, which Dahl portrays as 'a pretty facade on a ramshackle structure' (Dahl 1982: 121), he draws heavily upon Charles Lindblom's criteria for the possibility of rational, central or synoptic planning:

> (1). If the problem at hand does not go beyond man's cognitive capacities and (2). if there exist agreed criteria (rather than social conflict on values) by which situations can be judged and (3). if the problem solvers have adequate incentives to stay with synoptical analysis until it is completed (rather than resort to rules of thumb, decision routines, guesstimates and the like).
>
> (Lindblom 1977: 322)

There are, Dahl accepts, no prototypes of democratically-controlled, centrally-directed economies to work from, and in practice the synoptic decisions are guided by intuition or are ideologically motivated, with considerable scope for abuse by a conscious, cohesive and conspiratorial oligarchy. In any case, he suggests, polyarchal institutions appear to be an inappropriate means to secure such forms of central control of resources, growth, investment and the distribution of income. By contrast, Dahl argues that a decentralized democratic socialist society (such as Yugoslavia, prior to recent conflicts) offers tangible evidence of democratic enterprises operating in competitive market environments. Nevertheless, this form of social order still generates inequalities between enterprises which, without a shift in civic orientations, encounter the same problems as his proposals for capitalist societies. In both cases, strategic decisions should be taken by a democratically controlled state which serves to guarantee the legal framework for resolving conflicts and minimise political inequalities by establishing 'general norms of distributive justice'.

The establishment of a right to self-government in socialist and capitalist economic enterprises reasserts the importance of Dahl's first dilemma between this right and utilitarian considerations of efficiency and material well-being. If the decentralized economic order is fulfilling its goals, he suggests, the increase in satisfaction, well-being and respect should clearly outweigh any losses in material utility. The second dilemma of what constitutes the most appropriate demos within an enterprise (or, for that matter, what constitutes an enterprise) is also raised when considering the citizenship of full-time against part-time and temporary employees. In addition, the tension between equality among individuals and equality among organizations is also present.

In *A Preface to Economic Democracy* (1985), these arguments about the ideal and the imaginary are consolidated by Dahl's account of his proposed 'system of self governing enterprises'. In such a system, the conflicts between interests, objectives, perspectives and ideologies between citizens would be reduced (although the model would suggest their elimination). Of these conflicts, the tensions between employers and employees would no longer be adversarial. Workers would become stakeholders in their own enterprises. Dahl believes that this would engender an atmosphere of moral responsibility in industrial relations, particularly as the workers are also likely to be consumers and residents who are unable to escape the social costs of the firm's decisions. Dahl's account attempts to address the objections he anticipates (especially by supporters of the corporate capitalist economy). These objections fall into three main areas: the problem of inequalities in the new economic order; the need to ensure adequate levels of efficiency and investment; and the relationship between guardianship and democratic participation in economic enterprises (also taking into account the issue of scale).

First, the tendencies towards inequalities will not be eliminated by these arrangements. The combined consequences of history, geography, society and luck would ensure that differences in market conditions in terms of factor costs and demand factors affected the revenue base of the various self-governing enterprises. Similarly, within each enterprise, differences of reward would persist, although the final arbiter in such an arrangement would be, in this case, the citizens of the enterprise. In such cases, it is assumed that the wage differentials would be much smaller than in capitalist corporations. Dahl sums up the effect of such inter-firm and intra-firm differences:

> Although it is impossible to say precisely how far such a system, operating autonomously without externally imposed reallocations (e.g. by taxes and transfer payments), would verge towards equality in wealth, income and other resources, it is clear that inequality would tend to arise both *within* firms and *among* firms. In self governing enterprises, the members themselves would decide on the principles according to which wages, salaries and surplus were to be distributed among the members. Their choice of internal distributive principles would depend on factors that are very far from predictable, including their implicit and explicit beliefs about fairness, which in turn would be influenced by tradition, the prevailing culture, ideology, religion and the like; and on the extent to which they would find they would find it desirable or necessary to adjust wages and salaries to the supply of and demand for various skills.
> (Dahl 1985: 104).

For more highly paid managers in co-operative enterprises, the tendency is for the enterprise to pay a competitive salary, and exclude such positions from citizenship and its consequent entitlements and obligations in the economic enterprise (such as the Pacific North West plywood co-operative).

Second, on the grounds of efficiency, Dahl suggests that self-governing enterprises would be motivated by different concerns. Previously the managers would have been motivated by the concerns of stockholders, such as the maintenance or increase of their dividend (for example, an expansion of production through the hiring of more labour). A self-governing enterprise would be unlikely to expand when this would reduce the size of surplus in relation to the share held by a citizen of the enterprise (Dahl 1985: 121). An alternative source of investment would have to be forthcoming for enterprises to modernize their productive processes. Dahl's main defence of this form of production is the commitment that self-governing enterprises receive from their members (as stakeholders), who are much more willing to make sacrifices in lean times than the employees of a stockholder operation. He also draws from the experiences of worker co-operatives (particularly the Mondragon Co-operative Movement in Spain) in order to demonstrate that investment pools can work effectively in a range of enterprises. In addition, Dahl cites the Scandinavian plans for a period of transition from stockholding to workers' ownership and control. In particular, he raises the Rudolf Meidner Plan (adopted by the Swedish Social Democrats in 1976), which would have allocated 20 per cent of profits to wage-earner shares, so that majority ownership would transfer to the employees over thirty-five years; and the 1973 Danish proposals to tax the payrolls of 25,000 Danish companies to establish both a national investment fund and a social fund to allocate workers' shares in terms of years of service. Dahl concludes that the recent experience of low performance in corporate capitalism and bureaucratic socialism reinforces the need for alternatives, and that experience of co-operative enterprises demonstrates that self-governing enterprises can match these efficiency goals (Dahl 1985: 122–32). In addition, as in any socio-economic order, the goals of efficiency and growth will be balanced with goals such as fairness and the distributive principle of justice devised to achieve this.

On the role of guardianship in economic enterprises, it is commonly assumed that the application of the strong principle of equality would undermine the productive utilization of the most talented and best qualified in the positions of greatest responsibility. Dahl suggests that this is again comparing the theoretical ideal with the actual practices of self-governing enterprises, since in practice corporations do not appoint on the basis of ability. In addition, the strong principle does not hold that all citizens have equal competence, but that they should be competent to decide which decisions they are qualified to make, and the terms of reference for decision making delegated to other, more qualified members of the enterprise. Further, he suggests, this is complicated by considerations of scale, in that he does not envisage direct democracy operating beyond small to medium-sized companies, and suggests that representative government should operate in larger enterprises (Dahl 1985: 119). He is not suggesting that managerial skills materialize out of thin air, but that managerial and technical training and the development of innovation will be an essential feature of the new economic order he envisages. The preponderance of innovative strategies in the small firm sector, he argues, provides greater support for his contention that self-government and innovation work well together (ibid.: 154).

It is not only the variety of forms of control which attracts Dahl's attention. He also compares the various forms of ownership which have been associated with co-operative enterprises. In the case of *individual share ownership* by employees, such arrangements are often short-lived as successful enterprises often revert back to corporate management following public floatation of the company and the sale of shares by employees. In addition, such enterprises tend to deny access to new members who become conventional employees. The *state ownership* of enterprises suffers from its associations with the inefficiencies and authoritarianism of bureaucratic state socialism. Dahl considers the possibility of symbolic state ownership raised by David Miller (1977) whereby the state's involvement is merely through general legislation, but he rejects this on the grounds that the politicization of company affairs would be a continuous temptation. By comparison, the *social ownership* strategies devised within Yugoslavian market socialism appear to Dahl to be much more viable, because of the safeguards against bureaucratic socialism built into the arrangements. In such enterprises, the means of production are considered as social property, with the employees in each enterprise (through workers' councils and management boards) acting as trustees. Consequently the assets cannot leave the control of the enterprise, and the trustees must act within the terms of reference established by general legislation and a substantial and growing body of case law. In Yugoslavia, in practice, the social property was in danger of becoming the group property of the interests within the industrial sectors, and the political party which shadowed the state. Consequently, Dahl's preferred alternative is *co-operative ownership* in a market system (along the lines of the Spanish Mondragon experiment highlighted earlier) where ownership rights are held by the employees directly as the citizens of the enterprise. In co-operative ownership, the entitlement to a share of the surplus is channelled through individual membership accounts which receive the share of the surplus following the deduction of costs. This system avoids the problem of individual share ownership, preserves the integrity of co-operative ownership, and acts as a barrier to intrusive state regulation. In this way, he concludes, self-governing enterprises would ensure that individuals could achieve outcomes according to their own values (Dahl 1985: ch. 5).

Imagining polyarchy III: civic reorientation and equality

Any envisaged transformation from a centralized to a decentralized social order is only feasible in relation to a corresponding transformation of civic orientations, for 'the more democratic a regime, the less the distribution of income depends on economic structures and the more it depends upon civic consciousness' (Dahl 1982: 133). Yet the structural changes he has in mind are not going to secure civic virtue, since the 'structures and consciousness are loosely coupled' (ibid.: 138). At this point in his work, he wrestles with a contradiction between his defence of diversity, whereby a range of principles of justice compete, and the need for a collective decision which would apply a more egalitarian principle of distributive justice. In order to establish which form of civic virtue is appropriate for his own utopian construction, he reviews three forms of civic consciousness.

1 *Individualist civic virtue* attributes a superior position to the citizen over the community where conflicts arise between their respective goods. This is identified with Rousseau's social contract, whereby the citizens subjectively perceive harmonious interests, and this harmony also exists in objective terms. However, this position is difficult to sustain in large-scale societies, where the common good is defined in theoretical rather than practical terms.
2 *Moral civic virtue*, whereby the citizens believe in the entitlement of each person to equal consideration, which can override the interests of the individual citizen. This requires some degree of altruism and commitment when the scale of the society or community is such that the collective is beyond the citizen's immediate existence.
3 *Organic civic virtue*, when a perfect correspondence is assumed to exist between individual needs and the interests of others. This is illustrated by reference to Marxist conceptions of communism as unalienated existence. Dahl suggests that no 'convincing psychophysical model' of consciousness exists to substantiate this contention. Indeed, he argues that the Marxist conception of the process by which workers comprehend their objective interests does not provide a mechanism by which the practical knowledge of workers translates into the Marxist theory of the social world; Dahl is cutting the connection between democracy and socialism.

Even the voluntarist liberal model for establishing the rules and arrangements within which the selfish egoism of citizens produces, as an unintended consequence, the best outcome for all, does not overcome the need for some historically specific regulative structures to facilitate the conditions for civic virtue. In addition, as the scale of the economy increases, then the drive of self-interest will be realized through collusion with others to fix prices (for labour, goods and services) rather than through market competition. Both theoretically and practically, capitalist markets exist through benevolence and conscious co-operation, if only on a small scale. Indeed, Dahl argues that it is the co-operation of such small organizations which 'generate orientations more favourable to the norms of unselfishness. Organizations beget loyalties, attachments, sentiments of community and solidarity' (Dahl 1982: 153).

Dahl formulates his account of feasible democracy against the backdrop of the inadequate assumptions highlighted in individualist, moral and organic civic virtue. For polyarchal democracy to be applicable in large-scale societies, it must accept: the continual presence of conflict; that human behaviour will be motivated inconsistently by egoism and altruism (for a mix of orientations encourages concern for individual and collective interests);

that most citizens are not 'highly competent theorists or political philosophers' (Dahl 1982: 160); and that an adequate means of conflict resolution should be in place. Given that easy judgements are unusual, he argues that:

> Regulative structures and principles are less satisfactory to the extent that they preserve or create among citizens long-run conflicts in their fundamental interests, either objectively or subjectively; conversely, the more that regulative structures and principles reduce such conflicts of interest, both objectively or subjectively, the better they are. . . . The fundamental conflict of interest in the prisoners' dilemma would not be reduced, at least among rational prisoners, by exhorting them to be nicer to one another. The conflict is built into the very structure of the situation that prevents them from co-operating to achieve the common good.
> (Dahl 1982: 163–4)

This enables Dahl to specify limits to democratic pluralism which are inscribed within the very definitions which make polyarchy possible. An attempt to return to small autarkic communities to restore democracy would create new problems without resolving the original dilemmas. In addition, any attempt to resolve conflicting claims to autonomy and control cannot rely upon the grounds that autonomy enables one group to harm others, for all arrangements provide this capacity for harm. Nor can a utilitarian resolution provide a definitive solution, especially if it contests a fundamental right. Similarly, there are limits upon the decentralization of economic decisions to 'relatively autonomous units' such as enterprises, as well as upon the operation of markets, just as these in turn act as limits on the capacity for any guardians operating central controls in attempts to co-ordinate the social order.

This attempt to find a balance between social imperatives is also witnessed in Dahl's resolution of the problem of inequality in political resources. He focuses his response on the way in which many societies have created floors and ceilings on the use of such resources, to ensure a greater degree of political equality. The floors include social resources (such as free compulsory education, a welfare safety net and benefit entitlements). The ceilings are limits on the use of resources to further sectional interests (such as limits on campaign contributions in the USA). In the case of voting, the floor and the ceiling are identical. Dahl is particularly concerned with how social inequalities are translated into unequal political resources, as the following extract demonstrates:

> differences in education, occupation, financial resources, and access to organizations greatly affect the extent to which American citizens participate in political life, the ways in which they participate, and their effectiveness in gaining a response from government officials. Education appears to have the greatest impact . . . [which] is loosely correlated with other resources: occupation, income and access to organizations. Since it

would be preposterous to reduce inequalities in political resources by imposing a ceiling on education, the alternative is substantially to increase the minimum level of education.

(Dahl 1982: 171)

In relation to income inequality, he draws upon the experience of social-democratic societies (notably the incorporation of unions in policy making) to identify the means by which such inequalities can be ameliorated, and comments upon the unfulfilled promise of American political rhetoric on equality. Dahl attributes the unique outcome of great inequalities in America to a distinct ideological development. In this process, two forms of political rhetoric, federal republicanism (where democracy should adapt to the existing economic arrangements) and radical democracy (where property rights are subordinate to the right to self-government) were fused in the ideology of the agrarian democratic republicanism of Jefferson and Madison. This ideology was concerned with defending political equality from social and economic inequalities, but only through the spread of property ownership and especially through the ownership of land, as supported by Tocqueville.[6] This led, in the USA, to a situation where the polity was governed by democratic procedures but the economy, defined in terms of ownership, was left privately governed and beyond the scope of political interference. This equality of property had very different consequences in the urban environment, and it was these consequences which became a general feature of all American life as agriculture gave way to industry and corporate capitalism.

Dahl's imperative is to make economic inequality a political issue again, but within a political culture which refuses to acknowledge the relationship between economic and political inequalities. He believes that low economic growth since the post-war boom has intensified competition for available resources, and that consequently this has increased awareness of the importance of distribution. However, he suggests that the civic reorientation he has in mind involves the recognition of the misperception involved in treating large economic structures as private (Dahl 1982: 181–2). In particular, he challenges the prevailing view that growth is the product of entrepreneurial risk-taking, by drawing upon evidence from human capital theory which suggests that growth is the product of the size and quality of the labour force, and economies of scale. In this line of argument he suggests that, as public entities, enterprises should be subject to the same forms of governance as the government of the state:

> A large firm is inherently a social and political enterprise. It is inherently social in the sense that its very existence and functioning depend on the contributions made by joint actions, past and current, that cannot be attribute to specific persons: the arrow is released by 'social forces', history, culture and other poorly defined agents. Without the protection of a dense network of laws enforced by public governments, the largest American

corporation would not last for a day. Without a labour force the firm would vanish. It would slowly languish if the labour force were not suitably educated.... Language comes free.... Concepts, ideas, civic orientations like the famous Protestant ethic, the cognition of science and technology: these are social.... A large firm is inherently a political system because the government of a firm exercises great power, including coercive power. The government of a firm can have more impact on the lives of more people than the government of many a town, city, province, state.

(Dahl 1982: 183–4)

Four defences of corporate capitalism are raised by Dahl for consideration. First is the argument that the existing arrangement of relatively independent economic enterprises is supportive of polyarchal democracy. He suggests that this is merely a defence of decentralization, and therefore applicable to both privately owned and employee-owned firms. Second is the argument that corporations are 'stockholder democracies', which is a violation of the equal-vote principle and ignores the claim of employee rights. Third is the argument that decisions in this area are private voluntary acts of exchange (and as such the consequences of free exchange are just). For Dahl, this involves a failure to distinguish an imaginary construction from actual conditions where the original distribution is unjust, access to social resources unequal, and all transactions run the risk of affecting those not involved (externalities). Finally there is the argument that corporations make decisions on behalf of the private concerns of owners (resting upon the Lockean principle of private property as anything with which an individual has mixed his labour), which ignores both the contribution of employees and the social contribution to the productive process (Dahl 1982: 199–202).

It is on these assumptions that Dahl argues that the same justifications which are applied to the government of the state can be applied directly to the government of an economic enterprise.[7] The extension of democratic principle from the polity to the economy would undermine the differences in wealth, income, status, information control and access to political leaders, which lead to significant disparities in capacities and opportunities for political participation (Dahl 1985: 55). The shift in the distributive principle of justice which this would require is elaborated in three phases. First is a *civic phase*, which would open up the distributive principle for discussion before a new one became binding. Second is a *catch-up phase*, which would seek to use the existing powers of the state on employment, income and taxation (along social democratic lines) until electoral resistance to taxation and the undermining of incentives affected efficiency. Third is the *phase of structural change* in the economic order, which would deliver democracy in economic enterprises and greater political equality, at the same time as maintaining incentives and efficiency.

To achieve this, Dahl proposes that *enlightened civic virtue* is promising as an alternative to American civic egoism. This would foster a deeper concern with the reinforcement of civic virtue, by seeking a convergence of interests and the resolution of conflict, so that the interests of those involved are 'complementary'. At the same time it embraces the existence of political conflict within large-scale democracies as a fact of life. For Dahl:

> Perfect complementarity is no doubt rare. But interests are often imperfectly complementary, in the sense that for each actor the gains from co-operating with others outweigh the costs on balance. Conflicting interests make political life necessary; but complementary interests make it possible.
>
> (Dahl 1982: 188)

This convergence of interests, he hastens to add, presumes the diminution of inequalities of resources. He also suggests further integrative measures for developing polyarchy in America, such as the creation of a multi-party political system to replace the existing fragmented two-party system and to facilitate more integrative coalition building, and a centralized negotiation and bargaining framework for building integration between economic associations, to replace decentralized bargaining by exclusive associations.

To summarize this complex series of arguments, the establishment of full polyarchy would involve the encouragement of greater diversity, decentralization and dispersion of power and political resources. The distribution of wealth and income would have to be much fairer than at present, and individual decisions in economic enterprises would be subject both to market controls and to regulation and control by an appropriate demos (which in economic enterprises would include all employees with an equal vote). This could mean that different decisions in the same organization could be controlled by different groupings of citizens, building considerable flexibility into the system. To return to Dahl's initial influences, where Tocqueville was worried about the dangers of democracy to personal independence, and the framers of the American constitution with the dangers to property rights, Dahl explicitly attempts to develop a case for democracy and political equality without any loss of personal independence or autonomy. The extension of the argument for the inalienable natural right of private property to contemporary corporate capitalism, he argues, makes a series of unsustainable conceptual leaps. He concludes that the right to self-government is theoretically prior to that of the ownership of property. Otherwise the control of resources by the propertied few empties the democratic process of its content (Dahl 1985: 62–76).

Dahl contends that contemporary America is torn between two visions of democracy, in which the right to self-government is superior to the right to property or, alternatively, the right to property is superior to the right to self-government (Dahl 1985: 161–3). At this stage it is useful to identify the key principles which constitute the content of democracy within this neo-pluralist approach. For Dahl, the nature of the democratic process can be summarized in seven assumptions.

- Within an association or collectivity, decisions should be binding upon all members.
- These binding collective decisions should involve both a period in which the agenda is defined and a final decision-making stage.
- Binding collective decisions should only be binding on those individuals affected by the decision.
- The 'good' of each person is entitled to equal consideration (the *weak principle of equality*).
- Each person in the collective association is the final judge of his or her own interests, with the onus of proof falling on those who wish to establish exceptions (the *principle of liberty* but re-labelled as the *presumption of personal autonomy* in 1989).
- Each adult individual is as well qualified as any other to decide which matters are in need of a collective binding decision (the *strong principle of equality*).
- Scarce and valued objects should be allocated fairly (the *elementary principle of fairness*) (Dahl 1985: 56–62).

On the last assumption, he raises the choice between two principles of fairness. First is fairness as 'person-regarding', taking into account the needs and deserts of individuals. Second is fairness as 'lot-regarding', ensuring that each individual receives an equal share or, if the object cannot be divided in this way, an equal opportunity (Douglas Rae, *Equalities* (1981): 82–103; cited in Dahl 1989: 87).

Building on this refined model of democracy, in *Democracy and its Critics* (1989) Dahl self-consciously attempts to combine normative political theory with empirical political science within a unified 'theoretical perspective'. He engages in an important elaboration of his position by rejecting the methodological individualism associated with rational choice theory, and by attempting to construct a human-centred approach. In particular, he rejects the treatment of political communities as aggregates, and views them instead as 'systems consisting of parts and their relationships'. In this way, by drawing upon the Kantian concern for respect for persons, Dahl claims to be more consistent with the definition of interests as social and value-laden, that is, in terms of the values of love, altruism, friendship, fraternity, justice, order, loyalty, security and so on (Dahl 1989: 72–6). In addition, Dahl pays more attention to one particular assumption involved in the democratic process, the strong principle of equality. He breaks the strong principle into two components, the *presumption of personal autonomy* and the *idea of intrinsic equality*. The presumption of personal autonomy involves the assumption that no other person is capable of being a better judge of one's own interests than oneself (ibid.: 84–105). Of the various conceptualizations of equality on offer, Dahl draws upon the idea that the good of all individuals can be achieved through the equal consideration of interests (the weak principle of equality). The democratic process is simply a necessary, although not a sufficient, means for securing one's interests. However, there is some discord over whether democracy is instrumental in facilitating self-determination (Rousseau), self-development (J. S. Mill) and/or the protection of personal interests (Mill again). Dahl is particularly keen to separate the role of democracy in the 'maximization of the satisfaction of wants', from the provision of a framework which maximizes *opportunities* for satisfying these wants. Dahl thus treats the democratic process and political equality as the essential means for achieving the ends of a just distribution of freedom and fairness in opportunities for self-development.

This leads Dahl to address his own treatment of the common good. This is achieved through an engaging critique of Michael Walzer's *Spheres of Justice* (1983). Walzer's analysis focuses on distributive justice, which Dahl takes as a form of common good. Dahl cites 'four aspects' of Walzer's account: that goods such as money, welfare and security constitute different spheres of justice; that social standards exist for each sphere, which derive their meaning from those involved; that justice is culturally relative and located in a historically specific social setting; and that the decisive arbiter of the social meaning of such forms of justice is the political community. In this account, no universal standards of justice or the common good prevail and 'the highest court of appeal is social meaning' (Dahl 1989: 304). For Dahl, putting aside his point about the diversity of political communities, this confirms his own view that there are significant problems in establishing universal substantive principles of justice. However, he raises the neglect of procedural justice in Walzer's account. Dahl's account of the common good is distinctive in attempting to relate it to both substance and process. In particular, his elaboration of polyarchic democracy examines the complex interrelationship between procedural and substantive aspects of the democratic process. The *enlightened understanding* of choices in the light of relevant alternatives presumes some understanding of one's interests and their relationship to the meaning of the common good (ibid.: 303–8).

Conclusion

A significant feature of Dahl's work on types of regimes is the tendency to neglect the internal features of the state within polyarchic and hegemonic societies. An insight into how this could be developed is present in his account of the shift from competitive *near polyarchies* in the nineteenth century towards *full polyarchies* in the twentieth century in the West. When considering governmental effectiveness, Dahl suggests that a significant role in the survival of emergent polyarchies has been played by the resolution of executive–legislative conflicts in favour of the former; so that the executive typically has considerable scope for exercising discretionary power. In addition, Dahl develops a classificatory set of types of political institutions, in order to establish the conditions for the variety of polyarchic systems in existence. However, this classificatory system focuses on the identification of constitutional norms and the most appropriate division of authority between the powers of government, as well as the fragmented subsystems within the state. He also considers the form of electoral and party system in operation, and the mechanisms established for the inclusion and exclusion of interest groups on 'key political decisions' (Dahl 1982: 65–7). Throughout his later writings, the focus of his attention is directed towards the decentralization of power and political resources.

This chapter has provided a metatheoretical reading of Dahl's major works on the state, politics and democracy, highlighting the epistemological and ontological shifts in the development of his theory of polyarchy. In the early, more descriptive, phase he adopts an empiricist position, grounded in a phenomenalist account of theory construction combined with an account of causality based upon regularity determinism. To achieve this, he constructs a closed-system model of eight conditions related to political influence. However, even here Dahl clearly has doubts about the extent to which the account is accurate in empirical terms. At this stage he does not adapt his approach to account for social complexity, which would allow him to move towards the idealist approach he later adopted. Instead, Dahl accepts Blalock's reworked version of causation as a form of correlation, using statistical controls to simulate a closed system in order to fit the evidence within his classification system of polyarchies (Dahl 1956: 87).

During the 1960s, Dahl began to acknowledge the complexity of social and political life, and the inadequacies of social-scientific research in attempting accurately to reflect such conditions. Consequently, he shifted towards a causal model based on intelligibility determinism which, although constant conjunctions retain a central place, recognizes that empirical regularities are not sufficient in themselves for establishing a causal law. The result of this shift is the development of a model composed of ideal types, constructed in terms of the extent of inclusivity of participation in the political process and the degree of public contestation. This enables Dahl to develop a simplified model which accounts for a range of regimes (forms of polyarchies and hegemonies), and which also enables him to speculate about the preconditions for the emergence and maintenance of fully polyarchal regimes. This last point perhaps contains the most significant clue in identifying the motivation behind Dahl's shifting positions. The most visible indication of a shift in Dahl's approach is his open endorsement of participatory democracy and, in particular, the extension of democracy to economic enterprises. By adopting an explicitly normative stance, Dahl acknowledges connections between the actual and the ideal which cannot be accommodated by empiricist social science.

The adoption of a neo-Kantian idealist epistemology is tied to Dahl's acknowledgement of the case for extending the right to self-government from the polity to other spheres when dealing with workers' control (Dahl 1985: 111). Dahl in practice modifies this categorical principle, on the empirical grounds that all political systems define their particular demos with some form of exclusion, such as the exclusion of children or, in some cases, certain adults (Dahl 1986a: 210–14; 1989: 124–7). This claim moves beyond the utilitarian justification of the positive benefits of self-governing enterprises and their potential for developing the democratic character in the populace. It is an application of the categorical imperative that for something to hold, it must be applicable to all members of the moral community; that human beings must be treated as ends in themselves rather than a means to an end. Thus democracy must be applied from motives which govern all actions. For Dahl the right to self-government, in his account of economic democracy, is exactly this sort of motive. Not only does he see the polyarchic democracy as the 'minimax' (least worst) solution from the regimes on offer, he sees it as the 'maximax' (best possible) outcome for human beings as social beings (Dahl 1989: 78).

Even though Dahl's intellectual position on politics shifts considerably, there are important elements of continuity. He remains committed to the identification of empirical variables and their regularities in the models he develops in his research practices on comparative politics. For Dahl the comparative and historical method, often expressed in the maxim 'what cannot be sensibly compared, can be usefully contrasted', generates a useful set of criteria for establishing some of the parameters for research. This allows him to recognize the problems of increasing complexity as the scale of political communities increases, including recent trends towards globalization.[8] These tendencies prompt him to worry about the dangers of a move away from democracy towards guardianship, although he remains hopeful that the communications revolution will facilitate a technological solution to access to information as well as serve as a mechanism for facilitating greater political participation (Dahl 1989: 322–41). Nevertheless, the internal structures and mechanisms of the state, the articulation of the institutional relationships across conventional constitutional boundaries, the relationship between the formal rules and procedures and the informal practices which shape the operation of policy making and implementation, are all conspicuously absent from Dahl's analysis. Understanding these remains a precondition for working through an adequate analysis of the relationship between political institutions and their cultural conditions.

4 The horizon of catallactic possibilities

Introduction

Hayek's concern with political philosophy emerged as an attempt to resolve a series of problems which he encountered in economics and the methodology of the social sciences from the 1920s to the 1940s. The substantive clues in explaining his supposed 'break' from economics, and his movement towards philosophy and the moral sciences, can be traced to the epistemological concerns which arise throughout his work. These concerns about knowledge construction reveal a greater degree of consistency in his development than is commonly recognized in Hayek scholarship to date. There is a tendency to lump Hayek together with other 'new right' thinkers on the grounds that they all advocate free market solutions, without considering their compatibility in epistemological terms. A closer examination of Hayek's social and political thought reveals that his attempts to resolve the problems of philosophy, politics and economics lead him in a direction which leaves his approach incompatible with rational choice theory, at least as it has presently been taken up and used within the neo-liberal tradition.[1] In addition, attempts to periodize Hayek's work solely as an economist (1920s–40s), as a philosopher (1940s–60s) and as a prophet (from 1970s onwards) are also misleading, for they neglect the unfolding character of his writings and the way in which his studies in economics, political philosophy and social-scientific methodology actually complement and reinforce one another.

This chapter contends that, in addressing the problematic standing of time and the social distribution of knowledge within economic theory, Hayek forges a creative synthesis between the Kantian critique of rationalism and phenomenological explanations of social action.[2] The phenomenology invoked is specifically that of Alfred Schütz's 'mundane' phenomenology, rather than the 'transcendental' phenomenology of Edmund Husserl.[3] The concept of the market in Hayek's approach therefore undergoes a significant transformation from an ahistorical abstract formulation in neo-classical economic equilibrium theory into *catallaxy as a condition of intersubjectivity* whereby the process of competition between participants enables mutual discovery and the co-ordination of plans. The mechanical formulation of the invisible hand of the price mechanism (taken by both sympathisers such as Israel Kirzner (1992), and critics such as John O'Neill (1989), as the defining feature of Hayek's resolution of the co-ordination problem) gives way to a focus on rules of conduct as the shared structures of meaning, within which the crucial role of tacit knowledge is acknowledged explicitly.

Time and subjectivity: from praxeology to phenomenology

Hayek's early work in technical economics is characterized by two concerns, which are themselves linked by a third normative purpose to defend liberal values. These two main concerns are the development of an adequate conceptualization of the temporal dimension in social-scientific explanations (particularly economics where, in business-cycle theory, it was conspicuously absent) and the recognition that human values are subjectively defined and established during the course of mutual exchange and communication. In 'Intertemporal Price Equilibrium and Movements in the Value of Money' (1928), Hayek reveals his growing dissatisfaction with static equilibrium theory because of its simplistic and flawed theoretical foundations. In addition he was concerned at the way static equilibrium theory had been used to justify socialist calculation (that managers within a command economy had simply to fix prices at marginal cost to ensure equilibrium in terms of the standard model). It is this awareness of the potential of static equilibrium analysis for justifying an omniscient body rationally directing a planned economy that led Hayek to develop his conception of the market as a process. The underlying problem in equilibrium theory at this time was the abstraction from the 'temporal' dimension of economic reality, producing a synchronic account of the business cycle, or at least a series of synchronic analyses. While Hayek does not, at this point, seek to dispense with the equilibrium construct as it stands, he does argue for conceptual innovation through the development of a diachronic analysis of the cycle. Hence, he developed the idea of the dynamic *intertemporal price equilibrium*, an open-system analysis which also takes account of the role of money as a commodity, and which also allows the prices of technically equivalent goods to differ, as they do in a concrete economy moving through time.

In his earliest work, Hayek explicitly recognizes that closed systems, while retaining a heuristic function, are clearly inadequate for explaining dynamic complex social phenomena such as market relations and processes. In his 1933 Inaugural Professorial Lecture at the LSE on 'The Trend in Economic Thinking' (Hayek 1991), he was concerned to show that the 'co-ordination' of complex social phenomena was achieved by means which, although individually they were often regarded as objectionable and the product of selfish motivations, when aggregated together produced beneficial unintended consequences:

In short, it showed that an immensely complicated mechanism existed, worked and solved problems, frequently by means which proved to be the only possible means by which the result could be the result of deliberate regulation because nobody understood them. Even now, when we begin to understand their working, we discover again and again that necessary functions are discharged by spontaneous institutions. If we tried to run the system by deliberate regulation, we should have to invent such institutions, and yet at first we did not even understand them when we saw them.
(Hayek 1991: 26–7)

In the essay 'Economics and Knowledge' (1937), Hayek can be seen exploring the relationship between the acquisition of knowledge and the capacity of human actors to engage in actions and valuations. In addition, he recognizes the ways in which economic concepts, specifically the equilibrium construct, are inadequate to the burdens placed upon them. Hayek still does not dispense with the equilibrium construct. However, its role is transformed as he embraces *subjectivism* more wholeheartedly. To achieve this, he shifts his attention towards the co-ordination problem: how the divergent plans of the human actors involved come into a co-ordinated pattern in the context of competition within the market process. This argument expands upon his previous work, regarding the inadequacies of equilibrium analysis when it is applied beyond the pure logic of choice with an isolated individual. When this pure logic of choice is extended to account for societal equilibrium (as an aggregation of individuals), conventional neo-classical economists make the assumption that all the actors involved possess the same knowledge about their objective surroundings. However, for Hayek, this creates a tautologous circuit of explanation for 'the statement that, if people know everything, they are in equilibrium is true simply because that is how we define equilibrium' (Hayek 1949: 46).

As a result, Hayek turned his attention to the process through which actors acquire knowledge and communicate knowledge. He concludes that, due to the operation of a division of knowledge (conceived along the lines of the division of labour), knowledge is subjectively held and widely dispersed. Rather than perfect foresight being a precondition for equilibrium (when subjective data held by human actors correspond to objective facts of the external world), it is portrayed as a characteristic of the state of affairs where an equilibrium holds, indicating the mutual compatibility of individual plans, and lasting as long as the anticipations of those involved prove correct, which, in turn, is an empirical question (Hayek 1949: 33–56). From this point onwards, the 'co-ordination problem' becomes his main concern, and ultimately leads him away from technical economics towards the development of an account of the institutional preconditions for resolving it.

The normative thrust of Hayek's work was inspired by Ludwig von Mises. However, the direction in which it developed was a product of acknowledging that Mises presented an inadequate conceptual framework for understanding co-ordination. Mises had attempted to establish a universally valid science of human action, praxeology, where economics and sociology are fused as the 'science of human action', conceived in terms of the *nomothetic* method. In this respect, by emphasizing the universal (along the lines of logic and mathematics) over the particular, he is closer to the position of the Marburg School of neo-Kantian idealism. Praxeology is concerned with establishing universally valid knowledge rather than with the validity of values. Mises clearly distinguished his approach from empiricism, as the following extract, from the article 'The Task and Scope of Human Action' (originally published in 1933), suggests.

> [W]hat we know about our action under given conditions is derived not from experience, but from reason. . . . [E]conomising, preferring, the relationship of means and ends, and everything else that, together with these, constitutes the system of human action – is not derived from experience. We conceive all this from within, just as we conceive logical and mathematical truths, a priori, without reference to any experience. Nor could experience ever lead anyone to the knowledge of these things if he did not comprehend them from within himself. As an a priori category the principle of action is on a par with the principle of causality.
> (Mises 1981: 13–14)

However, in other respects he draws upon the position of the Baden School in the identification of the intentional and purposeful nature of human action and the importance of meaning within economic life. In *Theory and History*, he later argued, 'There are no judgements of values other than those asserting I prefer, I like better, I wish' (Mises 1958: 22). This emphasis upon the subjective character of values again raises the charge of relativism. His escape clause is the argument that the science of human action is nomothetic, so that subjective value judgements are taken to be 'facts, that is the way in which people really choose ultimate ends' (ibid.: 35) rather than having any transhistorical basis or relation to universal values. The explanation of value in terms of a means–ends structure, and the relations between human actors and between the actors and the object in question, rather than the identification of intrinsic properties, owe much to Carl Menger's *Principles of Economics* (1981). Following in Menger's footsteps, Mises and Hayek have been concerned to explore the conditions of valuation prior to the possibility of individuals engaging in acts of exchange. This conception of individuals as valuing and acting (without any predetermined content or quality) leads Mises into some interesting conclusions on the nature of prediction in economics, which are directly relevant to Hayek's account of the complexity of social life. In 'Sociology and History', originally published in 1929, Mises distinguishes between the role of 'quantitative predictions' within the natural sciences, and 'qualitative predictions' within sociology and economics, in a way which highlights his awareness of the distinctive characteristics of the object of analysis in social scientific enquiry:

Sociology cannot grasp human action in its fullness. It must take the actions of individuals as ultimately given. The predictions it makes about them can be only qualitative, not quantitative. Accordingly, it can say nothing about the magnitude of their effects. This is roughly what is meant by the statement that the characteristic feature of history is concern with the individual, the irrational, life, and the domain of freedom. For sociology, which is unable to determine in advance what they will be, the value judgements that are made in human action are ultimate data. This is the reason why history cannot predict things to come and why it is an illusion to believe that qualitative economics can be replaced or supplemented by quantitative economics. Economics as a theoretical science can impart no knowledge other than qualitative. And economic history can furnish us with quantitative knowledge only *post factum*.

(Mises 1981: 116)

Having extended economics into praxeology, the 'science of all and every human action' (Mises 1981: 233), Mises is left with the problem of delineating the scope of economics. This is achieved through the development of *catallactics*, a discipline whose object of analysis includes all market phenomena, their preconditions and their consequences. Mises is keen to distinguish this approach from the prevalent attempts in his day to examine the various motives which cause action and the goals to which actions are directed. The classification of human actions according to their motives was particularly marked in psychological and moral accounts of social life. Mises, however, saw this as 'inconsequential' in economics, which he argued was founded upon a subjective theory of value. This was a subjectivism which could not be reduced to a series of taxonomic categories. Catallactics as a form of analysis is therefore the study of actions taken as a form of economic calculation based on money prices within the conditions of (and hence conditioned by) market exchange (ibid.: 233–5). The use of the term 'catallaxy' by Hayek in preference to that of 'the market' draws upon this account of human action. For Mises, economics (conceived as the most advanced component of praxeology) is seen essentially as the method of 'imaginary constructions' through which all human beings comprehend existence; where commonsense constructions are 'more or less confused and muddled, economics is intent upon elaborating them with utmost care, scrupulousness, and precision' (ibid.: 237). Hayek ultimately came to criticize the rationalist elements in Mises' account of praxeology within the *Miseskreis*, the intellectual circle formed around Ludwig von Mises in Vienna. Nevertheless Hayek assimilated into the subjectivist theory of value the conception of the market economy as a catallactic process and the normative critique of socialist calculation.

In explaining the trajectory of Hayek's thought, it is possible to identify a central theoretical preoccupation (or unresolved question within his work) from the late 1920s through to the 'Scientism' essay: 'how is it possible to account for time?'(Hayek 1979 [1952]). Of course, he was not the first to ask this. Wilhelm Dilthey's contribution is especially significant. In order to accommodate the subjective propensities of lived experience and the historical character of human action, Dilthey had conceptualized 'meaning' as a temporal category (that understanding takes place where the past meets the future in the present). This temporal process of understanding, by which one mind grasps the mind of the other, bringing together the inner and the outer, is the starting point for the phenomenological approach. Indeed, this way of viewing the historicality of human action serves as an important reference point for Hayek's treatment of time. However, the underlying relativism of Dilthey, whereby there is no basis for making a judgement between competing life-worlds, is more problematic. It is also necessary to explore the Kantian and neo-Kantian dimensions of Hayek's analysis in more detail, particularly the role of Ludwig von Mises.

If Hayek was attempting to establish a phenomenological foundation for understanding the market system and the co-ordination problem at the same time as avoiding relativism (for relativism would nullify the normative dimension of his work), then the relationship with the Misean approach would be under strain. Certainly Hayek appears to be selective in the use of ideas from praxeology, and disagrees with the rationalist elements in the Mises approach. This becomes even more apparent when we examine Mises' own treatment of the concept of time in the light of Hayek's account of the historicality of human action. The central pivot of Mises' account is the relationship between action and reason, as the following quotation from *Human Action* reveals:

> [T]he subject matter of praxeology, human action, stems from the same source as human reasoning. Action and reason are congeneric and homogenous; they may even be called two different aspects of the same thing. That reason has the power to make clear through pure ratiocination the essential features of action is a consequence of the fact that action is an offshoot of reason.
> (Mises 1949: 39)

As Parsons points out, for Kant all the objects of possible experience were temporal, and time must be presupposed for action to take place. For Mises, however, action takes place within time while reason is beyond time. Kant viewed time and space as a priori conditions for the possibility of experience, mediating between knowledge and the objects of possible experience, although he pulled back from extending the relationship between knowledge and time to include reason as well, preserving the autonomy of reason and the role of the scientist (Parsons 1990: 307–14). Parsons provides a useful Kantian critique of Mises' nomothetic account of human action, which leads to some interesting conclusions about the way Hayek began to question the rationalist a priori nature of praxeology. It is in this context that Hayek worked through the problems of equilibrium analysis in relation to time and the social distribution of knowledge. It is significant that the publication of the essay 'Economics and Knowledge' (1937), which constituted Hayek's first clear statement of the subjectively held and widely dispersed nature of knowledge, is also his first clear break with Ludwig von Mises (although Mises never acknowledged it as such).

This brings us to the importance of the Schütz–Hayek connection. It is clear that Hayek gathered a wide range of theoretical tools from the sources discussed (particularly from his participation in the *Miseskreis*). However, it is the contention of this chapter that the aforementioned accounts of Hayek's intellectual development miss one vital ingredient. This missing ingredient in Hayek's 'recipe knowledge' is the writings of Alfred Schütz, particularly *Der sinnhafte Aufbau der sozialen Welt* (1932; translated as *The Phenomenology of the Social World*, 1967). This exploration of phenomenological sociology constitutes an attempt to outline the meaningful construction of the basic concepts of the social sciences. The similarity of the ideas of Schütz and Hayek has not gone unnoticed. Mark Peacock has highlighted the affinities between Schütz's account of 'typifications' (first-order constructs) and Hayek's version of anti-naturalism, as well as his account of the concept-dependent nature of the subject matter in the social sciences (Peacock 1993: 251). Similarly, Tony Lawson has identified a 'hermeneutic foundationalism' in Hayek's writings. However, if this is interpreted as an indication of the influence of Dilthey, it takes no account of the significant discrepancies between their accounts on the issue of relativism (Lawson 1994a; see Chapter Six for a fuller discussion). The personal links between Friedrich Hayek and other Austrian associates (Mises, Alfred Schütz, Fritz Machlup, Oskar Morgenstern) are barely documented. What is clear is that they shared a vision of the appropriate principles for establishing an adequate social-scientific method and of the peculiar problems faced in studying social life (see Smith 2000b).

A key role in the 1928–30 methodological discussions of the *Miseskreis* was played by Alfred Schütz. These arguments and ideas were developed by Schütz in *The Phenomenology of the Social World* (1967, originally published in 1932). They represent an attempt to draw together insights from Weber, Bergson and Husserl. Schütz attempted to construct an adequate account of social phenomena which could accommodate the condition of *intersubjectivity*, the social relationships through which the individual actors involved are able to grasp each other's consciousness. The key to the first part of the text is the identification of the interpretive and intentional character of the actors involved. While Schütz draws upon the emphasis placed upon 'meaning' in Weber's work, he remains dissatisfied with the ambiguity of Weber's attachment to the ideal types which had been deployed by objective social scientists. Schütz draws upon the ideas of Husserl and Bergson to identify clearly the subjective meanings of the actors as the source of understanding. The 'stream of consciousness' (within the deepest stratum of experience accessible to reflection) is identified as the ultimate source of meaning. In order to distinguish his position from Dilthey's attempt to establish hermeneutics as a foundation, Schütz draws upon Bergson's distinction between living within the stream of consciousness (the contents of which have no meaning in themselves) and living within the world of space and time:

> The stream of consciousness by its very nature has not yet been caught up in the net of reflection. Reflection being a function of the intellect, belongs essentially in the spatiotemporal world of everyday life. The structure of our experience will vary according to whether we surrender ourselves to the flow of duration or stop to reflect upon it, trying to classify it into spatiotemporal concepts.
> (Schütz 1967: 45)

Schütz draws together Bergson's conceptualization of the simultaneity of experience, the sharing of time and space by two individual actors involved in communication, and Husserl's conception of intersubjectivity, so that the process of understanding the other person involves grasping what is going on in the other person's mind, their lived experiences (Schütz 1967: 112–13). The idea that the alter ego coexists with one's own stream of consciousness provides Schütz with the basis for developing a sociological account of the social world constituted by typifications and recipe-knowledge, the *lebenswelt* (life-world) of everyday common sense.

Hayek's recognition that it was theoretically possible to ground the 'fatal conceit' of central planning upon equilibrium theory and the price mechanism led him to reformulate the 'central problem of economics' as the co-ordination of plans within the context of widely dispersed and subjectively-held knowledge. Indeed, it is through the writings of Schütz on phenomenology and rationality that Hayek was able to formulate a more adequate account of subjectivism and time within the tradition of Austrian economics. However, there was a price to pay. Hayek ultimately came to reject the praxeological approach of Mises as a form of 'rationalist-utilitarianism', radically transforming the concept of catallaxy in the process. The close intellectual links and their points of contact between Hayek and Schütz can be traced from 1921 to 1958. (Schütz died prematurely in 1959.)

With these aspects of Hayek's work in economics and the philosophy of social science in place, he identifies the limitations of contemporary economics as a discipline. He then proceeds to establish a state theory and political philosophy which, if embodied in institutional form, would act as the best possible shell for the unimpeded efficient operation of the market system conceived as catallaxy. The liberal state and the 'rule of law' in this approach are meaningful structures or sets of rules of conduct, within which mutual discovery can take place and individual liberty is enhanced. The normative intent of Hayek's theory of the state is fairly clear and subject to a wide level of agreement: that good or altruistic intentions exercised through the polity lead to disastrous social consequences (and potentially to totalitarianism); while respect for and non-interference in individual and self-interested desires lead to positive social consequences. Here, Hayek does not argue that the market will automatically provide the optimal solution to the co-ordination problem, simply that it is the least worst alternative to planning.

Hayek combines careful analysis with a programme for political change. The audiences which he sought to address in the post-war years, namely policy makers informed by the Anglo-American traditions of political philosophy and economics, led him to focus his attention on generating a revival of interest in classical liberal theory. However, the dynamic core of his intellectual project, a *phenomenologically informed transformative praxis*, remains intact throughout his intellectual development. His main concern is to explain how the emergence of the spontaneous order (although he prefers the less ambiguous 'self-generating order' or 'self-organizing structures' in the Preface to *Law, Legislation and Liberty* (1982: xix) is possible without the loss of human freedom. The targets of his invective were the growth of state intervention in the twentieth century and the political philosophies which endorse the emergence of totalitarian states in advanced industrial societies and hence undermine civilization.

The links between the phenomenological analysis of social relations, and Hayek's concern for the delicate cultural and moral fabric through which liberal social and political orders are sustained, are much more evident from the late 1930s. Certainly, when the liberal order is in peril in the face of the rise of fascism, the essays which comprise 'Scientism and the Study of Society' (reprinted in Hayek 1979), written in London during the Blitz, constitute a remarkable but neglected link in the developing problematic of Hayek's thought. This text is the epistemological equivalent of his critique of the devices of socialist calculation in economics. It is polemical in tone and clearly identifies the enemies of a free and spontaneous social order. These enemies are *scientism* and its various derivations of *objectivism*, *collectivism* and *historicism*. In contrast, Hayek wished to develop a social-scientific method which could take proper account of the complexity of social phenomena within open systems, and which could specifically 'explain the unintended or undesigned results of the actions of many men' (Hayek 1979: 41). His individualistic and compositive method examines social phenomena as though they are constituted through the actions and valuations of individual agents. Hence, Hayek takes seriously the 'subjective' perceptions and purposes of such actors in specific situations as the basic data of social science: 'It is probably no exaggeration to say that every important advance in economic theory in the last hundred years was a further step in the consistent application of subjectivism' (ibid.: 52).

The building blocks of Hayek's social and political philosophy are clearly established at this point: the humility of the individual and the role played by tacit knowledge in accounting for the emergence of the spontaneous order. Together, these provide the underlying thrust of the critique of state intervention. The place of tacit knowledge, of 'which we never consciously know, implicit in the knowledge of which we are aware, knowledge which yet constantly serves us in our actions, though we can hardly be said to possess it' (Hayek 1979: 150 n.9), is the binding element of Hayek's work and, as will become apparent later, a key to understanding the complex epistemological position that he constructs in his later work.

Knowing the social as mutual exchange: one principle and two postulates

Hayek's intellectual trajectory can be seen as propelled by two forces, one negative and the other positive. The first involves the rejection of state planning in the economy, unless a competitive solution cannot be found. Following the *Socialist Calculation Debate*, Hayek saw his main task as exposing as a myth the dominant explanation of the rise of Fascism and National Socialism as the capitalist reaction against socialism. His message to the British (and American) intelligentsia was simply that 'You're going the same way that they do' (Kresge and Wenar 1994: 102). Moreover, he saw this as part of the general trend towards collectivism or socialism in Western societies in the twentieth century. This is most tellingly explained in his famous intellectual joust with Charles E. Merriam and Maynard C. Krueger in Chicago in 1945:

> [T]he trend toward socialism was the main cause in putting greater and greater powers, over all activities, in the hands of the government. In Europe, once governments directly controlled a large part of the social activity, they had to tell the people in the service of what ends these activities had to be employed. Thus they had to shift from the control, merely, of our material activity to the control of our ideals and beliefs . . . I say that collectivism is a method that can be used for many different things and that the others [communism, socialism, totalitarianism and planning] are various specimens of collectivism. That method of central planning which is proposed as an alternative method of organizing production to take the place of competition means that a government, or some central authority, must take complete control of the resources.
> (Kresge and Wenar 1994: 117–19)

In response to Merriam's and Krueger's remarks on his idea of planning as incompatible with the rule of law, Hayek attempts to shift the terms of debate from:

> an old controversy – about whether the state ought to act or ought not to act. The whole effort of [*The Road to Serfdom*] was to substitute a new distinction for the older silly and vague idea. I had realized that some kind of state action is extremely dangerous. Therefore my whole effort

was to distinguish between legitimate and illegitimate action. I have attempted to do that by saying that, so far as the government plans for competition or steps in where competition cannot possibly do the job, there is no objection; but I believe that all other forms of government activity are highly dangerous.

(Kresge and Wenar 1994: 123)

The second concern in Hayek's intellectual project involves the clarification of the conceptual framework necessary for establishing a free and spontaneous social order which can weather the onslaught of constructivist rationalism (a twenty-year task of which the establishment of the Mont Pèlerin Society, as an international discussion group, was the first step). This intellectual project involved the development of an exposition of the forms of liberalism most compatible with the conception of the market as catallaxy. For this purpose, Hayek introduced the distinction between true and false individualism. He is concerned to distinguish the critical liberal tradition of John Locke, Adam Smith, Edmund Burke and Alexis de Tocqueville from its continental counterpart inspired by Cartesian rationalism (egoistic liberalism), notably the work of Rousseau, Comte and the Utilitarian tradition. The former, 'true' variant entertains a healthy sense of doubt when assessing the potential of the state for remedying the problems of society. The latter, 'false' individualism, in proposing the design and creation of social institutions to respond to these problems, contains the seeds of collectivism. In the development of his own political philosophy, Hayek also comes to the conclusion that John Stuart Mill's writings are contaminated by rationalist elements (see Hayek 1951). In the absence of perfect knowledge in the formulation of public policy, the underlying thrust of Hayek's argument is simply that the social order most capable of maximizing freedom is that which is the product of human action and not of human design.

In *Law, Legislation and Liberty*, Hayek suggests that this intellectual project involves an interdisciplinary task, drawing upon the collective effort of like-minded individuals from economics, legal theory, politics, ethical philosophy and, crucially for this discussion, sociology (Hayek 1973).[4] This involved both the identification of those elements of the liberal tradition that are compatible with these goals (and the denunciation of those that are not) and a fundamental reappraisal of the concepts within this tradition. These concepts, such as liberty, equality, freedom, merit, responsibility, tradition and progress, were to be stripped of their rationalist connotations and grounded in an account of the social which could accommodate the recognition of rational action as founded upon everyday, intertemporal, intersubjective experience.

The formation of Hayek's distinctive position in political philosophy can be seen as inspired by Alfred Schütz's engaging critique of the uses of the concept of rationality in the social sciences (Schütz 1943), as well as by those earlier contributions to the problems of establishing the meaningful construction of the social world that were considered earlier (Schütz 1967). Of note here is a critical review of Talcott Parsons' *The Structure of Social Action* (Schütz 1943), where Schütz was keen to contrast the peculiarity of Parsons' theoretical level of comprehension with the other levels of social experience explored in his own work. Hayek commissioned this review article (which was finally published in 1943), expressing his desire to see Schütz explicitly address the methodological problems of economics. Schütz focuses on the manner in which rationality, as the 'key concept' of social science, clearly constitutes:

> the differentiations between the points of view which we call levels. The meaning of such key concepts, therefore, does not depend upon the level of the actual research, but, on the contrary, the level on which the research may be done depends upon the meaning attributed to the key concept, the introduction of which has for the first time divided what formerly appeared as a homogenous field of research into several different levels. . . . [Hence] the introduction of the term 'rational action' as a chief principle of the method of social sciences is nothing else than the level of theoretical observation and interpretation of the social world.
> (Schütz 1943: 133–4)

Thus for Schütz the problem of the method of the social sciences is that any social object of analysis can be considered at different levels, and hence can only be resolved by the recognition that at all levels the process of 'typification' is underway: '[T]he transformation of an uncontrollable and unintelligible world into an organization which we can understand and therefore master, and in the framework of which prediction becomes possible' (Schütz 1943: 136).

To substantiate his conception of levels, Schütz provides an illustration from cartography to show how there are different ways of mapping the social. Taking the object of analysis to be a town, he contrasts the perspectives of three persons (or types): first, the cartographer, the detached scientist; second, the native dweller; and third, the foreigner or the stranger. The scientist would use established techniques such as aerial photography to gather the data, and hence proceed to establish the main points of population density, communication systems, and so on, in order to construct objective knowledge. This form of human activity, whereby scientific detachment allows only for cognitive interest and not for practical interest in the social, 'constitutes the archetype for rational interpretation and rational action' (Schütz 1943: 134). Its detached contemplation does not accept that human actions are performed with full responsibility for the consequences. For the native, the town has a special meaning, beyond the habitual and routine typicality of everyday life or practical knowledge, although, like the scientist, the native naively presumes that what has been verified as true will remain so. Finally, the stranger or foreigner recognizes the finitude of his/her knowledge, depending upon common-sense guidelines to get by (such as a map or asking directions), and like the scientist, remains detached from and external to the object in question. Ultimately all levels of social inquiry are based upon relations of mutual co-operation, influence and criticism even if their 'attitude' differs. For Schütz, all 'life worlds' are constituted: 'within the framework of the categories of familiarity and strangeness, of personality and type, of intimacy and anonymity. Furthermore, each of these worlds would be centred in the self of the person who lives and acts in it' (ibid.: 136).

At the heart of Hayek's political philosophy lies the conception of the naive man living in the natural world, wide awake to social phenomena and drawing upon 'heritage and education, from the manifold influences of *tradition, habits* and his own previous reflection, his stores of *experiences*' (my emphases; Schütz 1943: 136). Beyond this are the 'rules of conduct' which, for Hayek, constitute both the product and precondition of a free society. As the following passage reveals, lived experience:

> embraces the most heterogeneous kinds of knowledge in a very incoherent and confused state. Clear and distinct experiences are intermingled with vague conjectures; suppositions and prejudices cross well proven evidences; motives, means and ends, as well as causes and effects, are strung together without clear understandings of their real connections. There are everywhere gaps, intermissions, discontinuities. Apparently there is a kind of organization by habits, rules and principles which we regularly apply with success. But the origin of our habits is almost beyond our control; the rules we apply are rules of thumb and their validity has never been verified . . . [T]hese experiences and rules are sufficient for to us for mastering life. . . . [W]e are not interested in the 'quest for certainty'. . . . Our knowledge in daily life is not without hypotheses, inductions, and predictions, but they all have the character of the approximate and the typical. The ideal of every day knowledge is not certainty, not even probability in the mathematical sense, but just likelihood. Anticipations of future states of affairs are conjectures about what is to be hoped or feared, or at best what can be reasonably expected. . . . The consistency of this system of knowledge is not that of natural *laws*, but that of *typical* sequences and relations.
> (Schütz 1943: 136–7)

Clearly indicated at the heart of Schütz's approach is the sociological formulation often described as 'cookery-book' or 'recipe' knowledge: that we do not need to understand the origins of a particular set of practices in order to select the ingredients, bake the cake and 'eat and enjoy it' (Schütz 1943: 137). Such concerns are reiterated throughout his work from the 1940s to the 1950s (Schütz 1944a, 1944b, 1946, 1951, 1953, 1957, 1958). It is this conception of knowledge which lies behind Hayek's formulation of 'rules of conduct'. Schütz's next step is painstakingly to identify six ways in which the concept of rationality has been understood in relation to everyday experience.[5]

1 *Rationality as synonymous with 'reasonable'*, that recipes from our store of experiences are used in a reasonable and routine way within similar circumstances subject to reformulation if the actors involved cannot 'master the situation'.
2 *Rational action as deliberate* in the sense of 'a dramatic rehearsal in imagination of various competing lines of action' (J. Dewey, cited by Schütz 1943: 138) rather than routine types of everyday actions which do not consider alternative possibilities.
3 *Rational action as planned or projected* whereby the framework of a plan is presupposed to include the routines of everyday life, ends are realized by stages and only the actor knows his or her own subjective plans.
4 *Rational as predictable* and conceived as estimate of likelihood.
5 *Rational as logical*, that at the level of everyday experience the logical status of the rational act is problematized, for it remains an idealization, with the characteristics of clearness and distinctness, inapplicable to the situation of the actor and his/her stream of thought.
6 *The rational act as presupposing a choice* between two or more means, a single or many ends, with a selection of the most appropriate action in mind (Schütz 1943: 138–40). However, as the following extract reveals, it is a nonsense to talk of preferences when the alternatives are not in mind:

> It is erroneous to assume that consciousness of such alternatives and therefore choice is necessarily given before every human action, and that in consequence all acting involves deliberation and preference. This interpretation uncritically confuses selection in the sense of just singling out without comparison of alternatives and choice in the sense of electing the preferred which presupposes reflection, volition and preference.
>
> (Schütz 1943: 141)

At the centre of Schütz's approach lies an attempt to understand the problem of the social distribution of knowledge. Rational choice would only be possible if an actor knows: the end in relation to the framework of plans; the interrelations between ends and their (in-)compatibility; the (un-)desirable consequences which may arise other than the main end; the chain of means necessary for the accomplishment of this particular end; the interference of such means with other chains of means and their ends; and the accessibility of the means in question for the actor involved (Schütz 1943: 142). Here we have the nub of the problem of the co-ordination of plans, and the perplexing difficulty of anticipating the unintended, conveyed within a means–ends formulation, which proved to be so enticing for Hayek in the field of economics and later in political philosophy. When Schütz applies this to the social situation, further determinants come into play: the (mis-)interpretation of the act by other actors; the reactions of others and their motivation; the way that the actor attributes knowledge of means and ends to others; and the categories of familiarity/strangeness, intimacy/anonymity and of personality/type within our inventory of the social world. Hence, rational choices, can only be understood as taking place within a system of rational acts, and not through being viewed as a series of singular isolated acts (ibid.: 142–3). For Schütz, the scientifically-detached observer replaces the human beings observed as actors on the social stage by 'puppets' created and manipulated by the researcher:

> We typify, in daily life, human activities which interest us only as appropriate means for bringing about intended effects, but not as emanations of the personalities of our fellow men. The procedure of the scientific observer is on the whole the same. . . . In short, the ideal type is but a model of the conscious mind without the faculty of spontaneity and without a will of its own.
>
> (Schütz 1943: 143–4)

Two points should be highlighted here. First, the social is constituted by actors with free will who can, and will, behave in spontaneous ways not anticipated by the 'fictitious consciousness' or 'distributed experience' of the scientific model. Second, scientists employ the same procedures of typification as actors in everyday life (which means that they are not omniscient). Neither Schütz nor Hayek wish to dispense with scientific inquiry. For both, abstraction and generalizing from experience are legitimate activities, providing we regard them as 'intellectual shorthand' and do not let them interfere with the movement between levels of research.[6] For Schütz, it is plausible to collect 'facts and regularities' within the natural sciences, but not when faced with the problem of understanding social existence, the study of people and social relations. With the social sciences, the *principle of relevance* is invoked to take into account the motives, the means and ends and the planning of human actors. Two recommendations follow from these observations: the *postulate of subjective interpretation* whereby social science should attempt 'to ask what type of individual mind can be constructed and what typical thoughts must be attributed to it to explain the fact in question as a result of its activity within an understandable relation' (Schütz 1943: 147); and the *postulate of adequacy* so that:

> each term used in a scientific system referring to human action must be so constructed that a human act performed within the life world by an individual actor in the way indicated by the typical construction would be reasonable and understandable for the actor himself, as well as for his fellow men.
>
> (Schütz 1943: 147)

Schütz concludes this essay by focusing on the problems involved in developing a unified approach to the levels of social existence. The answer lies, he argues, in the location of a 'fundamental hypothesis' which 'defines the fields of research and gives the regulative principle for building up the system of ideal types' (Schütz 1943: 148). Finally, he returns to the postulate of adequacy and our uncertainty about the social world:

> Our scientific activity . . . is also performed within a means-ends relation, namely, in order to acquire knowledge for mastering the world, the real world, not the one created by the grace of the scientist. . . . The postulate of adequacy requires that the typical construction be compatible with the totality of both our daily life and our scientific experience.
>
> (Schütz 1943: 148)

It is significant that Schütz draws upon the history of economics to suggest that the 'fundamental hypothesis' of classical economics can be defined as the 'utilitarian principle', while for modern economics it is the 'marginal principle'. Hayek was later (following the death of his teacher and mentor) to describe his break with Mises as a direct consequence of the rationalist-utilitarian elements at work in the praxeological approach. However, Hayek remained deeply attached to the liberal political values and the commitment to subjectivism within economics which both Hayek and Mises held in common. To summarize, at the heart of Hayek's approach to the constitution of liberty lies a phenomenological approach to the constitution of the social. The private domain of liberal political theory is transformed from the realm of individual atoms into a shared world of meaning for all its members. That is the condition of intersubjectivity.

The key distinction in Schütz's account of 'mundane phenomenology' for resolving Hayek's problems in economics and political philosophy is that between the *umwelt* and the *mitwelt*. The *umwelt* involves the intimacy of 'we-relations', directly experienced communication taking place within shared time and space between consociates, whereas the *mitwelt* involves the anonymity of 'they relations' between contemporaries, subsuming individuality within the ideal types of subjective experience. Nevertheless, the *mitwelt* is grounded upon the *umwelt* (see Schütz 1967, ch. 4, which also contains a discussion of *folgewelt*, the indeterminacy of the future, and *vorwelt*, the determined existence of predecessors). Hayek uses these ideas to flesh out a transformed understanding of the lived experience of market relations as a catallaxy, where actors discover each other. Catallaxy is a process involving simultaneity, whereby human actors grasp the *alter ego* within their stream of consciousness. A unified approach to the problem of the existence of different levels is facilitated by the recognition that the typifications or recipes of everyday life (first-order constructions) within the life world, where participants assume the natural attitude, act as the basis for the construction of ideal types (second-order constructions) of what we take to be objective knowledge.

Hayek and the use of knowledge: competition as a discovery procedure

> Though we cannot see in the dark, we must be able to trace the limits of the dark areas.
>
> (Hayek 1960: 23)

With the origins of the trajectory of Hayek's intellectual development in place, I shall now focus more specifically on how Schütz's account of social action and the concept of rationality informs Hayek's discussion of the problems of liberalism in the face of the dangers of collectivism. These connections were developed in the context of the intellectual camaraderie of the closed circles of Viennese intellectual life in the 1920s and early 1930s, notably the *Miseskreis* and the *Geistkreis*. It is often assumed that the intellectual diaspora from Vienna separated the participants of these groups irreparably. However in the case of Friedrich Hayek, Ludwig von Mises, Fritz Machlup, Felix Kaufmann and Alfred Schütz, close intellectual and, in some cases, personal relationships were maintained. The relationship between these figures and Karl Popper is tentative in Vienna, and he only becomes significant in Hayek's intellectual development in the late 1940s.[7] Yet even here, Hayek views Popper's arguments on critical rationalism through phenomenological spectacles.[8]

In the essay 'The Use of Knowledge in Society' (1945), Hayek directs a spotlight on to what he considers as the fundamental problem of economics, from which all disputes within the discipline arise, that is, how to construct a 'rational economic order'. This is not the question of how to allocate resources based upon 'given data' but the 'problem of the utilization of knowledge which is not given to anyone in its totality' (Hayek 1949: 78). This is part of a passage in which he reiterates his previous criticisms of scientism (Hayek 1979) and central planning (Hayek 1935, 1937, 1939). Hayek goes beyond these concerns to raise the increased importance of technological knowledge and the dominant presumption that 'scientific knowledge is the sum of all knowledge' compared to the low status of 'the knowledge of the particular circumstances of time and place of the fleeting moment not known to others' (Hayek 1949: 80). This general perception of the downgrading of the importance of unorganized practical knowledge is then related to the 'belief that changes, or at least day to day adjustments, [and hence economic problems] have become less important' (ibid.: 82) thus legitimizing the role of central planning. He uses his well-known example of the tin market to illustrate the dispersal of knowledge and the role of prices as a symbolic medium of the catallaxy operating:

> as one market, not because any of its members survey the whole field, but because their limited individual fields of vision sufficiently overlap so that through the intermediaries [the means of the means of the means . . .] the relevant information is communicated to all.
>
> (Hayek 1949: 86)

Hayek does not see this mechanism as perfect, nor smoothly efficient, but argues that it works most effectively when the participants are not thinking about what they are doing and the consequences of their actions. He concludes that scientific knowledge, the interpretation of 'given data', does not fully comprehend the social situation. The price mechanism is not portrayed as a directing force, as many consider the notion of the 'invisible hand', but as a mediated field. These themes do not dissipate throughout his intellectual development, and can visibly be seen in his writings on competition. Hayek is concerned here to identify the misconceptions of the theory of 'perfect competition' within equilibrium analysis, and to provide an account of the dynamic processes involved which are appropriate to the problems of real life, the personal relationships between participants (acknowledging the contribution of Fritz Machlup (1942). In 'The Meaning of Competition' (1946), when commenting upon equilibrium analysis, Hayek writes:

> The economic calculus (or the Pure Logic of Choice) . . . consists of an apparatus of classification of possible human attitudes and provides us with a technique for describing the interrelations of the different parts of a single plan. Its conclusions are implicit in its assumptions: the desires and the knowledge of the facts, which are assumed to be simultaneously present to a single mind, determine the unique solution. The relations discussed in this type of analysis are logical relations, concerned solely with the conclusions which follow for the mind of the planning individual from the given premises. When we deal, however, with a situation in which a number of persons are attempting to work out their separate plans, we can no longer assume that the data are the same for all the planning minds.
> (Hayek 1949: 93)

Hayek argues that the artificial construction of perfect knowledge is founded upon the presuppositions of the homogeneity of commodities, facilities and opportunities; assumptions which can be disregarded in the analysis of competition. Hence, for Hayek, it is disequilibrium and hence change which paves the way for adjustment and progress, just as misunderstandings in communication provide the dynamic element in the Schützian characterization of intersubjectivity. By prompting the participants to find new ways of establishing mutually rewarding contacts, it is possible to help them 'discover new ways of doing things better than they have done before' (Hayek 1949: 101). For Hayek, there is no such thing as a long-term equilibrium (which, in fact, assumes the end of competition) in the complex competitive conditions of real markets. The issue is not whether the market is imperfect but whether competition exists at all. He concludes with a clear hint of the Schützian elements in his work:

> *Competition is essentially a process of the formation of opinion: by spreading information*, it creates that unity and coherence of the economic system which we presuppose when we think of it as one market. It creates the views

people have about what is best and cheapest, *and it is because of it that people know at least as much about possibilities and opportunities as they in fact do*. It is thus a process which involves a continuous change in the data and whose significance must therefore be completely missed by any theory which treats these data as constant.

(Hayek 1949: 106)

Twenty-two years later, Hayek was again to address these concerns in 'Competition as a Discovery Procedure' (1978) in discussing the methodological peculiarity of competition as it is treated in economics. Consequently, Hayek argues that such assumptions cannot be tested in those situations where they would be useful and interesting. He argued that such theories can indicate patterns but are unable to identify 'particular facts relevant to the achievement of specific temporary purposes' (Hayek 1978: 181). Again, he reiterates the fallibility of the theory of perfect competition in explaining 'activities' within markets. The concept of catallaxy, as a spontaneous order, has advantages for it recognizes the social distribution of knowledge: 'Knowledge that is used in it is that of all its members. Ends that it serves are the separate ends of those individuals, in all their variety and contrariness' (ibid.: 183).

At this point, there are indications of Hayek's growing interest in cybernetics and socio-biology, which were to be developed more strongly in *The Fatal Conceit* (Hayek 1988). However, in relation to his basic arguments, this is window dressing. It lends support to his position by making favourable comparisons with developments in the biological sciences, but it does not alter the underlying principle that market processes are constituted through human action. Hayek has delivered a phenomenological account of the process of exchange, and it is in this sense that market competition, the catallaxy, involves a process of discovery.

In Volume Two of *Law, Legislation and Liberty* (1976), Hayek relates these arguments on the market to the concept of justice and the problems of state intervention. The market order is treated as a special case of the spontaneous order generated through 'people acting within the rules of the law of property, tort and contract' (Hayek 1976: 109). At one point, he suggests that the conception of the economy as a catallactic phenomenon can operate as 'a standard by which all particular institutions can be judged' (ibid.: 113). He draws upon the Greek verb *katallattein* to identify how markets involve more than simply acts of exchange, and also to mean 'to admit into the community and to change from enemy into friend' (ibid.: 108). He distinguishes this understanding of exchange from that associated with approaches (such as Ayn Rand's 'objectivism') which celebrate selfish aims. For Hayek, the latter are inadequate for grasping the mechanisms through which the *great society* is generated:

> The important point about the catallaxy is that it reconciles different knowledge and different purposes which, whether the individuals be selfish or not, will greatly differ from one person to another. It is because

in the catallaxy men, while following their own interests, whether wholly egotistical or highly altruistic, will further the aims of many others, most of whom they will never know, that it is an overall order so superior to any deliberate organization.

(Hayek 1976: 110)

Given that the effective operation of the 'negative rules of just conduct' depends on the state avoiding the prescription of common ends or results, policy making in a free society is limited to creating an 'abstract order' which can act as a framework for individuals achieving their different ends and resolving the inevitable grievances which follow from disappointed expectations. He describes catallaxy as a 'wealth creating game', that is, a variable-sum game (rather than the zero-sum games associated with game theory) through which markets achieve 'the satisfaction of a greater range of needs than would otherwise be possible' (Hayek 1976: 115). In this variable-sum game, prices act as 'indicators of what ought to be done in the present circumstances' (ibid.: 116), reinforcing the importance of the actors engaged in mutual discovery rather reifying the price mechanism. This reformulation of the market is founded upon the acceptance of both human ignorance and uncertainty. By preventing interference with an individual's property and establishing a basis for trust, abstract rules can control some forms of uncertainty while retaining the capacity to adapt to change.

These abstract rules apply equally to all members of the social order, and should be distinguished from state intervention or interference. Such intervention in private relations in order to achieve a specific purpose is characterized as a 'command' (a subcategory of coercion). Thus, Hayek objects to state interference on two counts. First is the 'creation of disorder', for it undermines the mutual adjustment of the parts of the market order if the state confers privileges on some individuals at the expense of others. While inequities are seen as inevitable in a spontaneous order (an order which is not made, but grows or evolves) since 'as a matter of logic the chance of any person picked out at random being among the lowest 10 per cent must be one tenth!' (Hayek 1976: 131), he contends that rules of just conduct 'improve equally the chances of all' (ibid.: 129). Second, actions which impose purposes upon an individual and which are not of their own choosing are simply unjust.

Useful insights into this dimension of Hayek's work can be drawn from the oral archives on his intellectual development (conducted by the Department of Economics at UCLA). These reveal that Hayek was developing a conception of the market process 'as a stream instead of an equilibrating force ... in terms of the factors that determine the movement of the flow of water in a very irregular bed' (Kresge and Wenar 1994: 147). This reference to time as flow (in contradiction to the static aspects of equilibrium analysis) is a distinctly Schützian contribution to Hayek's thinking on this subject (as well as an indication of the role of Bergson's concept of the 'durée' within Schütz's account). The dynamic aspect of the catallaxy is its capacity to produce material wealth for the participants, and since the market is not conceived as a zero-sum game, wealth production can contract or expand depending on the horizon of catallactic possibilities. For Hayek, given that 'the market reaches this horizon when the greatest possible quantity of the particular combination of goods is being produced which in the circumstances can be produced' (Hayek 1976: 118), it is the nature and activities of the state which constitute the horizon of catallactic possibilities (Hayek 1976: 118–19; 1978: 186).

The phenomenological constitution of liberty: rationality, democracy and equality

> Liberty in practice depends on very prosaic matters, and those anxious to preserve it must prove their devotion by their attention to the mundane concerns of public life and by the efforts they are prepared to give to the understanding of issues that the idealist is often inclined to treat as common, if not sordid. The intellectual leaders in the movement for liberty have all too often confined their attention to those uses of liberty closest to their hearts and have made little effort to comprehend the significance of those restrictions of liberty which did not directly affect them.
>
> (Hayek 1960: 7)

This warning to his audience in the introduction to *The Constitution of Liberty* (1960) shows how Hayek is concerned to develop the same approach within the field of political philosophy that he had developed within economics. A close reading of the text also reveals that Hayek deployed the same analysis of the problem of the concept of liberty that Schütz had been concerned to deploy in his 1943 paper for *Economica* (Schütz 1943), a phenomenological critique and clarification. From the very start of the text, Hayek develops an approach towards the concept of liberty which draws upon the work of Schütz on the concept of rationality and the role of recipe knowledge. For Hayek, this is a necessary if 'barren task', to identify the dangerous 'verbal trap' of treating these liberties as 'different species of the same genus' (Hayek 1960: 18). Liberty was analysed as follows:

1 *Liberty as freedom in the vulgar sense* of one's relationship to other men presupposing an 'assured private sphere' whereby individuals can pursue their own plans and intentions within everyday routines:

> Whether he is free or not does not depend upon on the range of choice but on whether he can expect to shape his course of action in accordance with his present intentions, or whether somebody else has power so to manipulate the conditions as to make him act according to that person's will rather than his own.
>
> (Hayek 1960: 13)

This is not to be confused with the following.

2   *Liberty as political freedom,* the entitlements of citizenship such as participation in the selection of governments, the formation of legislation and monitoring the actions of the executive. Here, Hayek clearly distinguishes between collective liberty in the formal sense and the freedom of the individual.
3   *Liberty as inner,* metaphysical or subjective *freedom,* 'the extent to which a person is guided in his actions by his own considered will, by his reason or lasting conviction, rather than by momentary impulse or circumstance' (Hayek 1960: 15). This is the freedom to choose intelligently between alternative courses of action, as opposed to being a 'slave of one's own passions'.
4 and 5   *Liberty as the 'physical ability to do what I want'* and the *'freedom from obstacles'* which, put together, imply 'omnipotence'. For Hayek these lie at the heart of those philosophical traditions which use the concept of 'restraint' to mean coercion, so that 'liberty has been suppressed in the name of liberty' (Hayek 1960: 16). In this dangerous socialist conception of liberty as power lie the seeds of totalitarian states. Dewey is cited as a source in the formulation of this conception, indicating further elements of continuity with Schütz's post-war writings.
6   Liberty as power leads to the *identification of liberty with wealth* and hence justifies the role of the state in redistributing wealth. Liberty and wealth are both seen as desirable things by Hayek but, more importantly, they must not be confused.

For Hayek the last five of these conceptions of liberty are antithetical to individual freedom. To treat them as identical by virtue of using the same word is (drawing from his earlier work on scientism) tantamount to 'conceptual realism'. Liberty is thus counterpoised to liberties, that the latter exist when the former is lacking (Hayek 1960: 19). Hayek then proceeds to subject the concept of coercion to the same close scrutiny. Coercion is portrayed as the limiting condition to liberty and is defined as:

> control of the environment or circumstances of a person by another that in order to avoid greater evil, he is forced to act not according to a coherent plan of his own but to serve the ends of another ... he is unable to use his own intelligence or knowledge to follow his own aims and beliefs.... Free action ... must be based on data which cannot be shaped at will by another.
> (Hayek 1960: 21)

In this sense, the condition of coercion is one in which human actors serve the purposes of others rather than their own purposes, and alternative courses of action are likely to produce even worse outcomes. This is still a situation involving choice, although it remains a 'Hobson's choice'. Where the alternatives are determined in this way the condition of intersubjectivity is impaired. However, individuals can still anticipate the likely consequences of their actions in such conditions, and planning remains possible, even if the intelligence and creative powers of human actors are not used to their full extent as they would be in a truly spontaneous order. Hayek then goes on to distinguish this meaning of coercion from other meanings common to political philosophy such as the *power to coerce*. In particular, he highlights the confusion between the capacity of human actors to achieve their ends and their ability to force 'other men to serve one's will by the threat of inflicting harm' (Hayek 1960: 134–5). In a telling passage on market relations, Hayek defines the mutual exchange of services as non-coercive. Economic relationships are portrayed as no different from other social relations involving dinner party etiquette or posing for a painting. This is subject to the proviso that 'the services of a particular person are not crucial to my existence or the preservation of what I most value' (ibid.: 136), creating a monopolistic situation. The operation of leadership within large-scale private enterprises can be defended here as an exercise of collective power, subject to the proviso that it is the effect of a 'voluntary combination of effort under a unified direction in the sense of an extension of our capacities' (ibid.: 135). By comparison, the state monopoly of employment within a command economy would deliver 'unlimited powers of coercion' to those who controlled production.

A precondition of Hayek's preferred conception of liberty is the assumption that individuals bear the full responsibility for the consequences of their actions, and that this is closely related to respect for (the rule of) law. He attributes the decline of individual responsibility in the twentieth century to the fear of freedom (along the lines of Erich Fromm). This is, in part, attributed to the growing importance of those deterministic explanations in science which have been crudely transposed into social-scientific attempts to comprehend human conduct. In a deterministic account of human action, the actor is unable to act differently, and this, in turn, denies the role of free will, awareness of the consequences of one's actions and the efficacy of punishments or rewards. For Hayek, the concept of responsibility refers to processes which take place beyond general formal rules (such as the legal specification of obligations and entitlements), within the intersubjective domain of private life, where actors engage in relationships which lead them to consider the consequences of their actions in future situations. As the following extract reveals:

> The assigning of responsibility thus presupposes the capacity on men's part for rational action, and it aims at making them act more rationally than they would otherwise. It presupposes a certain minimum capacity in them for learning and foresight, for being guided by a knowledge of the consequences of their action. . . . Rationality, in this connection, can mean little more than some degree of coherence and consistency in a person's action.
> (Hayek 1960: 76–7)

The ethical conclusions he reaches are fairly standard in relation to liberalism. The individual actor is free to breach the normative constraints of the existing order, but must bear the full consequences of his or her actions. Responsibility and hence liberty are related to the capacity for reflexive choices within a moral community of similarly endowed individuals who cannot look into each others' minds or impose order through coercion. He adopts a narrow conception of the moral community by specifically excluding 'infants, idiots, or the insane' who are not in a position to respond adequately to the process of trial and error in everyday life (Smith 2001b, ch. 1).

At this point in the discussion, Hayek distinguishes between the 'intimate relations of private life' whereby we do come to know each other as 'unique individuals', and the 'freedom of public life' which necessitates that we approach each other as 'types' (Hayek 1960: 78). The implications of this distinction become clearer when he approaches the problem of altruism (our obligations to the needs of 'strangers'). In the public world where we do not know and hence care for particular people, altruism becomes 'a meaningless conception'. This is also closely related to Hayek's account of the subjective origin of values considered earlier, and it neatly dovetails with his conception of negative liberty. Welfare is identified as an expression of misplaced public altruism, an intrusion by some individuals setting themselves up in a position to judge the values of others. This is a theme which runs throughout many of the neo-liberal accounts of social or distributive justice, and it has been applied to the provision of welfare benefits and state education in recent years in Western societies. For Hayek, the prosperity and welfare of all the individual members of a society is best served by facilitating the most appropriate utilization of the skills and concrete knowledge of particular conditions of all individuals within a complex division of labour. The normative thrust of Hayek's politics, directed against Crosland's *The Future of Socialism* (1956), is particularly evident on this issue:

> To be effective, responsibility must be both definite and limited, adapted both emotionally and intellectually to human capacities. It is quite as destructive of any sense of responsibility to be taught that one is responsible for everything as to be taught that one cannot be held responsible for anything. . . . As everybody's property in effect is nobody's property, so everybody's responsibility is nobody's responsibility.
> (Hayek 1960: 83)

Hayek attributes this shift towards such an all-encompassing conceptualization of responsibility to the loss of community and the increased impersonality of social life. In this condition, the state acts as a sort of guarantor of security as part of a broader trend towards collectivism which, in turn, leads to further demands for greater state intervention, although these are usually camouflaged as both democratic and egalitarian. Hayek is therefore concerned not only to engage in political polemic but to expose the misleading conflations of different ideas which lie behind such concepts. Just as he drew upon Schütz's distinction between scientific and everyday conceptions of rationality to identify specific conceptions of liberty, freedom and responsibility compatible with his account of liberalism, so too he explores the implications of this analysis for equality, merit and democracy.

Hayek's premises are clearly apparent: individuals are portrayed as fundamentally different in terms of their 'capacities and potentialities'. He argues that these differences do not provide any justification for different treatment by government:

> Equality of the *general rules of law and conduct*, however is the only kind of equality conducive to liberty and the only equality which we can secure without destroying liberty. Not only has liberty nothing to do with any sort of equality, but it is even bound to produce inequality in many respects.
>
> (Hayek 1960: 85)

Within this approach, egalitarian projects are portrayed as misconceived and dangerous in that they attempt to 'impose upon a society a preconceived pattern of distribution' (Hayek 1960: 87), and hence dispense with the underlying precondition for a free society, that is, equal law. He makes two contentions here, that no individual or group can successfully determine the optimal outcome of the potential of other actors, and that any increase of the capacity to do things should be seen as a positive contribution to the collective outcome. The advantageous capacities of individuals which result from their family, inheritance and education (cultural and material advantages) are defended in much the same terms. He argues that the desires of parents to prepare their children for a better existence, through the transmission of traditions, morals, standards, tastes and knowledge, have the unintended consequence of accumulating 'socially valuable qualities'.

Although Hayek accepts that this material and cultural heritage, transmitted through informal channels of family and acquaintance, is the source of inequality and hence conflict, he claims that the such problems cannot be resolved through state regulation. Again, in answer to Crosland, he argues:

> However human, envy is certainly not one of the sources of discontent that a free society can eliminate. It is probably one of the essential conditions for the preservation of such a society that we do not countenance envy, nor sanction its demands as social justice.
>
> (Hayek 19960: 93)

Hayek makes similar remarks when dealing with the concept of merit. He makes a clear distinction between understandings of 'attributed meritorious' and 'maximum usefulness with minimum pain and sacrifice'. This effectively produces a mismatch between the value placed upon the contributions of individuals by others and the remuneration these individuals receive for their efforts. In a planned order, individuals would be assigned a reward according to some fixed scale of effort based upon a conception of dutiful or obedient behaviour. However, in a free society, the individuals concerned would receive their rewards regardless of merit so long as they made a contribution to the well-being of their contemporaries. This argument is again grounded upon an intersubjective conception of the private sphere, within which it is assumed that no human actor can determine the worth of another individual or what that individual could achieve.[9] Hence, Hayek argues that 'if nobody's knowledge is sufficient to guide all human actions, there is no human being who is competent to reward all efforts according to merit' (Hayek 1960: 97). The conceptual confusion which Hayek identifies in this case is a direct result of the conflation of value with merit, a confusion which undermines the system of incentives which enable human beings to make rational (in the sense of 'reasonable') decisions. For Hayek, rather than one scale of merit being imposed, so long as 'a multiplicity of organizations compete with one another in offering different prospects' (ibid.: 99) the range of choice to the individual is extended. So, in this way, the concept of justice is directly compared to that of liberty and coercion, as concerning the *deliberate* treatment of men by other men'. Hayek is concerned with the relations between individuals and the consequent application of an appropriate set of rules of conduct than with the consequences of these actions:

> Insofar as we want the efforts of individuals to be guided by their own views about prospects and chances, the results of the individual's efforts are necessarily unpredictable, and the question as to whether the resulting distribution of income is just has no meaning . . . equality of those conditions must lead to inequality of results.
>
> (Hayek 1960: 99)

So long as each individual's actions are voluntary, the social outcome is 'just'. In this way, the principle of distributive or social justice is characterized as an unfolding process, gradually extending to all aspects of society, to the point where 'authority decided what the individual was to do and how he was to do it' (Hayek 1960: 100). It is at this point in *The Constitution of Liberty* that Hayek highlights an inconsistency in the arguments of the supporters of social justice, that membership of a community ought to convey the entitlement to a particular standard of living (such as a minimum wage). For him, this runs contrary to the argument that rewards should be based upon personal merit.[10] Having stated these objections, he does defend the use of political institutions 'to make provision for the weak or infirm or for the victims of unforeseeable disaster' (ibid.: 101), although this is clearly made dependent upon the capacity of that community to produce wealth.

These themes are further developed in Hayek's account of the labour market, where he distinguishes the position of waged employees from those who earn their living independently. Employees are characterized as having little interest in freedom, in the sense of having the capacity to make decisions which affect their whole lives, for they do not have to be 'inventive' or 'experimental'. He goes further to suggest, rather provocatively, that the employed, by virtue of their position, are blind to the fact that their own freedom (such as it is) is a product of the creation of conditions which allow others in different positions to exert themselves and take risks. This freedom consists of choosing 'between complexes of advantages and disadvantages' (Hayek 1960: 120) and inevitably involves trade-offs between alternative plans. For Hayek, it is competition which enables employees to choose between a 'multiplicity of employment opportunities' (with the exception of periods of a large labour surplus). This is, in turn, dependent upon the activities of independents who 'take the initiative in the continuous process of re-forming and redirecting organizations' (ibid.: 124). Competition, it is argued, serves to ensure the absence of monopolies and hence limits the exercise of coercion in the market place. Individual choice is again a key aspect of this explanation, although it is clear from the preceding section that this could only effectively operate in an intersubjective social context. At times, it is hard to avoid the conclusion that Hayek has in mind the part-time scholarship of the *Miseskreis* and the *Geistkreis* (his memory of the scholarly meetings and activities back in Vienna which many of the members combined with demanding full-time business occupations):

> The fact of being employed will affect more than a man's initiative and inventiveness. He has little knowledge of those who control resources and who must concern themselves constantly with new arrangements and combinations; he is little acquainted with the attitudes and modes of life which the need for decisions concerning the use of property and income produces. For the independent, there can be no sharp distinction between his private and his business life, as there is for the employed, who has sold part of his time for a fixed income. While, for the employed, work is largely a matter of fitting himself into a given framework during a certain number of hours, for the independent it is a question of shaping and reshaping a plan of life, of finding solutions for ever new problems.
> (Hayek 1960: 122)

The political implications of this analysis are even more striking. He argues that mass democracy places the political institutions in the hands of the employed majority, and policies reflect the narrow vision associated with their position. Their determination of legislation and the organization of institutions and business practice effectively undermine the contributions of *the independent*. Hayek suggests that those who are paid according to merit (based upon the opinion of others) limit the potential of those who are paid for results. The progressive taxation system, the operation of credit and the 'paternalistic' social services are thus seen as based upon an employee's 'conception of income'.

It is in relation to the position of the independent that the concept of private property plays a vital role. For Hayek, 'men of independent means' have an indispensable part to play in the utilization of capital, as well as in providing services which contain no material gain for the benefactor, that is, public works and cultural leadership. This enables Hayek to come to the defence of idle wealth and the leisured classes who engage in 'conspicuous waste'. Here he makes a contrast between his experiences of Vienna and America, and warns against the dangers of allowing this social group to disappear, particularly in regard to 'gentlemanly scholarship':

> Quantitatively the wastes involved in the amusements of the rich are indeed insignificant compared to those involved in the similar and equally unnecessary amusements of the masses, which divert much more from ends . . . even the successful use of leisure needs pioneering. . . . [Thus] we owe many of the common forms of living to people who devoted all their time to the art of living.
>
> (Hayek 1960: 129)

For Hayek, it is the majoritarian tendencies of democratic systems which act as the motor propelling the 'principle of distributive justice'. Here, he again returns to his distinction between true and false individualism, with 'traditional liberalism' characterized by a concern with upholding equality before the law through the limitation of the coercive powers of government, while 'dogmatic democrats' confuse the 'majority rule' as a decision-making method with popular sovereignty, and narrowly define liberty as simply 'political liberties'. For 'dogmatic democrats', democracy has become good in itself, and is subject to further inappropriate extensions into private life. Hayek singles out two aspects of this 'extension'. The first is the extension of the franchise, which he designates a matter of expediency (incidentally, developing what he calls a 'reasonable' argument for excluding those employed by the state and 'recipients of public charity' from the franchise). The second is his main concern, the extension of the issues which are subject to democratic scrutiny and the possibility of 'collective control' and hence arbitrary power. These problems, he argues, are the consequence of conceptual confusions around the fringes of the concepts of democracy and liberalism. As a result, Hayek attempts to clarify the issues by identifying the opposites of democracy and liberalism (see Figure 4.1).

Democracy	⟷	Authoritarian government
Liberalism	⟷	Totalitarianism

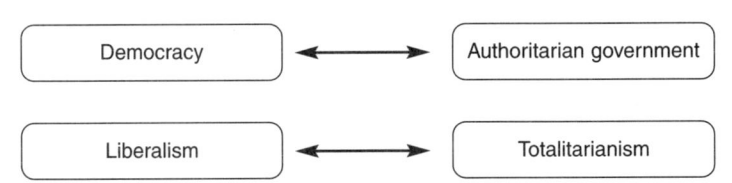

Figure 4.1 Hayek's conceptual terms of reference

On the basis of these distinctions, Hayek draws a contrast between democracy as a method of majority rule, and liberalism as a normative political doctrine: that is, what constitutes 'good law' (Hayek 1960: 103). Similarly he raises the illustrations of democracies wielding totalitarian powers and authoritarian governments acting upon liberal principles. Hence, democracy and liberalism are not automatically concurrent, although in an ideal situation they would be. While both democrats and liberals agree upon the importance of political liberty, they disagree upon the scope of state action subject to democratic decision making.

Hayek is suggesting that a fully effective private sphere is only possible when the state acts in a night-watchman capacity and does not violate the common principles which make a collection of people a community, even if positive consequences are envisaged from intruding upon private relations: 'A group of men normally become a society not by giving themselves laws but by obeying the same rules of conduct' (Hayek 1960: 106–7). Following this, he develops what he calls 'three conclusive arguments' for democracy:

1 *Democracy as a peaceful method for initiating change*, in that 'it is less wasteful to determine which has the stronger support by counting numbers than by fighting' (Hayek 1960: 107).
2 *Democracy as a safeguard for individual liberty* against the dangers of the tyranny of the majority.
3 *Democracy as an active agent in the formation of informed opinion*, using the argument that opinions should emerge independently of government.

In the case of the third argument, Hayek makes explicit reference to Tocqueville's points that, 'any minority opinion may become a majority one' (Hayek 1960: 107) and that knowledge and understanding progress through open discussion. He concludes his analysis of democracy by raising the same objections in state theory as he had earlier developed against equilibrium analysis, that democracy is best understood as a 'dynamic' process rather than a 'static' state of affairs. The problems of democracy can thus be resolved through an explicit reconsideration of the concepts of time and subjectivity, but this time in social and political theory.

At the heart of this reconfiguration of social and political theory lies the intersubjective basis of the spontaneous order, whereby learning occurs not just through discussion, but also through the everyday relations between human actors engaged in the pursuit of their own ends. In a condition of impaired intersubjectivity, where the state acts as if it possesses a 'superior wisdom', this merely leads to the accumulation of 'conflicting motives and aims' which bear no relation to each other except that they emerge from the decisions of 'shifting majorities'. In a free society, Hayek suggests, such mistakes and discontinuities can be corrected through the mutual adjustment of those involved and the reexamination of past precedents (as in legal evolution), so resolving the unintended negative consequences of collective decisions.

Even in relation to intellectual development, the distinctive Schützian qualities of Hayek's work stand out. He makes an important contrast between the role of politicians (elsewhere misleadingly described as experts), who are on the whole responsive to shifting public opinion, and that of intellectuals or political philosophers whose function is to speculate and generate original ideas which, in the long term (a generation) will come to shape politics, and ultimately acquire the status of common sense. It is hard to avoid the conclusion that Hayek had in mind the informal discussions of the Mont Pèlerin Society, and possibly the economic and cultural discussion group attended by both Hayek and Schütz in Vienna, which had no propagandist role as such but simply sought to encourage intellectual discussion and conceptual clarification between like-minded individuals in a variety of disciplines. Hayek characterizes the role of ideas within the process of social change as a 'cascading' process across different 'levels' from abstract generalizations (the realm of scientific knowledge) down to concrete circumstances (the realm of everyday experiences). Here, he is using distinctions which were clearly developed in Schütz's 1943 paper on rationality (Schütz 1943), in particular his account of the cartographer and the native, and reinforced in his other writings on belonging and detachment (Schütz 1944a, 1944b, 1946, 1951, 1953, 1957, 1958).

It is important to add that, for both Hayek and Schütz, it is only through the trial and error of everyday practice that an idea comes to be accepted by human actors in their social relationships. To use the language of contemporary phenomenology, progress is achieved through the acceptance of second-order constructs within the relationships constituting first-order constructs, subject to the proviso that the general abstractions do not damage the dynamic intersubjective existence of actors operating within both general laws and rules of conduct. Within the context of this system of ideas, Hayek develops his account of *the practical man*:

> The practical man concerned with the immediate problems of the day has neither the interest nor the time to examine the interrelations of the different parts of the complex order of society. He merely chooses from among the possible orders that are offered him and finally accepts a political doctrine or set of principles elaborated or presented by others.
> (Hayek 1960: 114)

The citizen, as such, remains passive on the fundamental issues of the day, and Hayek remarks at certain points in his work in economics and politics that human actors would have behaved more appropriately if they had been better informed. The philosopher or intellectual has a crucial normative role to play in his account, consistently developing liberal ideas which will persuade citizens in time following their experiences of the negative consequences of planning:

> The political philosopher cannot discharge his task if he confines himself to questions of fact and is afraid of deciding between conflicting values. He cannot allow himself to be limited by the positivism of the scientist which confines his functions to showing what is the case and forbids any discussion of what ought to be.
>
> (Hayek 1960: 114–15)

Throughout the work of both Schütz and Hayek, there is a clear agreement on the importance of these distinctions, between general laws, rules of conduct and transmitted inheritance over generations. Just as Hayek used Schütz's ideas on the meaningful construction of social life to ground his account of economics and politics, so too there are strong grounds for reassessing Schütz's own political motivations in the light of his background in Austrian economics and his affiliations with neo-liberal organizations after he left Vienna (such as his involvement in the 1938 Walter Lippmann Colloquium, his membership of the Mont Pèlerin Society and his ongoing contacts with Hayek, Machlup and Mises). In a backward glance to the impact of Walter Lippmann, Hayek reiterates the nature of this project of the revival of liberalism, laid out at the 1938 Lippmann Colloquium, when he states that 'democracy will remain effective only so long as government in its coercive action confines itself to tasks that can be carried out democratically . . . that it is not the fountainhead of justice' (Hayek 1960: 116–17).

The key insight within Hayek's work, which runs throughout both *The Constitution of Liberty* and *Law, Legislation and Liberty* and which highlights the dangers of democracy, is the distinction between spontaneous order and organization. Hayek is quite explicit on this, 'that unlimited democracy is riding for a fall and that it will go down, not with a bang, but with a whimper' (Hayek 1973: 3):

- A *spontaneous order* is an evolving set of institutions and practices within which individual liberty can flourish unhindered, while organization involves a rationally planned social order where individuals are subject to the arbitrary will of others (drawing upon Menger's distinction between organic and pragmatic institutions).
- Social or distributive justice is associated with *organization*, while individual justice is associated with a spontaneous order.

Social justice is meaningless within a spontaneous order, for here the rule of law operates as a regulative framework within which all individuals are treated as ends in themselves rather than as a means to an end. This approach to justice clearly indicates Hayek's attachment to Kantian accounts of the moral order, yet this is not applied through the identification of universal principles. His attachment to this account of justice appears to be shaped by the Burkean argument that the most effective rules are those which emerge out a process of trial and error. Nevertheless, without the careful maintenance of a spontaneous order, Hayek provides quite dire warnings of what would spring up in its place:

> the predominant model of liberal democratic institutions, in which the same representative body lays down the rules of just conduct and directs government, necessarily leads to a gradual transformation of the spontaneous order of a free society into a totalitarian system conducted in the service of some coalition of organized interests.
> (Hayek 1973: 2)

In the next section, we consider how these arguments about democracy and liberalism are developed in relation to the state and its role in sustaining or undermining a spontaneous order.

Rule of law as a political ideal: the two functions of the state

The main concern of Hayek's forays into political philosophy is to defend the private sphere, the field of personal liberty, and to ensure that individuals are free from the 'arbitrary' intrusions of the state, as the following passage reveals:

> In some degree all close relationships . . . provide opportunities for coercion. And a morose husband, a nagging wife, or a hysterical mother may make life intolerable unless their every mood is obeyed. Any attempt to regulate these intimate associations further would clearly involve such far-reaching restrictions on choice and conduct as to produce even greater coercion: if people are free to choose their associates and intimates, the coercion that arises from voluntary association cannot be the concern of government.
> (Hayek 1960: 138)

The role of the state, in possessing the monopoly of coercion, is to depersonalize the limitations on freedom by converting them into general rules or laws (and establishing 'rights' such as security). The rules of property and contract clearly mark the boundaries of permissible action and protect the private sphere. These rules are seen as assisting human actors in the pursuit of their own ends. Actors, by Hayek's account, need never be coerced if they anticipate where sanctions are to be imposed. The 'night-watchman state', in establishing the boundaries of the private, serves to remove the possibility of arbitrary coercive power. The interference of the state in private life is seen as permissible only where it is unavoidable and predictable (such as in the collection of taxation, the military defence of the society, the internal policing of violence against persons and property, and the regulation of fraud and deception). Thus the state, in Hayek's political philosophy, serves 'the sole purpose of enforcing known rules intended to secure the best conditions under which the individual may give his activities a coherent, *rational pattern*' (Hayek 1960: 144: my emphasis). Wealth is not seen as the decisive component in liberty, however: the means for the fulfilment of individual plans should not be the exclusive possession of a single agent. In such an intersubjective context, whereby the process of mutual discovery between strangers can take place, creativity will flourish and 'civilization' spontaneously emerge.

Hayek stresses the importance of the relationship between abstract rules and tacit knowledge in explaining the distinction between rules and commands. (In the case of the latter, it presupposes a personal application of a rule in a specific instance.)

> Abstraction occurs whenever an individual responds in the same manner to circumstances that only have some features in common. Men generally act in accordance with abstract rules in this sense long before they can state them. Even when they have acquired the power of conscious abstraction, their conscious thinking and acting are probably still guided by a great many such abstract rules which they obey without being able to formulate them.
>
> (Hayek 1960: 149)

He goes on to develop a remarkable illustration of the different levels of scientific explanation and everyday understanding. Whereas 'law' as an ideal type serves to inform the anonymous members of a community engaged in decision making irrespective of their personal circumstances, the ideal type of 'command' determines the action to be taken and prevents the use of the actors' own knowledge and initiative. To illustrate, he compares the guidelines operating for the head of a large household of servants with the specification of duties originating from the chief of a tribe. In explaining the transition from the specific customs to laws as abstract generalizations, we find Hayek wrestling with the same problems as Schütz, the relationship between subjectivity and objectivity in the social sciences: 'The rules merely provide the framework within which the individual must move but within which the decisions are his . . . specific ends of action, being always particulars should not enter into general rules' (Hayek 1960: 152).

Here he is concerned to clarify the distinction between status-based orders and contractual arrangements at the heart of liberal societies. Contractual law in this account must be seen as equally applicable to all, rather than the very existence of law being enough:

> Like the laws of nature, the laws of the state provide fixed features in the environment in which he has to move; though they eliminate certain choices to him, they do not as a rule, limit the choice to some specific action that somebody else wants him to take.
>
> (Hayek 1960: 153)

This reduction of freedom to the operation of general rules is strongly evident in Hayek's comments upon the confusions of legal theory. Here he distinguishes between laws at an 'abstract level' and laws as commands to human actors in specific situations. The confusion of these operates to the detriment of freedom. In effect, he is reinforcing a commonplace in liberal theory, that rule by laws is preferable to rule by men (that is, arbitrary rule). However, it is his line of argument which is distinctive here, in examining how law should relate to the human actor in order to highlight the inherent dangers of the rationalist tendencies in utilitarian thinking:

> The rationale of securing to each individual a known range within which he can decide on his actions is to enable him to make the fullest use of his knowledge, especially of his concrete and often unique knowledge of the particular circumstances of time and place. The law tells him what facts he may count on and thereby extends the range within which he can predict the consequences of his actions. At the same time it tells him what possible consequences of his actions he must take into account or what he will be held responsible for.
> (Hayek 1960: 156–7)

Here, it becomes somewhat clearer what role the discipline of economics plays within his overall approach to the problems of liberalism. The focus on markets directs our attention towards the problem of understanding the co-ordination of plans, in the absence of the omniscient mind posed by the utilitarian tradition, and given the need to recognize that ends cannot be specified in law.

With direct reference to Michael Polanyi's *The Logic of Liberty* (1951), Hayek concludes these arguments on the legal dimension of 'the social' by suggesting that a 'spontaneous order' is the product of 'interaction' between human actors operating in the context of general and impersonal laws. In an interesting citation, without an origin, Hayek reiterates 'that there is some kind of order, consistency and constancy in social life is obvious. If there were not, none of us would be able to go about his affairs or satisfy his most elementary wants' (Hayek 1960: 160).

So, in addition to defining the state as the horizon of catallactic possibilities, a second important function emerges in relation to the material and mental growth of civilization. The material success of the market system breeds a new problem, that our 'knowledge of the possibilities' of material growth begins to outstrip the capacity of the market order to deliver material benefits at the level of the expectations generated. In order to temper demands for such benefits among the populace, an effective liberal state should develop a mediating role between conflicting expectations or demands, and the capacity of the economy to deliver the goods. From Hayek's viewpoint, this tendency to demand more than the market economy is capable of delivering can be seen most clearly in the confusion over the concepts of liberty, equality, responsibility, merit and democracy which underlie the dominant conceptions of social justice in the post-war period in Western societies.

In short, Hayek attempts to establish a new foundation for the 'liberal principles of justice and political economy' (picking up on the subtitle of *Law, Legislation and Liberty*). His diagnosis of the problem at the heart of the present malaise can be readily identified:

> [T]he loss of the belief in a justice independent of personal interest; a consequent use of legislation to authorize coercion, not merely to prevent unjust action but to achieve particular results for specific persons or groups; and the fusion in the same representative assemblies of the task of articulating the rules of just conduct with that of directing government.
> (Hayek 1973: 2)

From the start, the underlying basis of his critique of constructive rationalism is the recognition of tacit (subjectively held, unorganized and widely dispersed) knowledge:

> that the rules of just conduct which the lawyer studies serve a kind of order of which the lawyer is largely ignorant; and that this order is studied chiefly by the economist who in turn is similarly ignorant of the character of the rules of conduct on which the order that he studies rests.
> (Hayek 1973: 5)

Hayek is particularly concerned to show the erroneous vain qualities of constructivist rationalism in assuming:

> that all social institutions are, and ought to be, the product of deliberate design . . . without at the same time greatly restricting the utilization of available knowledge. . . . [This] is closely connected with the equally false conception of the human mind as an entity standing outside . . . society, rather than being itself the product of the same process of evolution to which the institutions of society are due.
> (Hayek 1973: 5)

Lip service is paid to Popper in linking the spontaneous/organization distinction to Popper's account of critical rationalism. However, and here I agree with Bruce Caldwell, this does not alter the substance of his work (Caldwell 1994).[11] Hayek expressed a willingness to change his language to suit the audience, in order to ensure 'intelligibility' (Hayek 1982: xix). For him, constructive rationalism, the belief that actions are guided by known purposes, involves a misconception on the origins of civilization or the 'great society'. So, again the intersubjective understanding of the social order shines through the shift in terminology:

The tendency of constructivism to represent those values which it cannot explain as determined by arbitrary human decisions, or acts of will, or mere emotions, rather than as the necessary conditions of facts which are taken for granted by its expounders, has done much to shake the foundations of civilization, and of science itself, which also rests on a system of values which cannot be scientifically proved.

(Hayek 1973: 7)

The origins of constructivist rationalism are identified in Descartes, with reason or truth defined as logical deduction from explicit premises, assuming it is possible to have absolute knowledge of all relevant facts. Such an approach removes the validity of the rules of conduct (customs, habits and practices) and does not serve as a basis for man 'mastering his surroundings' (Hayek 1973: 11). Here again, we can see the eerie similarity to Schütz on the concept of rationality:

We live in a society in which we can successfully orientate ourselves, and in which our actions have a good chance of achieving their aims, not only because our fellows are governed by known aims or known connections between means and ends, but because they are also confined by rules whose purpose or origin we often do not know and of whose very existence we are often not aware. Man is as much a rule-following animal as a purpose-seeking one.

(Hayek 1973: 11)

For Hayek, the market order is characterized as much by a division of knowledge as by a division of labour, and to ignore this stark reality simply assumes away the central problem for human understanding. This error is summed up by Hayek's use of the synoptic delusion (the belief in omniscience) which 'is expressed with a touching naiveté by the enthusiasts for a deliberately planned society' as when one of them dreams of the 'art of simultaneous thinking: the ability to deal with a multitude of related phenomena at the same time, and of composing in a single picture both the qualitative and the quantitative attributes of these phenomena' (Hayek 1973: 14). While the citation is drawn from Lewis Mumford's introduction to F. Mackenzie's *Planned Society* (Hayek 1973: 148 n.12), it is significant that the close relationship between Schütz's stress upon simultaneity and the conceptualization developed by Mises on the difference between qualitative and quantitative prediction are also hinted at within the passage. The rules of conduct, upon which the spontaneous order is based, are the product of successful practices rather than being 'the recognized conditions for the achievement of a known purpose' (ibid.: 18).

The final paragraph of *Law, Legislation and Liberty* provides yet another indication of the epistemological basis of his work. It is explicitly linked to the normative project of demolishing socialism in all its forms. In the footnotes to this passage, Hayek stresses the continuity of his development over forty years, that *Law, Legislation and Liberty* represents the culmination of an abandoned project from the war years, 'The Nemesis of the Planned Society' (from which the Scientism essay emerged) and from a long process working through an 'original idea'. It is the contention of this chapter that this 'original idea' was the application of Schütz's account of intersubjective meaning to the market process within economics and, later, to the question of what would constitute the most appropriate state form to serve as the 'horizon of catallactic possibilities'. Following a call to battle in defence of liberty, the paragraph in question states:

> We ought to have learnt enough to avoid destroying our civilization by smothering the spontaneous process of the interaction of individuals by placing its direction in the hands of any authority. But to avoid this we must shed the illusion that we can deliberately 'create the future of mankind', as the characteristic hubris of a socialist sociologist has recently expressed it. This is the final conclusion of the forty years which I have devoted to the study of these problems since I became aware of the process of the Abuse and the Decline of Reason which has continued throughout that period.
>
> (Hayek 1979: 152)

The Schützian foundations of this account are much more explicitly revealed in Hayek's account of the origins of civilization and his exposition of the *common sense of progress* in *The Constitution of Liberty* (Hayek 1960). Here he argues, in criticism of 'utopian constructions', that 'though discussions of moral or social problems based on the assumption of perfect knowledge may occasionally be useful as a preliminary exercise in logic, they are of little use in an attempt to explain the real world' (Hayek 1960: 22). In this account, civilization is seen as the unintended product of past practices, as well as defining the scope for the pursuit of future human ends. Within this process, knowledge is taken to include all the adaptations of human actors to their surroundings and their shared activities, and he conjectures that ignorance accumulates with the advance of science and growth of civilization (ibid.: 26).In addition there are further attempts to develop an account of the intersubjective character of social life upon which his political philosophy rests:

> The successful combination of knowledge and aptitude is not selected by common deliberation, by people seeking a solution to their problems through a joint effort; it is the product of individuals imitating those who have been more successful and from their being guided by signs and symbols, such as prices offered for their products or expressions of moral or aesthetic esteem for having observed standards of conduct – in short, of their results of the experiences of others.
>
> (Hayek 1960: 28–9)

Throughout *The Constitution of Liberty*, and indeed the whole development of Hayek's work, there are the constant references to the problems of accommodating the dynamic elements of the transmission and communication of knowledge (in both conscious and tacit forms) and the importance of the conceptualization of time as a flow.

The model constitution and the dangers of discretion

> The little gap at which every man's liberty may go out
> (cited in Hayek 1960: 212)

With the epistemological basis of Hayek's work in place alongside both his account of the market order as a catallaxy and his critical evaluation of the confusions of political language, it is now possible to address his recommendations for a constitutional system which would foster a free society. He is not simply advocating a 'minimal state', for he does recognize the appropriateness of state provision of services, and by implication the collection of the necessary taxation to finance them, where the market is incapable of providing an adequate solution. It also follows that the areas where state intervention is appropriate will change according to circumstances. In particular, they depend on the nature of the problems encountered, the practical solutions available and the combination of elements in the market order at that point in time. Hayek's arguments for a model constitution can be seen developing throughout *The Constitution of Liberty* (Hayek 1960), particularly Part II. We can also find a more programmatic approach in volume III of *Law, Legislation and Liberty* (Hayek 1979), suitably entitled *The Political Order of a Free People*. He did not see his task as offering a blueprint which could be grafted upon, or which could replace, the existing constitutional structures of advanced Western civilizations. This would, of course, be antithetical to his whole intellectual project. Nevertheless, Hayek sees his recommendations as vital in considering developments beyond the context of Western nation-states, both in terms of fledgling post-colonial democracies and in the emergence of supranational political systems. To examine the issues at stake, Hayek starts with a consideration of the historical development of liberal constitutions in England, France, America and Germany.

The starting point for what can be called Hayek's 'genealogy of liberty' is the English legal tradition. In the peculiar case of England, continental absolutism had not eradicated medieval liberties. Customary understandings of freedom and justice were widely held beyond the elite. Hayek specifically identifies the seventeenth-century conflicts between political bodies as the cause of the advance of individual freedom, an unintended consequence of each authoritative body accusing the others of acting in an 'arbitrary' manner. The emergence of 'limited government' is thus conceptually tied to the understanding of *isonomia* in Elizabethan politics and society as 'equality of laws to all manner of persons'. He discusses both the formal and the informal or popular understandings in the Elizabethan period, in the latter case by reference to popular drinking songs on the assassination of tyrants. This dovetails with Schütz's exploration and discussion of the distinctions between concepts of equality in the opening passages of 'Equality and the Meaning Structure of the Social World' (Schütz 1957), and in his short paper on the concept of responsibility (Schütz 1958). In this sense, Locke's formulation of rule by laws, rather than by men, and the importance of trial before a known and impartial judge, adjudicating according to declared and received laws, becomes an expression of unique cultural achievement. The role of the courts is to enforce general rules, and obedience of the law becomes both an expression of, and a precondition for, freedom.

Similarly, this recognition of the cultural dimension of the social order allows for a reassessment of the relationship between Hayek's use of Adam Smith and the position adopted recently by Donald Winch, who has identified the inappropriate and inaccurate uses of Smith's work by contemporary neo-liberal approaches. Winch argues that to treat Adam Smith's account of the role of benevolence and self interest in exchange as an account akin to those of 'rational economic man' (as in neo-classical economics and in public choice approaches within political science) is a distortion of Smith's intent. He specifically raises the integrated nature of Adam Smith's project. The concept of 'interest' in *An Inquiry into the Nature and Causes of The Wealth of Nations* (Smith 1950) cannot be divorced from Smith's account of 'sympathy' in *The Theory of Moral Sentiments* (Smith 1812). In this account, acts of exchange create inescapable bonds through which conduct is stabilized and normalized within a context which involves limited foresight of the consequences of action (Winch 1996b). However, Hayek's work does not fall into the rubric of what Winch describes as 'negative libertarians', for it is also clear that Hayek has a keen sense of the relevance of the intersubjective nature of market relations and the importance of the social distribution of knowledge. There are remarkable parallels between Smith's account of sympathy and interest and Hayek's account of the market as catallaxy. For Hayek, the cultural achievement of the market was undermined, as noted earlier, by the 'rationalist-utilitarian' tendencies of nineteenth century liberalism, which can be traced from Bentham through to Keynesian policies in the twentieth century. Hayek even identifies rationalist tendencies in J. S. Mill (derived from Comte) while collating and studying the correspondence of Mill and Harriet Taylor (Hayek 1951).

In the case of English legal and political institutions, the rules of just conduct which had evolved in the legal system rested upon particular cultural premises. However, in Hayek's view, these were undermined by state interference. The American constitutionalist approach, by contrast, was a product of design. Hayek argues, as Burke suggested, that the American polity remained devoted to the English conception of liberty. But it was felt that the unlimited parliamentary democracy characteristic of the English political system was anathema to liberty itself, for no constraints existed upon arbitrary decisions. In England, two foundation stones were missing. The first was a fixed constitution distributing powers and sovereignty throughout the agencies of the state. The second was a representative government limited by a constitutional document which confers powers upon the institutions of the state. The American distinction between general laws (those without concern for the ends of the groups and individuals concerned) and particular laws (with specific ends in mind) is central. In this instance, it is analogous to the distinction between general legal principles and particular cases in the liberal judicial system. As such, the American constitution was an 'application of traditional principles to particular problems' (Hayek 1960: 184). Moreover, Hayek recognized that:

> This division of authority implies more than may at first be apparent. It implies a recognition of limits to the power of deliberate reason and a preference for reliance on proved principles over *ad hoc* solutions; furthermore it implies that the hierarchy of rules does not necessarily end with the explicitly stated rules of the constitutional law. Like the forces governing the individual mind, the forces making for social order are a multilevel affair; and even constitutions are based on, or presuppose, an underlying agreement on more fundamental principles – principles which may never have been explicitly expressed. . . . [A] group of men can form a society capable of making laws because they already share common beliefs which make discussion and persuasion possible and to which articulated rules must conform in order to be accepted as legitimate [for] . . . all rational thought moves within a non rational framework of beliefs and institutions. Constitutionalism means that all power rests on the understanding that it will be exercised according to some commonly accepted principles, that the persons on whom power is conferred are selected because it is thought that they are most likely to do what is right, not in order that whatever they do should be right. It rests, in the last resort, on the understanding that power is ultimately not a physical fact but a state of opinion which makes people obey.
> (Hayek 1960: 181)

In this sense, Hayek shares with Adam Smith the rejection of the Hobbesian conception of sovereignty as an indication of false rationalism, that of self-determining reason (Hayek 1960: 181). The reference to the social order as a multi-level affair is also another link to Schütz and the mundane phenomenological approach to the non-rational. Although a bill of rights was initially seen as problematic, in that any list will exclude some rights, for Hayek this became more significant within the context of the separation of powers and the development of the process of judicial review.

Even in what is regarded by critical liberals as the hopeless case of the French Revolution, Hayek finds some surprising positive qualities. He suggests that the *Conseil d'État*, initially designed to implement the intentions of the legislature, in fact provided more effective protection of citizens from administrative discretion than was provided in England. However, the French constitution retained the fundamental flaw of exempting administrative actions from judicial scrutiny and control. In the final case, that of the Prussian constitutional monarchy, Hayek examines the potential of the *Rechtsstaat* (state of law), or justicialism. He describes this development as an attempt to construct an institutional embodiment of the principles often expressed in terms of Kant's 'categorical imperative', in conjunction with the arguments of Humboldt in *The Sphere and Duty of Government* (Humboldt 1854). All moral measures or legislation, if they are to be understood as just, should apply universally, extending the basic principles of the rule of law to ethics (that laws and ethics, as argued earlier, should have the form of being both abstract and general).

For Hayek, the distinctive development in Prussia was the recognition that to be fully effective, the rule of law could only operate in situations where public administration was closely monitored and strictly controlled. He cites the example of the belated attempt from the 1860s to replace administrative jurisdiction, the quasi-judicial bodies inside the administration whose function was to monitor the execution of the law. In their place, independent administrative courts sought to monitor administrative measures by reference to pre-existing general rules. In practice, the context was not auspicious for this development, and loopholes allowed for the development of discretionary powers, especially as Bismarckian welfarism gathered pace. However, Hayek remained convinced that the separation of those courts which adjudicate on private matters from those courts concerned with administrative disputes was both feasible and desirable; although the latter were to be limited to protecting the individual against interference only in so far as it was against the intentions of the government. The Prussian legacy, he concludes, is theoretical rather than practical, and more appropriate to the conditions of the twentieth century than to the time of their emergence. This is because the distinction between the concerns of ordinary jurisdiction and the judicial control of the administration is not so clear in the absence of a 'body of detailed legal rules for guiding and limiting the actions of the administration' (Hayek 1960: 201), and this leads to the confusion of general rules with those rules engaged in the pursuit of policies.

Hayek raises the conceptual confusions, particularly on the part of economists, around the interpretation of state interference in the context of his discussion of rule of law. On this score he argues, consistently with the work of Adam Smith, that it is important to consider the qualitative as well as the quantitative dimensions of intervention in the market. Economic freedom is more than simply 'freedom under the law'. Hayek avoids the knee-jerk reaction, common amongst libertarians, of proscribing all state services. He cites the function of the rule of law in providing a yardstick for assessing whether measures are compatible with the catallaxy. This is to be distinguished from policies which, when appropriately understood, seek to establish the specified ends of government. For Hayek, policies should be subject to general and abstract laws. Such general laws are opposed to the chaotic conception of 'policy' when it is taken to indicate all kinds of legislation, and converts legislation into the 'instruments of policy'. Both of these uses are then distinguished from the 'policy of the law' which relates to general principles (such as the protection of good faith, the preservation of public order, and the non-recognition of contracts engaged upon for immoral purposes). These are not enshrined in legislation for they also specify ends, and neither do they constitute rules of conduct (Hayek 1960: 214–15). Interestingly, he also suggests that the rule of law is necessary but not in itself sufficient for securing the effective operation of a spontaneous market order, and that legal frameworks also need to encourage the confidence of individuals in their own plans and the predictability of market conditions in order to realize their own ends:

> The habitual appeal to the principle of non-interference in the fight against all ill-considered or harmful measures which are and those which are not compatible with a free system. And the opponents of free enterprise have been only too ready to help this conclusion by insisting that the desirability or undesirability of a particular measure could never be a matter of principle but is always one of expediency. In consequence, a government that is comparably inactive but does the wrong thing may do much more to cripple the forces of the market economy than one that is more concerned with economic affairs but confines itself to actions which assist the spontaneous forces of the economy.
> (Hayek 1960: 221–2)

Hence, the scope of state intervention is tied to the distinction between 'the exercise of coercive measures' and 'pure service activities' (where coercion only takes place in order to raise tax revenues). In the case of public service activities, state involvement is simply assessed 'where the benefits are worth the cost' (such as factory legislation on health and safety, working conditions and technological experimentation, working hours and holidays) and where trust is facilitated in market conditions through the acquisition of 'reliable knowledge' (such as weights and measures, land registration and surveying).

Startlingly, for many contemporary leftist critics and rightist supporters, Hayek provides an extensive list of areas where he considers state involvement as unquestionably desirable: health and sanitation; road maintenance and construction; municipal services and public works; the provision of military defence and the maintenance of law and order; and finally the advancement of knowledge. This is hardly a libertarian manifesto. For Hayek, 'What is objectionable here is not state enterprise but state monopoly' (Hayek 1960: 224), and extensive discretionary powers would be permissible subject to the constraint of judicial review by an impartial court, adjudicating upon whether a policy with a specific purpose achieved the goals established in legislation. The examples raised here are disease control in livestock, demolition to prevent the spread of fire, prohibiting infected water supplies, safety regulations in public places and in buildings, and protective measures against electricity cables. All such areas, he argues, function more effectively through general rules than through 'particular preferences'. However, Hayek argues that some forms of state interference are, within the context of the rule of law laid out above, excluded in principle for they involve 'arbitrary discrimination between persons' (ibid.: 227). For instance, we can see this in the labour market or in the operation of price controls in determining 'what is produced by whom and for whom' (ibid.: 228). The general rules permitted in such markets are related to maintaining the condition of trust when faced with difficulties in the enforcement of contracts, the protection of private property, rules ensuring fair competition, and the prevention of fraud and violence.

In these areas Hayek clearly accepts the need for discretionary powers, but in so far as this constitutes a problem, it is one which relates to the 'scope of administration in general' in interfering with the private sphere, the realm of the citizen and his property (Hayek 1960: 213). This brings Hayek to the problems of formulating what would safeguard individual freedom or liberty, and of what institutional framework would be most appropriate for successfully delivering such a condition. In short, what are the conditions of possibility of the market conceived as a condition of intersubjectivity, as a catallaxy? These preconditions involve the operation of government coercion under known rules, that true laws are known and certain, that equality exists without the determination of ends and that, as a consequence, the operation of the rule of law is just in the strictly limited sense that all laws are general and abstract, and bearing in mind that particular laws can be just or unjust. This approach places a great deal of stress on the intersubjective dimension of legal relations and the 'complex of principles' invoked by any fully effective condition where the rule of law holds. Hayek argues that the rule of law as a political ideal:

> will be effective only insofar as the legislator feels bound by it. In a democracy this means that it will not prevail unless it forms part of the *moral tradition of the community*, a common ideal shared and unquestionably accepted by the majority. . . . If the ideal . . . is represented as an impracticable and even desirable ideal and people cease to strive for its realization, it will rapidly disappear.
>
> (Hayek 1960: 206)

The consideration of the rule of law prior to the procedural safeguards of habeas corpus and trial by jury is deliberate, but it is not intended to be disparaging towards the latter. For Hayek, the contention that laws should be certain is not meaningless but a worthy ideal (just as with equality before the law). However, to exaggerate the uncertainty is damaging for the rule of law which, of course, rests upon trust. The consistency and predictability of the practical operation of the courts involve the discovery of rules in much the same way as identified earlier (in relation to the market as catallaxy) and are a manifestation of Hayek's conception of the construction of knowledge: 'Probably all generalizations that we can formulate depend on still higher generalizations which we do not explicitly know but which nevertheless govern the working of our minds' (Hayek 1960: 209).

In *The Constitution of Liberty* (Hayek 1960), he hints at the key elements of his later proposals for the model constitution. Starting from the premise of the desirability of separating the formulation of material or substantive laws (the regulation of relationships between citizens and/or the state) from laws pertaining to servants of the state and the direction of administration (a hierarchy of rules whereby general rules from a superior authority govern the particular rules of a delegated authority), he proposes a bicameral constitutional solution. In the former case, he suggests, one chamber will be purely concerned with the provision of general abstract rules as 'essentially long-term measures, referring to yet unknown cases and containing no references to particular persons, places or objects. Such laws must always be prospective, never retrospective, in their effect' (Hayek 1960: 208).

In the latter case, a chamber would be purely concerned with the orders given to the administrative apparatus, subject to the proviso that executive action cannot be exercised coercively or arbitrarily in relation to private citizens and their property. Hence, this separation of powers also suggests that there is a need for an independent judicial review of both chambers, a legal limit on administrative discretion or delegated legislation. In the case of the second chamber, it is particularly important to ensure that executive actions comply with general rules, and to avoid the dangers of decisions automatically having the force of law (which would make judicial review impotent). Again, the intersubjective conception of the social is invoked to clarify the conceptual confusions over the concept of discretion. Hayek has in mind the rules of conduct at work in the legal sphere, rather than the power or authority (these terms are used synonymously here) of a judge to interpret legal rules or the discretion delegated to an official in the government hierarchy:

> The task of the judge is to discover the implications contained in the spirit of the whole system of valid rules of law or to express as a general rule, when necessary what was not explicitly stated previously in a court of law or by the legislator. . . . [Hence] the dispute must be settled by an appeal to the rules and not by a simple act of will.
> (Hayek 1960: 212)

In vol. III of *Law, Legislation and Liberty* (Hayek 1979), Hayek develops his earlier constitutional ideas on the relationship between the nature of political frameworks and his conception of social conduct as embodied by both rational and non-rational elements. He justifies his advocacy of an ideal constitution on two grounds, and is careful to qualify his approach by reference to those countries which possess a 'strong constitutional tradition' and presumably do not need to take his advice. First, many countries have experienced the failure of democratic procedures following decolonization and this, he suggests, is a result of the application of inappropriate institutions to conditions where the tacit acceptance of certain principles is lacking. Second, he notes the possible emergence of supra-national political institutions and the need to restrict international law to general rules (Hayek 1979: 107–9). He sets out his analysis of the model constitution against the dangers of an 'omnipotent sovereign parliament', and states in clear terms that the sovereignty of an unlimited parliament is irreconcilable with sovereignty of the law. For Hayek, the choice is clear: 'we can either have a free Parliament or a free people' (Hayek 1979: 102). Hayek's stridency against the interference of the state is much stronger in these passages, in which he ties the 'legalized corruption' of the state to the failure to divide the power of the legislative body along the lines of substantive and directive legislation:

> Two such distinct assemblies would, of course, have to be differently composed if the *legislative* one is to represent the *opinion* of the people about which sorts of government actions are just and which are not, and the other *governmental* assembly were to be guided by the *will* of the people on the particular measures to be taken within the frame of rules laid down by the first. . . . [T]he existing parliaments are largely unfit for legislation proper. They have neither the time nor the right frame of mind to do it well.
>
> (Hayek 1979: 104)

In the case of Britain, he recommends a division of functions as opposed to the existing division of classes between commoners and nobility. The House of Commons, he argues, would serve well the task of monitoring and controlling the exercise of power and the resources of the government, the personnel of which would be drawn from amongst its number, as is presently largely the case (Hayek 1979: 106–7). Hayek's proposals for the second chamber or legislative assembly are more novel. He develops his ideas on what role legislation would play if it were to be conceived without consideration of its application to future instances or specific purposes, indicated by his use of the concept of *nomos*. Here, the language changes from his earlier writings but the argument does not, for *nomos* simply refers to situations where laws operate in such a way that 'men could be restrained from doing what they wished or coerced to do particular things, only in accordance with the recognized rules of just conduct designed to define and protect the individual domain of each' (ibid.: 109).

Hayek argues that the most effective check on the capacity of the governmental assembly would be to devise an alternative form of representation to avoid the duplication of the same levels of support for the same parties, undermining the division of labour implied by having two chambers. He certainly wanted to avoid the American answer to this problem of holding staggered elections. Hayek suggests that this leads to dislocation, immobilism and unnecessary conflict. While the governmental assembly would have conventional political party representation, to facilitate the smooth succession of governmental teams, the distinctive task of the second chamber in upholding justice impartially demands a different electoral solution.

For Hayek, the classical theories of democracy are inappropriate for this task. Instead, he suggests a restricted franchise on the criterion of age. Each annual cohort on attaining the age of forty-five should select from among their number a group of public-spirited and reputable representatives for a term of office of fifteen years. This is premised on the assumptions that a person's contemporaries are the best judges of a potential representative's character and calibre. The length of appointment would ensure a degree of independence from political parties. In addition, the representatives would be provided with adequate means to minimize corruption (a pay formula based upon an average of the twenty highest paid government posts), and the prospect of further public employment as 'honorific but neutral lay judges' once the term of office was complete. Further safeguards, such as excluding party members and governmental assembly representatives, procedures for removing representatives on the grounds of neglect or misconduct, and an electoral college of regional delegates to elect representatives, ensuring regional spread, could also be added. Hayek suggests that the moral fabric of urban societies would benefit from the formation of local clubs of contemporaries formed from school age onwards. These would function as a training ground for future representatives, foster the ethos of voluntary commitment, and facilitate this distinctive generational form of representation.

This legislative chamber composed of men and women from the ages of forty-five to sixty (with one-fifteenth replaced each year) would not only be youthful in comparison to most legislatures, but was considered by Hayek to provide the most appropriate means for fulfilling the distinctive task of what he terms 'legislation proper', that of formulating general and abstract laws without regards for specific ends. In addition, this assembly would be charged with the laborious task of reviewing 'all enforceable rules of conduct', from taxation and public order to regulating market competition in its myriad forms. This would, he argues, prevent the bureaucratic apparatus or executive agencies taking on the role of defining everything they do as having the force of law, and hence exercising arbitrary power. In effect, Hayek is seeking to resurrect the conception of the representative as 'a man of independent means' (Hayek 1979: 112–19).

In order to regulate any conflicts of competence between the governmental and legislative assemblies and to prevent both chambers initiating coercive measures, it would also be necessary to establish a constitutional court. Hayek suggests a composition of senior professional judges and former members of the legislative assembly who had distinguished themselves. The task of such an institution would be initially to establish and develop a body of known and established constitutional law which would then serve as precedents for future judgements. Judicial appointments would be separated from the executive and placed into the hands of the committee of former members of the legislative assembly, who would also decide on the employment of their peers as lay judges. Judicial salaries would reflect the same pay formula as that established for elected representatives. The executive would retain responsibility for the technical provision of the courts (Hayek 1979: 120–2). Hayek then leaves the finer points of discussion for the future.

In these conditions of dispersed sovereignty and an evolving set of political institutions, Hayek argues it would be possible to identify the endogenous emergence of a grown or spontaneous order, a *kosmos*. The properties of such an order are the existence of purely abstract relations, where rules do not presuppose specific purposes (described as *nomos*) as indicated earlier. As a result, human arrangements can realize unexpected and bewildering levels of complexity. He declares that the belief in the need for some ultimate unlimited power is fallacious. In a directed or exogenously created order where deliberately designed laws are geared towards particular purposes (described as *thesis*), a closed system, only one outcome can be witnessed, and evolutionary growth is replaced by the stultifying monotony of an omnipotent state control with omnipresent surveillance. This account of the most appropriate constitution for catallaxy is one which specifies strict limits for the exercise of state power. There remains a place for *thesis* within a separate institutional context, and subject to the overarching existence of general and abstract rules created by a separate legislative assembly and interpreted by an independent judiciary. In such conditions, Hayek argues, the foundations of the great society, of peace, freedom and justice, will have been laid.

Conclusion

In the place of 'glamorous constructivism', Hayek makes a plea for 'humble and quiet evolution' (Hayek 1973). This account of the economy, the state and law is grounded upon a phenomenological conception of the dispersed distribution and intersubjective character of knowledge at all levels of the social order. The role of Alfred Schütz in articulating the 'mundane phenomenology', and indicating the practical consequences of the study of social life in the manner of a detached scientist, is central to Hayek's reassessment of the central concepts of political philosophy and his clarification of conceptual confusions within actual political institutions. These relationships are neatly expressed in one final passage:

> It is that all men in the pursuit of immediate aims are apt – or, because of the limitation of their intellect, in fact bound – to violate rules of conduct which they would nevertheless wish to see generally observed.

Because of the restricted capacity of our minds, our immediate purposes will always loom large, and we will tend to sacrifice long-term advantages to them. In individual as in social conduct we can therefore approach a measure of rationality or consistency in making particular decisions only by submitting to general principles, irrespective of momentary needs. Legislation can no more dispense with guidance by principles than any other human activity if it is to take account of effects in the aggregate.

(Hayek 1960: 179)

Hayek's vision of a free society is thus characterized as one in which the results are uncertain, and where disappointment and failure are as valuable as success. In particular, it is one where the 'non-rational' aspects of life (he is referring to habits, customs and rules of conduct rather than to the concept of the 'irrational') are a vital component in the constitution of institutional existence. Within such a society, individuals would be able to pursue their own plans within the context of shared structures of meaning, and a competitive environment free from the coercive intrusions of exclusive monopolistic organizations (particularly, but not exclusively, those of the state).

Constructivist rationalism is characterized as the attempt to predict and control, and is seen as antithetical to the further progress of human civilization. The most that scientific explanations should hope to achieve is to identify the kind of forces which could bring future states of affairs into existence (a form of pattern prediction). The phenomenological undercurrent in Hayek's work allows for the recognition of complexity and the absence of closure in social life. However, he resolves these difficulties by adopting the idealist solution, adopting the position of 'intelligibility determinism' in establishing causal laws. For Hayek, like Dahl, complexity precludes the assumption that constant conjunctions of events are both necessary and sufficient for establishing a causal law. Some form of causal-genetic explanation remains his goal, with empirical regularities as necessary although not sufficient to establish a causal law. This is also subject to the limitations of accommodating the level of everyday experience and tacit knowledge within explanatory accounts. Hence Hayek remains wedded to an empirical realist ontology founded on the concept of the empirical world (informed in this case by life philosophy), combined with a transcendental idealist epistemology, indicated by his account of the place of causal laws. The significance of this approach to knowledge construction will be addressed in Chapter Six.

5 Capitalism, the state and societalization

Introduction

This chapter examines the contribution of Bob Jessop to neo-Marxist theories of the state by tracing the evolution of his work from the late 1960s. Where in Chapter Three Dahl's work was shown to demonstrate the evolution of an approach from empiricism to transcendental idealism, and in Chapter Four Hayek's approach was shown to reveal a creative synthesis of neo-Kantian and phenomenological insights within the idealist approach, Jessop's work in political sociology and political economy demonstrates the complex relationship between idealist and realist concerns. In relation to substantive concerns, just as Dahl and Hayek developed an account of the state in terms of the limits and possibilities placed upon (their different conceptions of) the social, Jessop also constructs state theory in relation to the constitution of the social order or, as he later describes it, the process of societalization, the contingently necessary process through which 'society effects' are produced.

Throughout the development of Jessop's work, there is a clear attempt to draw upon a technique of theoretical synthesis drawn from Willer's account of the symbolic model. It is also possible to identify a set of *triadic parameters* in Jessop's intellectual evolution which are brought together through a concern with the constitution of the social order. In Jessop's early work, the triad is composed of theories of normative consensus, of constraint (in Weberian and Marxist senses) and of exchange. The middle work consists of a directly focused attempt to re-theorize economy, polity and ideology within Marxism, in both theoretical and substantive terms. More recently, Jessop has brought together the concerns of his earlier symbolic models into an account of societalization founded upon regulation theory, Laclau and Mouffe's discourse analysis, and an account of the state which draws together the insights of both Poulantzas and Foucault. The synthetic element in this moment of Jessop's intellectual evolution is the systems theory of Niklas Luhmann. This also provides him with the means of resolving the substantive issues surrounding any attempt to provide an account of 'society effects' without resorting to the construction of a 'grand theory'.

This chapter focuses upon the neo-Marxist approach to the state and the relationship between the political, economic, cultural and social dimensions of contemporary capitalism. In comparison to many other contributors to this approach in the late 1960s and 1970s, Jessop maintains a commitment to the characterization of economic life as grounded upon the labour theory of value. At the same time, Jessop has consistently addressed the difficult questions which have confronted neo-Marxism. In addition, he developed some novel ways of reinterpreting the relationship between the capitalist infrastructure and the 'superstructural' dimensions of social life. Jessop's contributions to neo-Marxist political economy involve one of the most consistent attempts to elaborate a state theory without either reducing the political dimension to some epiphenomena of more fundamental processes and relations, or treating the state as an autonomous actor in relation to other dimensions of social life.

It is the contention of this chapter that Jessop attempts to resolve the problems of neo-Marxist theory, particularly the conceptual dead-end of *relative autonomy*, through a creative synthesis of realist and idealist approaches to the constitution of social life. The role of economic determinism (in the last instance) in reducing the political, ideological and cultural to a manifestation of deeper essential causes is sustained in some branches of neo-Marxist thought. However, the most common outcome for neo-Marxists such as Paul Hirst, Ernesto Laclau and Stuart Hall has been to reject Marxism as a 'finished project', in favour of a more broadly based reformist or radical project around the theme of cultural transformation. These post-Marxist theorists have rejected Marxist political economy in favour of prioritizing the cultural dimension, especially through post-structuralist and postmodern interpretations of language, discourse and culture. Jessop, however, has sought to weave together such insights into an increasingly elaborate theoretical account of the complex relationships between the economic, political and ideological dimensions of social relations.

In some respects, Jessop entered the debates on the crisis of Marxism in the 1970s later than many other contributors. These critical interventions started from a vantage point which drew widely from sociological theory on the complexities of the constitution of the social. In the two attempts to periodize Jessop's work (Ling 1991; Bertramsen, Thomsen and Torfing 1991), the late 1970s are taken as the benchmark against which to compare the subsequent development of his work. This leaves the trajectory of Jessop's intellectual development, as simply a response to the problems of European Marxism, unquestioned, and it treats his subsequent innovations as an anti-reductionist response to these problems. Ling's analysis treats Jessop's intellectual development as the 'high road' in recent state theory compared to the 'low road' which (in failing adequately to resolve the problems of economic determinism) ultimately led to the treatment of the state as an autonomous actor. Ling's story line on Jessop's intellectual development starts with a narrow focus and moves progressively towards a more inclusive and theoretically sophisticated account of the role of the economy and the state in the processes and relations involved in societalization. This story line is punctuated by the acquisition of insights from Poulantzas, Offe, Lipietz, Hirsch, Laclau and Luhmann. However, this chapter contends that many of the formulations and substantive areas of concerns of Jessop's work predate the late 1970s, and that Jessop's utilization of Luhmann's account of autopoietic and allopoietic social systems, and his attraction to Foucauldian interpretations of power and governance, are a reworked extension and reintegration of his early 'culturological' concerns with the constitution of social change and social order.

Jessop's recent calls for a Luhmannian reinterpretation of Marx can be understood more effectively when they are placed in relation to the full development of his work to date. In his early theoretical work, Jessop attempted to integrate normative functionalism, Dahrendorf's conflict theory, Blau's exchange theory and Avineri's account of Marx's concept of alienation. In the light of this early work, the integration of Luhmann's account of the dynamics of social systems makes a great deal more sense. In particular, it helps to make clear the significance of the Poulantzian appropriation of Foucault and the impact of Laclau's account of 'articulation' in ideological and political discourse within Marxist theorizing. These approaches are explored and developed by Jessop within the context of an anti-reductionist account of Marxist regulation theory (developed by Alain Lipietz). In addition, the early work explicitly acknowledges the use of Willer's account of symbolic models as a means of theoretical innovation. This can be seen repeatedly throughout his work to date, accounting for the diverse range of sources and influences. In the early 1980s, in addressing the relationship between the abstract and the concrete in his writings on state theory, Jessop also explicitly acknowledges the use of Roy Bhaskar's scientific realist account of theoretical construction and causal analysis. This enables him to find a way of rejecting determinism, reductionism and essentialism without rejecting the use of determinations in accounting for causal processes and social relations.

Nevertheless, the use of symbolic model construction as a means of achieving theoretical synthesis and innovation continues to remain a distinctive feature of Jessop's work throughout the 1980s and early 1990s. This also appears to correspond with his move from an exclusive focus upon the relationship between state and the economy, towards an account of societalization and the empirical application of his theoretical system (within overdetermined social formations). Jessop's approach thus provides a unique case study in the consistent deployment of neo-Marxist assumptions in political economy, combined with the recognition of the cultural and social dimensions of political relations. Jessop has an epistemological and ontological self-awareness rarely seen in accounts of the state. In this way, his work not only provides us with a theoretically sophisticated account of the state as a social relation, but implicitly provides a basis for working towards the conceptual clarification of realism itself.

Exchange, power and institutionalization: the idealist foundations in Jessop's early work

Jessop's first contributions to sociological theory in the late 1960s and early 1970s provide a useful guide to the concerns which have characterized his work over the last thirty years. At the centre of Jessop's analysis was the theorization of consensus, conflict and change in order to provide a framework for the organization and analysis of empirical evidence of order, reform and revolution in concrete societies. Jessop sought to identify the necessary features of reform and revolution within their socio-cultural context. In particular, he established the way in which revolutionary movements came to be defined as such only through derogatory labels applied by the powerful. In similar terms, reformist movements were only characterized as such in relation to their degree of institutionalization in the social order in question. Existing approaches towards such movements were therefore unable to account for the substantial empirical differences between movements which had been institutionalized (and their differences from those which were not). This led Jessop to reconsider the theoretical frameworks available in political sociology at that time.

Jessop's initial interventions sought to establish a synthesis of the insights of consensus theories (the normative functionalism of Talcott Parsons) and conflict theories in sociology (particularly that of Ralf Dahrendorf) through the use of the assumptions and concepts of exchange theory (the early work of Peter Blau). Utilizing the symbolic model-construction techniques of David Willer (1967), Jessop attempts to synthesize these macrosociological models of social structure (or at least the dimensions of power and exchange within them). For Jessop, each theory offers a useful pathway, yet each theory is also limited by unrealistic assumptions about the social order. The concern with normative constraints in Parsonian functionalism is brought together with the characterization of non-normative aspects of social life raised by conflict theory; in particular, their focus on interests, coercion and structural contradictions within the context of centre–periphery relations. In this regard, Jessop wishes to address 'centres' as 'purely structural phenomena' composed of individuals, groups and organizations. He argues that 'centres' exercise power regardless of the 'normative distribution of power'.

The definition of power at this stage is a useful litmus test in the development of Jessop's approach. In his examination of power as a 'zero-sum' game, in largely Weberian terms, Jessop introduces the proviso that the power holders and the powerless are not always in conflict and that power holders can act in the interests of the powerless.[1] This provides useful clues as to the epistemological and ontological assumptions at work in his early sociological interventions. In identifying the 'generic' character of power, Jessop raises the existence of four analytical (that is, not empirical) types of power relationship.[2] All four analytical types of power could be combined with a range of resources, and together they provide some indication of the complexity of the model under construction (Jessop 1969; 1972: 54–7).

- *Economic power* involves control over the means of production, distribution and exchange.
- *Political power* is control of the means of coercion (including that of the military).
- *Social power* is control of the means of status attribution.
- *Cultural power* is control of the means of value creation, interpretation and maintenance.

In relation to each of these primary bases of power, he identifies their respective outputs (goods and services, force, status and value commitments) as corresponding secondary bases. In turn, the institutional conditions of their operation are portrayed as tertiary bases of power. In each case, power involves the control of the means (whether this is control of production, coercion, status and/or values), as distinct from the end product. (Later neo-Marxist formulations defined power as visible in its consequences.) In particular, he redefines the concept of 'status attribution' from being concerned merely with the terms of membership of status enhancing collectivities and roles, to being about the differential control over access to resources. This subordinates social power to cultural power, which defines what is culturally valued in the first place, but at the same time he does not reduce social power to cultural power (Jessop 1972: 57–69). These four types of power are seen as empirically differentiated with no necessary correspondence. Nevertheless, they are also interdependent and are characterized by interpenetration. The judicial system is highlighted as a useful illustration of the interlocking of power systems; judicial institutions sanction coercion, allocate economic costs and benefits, attribute status and interpret norms (ibid.: 70).

The use of conflict (or constraint) theory, particularly Dahrendorf's 'revision' of Marxist assumptions, provides Jessop with an account of the relations of superordination and subordination in the power relations of each specific substratum. In this way, he secures the correspondence of a symbolic model of class conflict with his symbolic model of normative constraints. Whereas functionalism could only accommodate cultural variation in terms of institutionalization and anomie, constraint theory could accommodate three states of consciousness: *institutionalization* (a broad commitment to the institutional framework which one inhabits), *economistic consciousness* and *genuinely conscious opposition*. Jessop applies this distinction across the centre–periphery relations of all the substrata in order to generate the distinction between exploitation, reciprocity and benefaction. Even at this stage, there is an early indication of the focus upon Marxist assumptions in relation to production and exchange, with the identification of the substratum of 'forces and relations of production, coercion, status attribution and value creation' (Jessop 1969: 419; 1972: 59–60).[3]

Alienation is defined in terms of a lack of control over these four means and, as such, is a characteristic of the periphery in the centre–periphery relationship. He does stress the contingency of these characteristics of powerlessness (in conditions of reciprocity and benefaction) rather than treating them as objectively necessary. In a strong hint of his later embrace of Marxist theories of political economy, he integrates Avineri's account of Marx's theorization of alienation. The three senses of alienation are:

- *Objectification*, as the process whereby the product of the periphery's contribution becomes a further means of control over the periphery (with reification as its cultural component).
- *Dehumanization*, with the degradation of the intrinsic value of those occupying places within the periphery.
- *Self-estrangement* (with false consciousness as its cultural component) where the contribution of the periphery is merely instrumental to the needs of the substratum concerned, and does not serve the needs of the periphery or act as a means to their self expression.

In each case, as demonstrated in Table 5.1, there are economic, political, social and cultural forms of these processes of alienation (Jessop 1969: 421–2).

Table 5.1 Jessop's synthesis of functionalist, conflict and exchange theories

	Objectification	*Dehumanisation*	*Self-estrangement*
Economic power	The *product* of the periphery becomes an additional means of control	Degradation of intrinsic value of periphery in terms of *productivity*	*Instrumentality* of the periphery as the means to the ends of the centre
Political power	*Obedience* increases control and ability to coerce of the centre	Degradation of intrinsic value of periphery in terms of *loyalty* of periphery	*Avoidance* of coercion rather than the realization of the ends of the periphery
Social power	*Deference* secures the status and potential influence of the centre	Degradation of intrinsic value of periphery in terms of the *humility* of the periphery	*Deference* secures *approval* but not as an expression of value of its own worth
Cultural power	*Commitment* to central values by the periphery increases the legitimacy of the centre	Degradation of intrinsic value of periphery in terms of the *orthodoxy* of the periphery	*Periphery unaware of its own interests* increases the commitment to central values

Source: Adapted from Jessop 1969: 417–22; 1972: 81–97

Of particular significance for Jessop's later theoretical development is the use of Louis Althusser's characterization of the role of contradictions and overdetermination in relation to the structural contradictions within a hierarchical and differentiated social order (Jessop 1972: 85 n5). In particular, he identifies four structural contradictions which act as sources of conflict:

1. The contradictions inherent in the relations between centre and periphery in the distribution of control over the bases of economic, political, social and cultural power.
2. The contradictions and the conflicts over the exchange relations between different power centres, as well as over the distribution of any surplus for reinvestment and consumption.
3. The contradictions between the forces and relations of production within each power system, which emerge if the forces of production create a potential for redistribution of power.
4. The contradictions which emerge within relations of different power systems, if the developmental tendencies of the forces of production of one or more power systems come into conflict with those of the other power systems, possibly intensifying the conflicts in each.

These theoretical constructs act as a means of building a model which can accommodate the contradictory coexistence of both unifying and discordant social forces, as the contingent outcome of the dynamics of power systems. At the same time, Jessop provides an account of the constitutive role of human beings in the emergence of complex social structures.

Exchange theory provides the necessary dynamic theoretical core for synthesizing the normative constraints and regulation of human interaction with the identification of power relations within each centre–periphery relation, and between the economic, political, social and cultural substrata. In addition, the integration of exchange theory into his theoretical scheme provides a means of integrating the emergence of macrosocial institutional structures from microsocial interaction. The exchange theory developed by Peter Blau in *Exchange and Power in Social Life* (1964) does not attempt to reduce the level of collective social institutions to that of small group interaction. Instead, it attempts to address the role of values and norms in the mediation of social transactions beyond the immediate contacts between individual actors and groups. This was a significant alteration of the behaviourist attempts to develop causal explanations around the principle of operant conditioning. In this way, Blau offered a bridge between the acts of exchange (and associated entitlements, obligations and rewards) and the individual and collective levels (Blau 1964: 253–64).[4] Blau's typology of exchange relations was founded upon the cross-classification of modes of exchange (as reciprocal or unilateral) and objects of exchange (intrinsic or extrinsic), as represented in Tables 5.2 and 5.3.

Table 5.2 Blau's constitution of the social 1

	Reciprocal	*Unilateral*
Intrinsic	Mutual attraction	One-sided attraction
Extrinsic	Exchange relations	Power relations

Source: Adapted from Jessop 1972: 34.

Jessop is particularly concerned to identify the emergent properties or mediation mechanisms through which personal interactions are translated into shared values and institutional structures. He specifically identifies deference as the missing link in Blau's framework.

It is the unresolved problems associated with understanding deference that Jessop attempts to address in his study of political culturology, elaborated later in this section (Jessop 1971; 1974). In effect, his empirical research on deferential voting patterns in Britain attempts to flesh out the operation of unilateral modes of exchange in relation to intrinsic objects of exchange at a macrosocial level (status is defined as only meaningful through deference). In common with both Dahl's account of polyarchic civility and Hayek's account of catallaxy, Jessop's culturological analysis draws upon Wagner's (1963) phenomenologically-informed interpretation of Blau's account of 'emergent properties', to identify the relations between the formal rules and the informal rules of conduct and tacit knowledge governing both personal and institutional life. As Jessop demonstrates:

> Shared values facilitate the extension of interaction beyond the limits of particular face-to-face groups both in time and space. The complex patterns of social interaction mediated by common values become

Table 5.3 Blau's constitution of the social 2

	Reciprocal	*Unilateral*
Intrinsic	Shared values and integrative solidarity	?
Extrinsic	Economic institutions	Political institutions

Source: Adapted from Jessop 1972: 34–5.

institutionalized and are thus perpetuated from generation to generation. Successful institutionalization depends on three conditions. Firstly, the organizational principles and procedures must be formalised and embodied in offices and structures rather than specific persons. Secondly, the social values that legitimate these institutions must be transmitted in the socialization process. And, thirdly, the dominant groups in the community must be strongly identified with these values and support them. Once institutionalized these values and organizations will constitute external constraints.

(Jessop 1972: 36–7)

Within such a social order, latent counter-institutional principles are also embodied within the cultural traditions which solidify the social order. This facilitates legitimate dissent in a situation where the actual social order is very much at odds with the ideals of the social order.

The special type of exchange on which Jessop specifically focuses is 'exploitation', which he defined as an 'imbalance of exchange between substrata to the detriment of one or other substratum or between centre and periphery to the detriment of the periphery' (Jessop 1969: 419; 1972: 70–5). The exchange relationships with which Jessop is concerned are those which exist between substrata, and those which pertain to the centre–periphery relations. In practice, the exchange relations (of secondary and tertiary resources) between the substrata are exchanges between economic, political, social and cultural centres. This allows him to consider the position of the peripheral as marginalized in any of the four relations so defined. The sources of the contradictions in the social order are inscribed in the operation of centre–periphery relations in relation to the four means, as Jessop states:

> The maximum possible reward for the periphery is clearly the total production in the relevant substratum over a given period. The minimum possible reward is the 'subsistence level' requirements of the periphery necessary to sustain its labour, obedience, deference, and commitment. For the social and cultural substrata, 'subsistence level' will refer to the minimal amounts of social approval and integrity necessary to maintain the morale of the periphery. Exploitation is total when the contributions of the periphery go unrewarded – when the labourer is starved, the obedient punished, the deferential despised, the committed deceived. Exploitation decreases to the extent that these rewards go beyond the minimum.

(Jessop 1969: 420)

Jessop raises the problem of identifying general relations and the particular forms of these relations when combined in historically-specific social situations. His close attention to the conceptualization of 'contradiction', which was to achieve a centrality when he reassessed the concept in the neo-Marxist framework in the late 1970s and early 1980s, played a key role in his development of a typology of social orders. He argued that the constitution of a stable social order required both the existence of consensus and some degree of institutional integration although the precise form of these preconditions, and thus the emergence of conflict, were governed by the complexities of the society in question.[5]

The idealist foundations of Jessop's early work can be seen in the role played by models of power. He rejects the stance that only one model is appropriate for all circumstances, and presents the case for selecting models according to variable and changing empirical conditions. He problematizes the tendency to describe power in zero-sum or variable-sum terms as too simplistic: the former is associated with both pluralism and Marxism, and the latter with functionalism. He describes zero-sum models as redistribution models, for they assume that the stock of available utilities is distributed, and therefore the gains of some would have to be offset by the losses of others. Alternatively, he considers constant-sum models (where participation can leave participants better or worse off). In the constant-sum situation, the stock of utilities is not fully distributed. This represents the maximum potential distribution of a given set of resources at a 'given level of economic, political, social and cultural technology' (Jessop 1969: 424). While the first offers redistribution, the second provides simple distribution. Once it is accepted that participants can cooperate and/or conflict in these arrangements, and that the stock of resources can either expand or contract, then we reach the mixed-sum model.

Willer's account of symbolic models in *Scientific Sociology* (1967) is explicitly adopted as the methodological framework for Jessop's early accounts of the social order and social change (Jessop 1969: 1972). A *symbolic model* operates through the 'meaningful interconnection of concepts' within the model itself. For Willer, 'Models of this sort are symbolic in that: (1) their general rationale consists of allowing a set of connected concepts to symbolise a set of phenomena, and (2) their symbols or concepts are the source of their mechanism' (Willer 1967: 52). This is contrasted to analogue models and iconic models. *Analogue models* are based upon the assumption that it is feasible and effective to transfer an explanatory mechanism from one situation to another, and the concepts are connected to the mechanism through the replacement of old concepts with new ones appropriate to the new application, such as with the organic analogy (ibid.: 29–37). *Iconic models* attempt to translate the phenomena of experience into theoretical concepts, and are associated with Weber's and Durkheim's use of ideal types to accentuate an aspect of empirical reality (ibid.: 37–52). Both the iconic and analogue models, Willer argues, are inadequate in the face of social complexity. In the iconic model, the theories lose contact with the phenomena represented because of the high levels of abstraction necessary to represent social objects. Hence, the uses of such a model are limited:

> Conceptual schemes centering around the ideas of institutions, roles, social action, meaning, symbolic interaction, statuses, the interrelations of class, status, and power, and norms, values, sanctions, attitudes, and

mores are all characterized by an iconic rationale of representation of phenomena. . . . What can 'role theory' say about the father role of a Buchenwald camp guard? Is he nasty to his children or does he 'choose' a 'Dad role'? Perhaps the question about a single individual is unfair. What, then, can role theory predict about the typical father role of Buchenwald guards? It can predict nothing because it has no mechanism. This is the difference between a conceptual scheme and a model.
(Willer 1967: 39)

Such conceptual schemes are not unattractive, however, for it is always possible to explain already established results in this way as having an 'inherent *post facto* isomorphism' (Willer 1967: 40). In symbolic model construction, the initial starting point is usually drawn from existing social theory, which ensures that this is the most formal model of the three. As Willer states, 'The starting point is not as important as the consistency of meaning within the total conceptualization when it is completed. This consistency of meaning refers to both the definitions themselves and to the connections between them' (ibid.: 53).

The examples drawn from sociology by Willer include the sections of Weber's work on the concepts of domination, organization, power, legitimacy and authority, which facilitated his iconic models of organizations. Significantly for the concept of 'interest' in Jessop's early work, Willer cites Ralf Dahrendorf's *Class and Class Conflict in Industrial Society* (1959). Fusing Marx's class analysis with Weber's definition of domination between organized groups enables Dahrendorf to identify the conflicting interests of different groups as located within the 'structure of domination' (prior to the understanding of the participants). This treatment of models and Willer's discussion of Dahrendorf's account of manifest interests (consciously articulated orientations of behaviour) and latent interests (orientations of behaviour inherent in the social positions held within any imperatively co-ordinated group) influenced Jessop's approach at this stage in his writings. (See Figure 5.1.)

In Willer's account, an interest (or quasi-) group is defined in terms of the organized aggregation of the manifest (or latent) interests of members of the group (Dahrendorf 1959: 237). For Willer, the mechanism involved is not dependent upon an analogue or the exaggeration of an aspect of empirical

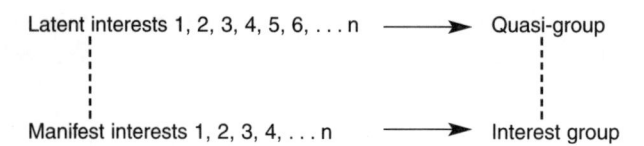

```
Latent interests 1, 2, 3, 4, 5, 6, . . . n   ⟶   Quasi-group
           ┊                                         ┊
           ┊                                         ┊
Manifest interests 1, 2, 3, 4, . . . n       ⟶   Interest group
```

Figure 5.1 Willer's representation of Dahrendorf's conception of interests
Source: Willer 1967: 55.

reality, but merely exists by virtue of its place within the system of relations so defined.[6] The fusion of the concerns of consensus and conflict theory is also apparent in Jessop's account of the role of the material and cultural determination of interests. Drawing upon his reconceptualization of the fourfold Parsonian division of spheres of the social system, he distinguishes political interests (the control of physical coercion), social interests (the exercise of persuasion) and cultural interests (control over commitments) from economic interests (control over the availability of inducements) (Jessop 1972: 49–52).

Jessop's account of the social order and the possibilities of social change is constructed around two forms of structural differentiation: the contradiction characterizing exchange between centre and periphery, and also that between the (economic, political, social and cultural) substrata of society. The forms of alienation identified earlier (see Table 5.1) are portrayed as aspects of the centre–periphery relation. In a situation where the periphery is in a position of objective powerlessness, alienation can only be resolved through the 'incorporation' of the periphery into the centre. In this way, the centre–periphery relations are transformed from relations of alienation into ones involving reciprocity and benefaction. It is unclear, at this stage, whether Jessop is referring to the amelioration of states of affairs or to the more substantive goal of socio-economic emancipation which clearly drives his later work. The approach adopted in Jessop's early writings should inform our interpretation of his subsequent intellectual evolution; however, one crucial shift did take place. At this point, he was still explicitly engaged in an attempt to construct a grand theory of social life, a task which he came to recognize as not only fruitless but also an inhibitor of conceptual innovation. The useful elements in this work, which were to be sustained in combination with transformed epistemological and ontological assumptions, stem from the 'interpretative, imaginative application of conceptual schemes and assumptions, rather than through an undirected examination of the data' (Jessop 1972: 5).

This theoretical framework was developed to facilitate the examination of Jessop's empirical research into the nature of deference and civility in theories of political socialization and culture. *Traditionalism, Conservatism and British Political Culture* (1974) represents the operationalization of Jessop's idealist (specifically neo-Kantian) epistemological framework in the specific field of psephological research. This empirical research also represents an attempt to fill the theoretical gap in Blau's account of the social order. Jessop begins to formulate his response to the problems of empiricist accounts of the causes of 'deviant class voting'. This helps him to clarify his objections to the tendency in voting behaviour studies to rely upon the Humean concept of causality (that is, regularity determinism). He suggests that empirical and theoretical work in this field has been dominated by two inadequate explanations: the account of political stability in the UK in terms of the 'civic values of submission to authority' (compounded by infrequent electoral participation) and the explanations of working class conservative voting in terms of deference and the pragmatic interpretations of self-interest by voters. He is particularly concerned to demarcate the confused realms of political structure and political culture. By structure, he refers to the legal and institutional structure, as well as patterned interaction relationships which characterize the exchange relations of political life. Culture in this field refers to the orientations to political action situations which had been used to subsume all explanations of political behaviour, and which have tended to re-describe rather than explain voting behaviour.

Rather than assuming that the constant conjunction of events is necessary and sufficient for establishing a causal law, Jessop introduces a key feature of his later work, the conceptualization of causality as 'contingent necessity'. However, the theoretical framework in which it is placed remains a neo-Kantian one. Hence, the ontology upon which this epistemology is predicated remains empirical realist, even though it is able to accommodate the ambiguity and uncertainty evident in the complexity of orientations and actions in actual political cultures. In identifying the difference between orientations and actions, he is able to develop an account of how social deference need not be associated with conservative voting (even though in some circumstances they can be associated). He recognizes that a constant conjunction of events is necessary but not sufficient for establishing a causal law, or in this case a causal explanation, of voting behaviour. For Jessop, existing deference explanations fit those studies which assume that individual orientations and political behaviour are constantly conjoined, and that such an empirical regularity is (both necessary and) sufficient for establishing a causal explanation (Jessop 1974: 15–20).

Studies of civility, however, raise further complications, for they examine the causal relationship between social acquiescence and the stability of the political system, shifting the focus away from individuals towards the relations between the different attitudes of individuals within a social system (as explored in Almond and Verba 1963). These approaches treat politics in Western industrial societies as an institutionalized version of class conflict within a democratic political system. For Almond and Verba, stable democratic polities rested upon a balance of, one, emotional and instrumental orientations towards political activity, two, consensual and conflictual orientations, and three, the diffusion of trust. Such approaches attempted to establish the effects of political structure upon attitudes and orientations, but neglected the distribution of power. By contrast, Nordlinger had suggested that these features could be accommodated within a dualistic approach of 'acquiescence rooted in trust' within civil society. Jessop argues that it is feasible to examine the relationship between actions and orientations as a two-way causal process, rather than to opt for one or another approach. Thus it becomes possible to construct a 'meaningful conceptual framework' to specify which orientations fit which actions for which people. Such a framework would overcome the separation of analytic and synthetic statements characteristic of empiricist research. It would also reintegrate the dynamic role of interaction in constituting political values and orientations within the context of the power relations between centre and periphery (Jessop 1974: 20–1). In respect to hegemonic societies, Jessop suggests that we should remain concerned with 'the complexities, tensions, and inconsistencies of the civic culture' (ibid.: 50) as part of an adequate theory of institutional structure and power distributions. Thus, he has serious doubts about the efficacy of both deference and civility explanations in providing adequate accounts of working-class (or middle-class) conservative voting patterns.

In this respect, Jessop is concerned with the formative role of the powerful groups upon the central values of the political system, and the generation of a framework within which the contestation between value systems does not enable contending interests to undermine the basis of the social order. This approach is concerned to illustrate the role of power within value systems within unequal social orders. In this way, it distinguishes between the bearers of the dominant or central value systems, deferential or aspirational value systems (reinterpreting the attachment to the central values) and the subordinate or peripheral value system (accommodating or acquiescing to central values). He also adds the possibility of oppositional contra-cultural value systems, and those localized parochial subcultures which have survived the tendencies towards greater integration within more complex societies. For Jessop, empirical research should also accommodate the possibility of inconsistencies and ambiguities which follow from the combination of elements for all four forms of non-central values in actual political cultures. These 'value system' categories are thus ideal-type concepts against which it is possible to compare and contrast empirical evidence.[7]

Utilizing a priori reasoning, Jessop selected specific variables from the data sets to construct causal models with the seven, and then eleven, variables cited as responsible for Conservative voting in the 1966 and 1970 elections. The correlations between variables (constant conjunctions of events) within this framework, are taken as indicative of the patterns which can be established. However, they are never sufficient in themselves to establish a causal law. Jessop adopts the position of 'intelligibility determinism' in the light of the complexity of the concrete empirical world. In conclusion, he identifies attitudes towards egalitarianism and traditionalism as effective indicators of conservative voting. However, these attitudes operate independently of each other, as well as of the structural influences identified (such as class background and union membership, although these also had their own independent effects). In the second sample, the strength of the relationships identified was greater in the middle-class responses than in the working-class responses. Jessop concluded that rather than class or local constituency being the most significant variables, as identified in empiricist studies of deference, it was more important to identify the location of individuals in relation to the periphery or the centre; in conjunction with their exposure to, or insulation from, the central value system.

These theoretical concepts and empirical evidence on the nature and content of political culture are also used by Jessop to identify the 'emergent properties of cultural systems'. These involve the extent of institutional integration of economic, political, social and cultural values, and the extent of consensus on the values of a particular social order (Jessop 1974: 21–6). This complexification of theoretical concepts enables Jessop to construct types of deference in political culture in an innovative way:

- *Political deference*, towards government regardless of the party or social composition.
- *Ascriptive socio-political deference*, towards a 'socially ascribed elite as uniquely qualified for political office'.
- *Ascriptive social deference*, towards those born into high status and wealthy families without political implications.
- *Socio-cultural deference*, towards a 'traditional social and cultural order'.

For Jessop, the latter two inclusive accounts of deference only have relevance in so far as some mechanism exists whereby non-political commitments can be translated into political ones. An example of this is the role of the Conservative Party in the 1950s and 1960s as the embodiment of the upper classes and traditional moral values. In addition other motivations, such as opposition towards trade unionism and even business, can be combined with such voting patterns (Jessop 1971 1–2; 1974: 30–48). For Jessop, empirical demonstrations of the transformations of a class-in-itself into a class-for-itself are the effect of the operation of relations of power, exchange and institutionalization, rather than denoting the truth or falsehood of class theory. In addition, he raises questions about the existence of unitary class interests by suggesting that they can be specified within concrete conditions, in contrast to the assumption that they are theoretically given. He concludes that the answers to such questions about the determinants of voting can only be identified in relation to:

> Historical party loyalties, microsocial pressures, the past performance of political parties, the 'nature of the times', general life-style, commitments to dominant or counter-cultural values, these and other factors can be expected to influence the choice. It goes without saying that these are the circumstances in Britain.
>
> (Jessop 1974: 45)

Thus, deference and civility are identified as relevant factors, as is class, in a complex overdetermined arrangement of structures and actions. This can be understood and explained within the context of exchange relations between centre and periphery, and between the substrata of an advanced class-hierarchical society constituted through both dominant and counter-cultural values and the distribution of power. Studies of civic orientations, he suggests, have neglected the role of populism and opposition values in peripheral groups, as well as the institutional integration of the central value system.[8]

Existing theories of stability based upon mass society theory, whereby activists and associations mediate between political decisions and citizens fostering acquiescence (Kornhauser 1959), or personality type theory, where key personality traits are associated with contributions towards (in-)stability (Greenstein 1969), are all seen as partial accounts of political culture. In Jessop's theoretical framework, it is possible to address the contingency of political relationships as well as to put existing theories of civility, hegemony and political culture to the empirical test. Jessop finds significant evidence to corroborate the hegemonic theory of political stability, that exposure to middle-class values has a disproportionate impact upon the level of commitment towards civility, regardless of structural location or personality types. Thus, a close investigation of insulation from, and exposure to, the central value system, acts as a key indicator of voting behaviour (alongside a range of other causal factors). Hegemonic theory, therefore, acts as a culturally non-specific nomothetic framework for the study of political culture (Jessop 1974: 227–69).

Jessop's work to the present day also involves the task of synthesizing existing theoretical frameworks and perspectives. In his early work, Jessop's grand theorizing (drawing upon Lenski 1966) led him to attempt conceptual elaboration:

> through combination, redefinition, conceptual connection and assumption . . . the transformation of categorical and polar concepts into variables . . . the decomposition of compound concepts into their constituent elements . . . establishing equivalencies between apparently different concepts . . . [and] contingent or variant relations between different concepts . . . the modification of assumptions and the specification of their respective spheres of influence.
>
> (Jessop 1972: 5)

This constant process of conceptual rejuvenation, developed during the early 1970s, continued with his explicit embrace of one of the most essentialist traditions of political economy, Marxism. This took place in the context of his rejection of the essentialism and reductionism associated with grand theorizing. In addition, and partly in response to this shift of focus, Jessop sought to establish an approach which could establish determinate explanations of social processes without falling into the trap of determinism. The focus on the relationships between the state and the economy, and between democracy and capitalism, became central to his concern, and the synthesis of sociological theories, which characterized his early work, receded into the background until it resurfaced in the mid-1980s.

Towards a theory of the capitalist state I: economy and polity

At some point in the middle of the 1970s, Jessop's participation in the Conference of Socialist Economists, particularly the state theory study group at the University of Essex (following his appointment to the Department of Government), led to a reorientation of his theoretical interests towards neo-Marxist political economy. Some of the concerns and themes which mark this reorientation were already present in his early work, although these were at times barely visible within the synthetic grand theory he had initiated. The previous clarity with which he defines the key elements of Marxist social theory and the relationship between forces and relations of production (already addressed in his account of centre–periphery relations) now occupied centre stage. Between the mid-1970s and mid-1980s, he directed his attention primarily towards the theoretical and concrete relationships between the economy and the state. In addition, the adoption of a Marxist mode of theory construction led to a reassessment and clarification of his own epistemological and ontological position. With the publication of *The Capitalist State* (1982), Jessop clearly identifies the realist epistemological and ontological assumptions of Roy Bhaskar (1978, 1979) as the most appropriate framework for a Marxist theory of the state. However, as early as 1975, the first edition of *Social Theory as Science*, by Russell Keat and John Urry (Keat and Urry 1982), (another CSE participant) raised the use of realist assumptions within Marx's account of the capitalist economy which were to have significant impact on Jessop's approach to knowledge construction.

The period of convulsion and crisis in Marxist theory in the mid-1970s is something of a watershed. Unlike Jessop, many of the participants of these debates have resolved to reject the project of socio-economic emancipation and wholesale transformation of capitalism, for the relative tranquillity of social reformist or post-Marxist cultural politics (notably Paul Hirst, Stuart Hall and Ernesto Laclau). While these critics have identified the problems of essentialism and reductionism as the reason for their disillusion with, and rejection of, the Marxist project, Jessop has turned these problems into the intellectual project of the rejuvenation of the Marxist approach by refashioning and reshaping its theoretical assumptions in order to take account of contemporary social transformations. The interrelated issues facing Marxism during this period include the following.

1   The questioning of class politics as an explanatory device and as the motor of social change, in the face of the emergence of new social

movements such as feminism, environmental and peace movements, ethnicity and other cultural identity movements.
2   The collapse of grand theorizing, essentialism and reductionism in the academy, and the recognition of the need to theorize contingency in relation to necessity, to resolve the problems of remaining committed to Marxist goals without the usual guarantees (that ideology was not simply true or false, that the state was not a simple instrument, and that revolution and socialist transformation was not inevitable).
3   The discussions within Marxism around the issue of relative autonomy, raising the need for a reassessment of the terms of reference of Marxist discussion of the state. This was in part the legacy of the rejection of the economic reductionism of Soviet Marxism by Western Marxists, and in part the consequence of increased dissatisfaction with the structuralist framework developed by Althusser in explaining the political, ideological and cultural dimensions of contemporary capitalist societies.
4   The practical problems associated with developing an effective political strategy which could effectively deliver the goals of the Marxist approach within the context of complex civil societies. Both this and the third issue had come to a head with the emergence of the Eurocommunist approach to social transformation through peaceful institutional means, and the appropriation of Gramsci as an alternative theoretical foundation to Lenin.
5   The unravelling and the later collapse of the balance between production and consumption which had maintained capitalist growth through the 1950s and the 1960s in the West (a transition later theorized as the transition from Fordism to post-Fordism), and the early phases in the restructuring of capital in the UK, which were to culminate in the Thatcher period.
6   The need to account for the dramatic shift in the relationship between economy, polity and ideology in Western capitalist societies since the 1960s (notably the collapse of the social-democratic consensus). Initially, this can be seen in the fiscal crisis of the state and the legitimation crises of capitalism. These were followed by the restructuring of capitalist economies and their corresponding state forms in the 1980s.

Jessop characteristically leaves no stones unturned in his investigation of Marxist approaches to the state. His starting point is the identification of the fragmentary and unsystematic comments and analysis of politics and the state in Marx's unfinished intellectual project to provide an explanatory account of capitalist society. In the 1960s and 1970s, Marxist scholarship was uniquely positioned to take account of the whole of Marx's political writings and personal correspondence, much of which had been published from the 1930s to the 1960s. In revisiting the reference points of classical Marxism (from Marx through to Gramsci), Jessop identifies six conceptions (or metaphors) of the state in Marxist thinking:

The State as parasitic The state is portrayed in Marx's early writings on Hegel as standing above the economy and as opposed to the common interest.

The State as epiphenomenal The state, or the operation of state power, mirror (or act as the surface reflections of) the property relations and class struggles within the economic infrastructure. (This is discussed in the 1859 Preface.) Jessop suggests this neglects the specificity of the political.

The State as the factor of cohesion The state as a regulator of the class struggle through repression or concession. For Jessop, this neglects the specification of the nature of the state and the mechanisms through which cohesion, and thus capitalist reproduction, are achieved. This runs through the classics from Marx and Gramsci to Nicos Poulantzas in the 1970s.

The State as an instrument The state as a neutral instrument of class rule, capitalist or proletarian. This approach is clearly demonstrated in Soviet Marxism–Leninism, but it runs into a number of difficulties. Jessop points to examples of the state being run by one class on behalf of another, state autonomy during periods of equilibrium in the class struggle (such as Bonapartism and Bismarckianism), dual power situations in revolutions, and the periods of transition between modes of production.

The State as a set of institutions The state as a public power corresponding to a particular moment in the development of the division of labour, as a distinct type of government monopolized by the officials specializing in administrative duties and the maintenance of order. This is apparent in both Engels (1884) and Lenin (1917).

The State as a system of political domination The state as political domination with a specific effect in the class struggle links the institutional structure of the state to actual historical conjunctures within the development of capitalism (in Marx's account of the Paris Commune). For Jessop, this focuses our attention on the ways in which the forms of political representation and political intervention by the state are (in-)adequate for securing the balance of social forces conducive for the long-term interests of the dominant class (fraction).

Jessop considers the characterization of the state as a pernicious manipulator of the masses for the benefit of the dominant class (in the *state as parasite* and the *state as instrument*) to be much too crude and inadequate to serve as an effective explanatory principle. In addition, the treatments of the state as empty or as a black box (in the *state as epiphenomenal* and the *state as a factor of cohesion*) neither identify the internal structure of the state nor specify the conditions in which cohesion is possible (or its limits). For Jessop, the treatment of the state as if it is operating in necessary correspondence with the economy (in crude versions of the base–superstructure relationship) ignores the contingency of the class struggle and the empirical variation of the development of the forces and relations of production. He opts finally to endorse the state as a set of institutions, in conjunction with the state as a system of political domination. This takes the form of the state and the role of state intervention seriously, but relates the institutional structure directly to the class struggle in historically and socially specific conjunctures. In particular, he argues that the function, effects and class nature cannot be established a priori, but only through the analysis of forms of representation and intervention in determinate conditions (Jessop 1977: 354–7; 1978a: 40–68; 1982: 1–31).

Jessop's concern at this stage is to think through the conception of relative autonomy, Althusser's problematic legacy to neo-Marxism. In attempting to resolve the question of why the Western state had not behaved in ways which economistic Marxism would have suggested, Althusser had distinguished between the operation of the state in abstract and concrete terms. In concrete historical conjunctures, the state could and did act against the perceived interests of capital; however, in relation to the reproduction of capitalism, the state was determined by the economic in the last instance. The explicit use of levels of abstraction which enabled Althusser to distinguish the determination of the economy, the shifting dominance of economy, polity and ideology, and the overdetermined operation of contradictions in concrete historical conjunctures, can also be seen in Jessop's analysis at this stage (Althusser 1977: 87–128; Althusser and Balibar 1970, *passim*; Althusser 1971: 127–86). However, the functionalist formulation in Althusser, which ensures that the 'lonely hour of the last instance' never comes (for the long term is just an endless sequence of short terms) poses significant problems for Jessop, just as the normative functionalism of Talcot Parsons was unsatisfactory within his early work. However, it is important to recognize that, for Jessop, Althusser provided a bridge to the Marxist approach which related closely to his earlier concerns with Parsonian functionalism.

Althusser's formulation of structural or metonymic causality places neo-Marxist accounts of social relations in a totalistic frame of meaning, where the relations involved can only be understood and explained by reference to the other relations in the system. In Althusser's account, the state in abstract terms is concerned with securing the preconditions of capitalist reproduction, while in concrete terms the state is engaged in policies and interventions which may harm the operation of individual capitals and impede the process of capital accumulation. Jessop uses the concept of contingent-necessity to begin to reformulate the problems involved. In particular, he reconsiders the levels of abstraction as involved in a relationship of articulation rather than mediation. In the method of articulation, the concrete can be seen as the non-necessary correspondence of relevant factors, whereas in the method of mediation, there is always a unified underlying explanatory cause of events and states of affairs (such as the class struggle or the interests of capital). This enables Jessop to break with the reductionist and essentialist tendencies of classical Marxism, which views the operation of the state as a manifestation of deeper economic processes and relations, and in the process to reformulate the base–superstructure metaphor within the neo-Marxist approach.

In 'Recent Theories of the Capitalist State' (1977) and at greater length in *The Capitalist State* (1982), Jessop redeploys the techniques of symbolic model construction, modified in this case by their insertion within the realist problematic of neo-Marxist thought. This enabled Jessop to transcend the issues which had led Marxist theorizing to become stagnant and circular, as well as to provide a more effective framework for empirical research. In the light of his reassessment of Marx's variations, Jessop examines a range of theories of the relationship between state and economy in order to achieve a theoretical synthesis which can ensure both 'theoretical and political progress' (Jessop 1977: 369). This involved identifying the aspects of existing state theory which were (in-)consistent with the conception of the state as a set of institutions and a system of political domination with specific effects on the class struggle. The state theories specifically under consideration were those developed in the unfocused debate between Ralph Miliband and Nicos Poulantzas, the neo-Ricardian position, theories of state monopoly capitalism (associated with the Soviet and French communist movements), theories of the form and function of the state derived from the capitalist economy (considering both capital-theoretical and class-theoretical variants) and neo-Gramscian attempts to provide a stronger foundation for the relationship between the economy, polity and ideological hegemony. Jessop engages with these positions to provide a non-essentialist account of the operation of the economy, polity and ideology in capitalism (at various levels of abstraction).

Jessop argues that the Miliband–Poulantzas debate is misconceived, and in effect sterile, because it misses the crucial points involved in the construction of an adequate state theory within the capitalist mode of production. Miliband (1969) is engaged in a critique of liberal-pluralist accounts of the polyarchic democracy, the state and civil society. For Miliband, this is empirically demonstrated through the common social composition of economic and political elites, and by developing the argument that class power is visible in its consequences (in terms of the unequal distribution of wealth and income). Poulantzas formulated a direct challenge to the tendencies towards reductionism and instrumentalism in the existing body of state theory. Poulantzas rejects the Miliband route as a concession to the 'genetic principle of the social actor', which falls back on 'bourgeois' epistemological and ontological assumptions and treats the state as a thing-in-itself in isolation from the economy (Miliband 1969, 1970; Poulantzas 1969; Laclau 1977: 51–79). Jessop endorsed the Poulantzian critique of the foundations of Miliband's work. Both Miliband and neo-Ricardian approaches focus on the distributive consequences of capitalist relations of production, and the role of the state in policy making and implementation. Class relations are translated into political struggles over the distribution of income (particularly over taxation and state spending on welfare and subsidies) in relation to social classes (Glyn and Sutcliffe 1972; Boddy and Crotty 1974; Gough 1975; 1979). For Jessop, this *exchangist* approach is not only instrumentalist and economically determinist, it also neglects both the importance of social relations involved in capitalist production and exploitation, and the explanation of the relationship between the class character and the internal structure of the state, and the rationale for state intervention. This points to the need to integrate existing evidence on the role of the state into the productive and exchange elements of the circuit of capital, in order to construct an adequate theory of the capitalist state (Fine and Harris 1979; Jessop 1977: 357–60; 1982: 13–16).

Jessop has by this stage become increasingly influenced by Poulantzas in his attempts to develop a non-instrumentalist and non-essentialist account of the state, although he manages to keep a critical distance from what he considers to be politicist tendencies in this work. To achieve this, he has to identify the useful elements of existing economic determinist approaches to the state. This leads Jessop to consider the *stamocap* (state monopoly capital) theories associated with Marxism-Leninism, and their treatment of the state as the 'fusion of the state and monopoly capital' in relation to the dominant fraction of the dominant class in the capitalist mode of production. In particular, Jessop identified a fundamental inconsistency between the treatment of the state as an epiphenomenon and the assumption that the state can be utilized as a means of effecting the transition from capitalism to socialism, creating a disjunction between the theory of the tendencies of capital accumulation and the role of the political struggle between classes. In concrete strategic terms, this had been used in the justification of building class alliances between the working class, the petty-bourgeoisie and small and medium capital, a feature of post-war European communist party strategy.

By Jessop's criteria, stamocap approaches neglect both the form of the state and the effects of state intervention in historically specific conjunctures. However, he does draw significant implications from the temporal dimension of this work on the periodization of capitalism. The stamocap periodization breaks capitalism into three stages:

- *Competitive capitalism*, a self-regulating period in which a *laissez-faire* or 'night-watchman' state corresponds to the operation of forces and relations of production, giving way to:
- The transition phase of *monopoly capitalism* (a product of the concentration and centralization of capital, characterized by falling profit rates and severe and periodic economic crises) which is resolved through:
- The emergence of *state monopoly capitalism*, in which the interventionist state stabilized the relations and forces of production in the post-war Western capitalist societies to ensure a stable phase of capital accumulation.

For Fine and Harris, this transition is closely bound up with the shifting balance between the expropriation of absolute and relative surplus value (Fine and Harris 1979: 112–45; Jessop 1977: 360–1; 1982: 32–77). While both Poulantzas and Jessop modify and complexify the periodization of capitalism, the identification of an underlying temporal sequence, and the broad relationships between state forms and the relations and forces of production, remained consistent features of Jessop's work until the mid-1980s. The main weakness of the stamocap approach is the methodological tendency to subsume particular cases under general explanations (often resulting in a crude confirmationist use of empirical evidence). Hence, it did not acknowledge the movement from the abstract to the concrete and the generation of rational (as opposed to chaotic) conceptions as characteristic features of Marx's approach to political economy (Marx 1857: 100–8).

In order to identify substantive concepts for the analysis of the complex articulation of the state form and capitalist relations, Jessop considered the debates over the form and function of the state in relation to the capitalist economy between the capital-logic or class-logic schools (based in West Berlin and Frankfurt respectively). These were a fruitful source. In particular, the *Staatsableitung* debate provides the first significant attempt specifically to address the complexities of the relationship between capital and state within the terms of Marx's method of abstraction. The capital-logic approach associated with Elmar Altvater (1973) and Blanke, Juergens and Kastendiek (1976) treated the state as a distinct political institutional structure, although it remained in correspondence to the needs of capital-in-general, as the *ideal collective capitalist*.[9] This approach attempted to identify the emergence of the state as separate from the institutions of civil society, in response to the emergence of a form of commodity production which no longer needed the involvement of extra-economic coercion in order to realize and expropriate surplus value (as in the case of pre-capitalist modes of production). The role of the state is therefore to facilitate capitalist expropriation through the development of a legal framework in which property rights and duties are clearly defined, and a monetary system in which the trust necessary for private exchange and rational calculation is fostered (based on reasonable expectations of the likely consequences of actions). The identification of trust as a significant aspect of the creation of legal and economic subjects becomes a major feature of Jessop's later writings, drawing upon the systems theory of social differentiation and autopoiesis.

A particular focus of the capital logic approach is the identification of Marx's 'Law of the tendency of the rate of profit to fall' and its 'Counteracting tendencies' in Volume III of *Capital*, as a significant explanation of state intervention in order to mobilize the counteracting tendencies which increase the rates of absolute and/or relative surplus value in order to counter a decline in profitability. State intervention can take the form of maintaining demand or, more importantly for explaining the development of capitalism, the restructuring of capitalist productive relations and the modification of the balance of class forces. For Jessop, this represented a significant advance, although he also highlighted its neglect of the concrete circumstances in which the needs of capital are satisfied, and the complex relations of mediation within the legal and monetary systems through which states intervene, often without interfering with the private decisions of particular capitals (Jessop 1977: 361–4; 1982: 78–101).

The operation of the law of the tendency of the rate of profit to fall, and its ultimate primacy over the counteracting tendencies (which, it is argued, have insurmountable limits), demand the construction of a sophisticated account of levels of abstraction, to accommodate the identification of causal laws as tendencies and powers rather than as empirical regularities (whether in terms of regularity or of intelligibility determinism). In response, Jessop explicitly adopts the realist position characterized in Chapter Two as 'ubiquity determinism', which asserts that a constant conjunction of events is neither necessary nor sufficient for establishing a causal law. Rather than treating causal laws as manifested in empirical regularities, in this neo-Marxist approach they are portrayed as normic abstract tendencies which, by definition, can only be observed in conjunction with other causal mechanisms. In this context, the objects in question are constituted by internally necessary relations which have definite properties but whose operationalization is contingently dependent on their combination with other such social relations in concrete historical conjunctures. In this case, the law of the tendency of the rate of profit to fall exists, by definition, at a more abstract level of analysis than the law of counter-acting tendencies. Nevertheless, the concrete is always the contingent result of multiple determinations rather than the direct expression of abstract tendencies. Hence there are no guarantees of the primacy of specific tendencies. It is the construction of a theoretical response to these issues that concerns Jessop in *The Capitalist State* (1982).

The class-theoretical approach provides the missing elements in the account of state and capital within the capital-logic approach. The class-theoretical approach provides an 'internal critique' of the neglect of the antagonistic relation between capital and waged labour in the capital-logic account of relations between competing capitals. In this case the institutional structure of the state is recognized but it is understood only in terms of how it functions in historically specific class struggles (Hirsch 1978; Holloway and Picciotto 1978). This account provides Jessop with a better sense of the dynamic processes shaping the development of capitalism and the role of the state in the restructuring of capital and class relations during periods of transition, a theme he was to unpack in his concrete research on British social formation and on the relationship between democracy, the nation-state and capitalism (Jessop 1978b; 1979; 1980a; 1980b; 1983d; 1989b). In particular, this approach raises the prospect of theorizing contemporary transformations in the relationship between the state and the economy, just as the social-democratic consensus began to crumble in Jessop's own conjuncture, (leading to the crisis phase of post-war capitalist development in Britain, which came to a head in the 1970s). The class-theoretical approach explains crises as the failure of capital to maintain its exploitative relations with labour in a way which permits the continuation of capital accumulation at a level sufficient to ensure the reproduction of capitalism. Accumulation is portrayed as the disorganized consequence of the capacity of capital, in conjunction with the role of the state, to maintain exploitative relations between classes. State intervention is seen as reactive rather than proactive, and economic crises act as the most important 'steering mechanisms' for state policy. No necessary correspondence between the needs of capital (the infrastructure) and state intervention (as an aspect of the superstructure) is assumed. Crises are portrayed as the complex outcome of contradictions, as well as having differential effects on the classes involved. Yet, for Jessop, by emphasizing the role of the class struggle in relation to historically-specific conjunctures the class-theoretical approach neglects the constraints imposed by the general laws of capitalist production, and it lacks the key concepts for historical analysis because it adopts an over-restricted definition of class struggle (Jessop 1977: 364–7; 1982: 101–41). These differences were to resurface in Jessop's debates with key members of the Conference of Socialist Economists in the pages of *Capital and Class* in the mid-1980s (Bonefeld and Holloway 1991; Clarke 1991; Jessop 1988a; 1991a). The most important implication of his synthetic reassessment of the capital-logic and class-theoretical variants of the form-derivation discussions is the recognition that the form of the state problematizes the functioning of the state for capital accumulation. This entails a drift away from highly abstract functionalist accounts of the state and the social order, towards an attempt to integrate these approaches with accounts of historically-specific conjunctures.

A particular important contribution to Jessop's framework on this point (mediated through the work of Hirsch and Poulantzas) came from the state theory of Claus Offe. Although Jessop was critical of Offe's neglect of the productive dimension of the economy, Offe's account of the principle of structural selectivity in the relationship between the state and the organization of capitalist production provided a stimulus in Jessop's characterization of the relationship between the structural and strategic dimensions of the state. Offe focused on the structural features of the state in capitalism, and the exclusion of the state from direct involvement in the organization of the production of capital. Hence, the state can have an impact on capital accumulation only in an indirect way. Three features are of note:

- The institutional separation of state and economy, so that the state's performance is dependent upon taxation revenues.
- Capitalism is not self-regulating nor is it self-sufficient. This provides the state with a mandate for intervention in the conditions for accumulation without violating its private character.
- In this position of exclusion and dependence, the state has to equate the needs of capital-in-general with the national interest in order to secure active popular consent for policy measures.

Offe's account of the relation between state and capital widens the scope of analysis by focusing on the political conditions of existence of the commodity form and its relationship to non-commodity forms. Crucially, Offe identifies the contradictions and dilemmas between the imperatives of capital accumulation, and bourgeois legitimation in relation to state interventions in response to the problems of factor supply and market failure. He also explores these contradictions within the organization of the welfare state, through the participation of representatives of capital and labour. In such a position, the state acts as a sorting, sifting and filtering mechanism which selects and excludes issues for consideration. In this way, the capitalist state maintains its putative neutrality in relation to its citizens yet ensures, more or less successfully, the continuation of capital accumulation. For Jessop, Offe's account of this aspect of the state provided a crucial link in accounting for the material concessions to working-class demands through the decommodification of some of the preconditions of capital accumulation (within the sphere of social policy) and the emerging crises of the state, without treating the state as a simple instrument.[10] Offe concludes that the state is only capitalist to the extent to which it contributes towards capital accumulation and the reproduction of capitalism (Jessop 1977: 366; 1982: 106–12; Keane 1984; Offe 1984: 119–46 and *passim*).

Towards a theory of the capitalist state II: ideology and polity

In order to develop an adequate analysis of the concrete conjunctures, Jessop turns to the most original development in Marxism in the 1960s and 1970s, the uses of the *Prison Notebooks* of Antonio Gramsci (1971). This enabled Jessop to develop the analysis of ideological hegemony in complex civil societies within western European social formations. Gramsci's writings became widely available in the late 1960s and early 1970s, at the same time as the Western European communist parties were attempting to develop an alternative Marxist approach to the Leninist model of social transformation, as their response to the treatment of the Eastern bloc by the Soviet state (a process actually initiated as early as 1958, by Italian communist Togliatti). The neo-Gramscian approach to politics and ideology focused on the role played by the state in the unification of the dominant class (fraction) and allied classes, fractions, categories and social forces. In this account, the state secured the organization of ideological domination within a power bloc, at the same as disaggregrating and mobilizing the consent of the dominated classes, fractions, categories and social forces. Unlike other neo-Marxist theorists:

> Gramsci nowhere suggests that state power in a capitalist society is necessarily bourgeois in character nor that there is any guarantee that bourgeois domination can always be reproduced through an appropriate mixture of coercion and consent. Indeed, far from adopting such essentialist ideas, Gramsci emphasises the obstacles in the path of the bourgeois *integral state*

(in which force is combined with hegemony) and stresses the fragility of the *unstable equilibria of compromise* on which such hegemony is premised.

(Jessop 1982: 150)

Therefore Gramsci's 'decisive contribution' to the analysis of state power in capitalist social formations is the questioning of both the treatment of the state in instrumental terms, and the conceptualization of classes as automatically unified through the common position of their members to the relations of production (Jessop 1982: 142–53).

Gramsci's account of hegemony, as political, intellectual and moral leadership, is a radical break with the Marxist tradition's economistic and reductionist accounts of ideology as false consciousness. The success of a hegemonic project is dependent upon the mobilized support of the dominated classes and fractions (such as sections of the working class), social categories (such as intellectuals, the military and state officials) and significant social forces which can affect the outcome of the class struggle, formed around identity politics and/or single issues (ethnic-minority movements, feminist movements, environmental and peace movements, or religious or moral movements). The articulation of a popular-democratic hegemonic project generates the active consent of the people through the incorporation of interests and aspirations within a common world view (Gramsci 1971, *passim*; Laclau 1977: 94–111). For Jessop, drawing on Poulantzas, as well as on concrete illustrations from his earlier work on the constitution of the social order, a power bloc (such as the British 'establishment') involves a 'fairly stable alliance of dominant classes or class fractions, whose unity depends on a modicum of mutual self sacrifice of immediate interests and on their commitment to a common world outlook' (Jessop 1977: 367).

For advocates of neo-Gramscian Marxism, such as Stuart Hall, the concept of hegemony, understood as the struggle for the hearts and minds of the popular masses (Hall 1980), serving as a precondition for social transformation (as a long-drawn-out war of position prior to the war of manoeuvre), opened up a vista of opportunity. In particular it helped Marxists to piece together the dramatic shifts in the economy, polity and ideology in Western capitalism, as the state engaged in redefining itself alongside other spheres. These transformations will be elaborated in the following section, which examines the theoretical responses within neo-Marxism to the collapse of the social democratic consensus and of corporatist interventionist state strategies, and the debates between Jessop and Hall on the character of Thatcherism. These debates focus on the relationship of the state to the restructuring of the relationship between production and consumption in late-twentieth-century capitalism.

Within the neo-Gramscian approach, the work of Nicos Poulantzas adds a crucial dimension to the development of Jessop's account of political strategy and the place of the state in relation to the economy and ideology within capitalism. Poulantzas is perhaps the most significant influence on Jessop's intellectual trajectory for two reasons. First, Poulantzas provides a means of reformulating state theory which can avoid the theoretical cul-de-sac of the conceptual couplet of relative autonomy. Second, Jessop's intellectual biography of, and critical commentaries upon, Poulantzas' intellectual development led him to reassess the relationship between structures and strategies in neo-Marxist accounts, and to question the attachment of neo-Marxism to the totalistic and hermetically-sealed conception of social formation (Jessop 1985a). By the mid-1980s, Jessop acknowledged this shift by defining his own position as post-Poulantzian. However, this shift is mediated through his intellectual encounters with systems theory in the study of law, and his critical dialogues with the post-Marxist account of political discourse developed by Ernesto Laclau and Chantal Mouffe in *Hegemony and Socialist Strategy* (1985).

Poulantzas initially engaged in the task of fulfilling the Althusserian project to identify the gaps and missing links in Marx's theory of historical materialism. Althusser suggested that while Marx had contributed to a *general theory* of modes of production, a *particular theory* of the capitalist mode of production and a *regional theory* of the economy within capitalism, the works of Marx remained incomplete. Althusser pointed to unfinished areas of research raised by Marx in the final sections of *Capital* (Marx) and elsewhere. At the level of historical-materialist general theory, there remained the task of theorizing class-divided social formations, the state and politics, and ideology, and at the particular level, the elaboration of Marx's scattered commentaries on pre-capitalist modes of production and the transitions between them. At the regional level in the capitalist mode of production, there remained the tasks of elaborating a theory of the state and ideology. Althusser and Balibar, in *Reading Capital* (1970, originally published in 1968), had fleshed out a general theory of social formations and had attempted to clarify Marx's contributions to this grand theoretical project. In addition, Althusser had added some preliminary comments from January to April 1969 in 'Ideology and Ideological State Apparatuses' (Althusser 1971: 127–86). This short essay on ideological state apparatuses can be taken as the start of a regional theory of ideology within the capitalist mode of production. Poulantzas initially attempted to develop a regional theory of the state and politics in the capitalist mode of production, as well as to contribute to a general theory of the state, social classes and power (Poulantzas 1973; Jessop 1982: 158–62). In addition, Poulantzas attempted to elaborate an account of the movement from abstract relations to concrete events. This can be seen in the way he identifies the operation of state power in historically-specific conjunctures in *Fascism and Dictatorship* (Poulantzas 1974) and in *The Crisis of the Dictatorships* (Poulantzas 1976).

Jessop's work can be interpreted as a critical commentary on the possibilities and limits of the Poulantzian project. Jessop draws on the later writings of Poulantzas to develop a non-reductionist and non-essentialist theory of the relationship between the state, the economy, ideology and the social formation. Jessop initially uses the Poulantzian characterization of the relationship between public and private spheres in the constitution of the state and the legal system. For Poulantzas, the institutional separation of the economy from the political institutions within capitalism is achieved through the coupling of two processes. In the first process, *private individuation*, Poulantzas identifies the interpellation of legal subjects who are individually endowed with formally equal rights and duties, regardless of their position in the social division of labour or the precise form of inequality within the context in question. Second, these atomized legal subjects are bound to the nation-state as the expression of the common interest and *public unity*. The political equality embodied in these relations (including both the 'isolation effect' and the 'unifying effect') is portrayed as a mirror of the fetishized relations between economic subjects within a commodity-wage-labour economy. This undermines attempts to construct political projects around working-class interests and leads to the identification of workers' demands as being against the national interest, and hence sectional in nature, while the interests of capital are portrayed as being in the interests of all members of the society in question.

In this context, the legitimacy of bourgeois political domination is reinforced through periodic elections, electoral competition and the existence and effective operation of strong parliamentary institutions. This corresponds to Dahl's preconditions for polyarchy, inclusivity, contestation and a strong civic tradition, as explored in Chapter Three. For Poulantzas, however, this state form is only a feature of the normal conditions of capitalist democracy. To provide an adequate explanation of the variations in political regime, he draws on Gramsci's approach to the *integral state* (as hegemony armoured by coercion). This formulation of the state enables Jessop to demonstrate the operation of the state in relation to the power bloc, and the maintenance of the division between public and private spheres which acts as the crucial precondition for the operation of liberal democracy (Jessop 1982: 162–7).

Yet to regard such conditions as a normal feature of capitalist social formations is clearly at odds with the comparative-historical evidence on state formation. In practice a range of state forms, more or less inclusive, more or less open to contestation, and with varying degrees of stability in their parliamentary institutions, have been compatible with capitalism. In recognition of this, Jessop suggests that neo-Marxism has to accommodate the fact that the relationship between capital and the state is less conditional than had previously been assumed. This form of 'Marxism without guarantees' focuses on the extent to which a *power bloc* takes account of the interests and aspirations of the dominated classes (such as demands for welfare) when formulating policies designed to secure the smooth continuation of capital accumulation. This also means that the 'rule of capital' should be seen as a contingent outcome of the ways in which the state is able to take advantage of the changing balance of class forces and economic crises, in order to secure the reorganization of production and to facilitate sustained capital accumulation. If bourgeois democracy does not facilitate such restructuring processes, then the economic crises which result can lead to situations where exceptional forms of state control may emerge, such as military dictatorships or fascist regimes. The role of the state is seen as a dual one. First it ensures that the members of the power bloc are unified and that the dominant classes and/or fractions are not economically isolated. Second, it ensures continued hegemony over the dominated classes and/or fractions, to which end the state must also ensure their disorganization and economic isolation (Jessop 1982).

Economic crises can often only be resolved through a reconfiguration of other elements of a particular social formation. In such situations, political struggles can become dissociated from the institutional bodies of representation, and this may be accompanied by the dissolution of hegemony (whereby the masses are detached from bourgeois moral, intellectual and political leadership). However, the conditions within which different forms of exceptional state can emerge are also periodized in terms of the overall development of the capitalist mode of production, as identified in stamocap theory. Fascist regimes are located in the monopoly capitalist crisis stage (Poulantzas 1974) whereas tendencies towards authoritarian statism within democratic states are associated with the crisis of contemporary capitalism and the failure of interventionist states to secure the conditions for monopoly capital accumulation since the 1960s (Poulantzas 1978; Jessop 1977: 368–9).

In relation to Jessop's intellectual project, the most important shift in the Poulantzian approach is the replacement of the Althusserian frame of meaning accompanying the regional theory of the capitalist state with the adoption of the relational theory of the state and politics in *State, Power, Socialism* (Poulantzas 1978: 128–9). This avoids the functionalist and class-theoretical treatment of the state as a factor of cohesion (as in the case of Poulantzas' historical-materialist general theory of the state, abstracted from particular modes of production and their distinct forms of expropriation). In the particular theory of the political region in the capitalist mode of production, the economy and the polity are institutionally separate. This means that the state specializes in managing contradictions and building cohesion, reinforcing this interpretation. The regional theory of the state allowed for specific institutions of the state to be identified as both a structural ensemble, within the structural matrix of the capitalist mode of production, and a political practice. This is a reflection of the attempt to integrate both Althusserian and Gramscian approaches (Poulantzas 1973). Jessop suggests that in the Poulantzian account, the state is neither an instrument of, nor is it autonomous from, the capitalist economy. Instead, the state is a 'form-determined field of social relations in which the regional structure of the political has definite effects on the political class struggle' (Jessop 1982: 160). Nevertheless, the state is still characterized by the differential presence of competing dominant classes and/or fractions in the branches (legislative, executive and judiciary) or power centres of the state, unified through the dominance of one of the branches (the legislative in competitive capitalism, and the executive in state monopoly capitalism).

This relational theory of the state allows for the identification of the operation of both dominant and dominated classes and/or fraction forces within the state apparatus itself, so that both ideological and repressive state apparatuses become the sites of hegemonic contestation. In his later work, Poulantzas provides an account of the role of the state as the mediator of contradictions within the power bloc, in terms of both the formal institutional structure of the state and the political practices of classes, fractions, categories and social forces, widening the range of agencies at work in the state. The political practices raised in this account include the short-circuiting of decision making, the selective filtering of policy implementation, and non-decision making. Jessop identifies some inconsistencies in the emergence of this new position, particularly the correspondence of state power in typical capitalist states to the interests of the power bloc, and the role of political struggles within the state.

When examining the role of ideology, Poulantzas similarly provides an account which reveals a break both with class reductionist assumptions and with approaches which assume the unified ideological content determined outside the ideological class struggle. For Poulantzas, a condition of the successful establishment of social cohesion in a class-divided social formation is the combination of ideological elements expressing petit-bourgeois and working-class interests within the dominant ideology itself. In this way, the forms of resistance to the power bloc are structured so that they do not endanger the reproduction of capital. Ideological hegemony, as a field of political and ideological class practices, is portrayed as closely related to the state form. The night-watchman state is identified as the best possible political shell for competitive capitalism, and (following the displacement of dominance from the economy to the polity in the structural matrix of capitalism) the interventionist state plays the same role for monopoly capitalism. However, these remain as limits upon the possible variations in dominance within the power bloc, for it is possible for a range of different fractions of capital to assert hegemonic leadership (Jessop 1982: 173–7).

The shift of Marxist political strategy which Poulantzas suggested can be seen most clearly in *State, Power, Socialism* (Poulantzas 1978). In the 1970s, he had already shifted considerably from the Leninist strategy for the mobilization of the working class through the vanguard party. In its place Poulantzas asserted the primacy of political struggle, and the development of alliances with other classes, fractions, categories and social forces around an alternative transformist hegemonic project against the power bloc dominated by monopoly capital. These alliances were seen as more than the product of short-term expediency. They were identified as part of a wider strategy to secure the unity of the oppositional alliance (through the modification of class positions) so that its members came to share the world view of the working class in the transition to socialism. In this context, the state was portrayed no longer as a monolithic apparatus dedicated to the promotion of bourgeois hegemony, but as a terrain in which these struggles would take place, and alliances be secured and fostered. This strategy promoted hegemonic struggle on two fronts. First it would take place within the state, to intensify the internal contradictions of the power bloc, to create real centres of power in the state and to secure active consent for the oppositional alliances. Second it would take place beyond the state, in the construction of centres of resistance and, ultimately, an alternative state appropriate for the transition to socialism.

Jessop's conclusions on the relevance of Poulantzas for contemporary state theorizing are drawn from the positive insights of his investigation into the *form derivation* debate. In particular, he highlights the politicist tendencies of Poulantzas, which lead him to treat economic determinism in the last instance as a warrant for political determinism in the first instance. This tendency was reinforced by his description of the state as a factor of cohesion, and the treatment of the capitalist state as uniquely specialized in this task (given the institutional separation of economy from polity in the capitalist mode of production). For Jessop this occurs at the structural level, with political class domination embedded within the institutional form of the capitalist state, as well as at the level of hegemonic practices of the power bloc (that is, in terms of the structural matrix of the mode of production and the overdetermined struggles within each conjuncture).

The conundrums which beset structuralist Marxism resurface in other ways. For instance, the problems created by the *relative autonomy* of the state from the economy do not disappear with the shift of focus towards the institutional autonomy of the state. This issue resurfaces in the distinction between the incoherence and contradiction of the short term, and the correspondence of state form to the political interests of the dominant class in the long term. Jessop concludes that this can be resolved through the establishment of the theory of the state as a form-determined condensation of social relations. By accommodating the institutional materiality of the state form and its role in the balance of social forces, he identifies the ways in which the capital relation imposes constraints upon state functions and the exercise of state power, and also recognizes the complex interrelationship between the economy and polity.

The final ingredients in Jessop's symbolic model of the capitalist state are the newly-emergent discourse approaches which have assumed a greater centrality in his latest work. The discourse-theoretical approaches, notably those developed by Ernesto Laclau (1977: 143–98) and Chantal Mouffe (1979), brought together the Gramscian focus on historically-specific conjunctures with the contemporary insights of post-structuralist thinking, particularly Laclau's appropriation of the Derridean approach to the production of meaning. Mouffe identifies the underlying problems with economism in Marxist theorizing since the Second International, and the steady move away from this in the work of Korsch and Lukacs (rejecting epiphenomenalism in the characterization of the politics and ideology), as well as the prison writings of Gramsci (rejecting the reductionist account of classes as a priori subjects in the production of ideological practices). Thus, in their different ways, both Laclau and Mouffe highlight the aspects of Gramsci's writings on hegemony which assume that political forces and ideological elements, at the national-popular level, do not necessarily correspond to class positions. This reading of the hegemonic principle in Gramsci's work identifies the 'ideological expressions of class interests' as having different characterizations depending on their articulation with a combination of ideological elements (a specific discourse).

Laclau extends this analysis by locating a unifying principle of class ideologies in a concept of subjectivity, such as 'race' in the Nazi fascist discourse (Laclau 1977: 81–142). It was this account, which retains class as a foundational basis for political and ideological struggle, with which Laclau and Mouffe were finally to break in *Hegemony and Socialist Strategy* (1985). In particular, this break was marked by their treatment of the concept of 'historic bloc' as discursively constituted, rather than the conception of the material base as an extra-discursive determinant of the discursive. In this way, class subjects are no longer privileged over popular democratic forces, and the hegemonic struggle is transformed in the continual disarticulation and re-articulation of ideological elements in the formation of discourses. This was already having an impact on Jessop's thinking in his account of 'The Political Indeterminacy of Democracy' (Jessop 1980b), although the full implications of the discourse-theoretical approach only became apparent in the later 1980s, as Jessop sought to resolve the unresolved issues he identified in the work of Poulantzas. At this stage, Jessop sought to highlight the problems involved in privileging the political or the ideological in response to the rejection of economism. In the case of Laclau and Mouffe, he was largely concerned to avoid the ideologism and textual reductionism in their approach. In summation, Jessop's break with grand theorizing, and with the associated forms of essentialism and reductionism within neo-Marxist theory, led him to criticize tendencies towards economism, politicism and ideologism. In terms of his own intellectual development, there is a great deal of consistency between this aim and his earlier attempts to utilize symbolic modelling to reformulate sociological theories of the social order and social change. In both instances, he sought to emphasize the interpenetration of economic, political, social and cultural substrata or regions, without reducing one to the others. However, this time Jessop's adoption of the neo-Marxist approach led him to divide the social into three fields of inquiry rather than four: that of the economy, state and civil society.

The Capitalist State (1982) also contains the first clear statement of Jessop's epistemological and ontological assumptions since his identification of Willer's symbolic modelling in his early writings. In rejecting reductionist, essentialist and economist assumptions in the vast bulk of Marxist theorizing, he is forced to rethink his relationship to the methodological assumptions of Marx's approach. In particular, he replaces the more or less complex *logics of mediation* (which characterized the derivationist approaches to the form and function of the state in relation to the capitalist economy) with an account of the *logic of articulation* as an alternative set of methodological premises. The method of articulation, he suggests, can be identified explicitly in a brief passage of Marx's *Grundrisse* (Marx 1857: 100–8), and more or less implicitly in Marx's method. This passage identifies the distinction between the 'real-concrete' and the 'concrete-in- thought' in a way which is consistent with the distinctions between transitive and intransitive domains within the realist analyses of science. This treats the conception of causality as the complex synthesis of multiple determinations. The identification of the real-concrete as stratified into various layers and differentiated into regions, each of which require specific and appropriate concepts and principles of explanation, fits well with the use of abstraction in Marxist theory, as demonstrated by Fine and Harris in *Reading Capital* (1979) and in a range of sources in the philosophy of science and social science (Bhaskar 1978, 1979; Keat and Urry 1982; Sayer 1992). Of particular importance for Jessop's account is the identification of the movement from simple abstract theoretical relations to complex concrete conjunctures. Jessop is particularly concerned to identify how the abstract laws of motion of capitalist production emerge within actually existing economies, as well as the interrelationships between the economy and the political and ideological spheres of social existence (see Jessop 1982: 211–59).

The realist approach offers a means of identifying the emergence of abstract relations as tendencies within overdetermined historically-specific conjunctures. For instance, if we take the example of the value form and how it operates in the capitalist mode of production, it is feasible to move from definite abstract relations, gradually introducing greater levels of complexity and the impact of other determinations, to approach a more concrete level of analysis. In this example, this would involve moving through the circuit of capital, the interrelationship between economic, political and ideological relations, the periodization of the mode of production, to consider the concrete conjunctures and the strategic agents involved in the reproduction and/or transformation of the relations concerned. The use of Althusser's conceptualization of contradiction and overdetermination provides a means of privileging the concrete relations as determinate within the range of social relations present in a particular conjuncture. This also means that this form of analysis can accommodate the co-presence of competing economic, political and ideological relations, such as the coexistence of different modes of production or state forms in a particular concrete situation. In this way, for Jessop, it was feasible to identify determinate causes in concrete relations without falling into the traps of determinism, reductionism or essentialism, or privileging the role of one sphere of social existence over the other spheres (as in the cases of economism, politicism or ideologism). For Jessop, theory formation should take into account the specific 'contingently necessary' conditions within which the degree of complexity and level of abstraction are defined. In the next section, I consider how this approach to the state was deployed in the 1970s and 1980s.

From corporatism to Thatcherism: characterizing the conjuncture

Jessop's analysis of his own historically-specific conjuncture is particularly useful for identifying the problem he was wrestling with at this time, namely a root and branch transformation of the neo-Marxist approach. He attempts to draw on his theoretical framework in order to account for the complex patterns of economic, social and political change in post-war Britain and, in particular, the crisis phase from the early 1970s to the 1980s. This period witnessed the collapse of the social-democratic Keynesian welfare state and the emergence of the Thatcherite neo-liberal accumulation strategy. In particular, he felt that it was appropriate to develop an account of the capitalist state which adequately reflected the relationship between contemporary political transformations and the processes of restructuring in the capitalist economies in Western industrial societies. In addition, he sought to account for the restructuring of the internal aspects of the state in concrete terms. Characteristically, Jessop uses the symbolic modelling technique of theory construction, in this case directed towards the research literature on corporatist political economy and policy making. While this provides a useful basis for sketching the political crisis in the 1970s, it was to prove less useful for understanding the complex transformations of the 1980s and 1990s.

The debates on corporatism offered a more flexible and innovative field of analysis than the sterile and inconclusive discussions which characterized the debates between structuralism and instrumentalism, between reform and revolution, and between economic reductionism and state autonomy. In particular, Jessop drew upon the corporatist literature to construct an account of the state form which could accommodate a greater degree of contingency and make explicit reference to the two-way relationships between state and economy. He identified four features which deserved further investigation:

1. The analysis of the *capitalist mode of production* at varying levels of abstraction, and its articulation with economic and political determinations in different phases of capital accumulation (drawing from his own symbolic model of the capitalist state). Corporatist approaches tend to neglect the ways in which capitalist production is characterized as a valorization process as mediated through the class struggle, and the contradictions between the needs of capital-in-general and individual capitals.
2. The reorganization of the *forms of political representation*, so that Parliamentarism gave way in various ways to corporatism (drawing upon Philippe Schmitter's (1979) account of interest intermediation). Jessop is concerned to stress the ways in which political forces are in part constituted through political representation.

3 The reorganization of the *state apparatus* and the modes of conduct in political institutions (drawing on Ray Pahl and John Winkler's (1974, 1976) pessimistic account of the emergence of the corporatist state) whereby strategic discrimination replaces universal and impartial facilitation and regulation.
4 The reorganization of the *forms of intervention*, requiring the identification of the manner in which state intervention is articulated within the economic order, and an exploration of the institutional links forged for policy implementation, such as quasi-autonomous governmental and non-governmental organizations (drawing on Pahl and Winkler's account of policy-making shifts). Jessop thus establishes the links between representation and intervention in shaping and facilitating political forces.

To explore these issues, Jessop constructs an account of how, in the manner of Offe's account of structural selectivity, the state acts as an 'institutional complex of forms of representation and intervention' (Jessop 1979: 193). He also makes an explicit connection between these forms and the internal character of the state apparatus, by drawing on the complex typologies of normal and exceptional state forms from Poulantzas. The acceptance of contingency can be identified through his recognition that the articulation of forms of representation, state apparatuses and intervention which he identifies offers no guarantees for securing the expanded reproduction of capitalism. This enables Jessop to specify the institutional differences between Parliamentarism and corporatism (see Table 5.4).

The transition from Parliamentarism to corporatism has been associated, in the neo-Marxist approach, with periodization of capitalist phases, notably

Table 5.4 A brief outline of Parliamentarism and Corporatism

	Parliamentarism	*Corporatism*
Form of representation	Political participation of citizens through voting and mediated political parties	Political participation through corporations based on a functional political parties' division of labour
Internal articulation of the state	The legislative body is primary in the branches of the state apparatus	The executive body is primary in the branches of the state apparatus
Form of intervention	Intervention in the form of general legislation and politics enforced by a rational-legal bureaucracy	Intervention through the corporations who act as representational agencies

the shift from competitive to simple monopoly, then to state monopoly capitalism. It should also be noted that the forms of corporatism in the transitional crisis phase of capitalism in the early twentieth century, associated with Fascism, differ in important respects from post-war variants, notably within relatively stable liberal corporatist and social-democratic regimes. Jessop is clearly suggesting that no such succession of state forms can be assumed, and that much depends upon the balance and character of historically-specific social forces. In addition, in historically-specific situations it is feasible for elements of both Parliamentarism and corporatism to be articulated together, which he suggests is a distinctive feature of the British state. For Jessop, the peculiar crisis tendencies of this hybrid 'Tripartism' in Britain in the 1970s are a product of the contradiction between the formal survival of Parliamentarist forms of representation, and the emergence alongside them of corporatist arrangements for policy making and intervention between state bodies and the representatives of capital and labour. These arrangements increasingly bypassed the formal democratic arrangements, and these tensions and contradictions were reflected in the internal articulation of the branches of the state apparatus. The problems in Britain proved more difficult to resolve, because the Parliamentarist forms of representation and intervention were no longer relevant or effective, at the same time as the corporatist forms were inadequately formed to take their place and maintain the legitimacy of the arrangements. This provoked a crisis of hegemony in the late 1970s. In this case, the hybrid became a contradictory unity (Jessop 1978b; 1980a), although Jessop also came to accept that with an appropriate balance of social forces they could, in certain circumstances, have formed a functionally complementary unity (Jessop 1979).

The effectiveness of state power is therefore identified as being closely related to the balance of social forces and their mobilization in support of official policies. Jessop draws upon Ernesto Laclau's neo-Marxist writings from the seventies (Laclau 1977) to identify how the balance of social forces involves not only the class forces but also 'class relevant' forces. In particular, Laclau highlights how these interests were articulated through both economic-corporate and popular-democratic demands. Economic-corporate interests involve demands for economic improvement by a determinate class or fraction, whereas popular-democratic interests involve demands for the extension of citizens' rights, the establishment of politico-juridical equality, and rights to participate in the legislative and administrative branches of the state. Within parliamentary democracies, Jessop argues, two dimensions of the strategies which attempt to maintain bourgeois domination stand out. First is the degree of attachment to Parliamentary forms of representation in the subordinate classes (which cannot be based purely on class interests). Second is the articulation of the economic-corporate and the popular-democratic demands of the subordinate classes within political and ideological programmes which are conducive to the dominance of a power bloc organized under the hegemony of a dominant class or fraction (Jessop 1978b: 38–40).

Jessop suggests that, within an overdetermined historical conjuncture, social forces are located in both fields of struggle; so that the primacy of 'class formation' or 'people formation' is a contingent matter within the unstable equilibrium of compromise.

The interrelationship between class–class determinations (relations of economic domination) and officialdom–people determinations (relations of political domination between state and subject) is also contingently related to the social structures and the balance of forces in the conjuncture concerned. In addition, Jessop raises an interesting point on the relative autonomy problem: that just as the relationship between the interests of capital-in-general and capitals is a problematic one, so too are the relationships between the interests of labour-in-general and labours, and that between people-in-general and peoples (Jessop 1980b: 56–70; 1982: 247–52). In *The Capitalist State* (Jessop 1982), the problems of specifying power, interests, structural constraints and the relative autonomy of the superstructure from the economic base are all resolved in the same way. For instance, rather than regarding power or interests as defined a priori in relation to a given context, endowing them with an independent causal status, Jessop's relational approach places them within determinate social conditions. These concepts are not seen as appropriate explanatory concepts for social relations in general, merely for social relations in particular conjunctures and the complex combinations of social forces, actions, structural constraints and so on which characterize them. In effect, such concepts are demoted from being an *explanans* to being an *explanandum*. In this way, Jessop avoids the tendencies in social theory which link such concepts to voluntarist and determinist methodological positions, and so paves the way for his later formulations of the structure–strategy dialectic (Jessop 1982: 252–8).

In addition, the success of a strategy for organizing an adequate social and material basis for a balance of social forces, or for disorganizing opposing strategies, depends on an appropriate mix of repression, indoctrination and active consent. This can only be established within a determinate historically-specific conjuncture. In Laclau's analysis of populist discourses in Fascist and military regimes, the immediate presence of coercion as a means of resolving the crisis is more evident. However, even for Jessop's analysis, hegemony is defined in Gramscian terms as consent armoured by coercion. For instance, Jessop examines the class basis for corporatism in Fascist and post-war democratic contexts. He argues that the decline of the traditional petty bourgeoisie and other intermediate groups, and the growth of the salariat alongside the working class, have changed the balance of social forces to such an extent that far from being 'Fascism with a human face', contemporary liberal corporatism in European societies represents the 'highest stage of social democracy'. Indeed, it was the failure to secure the social and material bases of emergent corporatist arrangements that led to the fragmentation of support with organized labour and capital, and the crisis in representation through political parties, in Britain in the late 1970s (Jessop 1979: 204; 1980a: 75). In a short passage on the crisis of the Keynesian welfare state in this period, Jessop demonstrates how the complex relations between state forms and their social and material bases, between economic-corporate and popular-democratic demands and their operation in relation to the balance of social forces within historically specific conjunctures, can be identified. This involves:

> state intervention in the operation of market forces to effect a redistribution of income and/or to socialize the provision and costs of certain forms of consumption, it is also premised on the institution of citizenship (and welfare rights) and organized to support the family as a primary unit of civil society. In this sense, the welfare state both presupposes and reinforces the institutional separation of the state and civil society from capitalist relations of production and reflects the juridico-political forms of the parliamentary-bureaucratic system.
> (Jessop 1980a: 65)

While this provides us with a fairly useful account of the complexities of the post-war settlement in the face of a changing world system, the problems of securing the social and material bases for continued support in a period characterized by economic stagflation, it also demonstrates the fragility of such arrangements. With the emergence of alternative strategies on the left and the right for resolving the fiscal crisis of the state, the forms of representation and intervention in place in the British state apparatus proved to be incapable of maintaining these arrangements. It is to the emergence of the right alternative which sought to restore free-market competition and deregulation, neo-liberalism, that I turn in the second half of this section. While at various points Jessop has expected some form of corporatist arrangement to re-emerge in Britain, this has not been borne out by events. This had a significant impact in reorienting his work towards the role of economic, political and ideological strategies through which hegemonic projects are constructed, and causing him to place a greater emphasis on the role of social forces as strategic agents in the constitution of social structures. To understand how this shift towards a strategic-theoretical approach came about, it is useful to examine Jessop's collaborative research on Thatcherism in the 1980s.

Jessop's collaboration with Kevin Bonnett, Simon Bromley and Tom Ling in the *New Left Review* was initially a response to the characterization of Thatcherism as 'authoritarian populism' by Stuart Hall (Hall 1980; 1983a; 1983b), in particular, that it amounted to an ideological celebration of Thatcherism. Hall's account of the social transformations in the late 1970s and early 1980s is informed by two key positions. First is the identification of an emerging *authoritarian statism* in *State, Power, Socialism* (1978) by Nicos Poulantzas. Second are the conceptions of *passive revolution* and *hegemony* within the *Prison Writings* of Antonio Gramsci (1971), which had been used as a basis for conceptualizing populism by Ernesto Laclau.

Hall was particularly concerned with how the left focused too much on the economic relations of capitalism, to the detriment of their understanding of the struggles within the political and ideological superstructure. This became especially important as the political right had managed to monopolize the popular-democratic field just as 'the question of democracy became the principal site of struggle' (Hall 1980: 158). Hall's account is a plea to the left to take democracy more seriously, at a time when the political right were successfully articulating popular support against the social democratic power bloc (a passive revolution from below), around the theme of the defence of law and the social order in a complex war of position (an extension of the arguments of Hall 1978).

Since popular democratic discourses are constructed through the contradiction between the people and the power bloc, the treatment of the social-democratic power bloc as statist, bureaucratic and prone to creeping collectivism makes it a strong contrast to the individual choice, freedom and personal responsibility emphasized in Thatcherite populist discourse. Indeed, Thatcherism did capture the moral high ground in the 1980s. However, when the Conservative Party came to power in the UK in 1979, the populism shifted away from active mobilization of popular demands, and served merely to secure active consent against opposition within the party system and the state. This populist ventriloquism has accelerated the centralization of power within the state at the expense of Parliamentary representation. In this way the crisis is not portrayed as 'a mirror of politics' reflecting a given set of economic conditions, but as a strategic terrain of struggle and contestation for the construction of popular consent in support of an increasingly authoritarian regime. The polemical response from Jessop, Bonnett, Bromley and Ling (1984) misreads Hall's account of populist discourses of a historically-specific conjuncture as a fully comprehensive account of Thatcherism. In addition, its accusation of ideologism conflates Hall's position with that of the discourse-analytic approach of Laclau and Mouffe (1985).

Nevertheless, by identifying the range of determinations beyond Hall's account, Jessop *et al.* present a useful case study in conjunctural analysis within which authoritarian populism is located as the means through which policies are legitimated. While it is useful within such specific terms of reference, that is, the political and ideological struggle for hegemony and the disarticulation and rearticulation of the political agenda, this analysis of authoritarian populism should be supplemented by careful economic and institutional analysis. This ensures that the relationship between structures and strategies within conjunctures can be more clearly specified. In turn, Jessop *et al.* suggest, this avoids some of the strategic consequences of focusing just on authoritarian populism, and encourages the strategic response of focusing on the longer-term reconstruction of an alternative hegemonic common sense. In the short term, the left's responses to Thatcherism tended to be primarily defensive, surrendering the immediate strategic terrain to neo-liberalism and failing to articulate 'a medium term economic and political strategy' which could take advantage of the contradictions and tensions in the Thatcherite project. For Jessop *et al.*, drawing on the political strategy developed by Poulantzas, Hall's account missed crucial opportunities for engaging in contestation with the Thatcherite project both within and beyond the state apparatus, even though Hall clearly recognized that Thatcherism exploited the contradictions and struggles within the Keynesian welfare state (Jessop *et al.* 1984; 1985).

Jessop's previous work on the institutional state and capitalism plays an important part in this picture. Jessop *et al.* argue that the capacity of Thatcherism to reshape the economic, political and ideological terrain is in part the consequence of its emergence during the dual crisis of Parliamentarism and corporatism as modes of representation and intervention in the British state, identified earlier, and the underlying structural crisis in the capitalist economy. As a result, the Thatcher administration enjoyed considerable decisional autonomy as the economic and political crises at work intensified each other. Jessop *et al.* also developed Gramsci's account of the relationship between the war of position and the war of manoeuvre in relation to the concept of passive revolution. This provided a way of distinguishing between Thatcherite populism and the more expansive form of hegemony associated with the 'one nation' or social-democratic consensus it had replaced. In particular, they identified a continuum ranging from a fully expansive hegemony, which articulates active support of the people, through the use of material and symbolic rewards, to organically-integrated consent for the pursuit of national-popular goals (the one-nation strategy), to the wars of manoeuvre, which impose hegemony through force, fraud and/or coercion, associated with crises of hegemony. In between these two forms of hegemony lie a range of forms of passive revolution which attempt to reorganize social relations through the neutralization and channelling of populist projects towards the dominance of a particular power bloc and its constitutive interests, through the mechanics of compromise rather than organic integration (Jessop 1983b; Jessop *et al.* 1984).

For Jessop *et al.*, Thatcherite populism represented a 'two-nations' strategy which, in descriptive terms, combined elements of both expansive hegemony and passive revolution. This form of populism articulates a privileged first nation of 'good citizens' and 'hard workers' against a subordinate and marginalized second nation which is excluded from the most significant rewards of the market. Social antagonisms, such as class, ethnic or regional differences, are discursively articulated and organized around the productive–parasitic opposition. The second nation is highly fragmented and constitutes multiple sites of resistance at the local level. This offered an inadequate basis for the Labour Party in articulating opposition to Thatcherism. In addition, the decisional autonomy of the state provided Thatcherism with an opportunity to reconstitute the power bloc. In the early stages the preference for policies which benefited certain elements of the circuit of capital to the detriment of others, privileging financial capital over industrial capital (particularly manufacturing and construction capital), undermined the possibility of reconciling the interests within the power bloc itself. This was partly a consequence of the global orientation of financial capital in relation to the national orientation of manufacturing (which meant that a global upturn could be consistent with relative decline in the UK). Particularly significant was the role of the privatization of public corporations in creating new sources of support for an emergent Thatcherite power bloc. At the same time, this policy reduced public borrowing and sustained the Thatcherite economic strategy; although the continued autonomy of the Thatcherite state also pointed to a failure to resolve the dual crisis of the state. It remained to be established whether authoritarian populism led to the mobilization of effective popular support (Jessop *et al.* 1984).

Jessop *et al.* were to return to these issues in subsequent articles in the *New Left Review* in 1985 and 1987 (Jessop, Bonnett, Bromley and Ling 1985; 1987), with a consideration of how the neo-liberal economic strategy related to the emergence of post-Fordist international capitalism. The deregulation of capital and the labour market, the export of investment capital, the decline of manufacturing and the expansion of the service sector established Britain as a low-wage European economy attractive to transnational investment. In addition, they identified the impact of Thatcherism on the state, and its relations with civil society and the economy. This involved the consolidation of its electoral coalition through redistributive policies to create new supportive social bases (through lower direct taxation and wider share ownership) and the denial of entitlements to those beyond the electoral bloc (such as the dismantling of socialist initiatives in the local state, as with the abolition of the Greater London Council).

This merely highlighted the need for consideration of a left alternative economic and political strategy. It also raised the urgency of developing a left supply-side approach to the problems of unemployment, of readdressing social policy and welfare, and the need for constructive alliances with new social movements (Jessop *et al.* 1985). Failure to do this, Jessop later suggested, led to the 'vivisection of the left', with the consolidation of both the Tory electoral coalition for popular capitalism in the 1987 Conservative election victory, and the relations between the neo-liberal economic strategy and the needs of flexible accumulation in the post-Fordist economy. In particular, they noted the increased permanence of skilled private-sector workers for the Thatcherite agenda, and the ways in which this dovetailed with the restructuring of the workforce in the post-Fordist economy. Nevertheless, the 'two-nations' strategy prevented the emergence of new national popular consensus and an organic power bloc. In relation to the search for a new role within the international division of labour, they also noted that economic policy had itself become a terrain of political and ideological hegemonic struggle, whereas in social democracy, political strategy was subordinated to economic strategies. The same processes of trial and error associated with institutional and organizational innovation appeared to be taking place within the state apparatus, in the operation of internal markets and the proliferation of quasi-autonomous (non-)governmental agencies (Jessop *et al.* 1987, 1988). Indeed, much of

Jessop's work in the 1990s focused on the complexities of institutional evolution. These complex processes of change were also reflected in the increased complexity of Jessop's theoretical approach in the mid-1980s, as he began to integrate systems theory and regulation theory into his strategic-theoretical analysis. It is to these theoretical innovations that I turn in the next section.

Towards the state as strategy

The closing sections of *The Capitalist State* (Jessop 1982) and *Nicos Poulantzas: Marxist Theory and Political Strategy* (Jessop 1985a) introduced a greater concern with political strategy. This was to transform Jessop's account of the state and economy, just as he responded to the rapid political, ideological and economic shifts identified in the previous section. Of particular importance is an article from *Kapitalistate* in 1983, 'Accumulation Strategies, State Forms, and Hegemonic Projects' (Jessop 1983b). This is the transitional work between his fascination with neo-Marxist political economy and his emergent attempt to situate his analysis of the state within a wider account of the social order. Strategic concepts are crucial in fleshing out the relationship between the identification of abstract tendencies and their actual operation in complex social relations within historically-specific conjunctures. Jessop is particularly concerned with generating middle-range concepts which link the abstract relations of capitalist production to conjunctural analysis determinations which can be identified without determinism.

The recognition that the method of articulation poses serious problems for the assumptions of neo-Marxist theorizing led Jessop to engage in a process of unravelling the whole approach, and initiating its reconstruction through the use of the structure-strategy dialectic. His work leading up to *The Capitalist State* (Jessop 1982) had uncovered a series of problems in the neo-Marxist attempts to formulate the relation between base and superstructure. In this respect, his reconceptualization of relative autonomy as a non-necessary correspondence between base and superstructure constituted a significant advance in this direction; correspondence as such becomes a conjunctural matter, and the formation of a historic bloc depends on the interrelationship between the structural conditions of that conjuncture and the balance of social forces involved. However, the temporal dimensions of neo-Marxist analysis of social and economic change, in particular the periodization of the capitalist mode of production, remained unchallenged.

Jessop attempted to identify the role of accumulation strategies in the expanded reproduction of capital and the operation of the abstract law of value as a process of valorization in the labour process. To do so, he drew upon the Gramscian account of the integral state (active consent armoured by coercion) deployed in his analysis of the capitalist state, in order to readdress the operation of the relations of articulation within the economy. In particular, he distinguished between economic determinism, domination and hegemony within the circuit of capital:

- *Economic determination*: that industrial or productive capital is determinate in the last instance.
- *Economic domination*: the imposition of the interests of one fraction of capital over the interests of the other fractions.
- *Economic hegemony*: when one or more fractions secure the active consent of the other fractions of capital in pursuit of a determinate accumulation strategy.

In this context, Jessop argues, the expanded reproduction of capital is secured through economic hegemony armoured by economic domination. Within the circuit of capital, competition and conflict between the fractions is assumed to be a consistent feature of a dynamic economy. Within a particular concrete conjuncture, hegemony/domination override economic determination. However, economic domination by one fraction of capital (such as finance capital) would undermine the integration of the circuit if the devalorization of total social capital were to take place, damaging the basis of production, industrial capital.

In this way, by taking account of the complex relations between fractions of capital and other social forces within the power bloc, Jessop suggests that there is no substantive unity to the circuit of capital, nor is there a predetermined course to capital accumulation or a unilinear or irreversible succession of stages which the capitalist mode of production must follow. This leads him to pose serious questions about the periodization of capitalism, and about the existence of definite breaks in its development. From this point on, Jessop becomes increasingly concerned with the specification of tendencies and trends in capitalist relations, the restructuring of the state and the emergence of crises and long waves, rather than the identification of definite stages. By focusing on the plurality of accumulation strategies (and a range of tactics within each strategy) within a specific conjuncture, the capital relation becomes an 'indeterminate terrain' for particular capitals to compete upon, as well as a means of establishing and reproducing/transforming the course of accumulation (Jessop 1983b).

At this stage, Jessop redeploys the familiar neo-Marxist triad of economy, polity and ideology, in the form of accumulation strategies, state forms and hegemonic projects. Although the development of the implications of the strategic-theoretical approach lag behind on the state, both capital and the state are defined as form-determined social relations. This is in part a legacy of Jessop's intellectual debt to Nicos Poulantzas in defining the state form as a condensation of class struggle, or of the balance of social forces within a given conjuncture. Consequently, the state is characterized as a terrain of contestation, articulating forms of representation, forms of intervention and forms of articulation of state apparatuses. Jessop develops this into an account of the ways in which the state, so conceived, acts as a mechanism of structural selectivity in privileging, transforming or excluding (and has different implications for) the competing accumulation strategies in a given conjuncture. In formal abstract terms, the state is defined as a factor of cohesion. However, a range of features of social existence can be defined as factors of cohesion. In addition, in Jessop's own terms of reference, cohesion constitutes an *explanandum* rather than an *explanans*. In terms of developing an explanatory account of superstructural relations, he shifts his focus to hegemonic projects as the interpellation (constitution as subjects) and the organization of class(-relevant) social forces under the political, intellectual and moral leadership of a particular class or fraction. In this sense, hegemonic projects compete across economic-corporate and popular-democratic fields and can be oriented towards a range of economic and non-economic goals (including military success, moral regeneration and economic restructuring).

Hegemonic projects, such as Thatcherism or Blairism, attempt to articulate and advance the interests of classes, fractions and/or social categories (such as intellectuals or the bureaucracy) in order to dislodge the existing power bloc, and to restructure social relations around a different configuration of interests, both within the power bloc and between the power bloc and the subordinate classes and the people. Successful hegemonic projects reconcile the competing interests of the power bloc as well as repudiating alternative configurations of interests. This involves providing material concessions within a framework for reconciling conflicts, and at the same time advancing the economic corporate interests of those social forces beyond. In addition, hegemonic projects play a vital role in maintaining the substantive unity of the state apparatus as an institutional ensemble, so that particular class(-relevant) interests are constituted as general interests. For instance, in Thatcherite populist discourse in the 1980s, the distinction between productive and parasite was operationalized around the social duty of individuals or companies to pursue risk-taking in order to create wealth and employment, so that the particular interests of capitals were constituted as the national interest (Jessop 1983b).

In the mid-1980s, Jessop identified a particular feature of Poulantzas' work which had dramatic implications for his account of the state. This new insight emerged alongside a renewed bout of symbolic modelling, with Jessop's integration of regulation approach and systems theory (with the concept of 'state system' replacing that of 'state apparatus'). This shift represents the culmination of Jessop's reformulation of neo-Marxist state theory. In *State, Power and Socialism* (Poulantzas 1978), Poulantzas integrated the ideas of Michel Foucault on state power, to generate his account of the state as a condensation of class forces. While there are significant differences between Poulantzas and Foucault, there are significant similarities in their analyses of power and domination. Both accepted that it was possible to theorize calculation without a calculating subject. Both Poulantzas and Foucault were also concerned with the relationship between power and resistance, and with the relationship between the multiplicity of micropowers and the emergence of macro-necessities. It should be stressed that their characterization of these relations, agencies and their formation differs considerably. Nevertheless, this enabled Jessop to reconsider his analysis of the state as 'site of strategy', and to indicate the crucial role played by the structure–strategy dialectic in his account. The relationship between this dialectic and the transformational model of social activity (outlined in Chapter Two) is explored in Chapter Six (see Jessop 1985a; 1990d).

By considering the state as a 'site of strategy', Jessop replaces the structural selectivity of the state with a focus on its strategic selectivity. The state thus becomes a system whose internal structure and mode of operation can be either open or closed to varying forms of political strategy which emerge from the social forces concerned, and which has a differential impact upon these social forces. Thus the unity of the state and the relations, contradictions and conflicts between its various branches are established through these strategies. As a consequence, the structural properties of the state are themselves the product of past strategic interventions and their interrelationships with previous forms of strategic selectivity. This leads Jessop to view both the state and capital as contradictory and constituted through strategic dilemmas and paradoxes. The application of this approach to the concepts of interests, class struggle and power, leads him to redefine them again in relation to the feasible alternatives within a specified 'horizon of action' (defined in spatial, temporal, material and social terms).[11]

In adopting this position, Jessop goes even further than the Foucauldian position of specifying the social as a global site of strategic calculation without a calculating subject. To achieve this, he draws on the approach developed by Gary Wickham (1984), who identifies global strategies as intersections of practices which are goal oriented, and which organize a plurality of sites of strategic calculation within their tentative boundaries, as well as serving as sites of strategic calculation within more global strategies. The term 'global' here refers to attempts to unify sites of strategic calculations, rather than denoting a specific total system of relations. This leads him to consider two issues. The first is the relationship between the state as a site of strategy and the process of societalization (the production of society effects which are themselves only partially constituted). The second is the need to assess the implications of integrating a system-oriented approach into a neo-Marxist theoretical framework in the terms of reference of realist epistemological and ontological assumptions (Jessop 1990d: 355–60).

The first tentative steps in this direction are taken when Jessop introduces Niklas Luhmann's distinction between production (whereby social forces control and co-ordinate a set of causal mechanisms in order to produce a range of events) and causality (the total or global nexus within which specific productions are themselves realized). Despite the idealist assumptions which underpin systems theory, Jessop remains committed to materialist assumptions about the real strategies, real calculations and real calculating subjects (social forces) which exist within concrete conjunctures, and the definite structural constraints and opportunities which exist within such historically-specific circumstances. Nevertheless, he does not explicitly address the implications of introducing an approach which identifies theory as a means of organizing empirical evidence, rather than as a means of identifying the abstract but real social relations which realists take as their objects of analysis. The reality identified in systems theory is an empirical reality rather than a structured and differentiated reality (Jessop 1990d: 248–72).

Autopoiesis and relative autonomy

This section examines the recent integration of systems theory into Jessop's account of the state, particularly the theory of autopoiesis developed and elaborated by Niklas Luhmann (1982, 1985a, 1985b, 1985c, 1987) and Günther Teubner (1985a, 1985b, 1987a, 1987b) in their application of this approach within the sociology of law. The legal system provides the ideal case for identifying the logics of social systems. These logics maintain their internal coherence and unity through self-reference, without resort to planned co-ordination. Because legal institutions develop through the application of general legislative principles (and previous precedents) to particular case studies, such institutions are particularly self-referential (autopoietic). The principles for their reproduction are contained within their sphere of reference rather than other institutional spheres. Jessop refers to this as 'a condition of radical autonomy' (Jessop 1990d: 320). There are some interesting parallels between these concerns and those identified in the Chapter Four on Hayek's account of the co-ordination of plans. In particular, there is a parallel focus on the interrelationships between formal institutional rules and the informal tacit rules of conduct in everyday existence, as was shown in the conceptualization of social and institutional orders as the product of human action but not of human design (to use Hayek's terminology).

In such cases, the system defines and maintains the boundaries and unifying codes through which the system operates, and in certain systems reproduction is achieved through closed circuits with their own 'laws of motion'. Jessop is clearly attempting to rethink the problems in the constitution of the circuit of capital which emerged as a key issue in his self-criticism of *The Capitalist State* (Jessop 1982). In particular, he draws on the autopoietic account of the ways in which a social system or subsystem (such as the capitalist economy) responds to environmental changes. Such changes perturb the operation of its unifying codes, boundary maintenance and programme implementation, generating system-specific processes for dealing with interference. If these responses do not prevent (or even aggravate) the disruptive forces involved, the system itself may disintegrate. This form of analysis shifts the focus from pre-given 'societies' or 'nation-states' towards the complex overdetermined processes through which social orders emerge; in short, the processes of societalization.

The highly differentiated and polycentric character of social systems in this system-theoretical account provides Jessop with a means of integrating into his thesis the arguments of Wickham on global strategies in relation to substantive objects (ranging from legal systems and the economy to politics and the state and welfare provision). If social systems and subsystems are constituted by autopoietic (self-referential) and allopoietic (other-referential) tendencies, then these are characteristically partially constituted and fragmentary and transitory in form. As sites of strategy, they can never be considered as fully constituted or as hermetically-sealed total entities. At most, Jessop suggests in a Hayekian moment in his work, any determining social logic among such autopoietic systems takes the form of 'societal guidance' and operates as the contingent outcome of the autopoietic and allopoietic tendencies of the systems subject to it. At all levels of these social systems, the unity and identity of each is a contingent and emergent property which results from the complex combinations of tendencies in each case. Nevertheless, it is clear that Jessop does consider specific social systems to have a greater degree of autonomy or density than others, both in their capacity to maintain their own boundaries and in sustaining their own internal logics. The economy and the legal system are seen as denser than art, health and ethical systems (Jessop 1986d; 1987d; 1990d: 320–1).

Jessop develops this autopoietic approach within the context of state theory in order to resolve some of the issues thrown up by the American social-scientific attempt 'to bring the state back in', notably by Eric Nordlinger (1981) and Theda Skocpol (1985). State-centred accounts had emerged to counter what were considered to be the problems of economy-centred or society-centred accounts of the state prevalent in neo-Marxism. This approach, notably that of Skocpol, places a greater emphasis on the institutions of the state, empirically defined, as the focus of analysis. In particular, the state is characterized as 'Janus-faced', or sandwiched between the international system and the respective societies of each nation-state. The state's powers are defined in the Weberian terms of its capacity to produce and enforce collectively-binding decisions within a given population and territory. As such, the state possesses the capacities to transform the institutional forms of other parts of the society, and to affect the balance of social forces as an independent causal agent. The autonomy of the state, and the role of state managers and public officials within the policy-making process, are given a crucial role over and above economic tendencies and the formation of civil institutions. In particular, Skocpol provides an account of the state as the central political agency, and in so doing relegates society to the status of a residual category in causal terms.

Within state-centred accounts, the precise form of the state actor is variable, for this is a product of its geopolitical position and its position within inter-state systems, the role of the state in securing internal order, the actions of state managers, and the relation of the state to internal and external crises. Jessop attempted to develop a middle way between the state-centred and society-centred accounts, suggesting that the state-centric approach provided a useful heuristic function in highlighting the importance of the state in any account of societalization. Within his account of society effects, he attempted to identify the specificity of the political while avoiding the problems of politicism. Ultimately, since state-centred theories treat society as a residual category, just as society-centred theories treat the state, any attempt at theoretical combination would repeat the problems of both. Just as functionalism provided Jessop with useful theoretical tools in his early work on the constitution of the social order, so systems analysis provided him with the conceptual apparatus for re-theorizing the state–society dialectic and transcending the relative autonomy problem. Autopoiesis provides a means of breaking the tendency to treat state and society (or state and civil society, or state and economy) as compartments:

> Once one allows for the complex interpenetration of social and political life, the circular flow of persons, power and resources, the contradictory matrix of functional interdependence and operational interdependence, the activities of intermediaries and gatekeepers, and other complicating factors, the attempt to demarcate state and society in black and white terms is sure to fail.
>
> (Jessop 1990d: 303)[12]

Jessop utilizes Niklas Luhmann's account of the political system to readdress the ways in which the state operates as a strategic terrain. For Luhmann, the state is constituted through communications about power and the making and enforcing of collectively-binding decisions. The modern state is portrayed as one of a number of autopoietic systems operating in varying ways in relations of interdependence and autonomy from systems in the same social order. In addition, the state is portrayed as simultaneously open and closed, a site of strategic dilemmas and contradictions for the social forces involved.

We can see here a transformation in the manner in which the state, as an object of analysis, is defined. The state simultaneously is open to emergent political demands (a source of flexibility), and presents limits to the delivery of the same demands, or faces overload by attempting to integrate the complexities and contradictions of other spheres within itself. The political system is reconstituted here as a circuit of power, and the state is viewed as a 'collective fiction' or 'semantic artefact'. Thus, the state provides the political system with a reference point in order to secure a degree of unity and the means of mobilization of social forces. As an object of analysis, 'the state' is thus a simplified self-description of the political system as a whole (Jessop 1986d; 1987d; 1990d: 325–7), a means of simplifying the overwhelming internal complexities of the political system. In this respect, he suggests, 'the discourse of the state serves to focus, unify and aggregate political action' (Jessop 1990d: 326).[13]

In contemporary liberal democracies, the binary code through which political power is translated is the distinction between public and private domains. The exercise of power depends on office holding and the restriction of political power to public officials, an important precondition for the emergence of autopoietic tendencies within the political system. The distinction between public and private thus becomes an important terrain of contestation between social forces both within and beyond the political system (in the organization and programmes throughout the social order). In the latter case, the distinction can be seen in four ways:

1 *Government and opposition*: the circulation of power within the context of the code of public office-holding setting clear limits to responsibility.
2 *Legal and illegal uses of power*, so that political power can be used for the lawful pursuit of private purpose.
3 *Progressive and conservative ideological codes*, in order to simplify decisions and facilitate alliances.
4 The development of codes to organize mobilization around the *choice of office holders and political programmes*.

The systems-theoretical approach of Luhmann provides Jessop with a way of identifying both the formal and informal forms of power, in a manner compatible with his own account of the relationship between the forms of representation, forms of intervention, the internal articulation of the state, and the balance of class forces. Luhmann identifies a circuit of power, from citizens to parliament to government to bureaucracy to subjects, against which the circuit of informal power flows in the opposite direction. For Luhmann, as the internal complexity of the political system develops, so too does the increased role of the informal circuit of power, particularly in the field of welfare politics (Jessop 1990d: 323–5).

By identifying the self-referential character of politics, Jessop initially suggests that Luhmann provides some of the conceptual tools for rethinking the relationship between the state and other spheres of social activity, notably the capitalist economy. In particular, the policy outputs of the political system are mediated through law and money, and legal and financial intervention have increased with the internal complexity of the political system. Consequently, the state has to live with the range of intended and unintended consequences of its own interventions. Jessop argues that the openness of such systems is a product of two features of complex differentiated social life. The first is the interdiscursive character of language, to facilitate communication between the systems and subsystems and their autopoietic discourses. The second is the fact that the subsystems are functionally interdependent and, as such, their co-evolution must be to some degree compatible if any global social formation is to be sustained rather than collapse (Jessop 1990d: 325–7). It is the conception of social systems as open, at the same time as they contain mechanisms which attempt to ensure closure, that led Jessop to reformulate the concept of society (and the functionalist account of social reproduction associated with studies of the welfare state) as a concrete process of societalization (the production of always-incomplete society effects).

In Jessop's discussion of Poulantzas and Foucault, it is clear that he found the proposition of 'strategic calculation without a calculating subject' unsatisfactory. However, he suggests that some forms of systems theory offer a useful way of generating insights into the relationship between the social relations and tendencies of the capitalist economy, and its relationship to other non-economic systems. Jessop notes the potential uses of theories of structural coupling, which identify the ways in which all systems and subsystems within a global social formation are connected, even if the systems involved are particularly autopoietic in character. In these theories, changes within one system necessitate changes in other systems, if the relatively smooth operation of the social order in question is to be sustained. Systems are understood to be interactive with the changing environment. In addition, the perturbing effects of a system's interaction need to be compensated for, and the tensions managed, if a more inclusive autopoietic social system (a society effect) is to be established and maintained. For Jessop, this offers a way of understanding the formation of historic blocs as the non-necessary correspondence of base and superstructure: as 'relatively stable structurally coupled blocs':

> In the case of autopoietic systems . . . it is their internal operations which determine how they will react to exogenous events. Whether a given event is merely perturbing and triggers self-reorganization or proves so disruptive that the whole system disintegrates may well vary in line with past changes in its structure due to earlier environmental perturbations and/or its own internal development. Thus the current operations and organizations of a system are always a result of its own dynamic and that of its environment. Through this sequential, path-dependent interaction the system comes to be *structurally coupled* to its environment. This structural coupling appears as a behavioural complementarity; the system tends to react in such a way as to maintain its autopoiesis. When a destructive interaction occurs, however, the process is interrupted and the system disintegrates.
>
> (Jessop 1990d: 328)

In a significant additional reference, Jessop identifies the role of co-evolution in constructing this approach, drawing on the work of Günther Teubner which highlights the role of institutional variation, selection and retention as a means of identifying the processes through which social organizations are reproduced and transformed. In particular, Teubner places a strong emphasis on the 'sequence of communicative interactions' through which systems are constituted and interact.

The interdiscursive dimension to the systems-theory account of communicative interaction (to ensure mutual understanding between, and reflexivity within, systems) provides the strategic terrain for social forces to engage in hegemonic projects, and their co-ordination within and across different fields. In addition, this account of autopoietic systems and organizations provides a means of re-conceptualizing the models adopted in policy making on the regulation of complex social institutions, and in particular, the regulation of economy by the state. The success of a particular form of regulation depends on its capacity to work through operational codes and procedures, and to facilitate self-regulation within the regulated system(s). By exploring these theoretical issues, Jessop was also addressing the central problems in accounting for the shifting patterns of state regulation since the disintegration of Fordism and the Keynesian welfare state (Jessop 1990d: 327–31).

The new synthesis: state theory, regulation theory and discourse analysis

The previous sections demonstrate how Jessop redefined the state as a site of strategy. This was tied to a reconceptualization of the processes involved in societalization, as the production of society takes effect through the autopoietic tendencies of social systems. This section focuses on the substantive problems of generating an account of the social order which can account for; one, the complex relations between structures and strategies; two, the relation between abstract and concrete levels of analysis; and three, the ways in which the relationship between economy, polity and ideology are re-conceptualized within Jessop's intellectual evolution. In particular, this section focuses on Jessop's endorsement of the regulationist account of capitalist economic development, and his critical engagement with post-Marxist discourse analysis. In 1990, the scope of this new synthesis was acknowledged in Jessop's account of 'Regulation Theories in Retrospect and Prospect' (Jessop 1990b). Here, he identified his intellectual project as synthesizing three approaches, each respectively oriented towards the economy, polity and ideological discourse:

1   *Regulation theory*, which explores the institutionalized relations of accumulation and regulation within the field of capitalist economic development.
2   *State theoretical approaches*, associated with the West German school of Joachim Hirsch, who had explored the relationship between state forms and regulation theory, and who treated the state in general terms as a factor of cohesion.
3   *Discourse-analytical approaches*, particularly the work of Laclau and Mouffe (1985) on the logics of equivalence and difference, which utilized Gramscian assumptions within the context of Foucauldian and Derridean conceptualizations of discourse.

In this familiar reworking of the neo-Marxist triad, Jessop is engaged in a renewed period of symbolic modelling in order to overcome what he considers to be the problems of one-sidedness associated with each approach (respectively, economism, politicism and ideologism). Nevertheless, he contends that a creative synthesis of these three sources can be justified on three grounds. First, each can operate within a realist ontological and epistemological framework. Second, each can generate concepts of the relevant causal powers and liabilities, and can specify tendencies and counter-acting tendencies in their respective fields. Finally, each can generate the middle-range concepts which serve to identify the institutional forms within which conjunctural analyses can take place. These claims are strongest in respect to regulation theory, and weakest in relation to discourse analysis. For Jessop, this synthesis is a vital component in his account of the process of societalization which he attempts to elaborate, using the modified systems-theoretical tools identified in the previous section in conjunction with the Gramscian account of the historic bloc.

Jessop's concern with regulation theory can be identified from the early 1980s onwards, as he began to consider the structural transformations related to the emergence and establishment of Thatcherism. The concern with the effects of state regulation emerged in French Marxist political economy as a means of finding a more flexible and appropriate way to explain capitalist reproduction (considered in Althusserian terms) while at the same time incorporating a degree of indeterminacy and uncertainty into the process. There is no one regulation approach predominating in Jessop's thinking, and he characteristically draws on ideas as and when they offer a useful way for rethinking — and possibly resolving — the issues he faced in different periods. Nevertheless, from the mid-1980s, Jessop's conceptual tools are largely derived from the French regulationists, notably Michel Aglietta (1979) and Alain Lipietz (1983, 1987). The focus upon regulation theory also furnished Jessop with the middle-range concepts which could operate between the highly abstract laws of motion of capitalism as a mode of production and the circuit of capital, and the operation of capitalist enterprises within historically-specific conjunctures and specific forms of state regulation. Such middle-range concepts could articulate the movements from simple to complex, and from abstract to concrete social forms, which remained central to Jessop's affiliation to the realist epistemology and ontology.

The regulationist account of Lipietz and Aglietta attempted to identify an alternative to the general equilibrium theories of neo-classical economics which had been the target of Hayek's criticisms in the inter-war period of the early twentieth century. From the standpoint of neo-Marxist political economy, the Keynesian critique of market relations had only gone part of the way towards resolving the problems of equilibrium analysis, since it retained the same conception of economic agency as the theories it sought to replace (those of the firm and the household at the level of exchange). In particular, regulationist accounts highlight the problems of treating time as a series of static time slices rather than as an expression of real movements. In Jessop's terms of reference, regulation involves the establishment and maintenance of a social logic of internal transformation, that is, 'regulation is a system transforming itself'. In this way, instead of treating reproduction and rupture (transformation) as discrete entities in opposition, economic relations are understood in terms of hierarchy rather than as functionally interdependent. In substantive terms, the regulationist approach was constructed to explore the interrelationship between accumulation and regulation, in order to overcome the problems of one-sided analysis of capitalist development. In this way, it was envisaged that it would be possible to identify the 'conditions and rhythms' of economic processes, their cohesion and crisis tendencies, and to relate these transformations to the class struggle (see Jessop 1990b).

Regulationist concepts identify the role of economic relations at varying levels of abstraction/concreteness and simplicity/complexity. Each concept is defined within the terms of reference of Marx's account of the abstract, simple and internally-necessary relations of production (where theoretical closure can be achieved). However, in order to operationalize these concepts they have to be combined with determinations which are themselves derived from relations at varying levels of abstraction and complexity in other fields. Precisely these problems provoked Jessop's earlier argument that 'form problematizes function' (Fine and Harris 1979; Jessop 1982; Sayer 1992). The level of exposition of these middle-range concepts (as indicated later) will remain general, as the focus here is to demonstrate the role of realist scientific method in Jessop's intellectual account. (For a useful survey see Jessop 1990b and Bertramsen, Thomsen and Torfing 1991.) These concepts provide Jessop with a way of identifying how the economy and its relations with extra-economic determinations are real processes, and as such structured, differentiated and changing.

Accumulation regime At the highest level of abstraction and greatest level of simplicity in the regulationist account, this denotes a pattern of production and consumption in abstraction from national economies (such as the Fordist pattern of mass production in relation to mass consumption).

Mode of growth The pattern of production and consumption of a national economy, and its place in the international division of labour (allowing for the identification of accumulation regimes, such as the ideal model of Fordism at local, regional, national, international and supranational levels).

Productive system This allows for the specification of the constitution of a mode of growth in more concrete detail, by identifying the relations of domination between sectors of production, and the distribution of skilled labour, expertise and technology in the different sectors. While Bertramsen *et al.* (1991) correctly recognize this as a more concrete level of analysis, by recognizing the national space as 'highly differentiated and heterogeneous', they should also recognize that the increase in internal complexity identified implies that this level deserves more systematic exploration and development.

Mode of regulation The institutional ensemble, complex of norms and patterns of conduct (acting as a form of societal guidance through which the dispersed decisions of economic agents are co-ordinated). It is through the mode of regulation that capitalism is reproduced within a definite historical and spatial context, in the face of the conflictual and antagonistic character of capitalist social relations. A range of organizational forms plays a part in the regulation of capital accumulation in the areas of competition, monetary exchange, legal procedures, educational and social policies.

Mode of development Alain Lipietz uses this term to identify the pattern of development associated with a dominant paradigm of industrialization, a specific accumulation regime and a mode of regulation (see Jessop 1990b).

Mode of societalization This identifies the ways in which the institutional forms of civil society relate to the organization of production and consumption in historically-specific concrete conjunctures (such as through the organization of work patterns, social security, care of dependants, family patterns, party systems and social movements, and consumption trends). This draws upon Joachim Hirsch's analysis of concrete conjunctures and modes of mass integration in the formation of historic blocs, unifying base and superstructure, and hegemonic blocs, whereby the state and party system secure the preconditions for effective societal regulation.

The exploration and utilization of elements of a wide range of regulationist accounts enabled Jessop to resolve some of the difficulties in the periodization of capitalist development which characterized his work on Poulantzas and the capitalist state in the late 1970s and early 1980s. In particular, the identification of specific accumulation regimes, in relation to variations in the production of value, enabled Jessop to overcome the apparent disjunctions between the periodization of stages of capitalism and the emergence of Fordism as an accumulation strategy. Aglietta's distinction between an extensive accumulation regime (involving the relative dominance of absolute surplus value and the expansion of capitalism into new spheres of activity) and an intensive accumulation regime (the relative dominance of relative surplus value, and capital accumulation through the reorganization of existing areas of capitalist activity) could only adequately be explained within Jessop's treatment of the circuit of capital as a contingent outcome.

Regulationist approaches distinguish the competitive mode of regulation (corresponding to the extensive accumulation regime) and a monopolistic mode of regulation (corresponding to the intensive accumulation regime). This distinction enabled Jessop to avoid the conflation of the Keynesian welfare state with Fordism which had characterized his earlier work. Fordism could now be defined as an accumulation regime, a mode of growth and a mode of regulation, although in each case, it remains the task of the researcher to specify how they operate in more detail, as the levels of complexity and concreteness are increased. The formation of a particular accumulation regime and mode of regulation, in so far as they secure the reproduction of capital in a particular time and place, also imposes certain rigidities on the capacity of the institutions to respond to change. As Jessop identifies:

> Far from regulationists assuming that accumulation regimes or modes of regulation somehow precede struggle, they argue that these are always the product of past struggles and are penetrated with present struggles. The legacy of past struggles is a structurally inscribed strategic selectivity which favours some class forces over others. Since there are no institutional guarantees that struggles will always be contained within these forms and/or resolved in ways that reproduce these forms, the stability of an accumulation regime or mode of regulation is always relative, always partial and always provisional.
> (Jessop 1990d: 309)

Changes in the international division of labour, the circuit of capital, the institutional configurations of the state and civil organizations and/or the balance of social forces in a determinate conjuncture, produce crisis tendencies which may destabilize the institutional forms in question. Consequently, any transitions embody the tentative outcomes of the struggles between social forces and institutional trial and error.

The distinction developed by Michel Aglietta between modes of regulation, in terms of both the wage form and the forms of competition, ensured that the extra-economic conditions of capital accumulation played a central role in regulationist explanations. In addition, through the specification of modes of growth, Aglietta was able to specify their correspondence to phases in the international division of labour (*pax Britannica* and *pax Americana* respectively). Finally, his account of the complementarity between the French and West German modes of regulation in the context of the emerging European Union could only adequately be understood as a form of structural coupling. The low-inflation and export-oriented mode of growth in West Germany was structurally coupled with the high-inflation and domestic-demand-led mode of growth of France. This led to the contingently necessary outcome of continued capitalist development, whereby the disruptive tendencies of each led to a situation of 'compensable perturbation' between the two social systems (Jessop 1990b; 1990d). The contingency involved in the analysis of Fordism, in terms of definite concrete conjunctures, can be seen in Jessop's account of the crisis tendencies of 'flawed Fordism' in the context of post-war Britain. In this situation, the attempts at modernization initiated by the British state produced an outcome where the public sector was considerably more Fordist than the private sector (Jessop 1992b).

The contingencies in any characterization of Fordism are relatively insignificant when compared with any attempt at understanding the range of possible features involved in any successive accumulation regime and mode of regulation. The distinctive features of the post-Fordist accumulation regime can be specified in very general terms as the emergence of flexible automation, and flexible specialization of the labour force with greater skill differentials between occupational sectors. Even here, Jessop has recently questioned the capacity of both Fordism and the range of characterizations of post-Fordism to provide an adequate taxonomy for the diverse and complex transformations in workplace organization. In terms of consumption, markets have become increasingly differentiated and subject to greater short-term fluctuations than within Fordism. It is also important to stress the large variations in actually-existing Fordisms (peripheral, flawed, neo-Fordism and so on) as opposed to an ideal model. Indeed, it is through the regulationist theoretical framework and its conceptual schemata of labour process, accumulation regime, mode of regulation, mode of societalization and the periodization of social processes, that Jessop is able to identify such empirical variation and problematize the transition to post-Fordism (Jessop 1992b). As Andrew Sayer's research suggests, Fordism does not exhaust the global range of systems of accumulation and regulation (Sayer 1989). Jessop's account of the problems in defining the transition from Fordism to some putative form of post-Fordist mode of regulation are beyond the scope of this study, but it can be traced through Jessop's work (Jessop 1989a, 1989c, 1990a, 1991a, 1991b, 1991c, 1992a, 1993; Jessop et al. 1988, 1990). These themes will be explored in the subsequent text which builds on the arguments of this study (see Smith 2002).

The regulationist account developed by Jessop therefore represents his most systematic attempt to construct a realist methodology for studying the processes of economic change. However, there are significant problems in this approach if it does not develop the same forms of techniques as have been developed in other social spheres, such as the constitution of the state form and the operation of ideological discourse. He specifically identifies the economistic tendencies of accounts which consider the extra-economic as external to (rather than interpenetrative with) the economy, which consider the role of the state and civil institutions only in so far as they serve some function within the productive system, and which treat the dynamic of the productive system as endogenous. In contrast, Jessop is concerned with the role of the state in regulating the relationship between wages, productivity and inflation, managing demand and generalizing mass-consumption norms within the Fordist mode of regulation (Jessop 1990c; 1992b). It is clear from the range of objects which involve regulation in some form (the wage relation, the articulation of accumulation with competition, the relation between the local, regional, national, international and supranational levels) that a more adequate characterization of the role of the state and processes of societalization is necessary. To do this, Jessop derives useful arguments and conceptual tools by returning to the West German regulation approach associated with Hirsch and, to a lesser extent, the American radical economists who developed an account of the 'social structures of accumulation' (Bowles and Edwards 1985).

Hirsch also attempted to construct an account of the state and its relation to civil society and the economy within the terms of reference of a realist ontology and epistemology. In this analysis, the real relations of the state are considered to be a complex structured whole composed of autonomous parts, which can be analysed at different levels of abstraction. In addition, the mode of presentation tends to adopt the movement from abstract/simple to concrete/complex forms. For Hirsch, the state plays an important role in initiating and managing the procedural regulation of the mode of societalization in order to deliver two goals. First, the state acts as a means of system integration within a given social formation and, if successful, contributes to the emergence of a specific 'historic bloc' (here defined as the structural correspondence of economic base and political and ideological superstructure). Second, the state secures an 'unstable equilibrium of compromise' between the relevant social forces, contributing to the formation of an hegemonic bloc, a relatively enduring alliance of class forces around the dominance of a fraction willing and able to exercise hegemonic leadership.

Hirsch identifies the connections between the capital penetration of society by the processes involved in the disintegration of traditional social structures, and the emergence of the 'security state' as a key constituent of the economic base itself. He also identifies the forms in which the Fordist state in crisis impacts upon the processes of societalization:

- The bureaucratization and centralization of mass parties and trade unions.
- The transformation of mass group representation through the mass-integrative steering, control and administration of life chances.
- The shifting relations between the state and fractions of capital within a more integrated global market (with consequent shifts in the power bloc).
- The growing contradiction between socio-economic steering conditions and political legitimation, with consequent conflicts between state and people.
- The emergence of politically organized but economically fragmented society.
- The emergence of new forms of state surveillance and social control.

Hirsch specifically highlights the way in which the state form and value form cannot, by themselves, offer an adequate account of the mode of societalization. This marks out his approach as more complete in mapping the conjunctural configuration of economic, political and ideological determinations than French regulation theory (Hirsch 1983; 1984; 1991; Esser and Hirsch 1989). Thus, Jessop draws upon earlier themes in his own work and places them within the context of the state as a site of strategic intervention and the dialectic of structure and strategy. To do this, Jessop places the strategically-inclined West German state theory within the context of the more structurally-inclined French regulation theory, with its emphasis on the structural constraints (in the sense of path dependency) of capital accumulation.

The final element in Jessop's theoretical triad, discourse analysis, is less easily integrated into a realist ontological and epistemological framework, which is itself based upon the assumed distinction between knowledge and reality. The discourse analysis of Laclau and Mouffe uses Gramscian conceptions of hegemonic struggle within the context of a post-structuralist account of discourse, within which knowledge and reality are themselves discursive categories. In this account, ideological and political discourses are seen as linguistically constituted through material practices around fluid and proliferating subject positions. Jessop has also commented on the limitations in adopting only a two-dimensional form of abstraction (the logics of difference and equivalence). He has explicitly criticized the focus on language to the exclusion of other things upon which, he suggests, discourse analysis is often based (Jessop 1990d: 288–301). There is little evidence that the realist assumptions he suggests exist within all of the three approaches he wishes to synthesize. By implication, in adopting the distinction between intransitive and transitive domains (see Chapter Two), Jessop adopts a more eclectic position with regard to the post-Marxist account of ideological discourse. For Jessop this approach provides a way of reformulating problems within his appropriation and modification of Luhmann's systems theory, and overcoming the functionalist tendencies of some forms of regulation theory.

Laclau and Mouffe's account of the relationship between floating elements within the interdiscursive field of language, and relatively fixed moments within particular discourses, provides Jessop with a means of identifying clearly the contingency within social relations. Jessop is particularly troubled about the problem of avoiding essentialism while recognizing that the objects of regulation pre-exist regulation itself. He argues that:

> they both pre-exist regulation and are constituted in and through it. They pre-exist regulation as so many relatively free elements which can become objects for specific regulatory practices. Once integrated into a specific mode of regulation, however, they are transformed into moments within that mode and thereby acquire a relative fixity. In Marxian terms, they become 'definite' objects of regulation. Moreover the same elements have points of articulation with alternative modes of regulation and can never be fully fixed within any mode of regulation. Thus regulation is always partial and unstable and the balance between fixity and fluidity (or . . . rigidity and flexibility) is complex and changing.
>
> (Jessop 1990b: 187–8)

The arguments of Laclau and Mouffe are partially based upon the insights of Lacanian psychoanalysis, particularly the concept of 'suture', and the Derridean approach to difference as both relational and deferred (see Smith 1998b ch. 6). This approach treats all attempts to construct meaning as attempts to construct a total frame of reference within which all the elements involved are constituted as moments. However, Laclau and Mouffe argue that all such attempts contain a surplus of meaning which subverts the possibility of total and final closure. This ensures that all the elements involved are open to disarticulation, and subsequent re-articulation as relatively fixed moments in configurations with other situated elements as related moments within another discursive formation (Laclau and Mouffe 1985). Without such partial fixity, relations of difference and equivalence would be impossible. They characterize hegemonic projects as just such an attempt to fix, once and for all, ideological discourse (but one which is doomed to have the elements continually rearticulated).

Jessop identifies an effective way of integrating the discourse-analytical approach with the systems-theoretical approach, within its treatment of systems as both open and closed, as both autopoietic and allopoietic. On these grounds, Jessop suggests that society, the state or any institutional form can be said to exist in so far as it is constituted through partial, unstable and provisional but nevertheless totalizing projects. In situating the discourse-analytical assumptions within the context of actually-existing institutional forms within definite conjunctures, Jessop avoids the difficult questions of integrating post-structuralist idealist conceptual formations within a broadly realist approach. In addition, this also enables him to utilize discourse-analytical terminology at the same time as slipping back into the conventional neo-Marxist distinction between knowledge and reality. This can be seen in the deployment of the distinction between the 'real-concrete' and the 'concrete-in-thought'. By pleading the fallibility of knowledge, Jessop's account of theory construction can accommodate his claim that the scientific specification of law-like tendencies of capitalism, or institutional forms in all fields, is tendential in two senses. First, causal mechanisms are actualized only within and through specific conditions. Second, the underlying causal mechanisms are themselves tendential, provisional and unstable. This reinforces his consistent endorsement of the logic of articulation as a methodology, in preference to the reductionist and essentialist assumptions associated with the logic of mediation (Jessop 1990b: 187–90).

Whither state theory?

The scope of this account prevents me from considering some of the interesting new work by Jessop on patterns of capitalist development (particularly at the local and regional levels), path dependency and forms of governance, the transformation of welfare into workfare in the field of social policy, and the consequences of his problematization of post-Fordism as an analytically useful category (with the exception of some preliminary remarks on his comments on regulation and governance). These aspects of Jessop's work are largely under way, and it is too early to establish their impact on his theoretical framework as it presently stands (although they form a significant part of the discussion in Smith 2002). This concluding section addresses the role of state theory in Jessop's account of societalization, and considers the 'long wave' of Jessop's theorizing on the state since the late 1960s. The epistemological and ontological issues raised by Jessop's complex creative synthesis of theoretical approaches will be explored in the concluding chapter.

The key issue for consideration here is whether Jessop's phased use of symbolic modelling introduces conceptual formations into his realist ontological and epistemological framework which produce discontinuities and contradictions within his theoretical framework. Jessop is concerned with the state and the economy as 'real-concrete' objects formed through 'concrete synthesis of multiple determinations within overdetermined historically specific conjunctures'. There are substantive grounds for using a range of idealist approaches to characterize the fragmentary and fluid character of institutional forms (as illustrated by the incorporation of systems theory and discourse analysis). Such approaches are less useful for constructing a conceptual hierarchy for the discussion of state forms along the lines adopted by Jessop for understanding the value form, the circuit of capital, the formation of accumulation regimes, modes of regulation and developing concrete relational conjunctural analyses. For Jessop, 'states are not the sort of abstract, formal object which readily lend themselves to a clear-cut, unambiguous definition' (Jessop 1990d: 340). However, the same problems exist in relation to understanding the capitalist economy. Jessop claims that by viewing the state as a form-determined social relation and adopting a spiral movement from abstract to concrete and from simple to complex, it is possible to generate a useful account of the state which avoids the problems of essentialism and reductionism.

Jessop develops an account which starts from three levels: the institutional separation of the state from other spheres (as an expression of the general interest); the nature of its internal organization, the modes of political calculation and operating procedures; and the political practices and discourses through which common interests are articulated (Jessop 1990d: 341–5). He suggests that a conceptual hierarchy would start from the idea of 'state as form' (comparable with Marx's 'production-in-general') as 'the emergence within a community of an institutionalized division of labour between an organization empowered to exercise force in implementing decisions binding on the members of that community and the community in its other modes of existence and activity' (ibid.: 344).

He argues that, in the absence of the distinction between officialdom (the administration) and the people, the state as such no longer exists. By starting from the position outlined in combination with the three levels, Jessop proceeds to outline states in modes of production, states in definite phases of a mode of production (indicating variations in the form of institutional separation of the state from the economy), normal and exceptional regimes (indicating dominance in forms of representation or in the internal articulation of state institutions) and, within these categories, regime types oriented to policy making and party systems. Nevertheless, this remains at odds with the transhistorical conceptions of people, nature, human labour and social relations of production which underlabour the Marxist characterization of the necessary and internal relations of class relations within capitalism.

The identification of the state at the highest level of abstraction, as a factor of cohesion, is an empty formulation which does not provide a similar explanatory principle to the conception of relations of exploitation which grounds Jessop's adoption of the Marxist approach to the economy. Indeed, the economy and ideology can all be conceptualized as factors of cohesion, and social cohesion is a conjunctural feature to be explained rather than something which operates as a distinctive explanatory principle (along with interests, power and relative autonomy). It is significant that Jessop offers an alternative research agenda for the impatient, in the form of concrete complex analysis of six dimensions: forms of representation; the internal articulation of state institutions; forms of intervention; the social bases of state power; the practices and projects which define the state's boundaries; and the discourses constructing the illusory community of the state within the framework of a given historic bloc. The research agenda for a conceptual hierarchy and the research agenda around these six dimensions appear to be unsynchronized, a curious side-effect of the synthesis of realist and idealist approaches with their different epistemologies and ontologies. It may be the problem of reconciling these research agendas which has recently led Jessop to explore the possibility of a Luhmannian reinterpretation of Marx.

As it stands, in *State Theory* (Jessop 1990d), Jessop identified six guidelines summarized below for an adequate strategic-relational account of the state. These guidelines are geared towards a research programme which explores the state in conjunction with social relations. (This was already implied in his definition of the state as the condensation and materialization of social relations.)

1. Adequate state theory can only be developed as part of an adequate theory of society (the political system and the wider environment), so that the distinctive organizational form and modes of calculation of historically-specific states are embedded in the societies within which they were constituted (despite the context of institutional separation and operational autonomy).
2. The complexity and differentiation of modern societies, with a variety of subsystems and centres of power engaged in relations of functional interdependence, means that no subsystem is determinant in the last instance.
3. The state is the embodiment of the paradox of greater autonomy combined with greater interdependence for, in the last instance, the state manages these relations. The state simultaneously is empowered to take collectively binding decisions, and operates as a condensation of the struggles within the overall political system. The success of the state depends upon its integration into an historic bloc (defined as a non-necessary, socially constituted and discursively reproduced relative unity)

which emerges from an evolutionary structural coupling of different institutional orders in conjunction with the strategic projects intended to secure some form of correspondence.
4. The state is a complex institutional ensemble, with its own modes of calculation and operational procedures, operating as a site of political practices deploying its institutions and capacities for specific purposes; the boundaries and character of the state system are contingent matters resulting from the combined effects of state projects in a historically and socially specific location.
5. The state, as an institutional ensemble rather than a real subject, cannot exercise power, although it is possible to identify the capacities of the state which are activated through definite political forces, with their own unacknowledged conditions and unintended consequences.
6. The structural powers, capacities and liabilities of the state, and their realization, cannot be understood except by reference to the political system and the wider environment. The strategic selectivity inscribed in the state (as an ensemble of centres) and associated institutional forms offers different opportunities to different groups (within and beyond the state) with different purposes, so that the powers of the state are always conditional and relational (adapted from Jessop 1990d: 365–7).

The whole development of Jessop's work on the social order, the state and, more recently the state within the societalization process, has a certain consistency at a number of levels. These will be explored in the concluding chapter. One of the difficulties in pinning down Jessop's position has been the continually renewed bouts of symbolic modelling, each involving a creative synthesis of additional approaches (and a revisitation of older ones) as a response to specific problems in social-scientific research. It is possible to distinguish the phases of these forms of symbolic modelling in terms of their scope, a function of the objects of analysis under investigation.

In the first phase, he is concerned with the broad problems of the constitution of the social order, and thus engages in a broad synthesis of functionalist theories, non-Marxist conflict theory, and neo-Marxism with exchange theory, providing a synthetic unity as well as linkages between macro- and micro-sociological levels. The epistemological position is transcendental idealist, and he remained committed to an empirical realist ontology. In the second phase from the mid-1970s to the publication of *The Capitalist State* (Jessop 1982), Jessop engages in narrow synthesizing within neo-Marxist political economy, attempting to avoid the manifestations of essentialism and reductionism in the economistic, politicist or ideologist writings within this field. The synthetic moment here is provided by Gramscian conceptualizations of hegemony and the historic bloc as a way of avoiding the conceptual dead end of the relative autonomy debate. In this work he develops a consistent realist epistemology and ontology, and he outlines his first clear statement on these matters in *The Capitalist State*.

The third phase of broad synthesizing is initiated through his self-criticism of the problems of politicism, both in his own work and in the writings of Poulantzas on the state as a social relation. This phase should also be understood in conjunction with Jessop's attempts to address the complex economic, political and ideological shifts in the 1970s and 1980s (particularly the emergence of the Thatcherite hegemonic project). The search for conceptually adequate tools leads him into post-Althusserian French political economy, regulation theory, and towards the appropriation of arguments from systems theory. This helps him to identify ways of reformulating the relative-autonomy problem. By the late 1980s, this coalesces into a synthesis of strategic-relational state theory, the regulationist account of the economy, and the discourse analysis of Laclau and Mouffe. The synthetic moments at the structural level of social-system integration are provided by a modified version of Luhmann's systems theory, while at the strategic level, Gramscian analysis relates this to the neo-Marxist characterization of conjunctural struggles and the overdetermination of structural determinations. The post-Poulantzian characterization of global strategic calculation without calculating subjects, combined with real calculating subjects at the concrete level, provides a means of mediating between these structural and strategic levels.

More recently the contours of this synthesis appear to be changing again. The reformulation of the state as a 'site of strategy' in the mid-1980s, the recent publications of systems theory approaches on governance and law, institutional economics, and the proliferation of Foucauldian studies of power relations in a range of institutional forms, have prompted him to explore the convergences between the diverse forms of regulation theories, systems theory and governance theories (Jessop 1995). Jessop's massive body of work is unique in two respects. The first is its consistent concern to explore the problems of political economy in the context of broader social relations. The second is the extent to which the epistemological and ontological questions raised by his research are addressed throughout his intellectual development.

6 Metatheorizing the state
Preliminary conclusions

Introduction

> [W]hen paradigms change, the world itself changes with them. Led by a new paradigm, scientists adopt new instruments and look in new places. Even more important, during revolutions scientists see new and different things when looking with familiar instruments in places they have looked before. It is rather as if the professional community had been suddenly transported to another planet where familiar objects are seen in a different light and are joined by unfamiliar ones as well. Of course, nothing of quite that sort does occur.
>
> (Kuhn 1970: 111)

It has been said by Thomas Kuhn, among others, that more information may spoil the activity of the imagination and undermine originality of insight (Parsons 1990: 317). Indeed, a characteristic feature of innovations within the philosophy of social science is their capacity to generate a 'bandwagon' effect. It is the purpose of this chapter neither to examine the psychological motivations of social scientists, nor to defend Kuhn's account of the history of science. It is merely to state that the mentality of 'me too' has recently begun to transform the intellectual project of critical realism, a project whose most influential exponent is Roy Bhaskar (1978, 1979, 1989a). The critical-realist project is in danger of being obscured and misunderstood in the dash to appropriate any set of ideas which bears some resemblance to realist assumptions, instead of utilizing the critical-realist account of science as a basis for generating original and new ways of understanding and explaining social phenomena.

Kuhn's socio-psychological account of paradigmatic shifts provides us with a vivid portrayal of theories of knowledge undergoing transformation, and a series of warnings about the contradictory processes involved. While the breakthroughs are the product of work on the fringes, or at least of those who are not committed to the taken-for-granted assumptions of a given scientific community, there is a tendency to reinterpret prevailing theoretical assumptions, ideas and conceptual frameworks in a way which allows for the retention of comfortable horizons and scenery. While I am not rejecting this as a source of inspiration, this chapter is a warning against the dangers of proceeding in such a way as to ignore the complex epistemological references of existing substantive bodies of knowledge.

The growing influence of critical realism can be seen in a number of fields of inquiry: from Rom Harré's investigations in psychology (Harré 1979), through Bob Jessop's and Andrew Sayer's contributions to political economy (for example Jessop 1995; Sayer 1996), Stewart Clegg's work on the analysis of power (Clegg 1989) to Paul Gilroy's *There Ain't No Black in the Union Jack* (1982), by way of a small sample. Predictably, this process has also involved exhuming realist insights from key figures in the development of the social sciences and social theory, notably Marx and Chomsky (Keat and Urry 1982; Sayer 1992; and of course, Bhaskar himself, 1978, 1979, 1986, 1989b) which made some sense in the light of the commitment of these authors to human emancipation. In the last decade, however, attempts have been made to situate Emile Durkheim (Taylor 1982; Pearce 1989) and, crucially for this discussion, Robert Dahl (Isaac 1987a) and Friedrich Hayek (Lawson 1994a; Peacock 1993) within a critical-realist framework. Such thinkers are problematic, for they do not sit easily in the categories devised to house them. However, it is possible to generalize that each in turn has developed a distinctive viewpoint in critical exchanges with both the empiricist and neo-Kantian positions in the philosophy of science. We should take care to avoid assuming that a critique of empiricism automatically leads to realist conclusions.

Dahl and realism?

Jeffrey Isaac, in *Power and Marxist Theory* (1987a), claims that there are elements in the later work of Dahl on polyarchy and democracy which can be useful for a realist theory of power and the state. In particular, he suggests that the shift away from his earlier behaviourist approach, towards power and political influence in empirical research, marks a watershed in Dahl's epistemological and ontological position. In his earlier work, Dahl affiliated his research methodology with the non-experimental empiricist methodology of Herbert Blalock, particularly the use of statistical techniques to simulate closure in accounting for empirical relationships in behavioural political science. While it is clear from my earlier arguments (see Chapter Three) that an epistemological and ontological reorientation did take place, Isaac's characterization of the shift is open to question. Indeed, the evidence he raises is rather flimsy when analysed in terms of the contrasts between and within empiricist, idealist and realist epistemological and ontological positions outlined in Chapter Two. Isaac claims that the shift from the search for behavioural regularities (in Humean terms) towards the analysis of the 'institutional conditions of pluralist democracy' represents an:

implicitly realist theory of political power, a theory distinguished by three general claims: (1) the political institutions of liberal democracies are relatively open, public, and responsive to the pressures brought upon them; (2) they are therefore neutral as regards the interests that can be articulated and the policies that can be adopted; and (3) under these institutional conditions there tends to be a plurality of competing groups and a dispersal of political influence among them.

(Isaac 1987a: 195–6)

Dahl appears to be engaging in a 'transcendental' questioning of democracy by attempting to identify 'the conditions of possibility of polyarchy', and there are certainly radical transformist overtones to the calls for the third wave of democratization of economic enterprises. Superficially it may appear that such a radical agenda has affinities or parallels with the realist approach associated with neo-Marxism, in terms of the attempt to transform social structures. However, transcendental questions have been associated with a wide range of diverse idealist position, at least since Kant. Isaac argues that the evidence of increased awareness of social and economic inequalities by pluralist researchers, and Dahl's shift to the loosely-labelled position of 'democratic socialism', are tantamount to an epistemological and ontological break in his work. This argument seems to rest on a common, straightforward contrast of empiricism and realism, a contrast which takes little account of the epistemological and ontological assumptions of each approach, and ignores the possibility of other approaches.

In a number of disciplines, such as economics, the contrast between empiricism and realism is a function of the debates in the field of knowledge (owing to the marginalization of idealist approaches in institutionalist and evolutionary economics). In politics and sociology, idealism has been both self-consciously developed and oriented towards empirical research, particularly since the dissemination of Weberian conceptual frameworks. Part of the problem lies in the characterization of causality in Isaac's text, particularly in relation to the concept of power. Isaac's argument moves from the Humean conception of causality as a constant conjunction of events (a behavioural or empirical regularity between observable variables) to a realist conception of causality conceived in term of causal powers (which can exist regardless of the existence of constant conjunctions of events). In the Humean approach a constant conjunction of events is both necessary and sufficient for establishing a causal law (regularity determinism), while in the realist approach, it is neither necessary nor sufficient to establish a causal law (ubiquity determinism). Isaac particularly highlights the importance of the account of causality established by Rom Harré, that objects possess causal powers by virtue of their intrinsic properties and structures regardless of observable effects, and recommends its adoption in the social sciences (Harré and Madden 1975; Isaac 1987a: 72–107, 192–8 and *passim*). This conflates an epistemological argument about causality with Bhaskar's account of the ontological assumptions of the empiricist and idealist positions. Isaac's treatment of Dahl's writing is a function of problem within realism which will be explored later in this chapter.

As was demonstrated in Chapter Two, it is common for social scientists to adopt the characterization of constant conjunctions of events as necessary but not sufficient for establishing a causal law, in conditions where the complexity of open systems in the analysis of social objects makes the possibility of closure (necessary for establishing constant conjunctions of events) unrealistic. The forms of closure associated with empiricist research (for instance, theoretical, statistical and experimental closure) are rejected by Dahl as he becomes dissatisfied with the descriptive and uncritical tendencies associated with empiricist social-scientific research. The adoption of regularity determinism means that the empirical evidence by the researcher is treated as a matter of observable fact (separate from values and the subjective propensities of theorizing), and as such our knowledge substitutes for reality. In addition, it also assumes that any explanation generated in this way has to be predictively accurate.

Dahl's account of polyarchy attempts to accommodate the existence of complexity, uncertainty and unpredictability in social life. He does this by constructing ideal type models to organize empirical evidence in the manner consistent with the idealist account of causality, that is, intelligibility determinism. The separation of facts from values clearly becomes an uncomfortable constraint upon Dahl's increasingly normative approach. In addition, the assumption of symmetry between explanation and prediction leaves little room for the existence of inadequate theories with a good predictive performance, and adequate theories which prove to be unsuccessful at predicting outcomes in open systems. More significantly, transcendental idealism, by recognizing the creative role of social scientists in constructing variables in the first place, raises problems about the ways in which empiricists see the relationship between theory and observation. Dahl's idealist position on the construction of knowledge and the intelligibility of experience clearly separates his writings after the 1960s from empiricism. However, we must be careful not to misread these developments as an indication of realism. This confusion is related to a more difficult problem. Roy Bhaskar has argued that both empiricism and idealism have a common ontological foundation, empirical realism (see Chapter Two). However, as we discover when we turn to Hayek, even this can be problematized when we consider the differences between empiricism and idealism.

Hayek and realism?

In assessing Hayek's intellectual development we must now return to the approach to knowledge construction upon which his accounts of economics, politics and the social are grounded. Explanations of Hayek's developing problematic have largely been couched in terms of a sudden break, with 'Economics and Knowledge' in 1936 (Hayek 1937) as the key moment. T. W. Hutchison in *The Politics and Philosophy of Economics* (1981) goes as far as suggesting that prior to and following this point in Hayek's development, there exist two different and opposed bodies of thought with their own internal consistency, dubbed Hayek I and Hayek II respectively. In Hutchison's account the transformation of the 'Austrian Economist' Hayek is attributed to the influence of Karl Popper (he cites a footnote revealing Hayek's awareness of the term falsification and of the text, *The Logic of Scientific Discovery* (Popper 1959; originally published in 1934)). Hutchison also cites the increased emphasis on the empirical tendency towards equilibrium as corroborating evidence, alongside Hayek's later praise for the testing of falsifiable statements, the role of prediction and forecasting in economics, and the demarcation of science from non-science (Hutchison 1981: 210–19).

Bruce Caldwell's response in 'Hayek the Falsificationist: A Refutation' (1992) convincingly claims that Hutchison has misinterpreted Hayek's methodological stance. First, he has taken certain statements out of context (Hayek's analysis of the inadequacies of static equilibrium analysis, and his increased concern with the 'co-ordination problem'). Second, he has neglected the crucial essay 'Scientism and the Study of Society', originally published in 1944 (Hayek 1979). The footnote citation of Popper appears to have been an afterthought and given that, as far as we can tell, they met for the first time in 1935 when Popper presented a preliminary version of *The Poverty of Historicism* (1957), influence of a strong kind is unlikely in the light of Hayek's earlier statements on 'The Trend of Economic Thinking' (see Hayek 1991). In addition, the whole trajectory of 'Economics and Knowledge' is to highlight the importance of a more sophisticated theoretical approach, rather than to reduce economics to a series of empirical questions. Clearly the shift in his work does represent a greater degree of attention to philosophical questions, as his own later comments suggest, but these are 'subjectivist' questions about the institutional preconditions for resolving the 'co-ordination problem' (with little evidence of a commitment to Popper's critical rationalist commitment to an 'objective third world'). Finally, on testing, falsifiability, prediction and the demarcation problem, Hayek clearly distinguishes between the character of objects of analysis in the natural sciences and those in the social sciences where the complexity of social phenomena precludes such categorization (Caldwell 1992: 1–15). There are also interesting differences, raised by Hayek, on the role of prediction when dealing with social phenomena, '[W]hat I have called earlier the mere pattern predictions to which we are increasingly confined as we penetrate from the realm in which relatively simple laws prevail into the range of phenomena where original complexity rules' (Hayek 1978: 33). These are cited by Caldwell but, as argued in Chapter Four, they are a useful indication of the tangible legacy of Mises on the differences between quantitative and qualitative predictions and their appropriateness within the discipline of economics (Mises 1981: 116–18). This also helps us to make sense of the conflicting interpretations of Hayek's statement that 'Prediction and explanation are two aspects of the same process' (Hayek 1967: 9). For

Hutchison, this is the most tangible evidence of the Popperian influence, whereas for Caldwell the distinction is simply a common way of addressing the issue in the 1950s, and Hayek does not explicitly state that unpredictable human actions cannot be explained. We can see this when Hayek pursues the point and relates 'degrees of explanation' to 'degrees of prediction'. When dealing with complex phenomena composed of a number of interdependent variables, he is referring not to the:

> individual event but always to phenomena of a certain kind or class [stating] . . . some and never all the properties of any particular phenomena to which they refer. In addition, each property stated will be expressed not as a unique value but as a range, however narrow, within which the property will fall. Because of the limitations of the possible precision of measurement this is true even of the most exact predictions of physics which, strictly speaking, never say more than that the magnitude in question will fall within a certain interval; and it is still more obviously the case where the prediction is not quantitative.
> (Hayek 1967: 9–10)

Taking into account Hayek's suggestion that we need to move from the familiar to the unknown in order to generate adequate explanations, we can see a continuous line of thought back to the 1930s in the development of the individualist and compositive method and the influence of elements of praxeology.

The recent interventions of members of the Cambridge Workshop on Economic Methodology, notably Tony Lawson, Mark Peacock and Steve Fleetwood, have provoked an interesting reassessment of Hayek's epistemological position, and this section is in large measure a response to this work. Tony Lawson presents an account of Hayek's intellectual development as a 'case of continuing transformation' (Lawson 1994a), although it would be more accurate to describe Lawson's account as one of periodization. Taking the work of Hutchison and Caldwell as his reference points, Lawson identifies the 'Economics and Knowledge' paper (Hayek 1937) as a key moment of transformation for Hayek, although he is keen to distance himself from the idea of a clean break. Lawson contends that Hayek's recognition of the subjectively held and widely dispersed character of knowledge, in working through the problems of equilibrium theory and its tendency to assume that data is given for the actors involved, can be characterized as the start of a hermeneuticized re-evaluation of positivist themes in his early work. While he maintains a positivist account of natural science, he advances an 'overstated subjectivist' account of social scientific inquiry.

In addition, Lawson argues that Hayek's treatment of social wholes as constituted by subjective preferences and individual actions, whereby human minds have a common structure, acts as an 'ontological premise' from which 'epistemological conclusions' follow. These are simply that social scientists should attempt to access the lay conceptions of individuals as they grasp their own existence, that interpretive understanding is necessary, and compositive analysis is sufficient, for constructing social scientific explanations (Lawson 1994a: 138–41). The 'Scientism' essay is thus a step on the path towards a resolution of the difficulties generated in social science by the acceptance of the 'concept dependence' of social phenomena. In Lawson's words:

> [T]he brute facts of positivism are in effect transformed into the brute opinions, beliefs, attitudes and interpretations of hermeneuticism; the self-evidence of the empirical world in positivism is reflected in the self-characterization of the social world in hermeneuticism; the empiricist foundations of positivist natural science translated into conceptual foundations in Hayek's hermeneuticised scientism.
> (Lawson 1994a: 147)

Lawson is suggesting that this constitutes a neo-Kantian displacement rather than a transcendence of positivism. However, as I have previously argued, such neo-Kantian idealist influences have shaped and facilitated Hayek's distinctive development since the late 1920s. Lawson presents a critique of Hayek's hermeneuticism, that the social world is not exhausted by its conceptual aspects and that human action has a material basis in real relations which remain inaccessible or only partially comprehended in sensory terms. This approach rests on the contrast he develops between transcendental realism and empirical realism. Yet Lawson's account does not adequately explore the variations in approaches which are committed to the broad-based assumptions of empirical realism.

More specifically, Lawson's account of the positivist displacement in Hayek's work makes references at various points to the neo-Kantian 'orientation', 'variation' or 'gloss' of positivist themes. This precludes a thorough investigation of the textual reference points in relation to which Hayek's work develops. This is possibly a reflection of the way in which the empiricist approach has dominated in economics, and faces a direct challenge from the transcendental realist position, whereas in sociology these challenges have been prefigured by, and mediated through, a lively neo-Kantian tradition. Lawson's critique of Hayek is founded upon the aforementioned distinction between two ontological accounts, empirical realism and transcendental realism. In Bhaskar's account of this position (as stated in Chapter Two), empirical realism involves an implicit ontology based on the category of experience, alongside three sources which together lend plausibility to its metaphysics and give credence to its philosophical form (Bhaskar 1978: 198). The first source is an implicit sociology based upon the 'model of man', with individuals conceived as passive 'sensors of given facts and recorders of their constant conjunctions: passive spectators of a given world rather than active agents in a complex one' (ibid.). This generates an ontological atomism and a predisposition towards epistemological, methodological and political individualism. The second source is 'celestial closure', that where constant conjunctions of events prevail (assuming the constancy of intrinsic states and external forces) it is possible to observe invariable regularities between events (ibid.: 68). Finally, the 'classical paradigm of action' involves the 'corpuscularian view of matter' where the motion of corpuscles accounts for aggregate observed behaviour, and the 'mechanical view of matter' whereby action consists of the impression of external forces upon these corpuscles (ibid.: 83).

Within this broad ontology, where experience, impressions and perception are taken to constitute the world, and where the objects are taken to be events and states of affairs, causal laws are seen as 'nothing more than constant conjunctions of the events of experience', fusing the domains of the empirical with the actual (Lawson 1994a: 134). This involves the utilization of the category of experience to define all that is real, and where experience is held to be certain, committing what Bhaskar has identified as the 'epistemic fallacy', that is, giving a particular 'epistemological concept a general ontological function' (Bhaskar 1978: 28), and dissolving the distinction between the transitive and intransitive domains (Lawson 1994a: 131–7; 1994b: 261–6). The crucial distinction between empiricist and Kantian positions is swept aside in a dismissive way, with the Kantian contribution portrayed as a 'surplus element' of mental constructions or conceptual entities (ibid.: 134).

The empiricist approach involves the premise that the truth of scientific statements can only be known through experimentation and/or observation, not through a priori categories, and that such procedures will simultaneously produce explanatory and predictive knowledge of the external world (Keat and Urry 1982: 4–50). The transcendental idealist philosophy of science, drawing upon Kant's identification of a priori categories as the conditions of possibility of experience, takes the epistemological standpoint that objects of knowledge are models or artificial constructs. According to Bhaskar: 'knowledge is given structure by a sequence of models rather than by a fixed set of *a priori* rules' (Bhaskar 1978: 27). Idealism rejects the empiricist account of science, whereby valid content is exhausted by atomistic facts and their constant conjunctions, in that while it does accept that a constant conjunction of events is necessary for establishing a causal law, it argues that this is not in itself sufficient. For Bhaskar, this is the position of 'intelligibility determinism', assuming that the causes of events are simply those that render an event intelligible to the human mind, unlike the empiricist position of 'regularity determinism' where a constant conjunction of events is both necessary and sufficient for establishing a causal law (ibid.: 163–4). In addition, the idealist position is capable of recognizing the 'transitive' objects constituted within discourse, although it is unable to identify the structures and mechanisms which exist and operate independently of our knowledge of them. Bhaskar poses a dilemma for empirical realism:

> Either theoretical entities refer ultimately to experience, in which case they can be eliminated or theoretical entities constitute experience (in whole or in part) in which case they cannot be eliminated, but must, given the equation of empirical realism, constitute the world (in whole or in part).
>
> (Bhaskar 1978: 163)

Hence it is feasible to account for some degree of complexity within the object of analysis and the concept-dependence of the social world within the terms of reference of transcendental idealism (ibid.: 15). This clearly has implications for assessing whether Hayek is a transcendental realist.

Lawson defines transcendental realism as involving the ontological claim that there is a clear distinction between the empirical, the actual and the real or 'deep' domains of reality. The 'deep' in this case refers to structures, mechanisms, powers and tendencies. The objects are not 'phenomena', as empiricism assumes, or 'social constructs', as in idealism, but real entities which exist, operate and endure quite independently of our experience, knowledge and the conditions which allow access to them. Realism thus makes a clear distinction between the transitive (objects constituted in knowledge or discourse) and the intransitive (the objects of knowledge) and is able to adopt a radically different conception of causality, that of 'ubiquity determinism'. This asserts that while every event has a real underlying cause or set of causes, nevertheless there is 'no presumption that the real cause of an event will also be intelligible to men' (Bhaskar 1978: 71). Causal laws, rather than referring to constant conjunctions of events, refer to causally efficacious transfactual mechanisms which may or may not be realized at the level of events. It is in this sense that objects in the natural and social world are both structured (irreducible to the events of experience) and intransitive (independent of the process of identification) (Lawson 1994b: 262–6).

The question is, does Hayek move beyond the phase in his development which Lawson attributes to hermeneutic foundationalism, where he retains his commitment to the empirical world? Lawson argues that in terms of two essays in the collection *Studies in Philosophy, Politics and Economics* (Hayek 1967), he does so in five ways. First, the language of 'opinions' and 'attitudes' in the 'Scientism' essay is replaced by 'rules that govern action' (Hayek 1967: 79). Second, the social is structured through discursive, tacit and unconscious levels of knowing or observing (ibid.: 87). Third, this opens a gap between the conscious reflections of individuals and the social structure, hence drawing our attention to the unacknowledged conditions of actions and the relationship between the internal impulses and external events in shaping individual actions (ibid.: 68–9). Fourth, given that social phenomena are seen as concept-dependent but are not reduced to concepts, the compositive method is replaced with that of conjectural history, which Lawson claims is retrodictive and hence transcendental-realist in character (ibid.: 75). Finally, the social objects of knowledge (rules and processes) are intransitive, in that they exist partially beyond the knowledge that individuals have of them (ibid.: 78–9). This leads

Lawson to conclude that Hayek's later work contains an embryonic transcendental realism, although he is keen to distance himself from the functionalist tendencies and the normative direction of Hayek's position. He also argues that these insights remain impoverished in Hayek's later work, as Hayek seeks to limit the transformist potential of such insights (Lawson 1994a: 151–7).

The arguments within these five points can be interpreted in another way, as being quite consistent with the influence of Schütz. For instance, the condition of intersubjectivity implies rules which are irreducible to action and which involve a tacit and unacknowledged character. If one takes the structure in this case as the structure of meaning, and the relationship between the internal and the external as a reflection of the condition of simultaneity (the process through which individuals attempt to grasp the interpretive procedures of other individuals), the argument that this is an embryonic transcendental realism is less convincing. The replacement of compositive theory by conjectural history can thus be interpreted as a recognition of the fallibility of attempts completely to reconstruct complex sets of relations. Interpreted in this way, the following source cited by Lawson (1994a: 153) can be seen in a completely different light:

> Conjectural history in this sense is the reconstruction of a hypothetical kind of process which may never have been observed but which, if it had taken place, would have produced phenomena of the kind we observe. The assumption that such a process has taken place may be tested by seeking for yet unobserved consequences which follow from it, and by asking whether all regular structures of the kind in question which we find can be accounted for by that assumption.
> (Hayek 1967: 153)

The Schützian response to the fifth point provides us with the crucial insight into this quotation. If we assume that the rules exist beyond the knowledge we possess as participants in social exchange, then the task of the social scientist involves the identification of the 'recipe knowledge' inscribed within the pre-constituted, meaningful, intersubjective life-world. All idealist approaches recognize the failure of scientific accounts fully to reconstruct the complex external world, but this does not necessarily mean that they also recognize that the real world is both stratified and differentiated.

Mark Peacock (1993) also identifies the close parallels between Hayek and Schütz, but leaves it at that, moving on to develop an account of the affinities between the account of open systems in Hayek's description of social science, and the critical realist account of scientific activity in both natural and social science. Peacock highlights the complexity of Hayek's position and the dilemmas it holds. On the one hand, his stance is anti-naturalist, yet this is premised upon the assumption that closed systems are independent of human intervention in natural science. On the other hand, Hayek's later work on pattern predictions hints at the use of a concept of 'emergent powers'. Yet he is firmly committed to the empirical-realist criterion for establishing a causal law (a constant conjunction of events) and does not identify the internal constitution of things as the prime consideration. Peacock also develops an interesting account of Hayek's later work, particularly on the connections between Hayek's account of the spontaneous order and the debates on social reproduction associated with Giddens and Bhaskar, as well as indicating the underlying problems with functionalist analysis within Hayek's work. These are a product of the use of socio-biological metaphors to explain the spontaneity of the market order, but they do not distort the mundane phenomenological thrust of Hayek's project. Peacock's account of Hayek's theory of agency, founded upon the concept of tacit knowledge and the emergence of rule systems as a manifestation of spontaneous order, can be subject to the same Schützian response as that deployed on Lawson's five points. However, it is still important to recognize that Hayek's position is characterized by epistemological complexity, and that the Schützian influence exists alongside other elements. Take, for example, Peacock's claim that Hayek's account of the complexity of social systems, and the weak nature of predictive claims when confronted with the absence of closure, mean that:

> [F]or Hayek the presence of a tendency in an open system delimits certain kinds or classes of events which can possibly ensue, although the specificities of these events will depend upon the contingent causes (data) with which the principle tendency interacts.
> (Peacock 1993: 253)

The identification of tendencies within complex social systems is contrasted with the lack of specification of structures and mechanisms which would substantiate the claims made by Lawson and Peacock, that Hayek's work contains implicit realist assumptions. In each case it is the commitment to an empirical-realist ontology which impedes Hayek's movement to a realist position. However, it is questionable that this is what Hayek had intended, which in turn raises the issue of whether it would be more fruitful to examine the continuities of Hayek's work from the late 1920s and the early 1930s onwards. Steve Fleetwood's examination of the realist potential of Hayek is useful here. Fleetwood raises the question of what constitutes complexity for Hayek, and whether this is in any way comparable to the definition of an open system within the transcendental realist tradition. For Hayek, he argues, complexity relates to the large number of elements prevalent in a system, which causes problems in identifying causal laws. Such complexity may take a visible form and simply prevent the social scientist from constructing new hypotheses (Fleetwood 1993: 15).

For transcendental realists the problem is not whether the social phenomenon in question is simple or complex, but whether it is possible to identify ontological depth. If we go back to Lawson's outline of transcendental realism and exploration of the relationship between the empirical, the actual and the deep as distinctive domains, then we can see why. These domains are portrayed as 'unsynchronized' in relation to each other; so that 'experience is out of phase with events, allowing the possibility of contrasting experiences of a given event, so events are typically unsynchronized with the mechanisms that govern them' (Lawson 1994b: 262). Hayek's attachment to the empirical-realist ontology of constant conjunctions of events clearly inhibits any developments in this direction. The grounds for questioning the explanatory role of prediction are therefore more closely related to Hayek's continuous concern with the inadequacies of quantitative economics (in the light of Mises' proposals for qualitative economics) than with any conception of ontological depth.

Jessop and realism?

Jessop's account is remarkable for its complexity, rapid changes and for the ways in which it demonstrates the problems of distinguishing between realist and idealist assumptions in social-scientific research. The first half of Chapter Five traces the way in which he shifts from a neo-Kantian idealist account of the comparative historical evidence on social order and change through an exploration of the interrelationship between power, exchange and institutionalization. In its place, he moved towards the realist epistemological and ontological assumptions of neo-Marxism. Unlike Dahl and Hayek, who have realist assumptions attributed to their work, Jessop explicitly adopts a realist approach. In his later work, the epistemological uses of symbolic modelling techniques serve as a means of theoretical construction; enabling Jessop to appropriate a range of idealist and post-structuralist conceptualizations (notably those of Luhmann, Laclau and Mouffe, and strands of Foucauldian thought) and insert them within the evolving neo-Marxist problematic he had developed since the mid-1970s.

Jessop's initial position is very close to the final position adopted by Dahl. His empirical method in the study of political culture (Jessop 1974) demonstrates the neo-Kantian assumptions within his early work. This research was designed to indicate political and social values and the forms of beliefs, deference, traditionalism, status and class consciousness which demonstrated a commitment to civic culture. He identified a number of themes which are pertinent to this investigation. First, political culture combines a respect for symbolic traditional institutions in general terms with strong criticisms of specific aspects. Second, there is a similar pattern of general consensus on the importance of central values, but it is combined with a populist indictment of the dominant order. Third, existing theories of deference and traditionalism fail to convey these complexities, and fourth, there exists marginal evidence of consistent co-variations in attitudes towards different dominant institutions. Together, Jessop suggests, these raise the need for a reformulation of deference and civility. The intention of the study was to accommodate the complex interactive process of opinion formation and voting behaviour. The data also facilitated statistical causal modelling along the lines established by Blalock (1964) for non-experimental research.

Jessop adopted symbolic model construction as a technique of social inquiry in order:

> to provide a more determinate and flexible mechanism for the generation of hypotheses and explanations . . . more amenable to manipulation and refinement in order to ensure greater precision in prediction . . . [and] greater understanding of the relations between variables than mere extrapolation or more rigid analogies.
>
> (Jessop 1972: 3–4)

This overcomes what Jessop considers to be the problems of inconsistency and contradiction which follow from comparing the incomparable, and the inadequate theorizing which often results from the adoption of regularity determinism. A further indication of the neo-Kantian epistemological assumptions underlying Jessop's political sociology can be seen in his treatment of values in social science in relation to the context of discovery and the context of justification. First, he followed Dahrendorf's (1968) position that the values involved in the choice of an object of analysis do not invalidate scientific research. Second, he acknowledges that the relationship between research practice, values and the perspectives adopted by social scientists is a complex one, for all causal explanations involve valuations in the specification of relevant causal variables:

> The length of causal chains, the relative specificity of selected causes, the possible neglect of by products and side effects of given causes, and the very multiplicity of such causes, all of these imply that causal explanation involves valuation and thus has ideological implications.
>
> (Jessop 1972: 9)

In his early writings, he also drew explicitly from Charles Taylor's 'Neutrality in Political Science' (1967) and, in the absence of a universally valid 'rational ethic', resolved these problems in Weberian terms through the adoption of the conception of 'value relevance'.

With the publication of *The Capitalist State* (1982), Jessop adopts an explicitly realist stance drawing upon the recently-published foundational texts by Keat and Urry (1982) and by Bhaskar (1978, 1979) on realist scientific method. This position was sustained until the early 1990s. He had already recognized the problems of generating scientific explanations in open systems in his exploration of the constitution of the social order. However, the realist approach allows for the specification of social relations at high levels of abstraction, and their relationship with complex and uncertain open systems at more concrete levels of analysis. The central issue for Jessop at this point is to find a way of resolving the problems of essentialism and reductionism in neo-Marxist theory. Realist analysis moves from the identification of simple and internally-necessary relations at a high level of abstraction, progressively towards the specification of more concrete relations where abstract simple determinations interact in overdetermined conjunctures. Consequently, contingency is prioritized over necessity. This enabled Jessop to readdress these problems in an innovative way, by developing an account of the 'contingently-necessary' operation of capitalist class relations in relationship to the state and ideology, without falling into the familiar Marxist trap of economism. Consequently, he was able to identify an analytically rigorous framework for Marxism without having to make any guarantees about the inevitability of revolution, or falling into circular accounts of the relationship between the state and the capitalist economy which Marxism often involved.

The realist approach attempts the reproduction of the 'real-concrete' as the 'concrete-in-thought' as a 'complex synthesis of multiple determinations'. At the same time, the analysis of overdetermined social formations involves 'determination without determinism'. The most frequently-identified example is the operation of the tendency of the rate to profit to fall in relation to counteracting tendencies. This is often cited as the archetypal form of contingently-necessary outcome that Jessop has in mind. Thus, the abstractions developed by Marxists such as 'capital' and 'labour', 'capitalism', 'modes of production', 'accumulation regimes', 'modes of regulation' and so on do not correspond to empirical observations. These rational abstractions identify social relations as real objects of analysis, with causal properties or powers which can generate empirical events through the complex articulation of causal mechanisms within specific conditions. For instance, he identifies labour power as an example of a real causal power, which exists independently of whether it is engaged in production (Jessop 1990b: 163).

Empirical regularities, or constant conjunctions of events, therefore tend to mask the complex determinations at work. These underlying determinations are difficult to specify in the complexity of concrete relations. The most effective demonstration of the double movement from the abstract to the concrete and from the simple to the complex in Jessop's work can be seen in his account of regulation theory, through the conceptual apparatus of accumulation regimes, modes of growth to modes of regulation (endorsed by Aglietta and Lipietz). In addition, the transformational model of social activity (see Figure 2.9) developed by Roy Bhaskar in *The Possibility of Naturalism* (1979) played a key part in the development of Jessop's concern with the interrelationship between structure and strategy. Jessop endorses Bhaskar's theorization of structures as the ever-present condition of agency, and strategic agency as the means through which structures are reproduced and/or transformed. This avoids the sterile debates on structuralism, and its treatment of agents as 'bearers' of social roles. The category of 'strategy' is used in preference to agency, because it focuses attention on 'concrete calculating strategic subjects' within the context of 'pre-existing social forms' (Jessop 1982: 211–20; 1990b: 162–6).

In his recent work, Jessop appears to take greater account of the possibility of moving from the complex concrete relations in open systems to the abstract simple relations in closed systems (also indicated in Bhaskar's writings in the mid 1980s). He also becomes increasingly aware of the problems in developing appropriate criteria for making judgements about the role of explanations in relation to the levels of abstraction/concreteness and simplicity/complexity. For instance, Jessop draws upon a third movement developed by Lipietz between the esoteric and the exoteric to characterize the relations between the objective relations so defined, and the fetishized enchanted world through which strategic agents reflexively define their own roles and behaviour (Jessop 1990b). The identification of two possible research strategies for the development of state theory, offering the alternatives of a conceptual hierarchy and of the concrete specification of six dimensions, offers a step in the direction of identifying a possible route for fleshing out the possibility of two explanatory schemes of retroduction and retrodiction (considered in Chapter Two). The incorporation of concepts from idealist approaches in Jessop's recent work may explain, in part, why we are faced with a choice of research strategies rather than an integrated package. The appropriation of systems theory which generates idealized models is a means of organizing experience, but Luhmann's analysis is also characterized by the absence of ontological depth. This seems to be acting as a inhibiting factor in the generation of conceptually-adequate means of moving from abstract/simple to concrete/complex levels. This is particularly the case in the specification of conceptual hierarchies in the superstructure, and the identification of political and cultural circuits and their relationship to the circuit of capital in the economic sphere. Indeed, in the absence of this two-way theoretical ladder, Jessop's recent work appears to offer priority to structural forms at the high levels of abstraction and strategies in concrete conjunctures, reproducing the distinction between structure and agency, and undermining his claim to have developed a dialectical approach.[1]

In his recent review of Holmwood and Stewart's *Explanation and Social Theory*, Jessop goes some way towards addressing these issues. Here, he considers actions as the performance of agents with a 'strategically calculating structural orientation', while structures are characterized by 'structurally inscribed strategic selectivity'. Jessop treats structures as concrete relational complexes of opportunities and constraints which 'do not exist outside of specific spatial and temporal horizons of action' (Jessop 1996: 126). The identification of emergent social structures in relation to partly socialized agents now appears as a dualism masquerading as duality. In conclusion, the strategic-relational approach appears to be propelled more by Luhmannian systems theory than by the specification of conceptual hierarchies, which he argues are needed to understand the concrete as the 'complex synthesis of multiple determinations'. As a result, Jessop's approach currently appears to contain two contradictory logics with different epistemological and ontological implications. It remains to be seen whether he can resolve these issues.

Problems in realism

In this section, I identify the implications of these three case studies in critical exegesis for the critical-realist approach itself and how it has been interpreted in the generation of social-scientific knowledge. In Lawson's account, the plausibility of realism as an approach in economics, there is a contrast between the empirical-realist and transcendental-realist ontologies, in a way consistent with Bhaskar's approach. Lawson distinguishes in a conventional way between the domains of the empirical (constituted by experiences, impressions and perceptions), the actual (constituted by events and states of affairs) and the real or 'deep' (constituted by structures, mechanisms, powers and tendencies). In empirical realism, he suggests, which accepts the existence of the actual and the empirical but not the deep, the realms of the actual and the empirical are fused together, so that empirical realism has a flat ontology (see Figure 6.1). By contrast, transcendental realism has a stratified and a differentiated ontology, within which the empirical, the actual and the real are out of phase with each other (as in Figure 6.2).

This characterization of empirical realism (which has been neatly captured by Lawson) is widespread, and the root cause of the problems of identifying the

Domain	Objects	
Empirical	experience impression perception	Different realms fused
Actual	events states of affairs	

Figure 6.1 Empirical realism
Source: adapted from Lawson 1994b: 263

Domain	Objects	
Empirical	experience impression perception	
Actual	events states of affairs	Different realms unsynchronised
Deep	structures mechanisms powers tendencies	

Figure 6.2 Transcendental realism
Source: adapted from Lawson 1994b: 263

difference between realist and idealist positions in the social and political theories identified in the preceding chapters (and increasingly elsewhere). For Lawson, who follows Bhaskar's contention that both empiricism and transcendental idealism have a common empirical realist ontology, then the epistemological differences between their accounts of causality have no ontological implications. Both empiricism and idealism reject the idea of ontological depth and do not admit the existence of unobservable structures, mechanisms, powers and tendencies. For idealism, structures are mental constructs, not real structures independent of our knowledge of them. However, in line with their acceptance of concept dependence, realism does not assume that structures can be understood without using existing conceptual frameworks, which partly explains some of the confusion. Nevertheless, we should take care not to slip automatically from considering what appear, at first sight, to be common features in empiricism and idealism (demarcating them from realism), into assuming that they have exactly the same ontology.

If we examine the differences between empiricism and idealism in terms of their account of causality, we can see that their epistemological standpoints have ontological implications which have been ignored. By adopting the position of intelligibility determinism, treating constant conjunctions of events as necessary but not sufficient for causal laws, a number of assumptions are built into an idealist model. It is assumed that theory and observation cannot clearly be separated, and that the empirical objects in question are open to a wide range of interpretations. In addition, the acceptance of the insufficiency of empirical regularities involves the recognition of complexity and uncertainty in generating causal laws. What this implies in ontological terms is that rather than a strictly flat ontology, transcendental idealism has a two-dimensional ontology which accepts that the empirical and the actual are out of phase with each other. Thus, while the recognition of complex open systems (or the absence of closure) does not necessarily entail a commitment to a realist ontology, it does mean that the standpoint in question is not empiricist. Finally, the difference between realism and idealism can be identified in terms of how it fulfils a specific task. This means that, in addition to the insights already gained from empiricist and idealist accounts, a realist approach should also recognize the existence of ontological depth, through the distinction between the domains of the empirical, the actual and the deep. Idealism, on the other hand, can accommodate the absence of closure but cannot recognize ontological depth.

There is another philosophical problem which exists for realist approaches to scientific activity and the production of knowledge, and it is the response to this problem which marks off critical or transcendental realism from other forms of realism. This problem concerns the (in-)adequacy of accounts of reality based upon a 'correspondence theory of truth'. The question is whether the social and natural world can accurately be reconstructed in thought, with certainty, or at least the clarity of understanding that is necessary for a transformative or emancipatory project to act as a plausible model for real change.

The normative position of Bhaskar is clear on this issue, for he adopts the *DEA model of emancipation*, that 'diagnosis', 'explanation' and 'action' follow each other in rapid concatenation (Bhaskar 1991: 160). The response of critical realism, based on its acceptance of the 'fallibility' of human knowledge (a point which flows logically from Bhaskar's fundamental distinction between the 'transitive' and 'intransitive' domains), is to reject any strict notion of 'correspondence'. Thus a dilemma emerges, which stems from the different logics which inspire the critical-realist approach, that of critical theory, and the realist theory of science. Initially, by suggesting that 'epistemological relativism is the handmaiden of ontological realism', Bhaskar attempts to have it both ways. To use his words, 'a proposition is true if and only if the state of affairs it expresses (describes) is real. But propositions cannot be compared to states of affairs, their relationship cannot be described as one of correspondence' (Bhaskar 1978: 249).

Isaac provides a typical realist discussion of these issues, when he attempts to examine the practical historical context of realism by providing a 'genealogical account' of the emergence of the critical-realist tradition. Isaac starts from the role of realism in articulating the growing dissatisfaction with the fundamental claims of empiricism within the post-positivist philosophy of science. He goes on to argue that realism avoids 'epistemological naiveté' by not insisting on the possibility of unmediated access to reality, and performs the difficult balancing act of incorporating the ideas of 'hermeneutics' while retaining some allegiance to causal analysis. Here lies the nub of the problem, for on the one hand critical realism provides an alternative ontology based on a transformed conception of causality, while on the other hand it endorses a 'robust fallibilism' by denying that absolute explanatory theories have any useful function (Isaac 1990: 3). Isaac (following Margolis 1986) defends realism by distinguishing 'epistemological relativism' from the 'radical relativism' of Paul Feyerabend and Michel Foucault who, he argues, tend to end in a position of 'epistemological nihilism'.

This kind of response to the complexities involved in representation is misleading for it over-simplifies the issues (these are explored in Smith 1998b chs. 6 and 7). This means that many realists have focused so closely on the intransitive domain, that they have neglected the way in which the production of meaning is itself a complex business. In particular, representation involves linguistic, discursive and cultural elements which can have a dramatic effect on social-scientific practice. For realists, epistemological relativism preserves the concepts of truth and falsity as constraints upon theorizing (in much the same way as Ian Hacking (1983) distinguishes between 'rationality/reason' and 'reality'). Similarly, Manicas writes of the 'adequacy' of theory in relation to reality, but this raises more questions than it answers (Manicas 1987: 262–3). Nevertheless, according to Isaac, the basis for such an adequate account of reality stems from the assumption that 'the world has a definite structure and is not a free play of signifiers, texts, discourses, conversations or what have you' (Isaac 1990: 9).

This kind of response can lead to a failure to recognize that the way in which meanings are produced has an impact on the ways in which social relations and processes operate. Rom Harré's recent contributions to this debate, by analysing the concept of reference, are particularly useful here. For Harré, 'referential realism based on things', rather than a search for truth or falsity, is grounded in 'material practice', conceived as a deictic practice whereby a person draws the attention of another, by any means to hand, to a being in their shared public space (Harré 1986: 97). Successful acts of 'reference' give the community 'epistemic' access and make a research programme into the properties of such beings possible. According to Harré, referential realism is epistemically modest and makes no assertions about the possibility of incorrigible existential claims (ibid.: 98). Hence, there is no need for reference to show that there is an incorrigible foundation of knowledge. Anti-realist arguments attack the notion of 'natural kinds' as based upon essences (as a sort of absolute foundation), but if one disposes of the idea that essences must be absolutes, this sceptical argument collapses. For Harré, 'natural kind' is a concept which can only be explicated in a double framework of practice and theory (ibid.: 97–107).

Three key assumptions or guidelines should be highlighted in order to identify realist approaches in the social sciences. First, a realist approach should demonstrate a recognition of complexity (this should include representational complexity) and the absence of closure beyond the artificial conditions created by human beings. This position is held in common with idealism, which clearly questions the existence of an external boundary in the closed-system model of scientific inquiry. Second is the specification of ontological depth and the clear distinction between the empirical, the actual and the deep. Third is the adoption of epistemological relativism, which should allow for the important role of the human imagination in theory construction, in conjunction with epistemic modesty, which ensures that we can make claims about the essential characteristics of the real world (while not treating necessary relations as absolute). To conclude, an epistemological and ontological vantage point which lays claim to the label of critical realism should recognize that reality is differentiated and complex, as well as stratified and changing.

Some preliminary comments on further research in state theory

This section contains no absolute maxims on the development of state theory in general, but draws on the case studies developed in the preceding chapters to identify fruitful areas for further research, for those willing to transgress the usual boundaries of neo-pluralism, neo-liberalism and neo-Marxism. In short, I want to encourage social scientists working on the state to explore the insights which can be identified through sensitive and careful intellectual cross-fertilization. The choice of the work of Dahl, Hayek and Jessop for this study was based on three grounds: their relevance for contemporary discussions about the character of the state; their distinctive focus on the relationship between the state and cultural and economic institutional forms; and their distinctive ontological and epistemological standpoints. The accounts developed in the preceding chapters raise some important issues about the role of state theory and the conduct of research. By conducting a critical exegesis of these case studies in state theory, it is intended that we should not only situate the existing bodies of theory more accurately in terms of their epistemological and ontological assumptions, but also generate new ways of thinking about the objects in question. One of the ways in which this investigation contributes towards this project is by defining the terms of reference of inquiry of further research.

While there are clear differences between the state theories in question, both in the way that they define the state and in the way in which they situate the state in the context of wider social relations, there are significant convergences. In addition, the distinctive focus of each theory has something to offer the other accounts. The divergences are clearly normatively driven, in that Dahl's neo-pluralist project is to identify ways in which the democratization process can be extended to institutions which many liberals (including Hayek) would see as in civil society, violating the public–private distinction as traditionally understood. Hayek's neo-liberal project aims to identify and promote the form of state in which a purely intersubjective catallactic market system can prosper and individual freedoms be established and maintained. Jessop adopts the left Eurocommunist strategy of transforming capitalism through struggle both within and beyond the state, to hasten the operation of contradictions which bring about social crisis and present opportunities for transformation. In each case, transformist strategies can be identified as the motor behind their respective intellectual projects.

More significantly, their conceptualizations of the state are closely related to the ways in which they attempt to theorize the social order. For Dahl, the polyarchic potential of political institutions is closely connected to the civic orientations and conceptions of citizenship prevalent in the social system in question, as well as the opportunities for mass participation and organized public contestation. These arguments for the democratization of civil institutions offer a variety of ways in which self-determination is possible, beyond the realms of the national state and associated institutions. For Hayek, the state serves as a horizon of catallactic possibilities; the state form is responsible for the degree to which the intersubjective capabilities of human beings can flourish. Hayek's account of the catallactic co-ordination of the plans of calculating subjects has many parallels with recent theories of governance (including Jessop's writings in the 1990s) and fruitfully explores the relations between various forms of formal and informal rules of conduct. Finally, for Jessop, the state is both a terrain of contestation and a site of strategic interventions, institutionally formed through the simultaneous interplay of structures and strategies. As the nation-state is redefined as part of the networks of governance through which social life is organized, these state theories offer fertile ideas and conceptual tools for rethinking our conceptions of the state and its relationship to other social spheres.

This kind of theoretical innovation cannot be limited to the identification of current trends in institutional change, for it must also address the epistemological and ontological issues generated by social-scientific practice (as has been demonstrated throughout the preceding chapters). By developing a better understanding of the ways in which existing theories and empirical accounts of the state have been constituted, we can learn some lessons about how to develop state theory, and avoid some of the problems that these writers have encountered. Each of these case studies provides useful insights into the kinds of problems and issues which must be explored if we are adequately to account for the historically and socially specific characteristics of actual states, and the ways in which the state relates to other spheres of existence.

What follows is a heuristic framework which helps us in the task of developing such an account. In a world which is complex, uncertain, interconnected and changing, such a framework must be able to accommodate the identification of the dimensions of object in question yet, at the same time, avoid reducing any of the dimensions to the status of a residual category. The model of inquiry adopted here involves a triangular pattern of abstractions; a triangle only makes sense in geometric terms through the connections between all parts, just as in social relations, the political, economic and cultural dimensions are each defined through their respective relationships with the other two dimensions. However, in order to develop an account of the social relations at work in a specific state, economy or culture, we also have to find ways of linking abstract-simple concept formation with the concrete-complexity of actual conditions. This framework places a special emphasis on the identification of two kinds of conceptualization developed in the realist approach, recognizing that the world is both differentiated and stratified. It also draws out the difference between the movements from abstract to concrete and from simplicity to complexity. This is represented in Figure 6.3.

In Figure 6.4, this framework is applied to the connections between the state, the economy and culture which have been stressed in earlier chapters. This does not mean that we can actually separate political, economic and cultural relations in concrete circumstances, for this framework remains an imaginative construct. We still have to acknowledge representational complexity in social-scientific practice. By moving from the identification of abstract and simple conceptual representations of economic, political and cultural relations, towards their concrete and complex articulations, we can also begin to explore how society effects are produced. This provides a stepping stone for developing an account of the state which can produce the 'conceptual hierarchy' which is missing from Jessop's account of the state. It can also accommodate the role of cultural and economic relations and processes, which have to be recognized and theorized in an account of the state, even at the highest order of simplicity and abstraction.

Metatheorizing the state 243

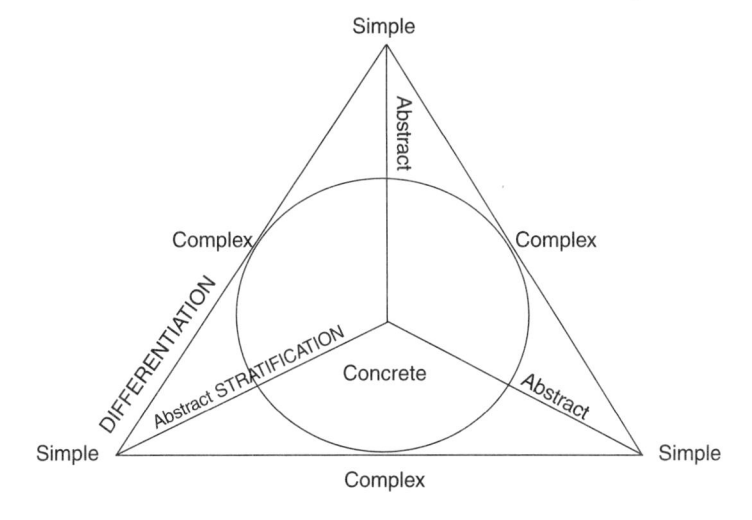

Figure 6.3 Triangular formation 1: from abstract-simplicity to concrete-complexity

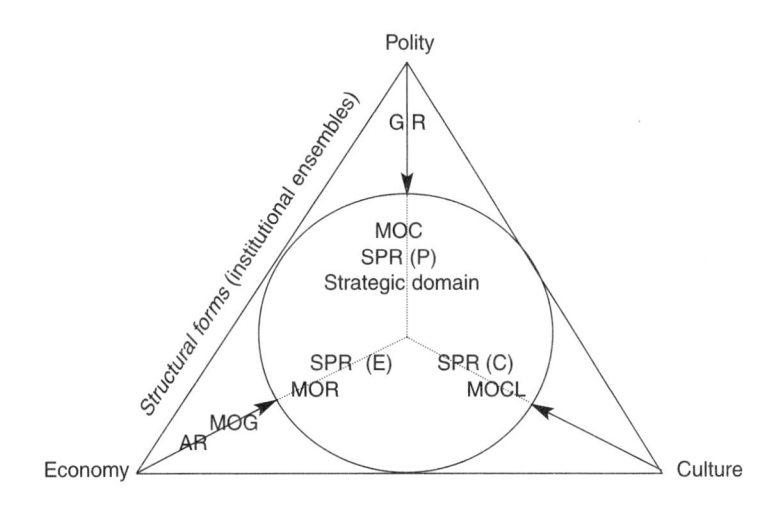

Figure 6.4 Triangular formation 2: a multidimensional framework for social-scientific research

Notes:
- AR — Accumulation regime
- MOG — Mode of growth
- MOR — Mode of regulation
- MOCL — Mode of cultural legitimation
- GR — Governance regime
- MOC — Mode of citizenship
- SPR — Social policy regime (E) Economic moment
    (P) Political moment
    (C) Cultural moment

In Figure 6.4, we can also begin to think through the ways in which theoretical construction can be made at different levels of abstraction and complexity. Moreover, this framework enables state theorists to acknowledge the role of actual social practices in social change, for human agencies are always involved in the reproduction-transformation of actual social structures. As Jessop has suggested, when we look at the examples of attempts to develop accounts of political economy (such as studies in regulation theory) it is the middle-range concepts which need more sustained attention and development. By comparison, the task of identifying the social relations involved in politics and culture has barely even begun.

Most accounts of neo-pluralist, neo-liberal and neo-Marxist state theories place them in irreconcilable opposition. This text cannot demonstrate all the connections between these approaches, but what can be identified through the earlier case studies is the need to rethink the specific relationships between the state and culture. I would argue that this is one part of a wider intellectual project, to find ways of developing theoretical accounts which can acknowledge the interconnectedness between political, economic and cultural dimensions of 'society effects'. It is precisely because this new intellectual project has been barely initiated that we should innovate in ways which transgress the usual normative divisions of social and political theory. In short, we should take this opportunity to break with the tendency to pigeon-hole state theorists, and look anew at their convergences.

In particular, this enables us to identify the way in which Jessop's account of the relationship between autopoietic and allopoietic qualities of social systems (including the political system) has strong affinities with Hayek's account of the institutional products of catallactic relations. In addition, Jessop's state theory, and his attempts to explain the concrete changes which take place in actual states, could benefit from a stronger emphasis on the intersubjective characteristics of social relations which are so important in the Hayekian intellectual project. The constitution of the state as the horizon of catallactic possibilities, which is the most innovative feature of Hayek's social and political theory, has affinities with Dahl's account of the cultural conditions of polyarchy. Both Hayek and Dahl stress the need to recognize the complex cultural conditions of the formation of states. Dahl's theoretical and empirical analyses of the close connections between cultural institutions and state formation, on the other hand, provide an account of the state which acknowledges the various ways in which actual states can have an impact, whilst Hayek is mainly concerned with the damage that the state can do to catallaxy. However, both Dahl and Hayek neglect the specific ways in which social forces operate across political, economic and cultural dimensions, which is a stronger, if unfulfilled, part of the promise of Jessop's project. In particular, Jessop accounts for the ways in which the internal institutional formations of actual states are intimately connected to the ongoing social relations beyond the state (although he is primarily concerned with agencies in the economy). This suggests that these three accounts of the state are better considered as accounts of the 'sociality of politics', since they all point to the need to examine the relationship of states to economic and cultural relations and processes.

As such, these approaches offer different ways of thinking through the aims and objectives of political research. The traditional focus of political studies, the national state, is presently in question. This opens up the possibility of a radical reappraisal of what political research should involve. If the state form, as traditionally understood, becomes less relevant in defining political relationships, this points to the need for a much clearer identification of the underlying relations involved in the political dimensions of the social. In this sense, one tentative avenue of inquiry compatible with the realist epistemological and ontological framework would be to specify the abstract and simple, internally-necessary social relations through which politics is the organizational dimension of the social order (just as the economy involves material production, and culture involves the production of meaning). The relations involved in the political dimension could be identified as that of dominator and dominated within a political circuit which, through the operation of consent and coercion, defines political relations in various ways (serving as the basis for effective collective decision making at more concrete levels of analysis). These relations could be identified in terms of movements from abstract-simplicity to concrete-complexity through regimes of governance and modes of citizenship, in a manner akin to the regulationist attempts to characterize accumulation regimes and modes of regulation. In turn, this would aid the generation of a more comprehensive characterization of the processes involved in societalization. The point of introducing this framework (which is really the start of a whole new project) at the end of a study such as this, is not to define clearly the way in which such an account should develop, but to indicate what the central concerns of the research agenda in future state theory should be. The suggestions made here are tentative, and are defined in a rudimentary way. It is hard to see, at this stage, what the limitations on such a development would be, since social-scientific practice, like all human activities, tends to have a range of unanticipated and unintended consequences. However, it is clear that this intellectual project to explore the connections between state, economy and culture opens up a wide range of new possibilities within political research.

Notes

2 Empiricism, idealism, realism

1 One of the most significant areas of confusion is the conflation of positivism with empiricism. The structure of this chapter is based upon a comparison between empiricism, idealism and realism; however, it remains essential to distinguish post-positivist empiricism from positivism. The remainder of this note is adapted from my account of these distinctions in *Social Science in Question: Towards a Postdisciplinary Framework* (Smith 1998b).

Norman Blaikie in *Approaches to Social Enquiry* (1993) suggests that certain general features of positivism can be identified without overlooking the significant differences between them. These six general features are:

1. Their common commitment to naturalism, that it is possible to transfer the assumptions and methods of natural sciences to the study of social objects, often referred to in textbooks as the unification of method. However, it is also possible to be naturalist without being either positivist or empiricist.
2. The assumption of phenomenalism, whereby only knowledge gained through observed experience can be taken seriously. Hence, if we cannot touch it, see it, hear it, taste it or smell it, then the object does not exist and is said to be metaphysical (beyond our physical senses).
3. The principle of nominalism in the construction of scientific concepts. This posits that mental constructs must be derived from experience, which means that concepts have no use other than as names. This reduces metaphysical terms to the level of meaninglessness, because they do not refer to physically identifiable objects.
4. All objects of analysis within observed experience are regarded as completely discrete and basic elements or atomic impressions, hence the term atomism. Collective objects are thus aggregates of their smaller components.
5. The proposition that the purpose of scientific laws is to generalize from empirically observed particular instances to other circumstances which display the same characteristics. This means that causal laws can be inferred from the consistent coexistence of two or more variables, often referred to as an empirical regularity. Such empirical regularities can be observed in different circumstances as well as over time (such as the empirical regularity associated with smoking and lung cancer).

6 The proposition that facts and values are distinct, with only facts being regarded as scientific since values cannot empirically be verified.

Empiricism is often used as a synonym for positivism, but it includes positions which can be described as post-positivist but are nevertheless empiricist. Since Popper remains committed to empiricism and describes his approach as post-positivist, positivism can be categorized as a sub-branch of empiricism. Hence, empiricism can be said unreservedly to accept the principles of phenomenalism, atomism, and the possibility of general scientific laws. However, it accepts that it is possible to reject the principle of nominalism, qualifies its acceptance of naturalism (by accommodating different criteria for demarcating science from non-science), and recognizes that the acceptance of meaningful interpretations in science can cause problems in clearly distinguishing facts from values, and that they should rigidly be constrained within the terms of reference of the strict application of the scientific method. (See Smith 1998b ch. 3 for a more fully developed analysis of these arguments.)

2 The distinction between noumena and phenomena is utilized to mark the distinction between the aspects of reality which can be taken to exist independently of human cognition (things in themselves) and those things which can be said to exist in relation to human cognition through the senses. The category of noumena does not involve an attempt to specify these things through pure reason, but signifies the 'unknown something' or the limits of sensibility. In other words, it indicates our inability fully to comprehend a complex and unpredictable external world. In short, the distinction is a way of marking out the peculiarities of the human condition, rather than a set of rational principles for constructing scientific knowledge. Kant identifies certain uses of the term noumena as inappropriate, that is, the uses which attribute some objectivity to the things in themselves separate from the intuitions of human beings. Kant's approach is founded upon the treatment of human knowledge as a synthetic unity of the intelligible world of ideas (mental constructs) and sensible phenomenal experiences (Kant 1987).

3 These arguments are often subsumed under the general label of the Duhem-Quine thesis. It is worthwhile disaggregating them to demonstrate the extent of Quine's originality. Pierre Duhem, in a series of articles published in 1904–5, reassessed the history of physics from Newton onwards, published in *The Aim and Structure of Physical Theory* (1914). The Duhem thesis states that an empirical test can never falsify an isolated hypothesis, but only the whole theoretical system of which it is a part. For Duhem this led to the questioning of the standards of theorizing which had been established by Francis Bacon in the seventeenth century. Bacon had recommended that true science involved the identification of all possible contending theories in the explanation of a specific phenomenon, and the use of experimental tests until all but one of the contending theories had been eliminated. In this way, absolute certainty could be established.

For Duhem, no such definitive test of a single hypothesis could be devised and applied. Hence, he suggested that it was only possible to examine theoretical systems against empirical evidence. In addition, when faced with a situation where the empirical evidence does not fit the existing theoretical framework, the choice between the modification of bedrock principles or the revision of contextual hypotheses becomes a matter for the 'good sense' of the scientists involved.

248 Notes to Chapter 2

In 'The Two Dogmas of Empiricism' (originally published in 1953), Quine developed a stronger version of the Duhem thesis by extending its scope to include not just a group of theories but all scientific knowledge (described as a sort of 'man-made fabric'). The whole field of enquiry of human knowledge is disturbed by the emergence of anomalies between empirical evidence and established theories in much the same way as a stone can cause ripples on the surface of a pond (Quine 1961).

3 Polyarchic civility and the state

1. Dahl seems to have in mind the legal conflicts over desegregation and the enforced political inactivity of American black people, as southern states in the USA gradually complied with case law on the abolition of discriminatory institutional practices and policies in voting, education, transportation and other public amenities. One might also add the legal tussles over abortion over the last three decades and, more recently, the debate over free speech and the censorship of pornography in relation to the First Amendment.
2. The prevailing academic norms of post-war political science suggested a retreat from the normative approaches, which were widely regarded as responsible for the processes which led into the destruction and violence of the first half of the twentieth century. This shift of emphasis towards the descriptive analysis of behaviour seems to have left analysts blind to their own normative standpoints; leading some social and political theorists to proclaim an *end of ideology* (for instance Seymour Martin Lipset 1959, and Daniel Bell 1960).
3. This definition recognizes both the capacity to act, presuming the possession of resources, and the successful attempt to exercise power. When these resources are utilized, they are subject to the uneven distribution of political skill, motivation and opportunity costs. Hence, Dahl recognizes the difference between potential and actual power (Dahl 1984: 31–3).
4. The reputational method is associated with the elitist approach to politics in the 1950s. This technique to establish the extent of influence of a particular ruling group or oligarchy involves a comparison of the subjective opinions of the general population (through surveys) with the identification of the holders of the chief command posts in economics, politics, the military and other social spheres such as religious organizations. If the survey evidence corresponds with the identification of command post holder, then, it is argued, a power elite can be said to exist. One of the problems of this approach is that it is designed to produce conclusions which confirm the hypothesis. However, this criticism could be raised against the pluralist method as well, for the narrow focus on actual observable decision making (to the neglect of agenda formation) is unlikely to produce concrete evidence of a power elite which is conscious, cohesive and conspiratorial. The elitist empirical approach is best demonstrated by Floyd Hunter's *Community Power Structure: A Study of Decision Makers* (1953).
5. Dahl cites Tocqueville's description of the USA (what follows is a little more selective):

> The social condition of the Americans is eminently democratic . . . [T]he germs of aristocracy were never planted in [America]. . . . But wealth circulates with inconceivable rapidity. . . . I do not believe that there is a country

in the world where, in proportion to the population, there are so few ignorant and at the same time so few learned individuals. Primary instruction is within the reach of everybody; superior instruction is scarcely to be obtained by any. . . . Men are there seen on a greater equality in point of fortune and intellect, or, in other words, more equal in strength, than in any other country of the world, or in any age of which history has preserved the remembrance.
(Tocqueville 1968: 48–55; cited in Dahl 1971: 72 n. 10)

Contrast this with Dahl's description of contemporary pre-industrial societies as

ordinarily bound by widespread illiteracy, a tradition-bound, preliterate, prescientific culture, weak or fragmented systems of communication, severe inequalities of wealth status and power, a tiny or non-existent independent middle class, and frequently a tradition of autocratic or authoritarian rulership.
(Dahl 1971: 72)

6   Tocqueville, even though he is embedded in a historically specific social location of nineteenth century America, serves as the main sounding board in Dahl's search for conceptual clarification in his attempt to reconcile equality and liberty. For Tocqueville, the increase of equality was an inevitable feature of modern life, although it was liberty which was given theoretical priority. For liberty to be guaranteed, barriers to the concentration of power had to be created and maintained. The problem for Tocqueville was the tendency of equality, in conjunction with democracy, to undermine liberty. In particular, he was concerned with the majority principle and the dangers of intimidation, and the conformity which follows from the domination of public opinion by a majority. Tocqueville's answer was to diffuse economic well-being, decentralize power, decentralize the constitution and enhance political culture (the manners, opinions and character of the people). Dahl adds two more dangers: that the majority oppress the minority through a strictly legal process; and that the people can voluntarily jettison liberties in favour of mass-based despotism. Dahl also distinguishes two kinds of equality – equality of power and equality of political resources – in order to demonstrate the relationship between the actual and the potential.

7   One of the most important objections to Dahl's identification of the relationship between government of a state and government of an economic enterprise focuses upon the assumption that, in each case, the collective decisions are binding. It is plausible to argue that, while the citizens of a state cannot escape the consequences of such decisions and are bound to follow them or face the consequences, the employees of an economic enterprise have the capacity to withdraw their labour and seek alternative employment. If this is the case then the analogy no longer holds. Dahl's response is to draw our attention to the actual operation of such relationships in states and firms. In practice, he suggests, the costs of exiting from employment are such as to deter most from making such choices; and in the case of the state there is empirical evidence of citizens moving locations to avoid being bound by local laws. He does not illustrate this, but the examples of tax havens and parents moving to secure residency in a catchment area for a particular school for their children will suffice. In the realm of the actual, as opposed to the theoretical ideal, the relationship between the citizen and the state (or an enterprise) is remarkably similar (Dahl 1985: 115).

8   Dahl shows sympathy with the intentions of Alaisdair MacIntyre's *After Virtue*

250 *Notes to Chapter 3*

(1984): 'Building a secure place for small communities amid the tempest of modernity and postmodernity is an appealing vision. It is one that I share' (Dahl 1989: 301). However, Dahl points to the empirical problems of establishing such viable small communities in the context of the modern world and, even if it were possible, the way that the dilemmas would merely shift to any co-ordinating authorities beyond such communities.

4 The horizon of catallactic possibilities

1 The use of the concept of rational economic man at the heart of public choice theory represents an uncritical transposition of the foundational assumptions of mainstream economics into the discipline of political science and state theory. While Hayek did not explicitly criticize this tradition, or James Buchanan in particular, he did begin to develop a critical stance on Milton Friedman's economic theories. Similarly, much of the literature on the 'new right' or neo-liberalism deals with each branch of the tradition as distinct, but fails to address the conceptual differences explicitly (Green 1987; King 1987). Nevertheless, as will become clear in this chapter, the whole thrust of Hayek's work (initiated by his early contributions on the problems of equilibrium analysis) is to undermine the foundations of such developments within the discipline of economics, by showing that they fail to address the problems of theorizing time and subjectivity as part of everyday existence and practical knowledge. It is clear that within the neo-liberal tradition, despite general agreement on the goals of the intellectual movement, there is a deep antithetical relationship between Hayek's account of the subjective and objective dimensions of knowledge, and his treatment of the concept of rationality compared with the concepts of rational 'minimaxing' behaviour developed within the public choice approach.

2 The remnants of this Kantian influence can be seen in Hayek's discussions of ethics, which have been developed most clearly by John Gray (1986). However, although Hayek is keen to point out that he did not 'study' Kant, he has accepted that his work probably acquired affinities through his reading the popular introductions to Kantianism by Alois Riehl in the early 1920s (Kresge and Wenar 1994: 139–40). This should hardly be surprising, given the importance of neo-Kantianism in Vienna during this period. Nevertheless, important differences existed within the neo-Kantian movement in addition to the debates with various kinds of logical positivism and life philosophy. Hayek viewed himself as taking up the analysis where Hume and Kant left off (this is ably explored in Chandran Kukathas' *Hayek and Modern Liberalism*, 1989). However, in order to move beyond them, Hayek develops a radically intersubjective account of the relationship between theory and observation drawn from Schütz's 'mundane phenomenology'.

3 Edmund Husserl's quest for certainty in the constitution of consciousness led him towards the transcendental reduction of consciousness of mundanity. Hence the cultural world, within which human actors naively accept common sense as given, is 'bracketed' allowing for the comprehension of the 'thing' world. To eradicate the naive fallacies and prejudices inherent in objectivistic and naturalistic conceptions of detached and rational science, Husserl attempted to transcend the separation of subjectivity from the objective world. Within this domain of transcendental subjectivity (pure consciousness) the existence of other

(transcendental) egos poses a problem. However, in Schütz's mundane phenomenology the existence of others within the 'paramount reality' of everyday experience is taken for granted. As Schütz himself argued:

> It is to be surmised that intersubjectivity is not a problem of constitution which can be solved within the transcendental sphere, but is rather a datum of the life-world. It is the fundamental ontological category of human existence in the world and therefore of all philosophical anthropology. As long as man is born of woman, intersubjectivity and the we-relationship will be the foundation for all other categories of human existence.
> (Schütz 1964; also see Schütz 1959)

4 Regarding the close intellectual positions of Kaufmann, Schütz and Hayek in the 1930s, Felix Kaufmann developed a phenomenological critique of the neo-Kantian foundations within the sociology and philosophy of law in the 1920s, and introduced Schütz to these ideas in the late 1920s. He also recognized the 'intertemporal, intersensual and intersubjective' nature of social existence (Kaufmann 1944: 11) as well as the role of different levels or strata of experience in *Methodenlehre der Sozialwissenschaften* (1936, later translated and truncated as the influential *Methodology of the Social Sciences*). All three seem to have taken steps to ensure that their respective audiences understood their work, and they couched these arguments in accessible terms: Kaufmann through the formal language of logic and philosophy of science; Schütz through the use of pragmatism in the USA; Hayek through the use of the terms of reference of Anglo-American political philosophy. One might also add Fritz Machlup in economics, where he explicitly acknowledges Schütz in his construction of the theory of the firm and of the role of verification in economics (Machlup 1955, 1960, 1967). Rarely do they acknowledge this common bond and shared perspective, particularly Hayek. However, their work can all be taken to represent the progressive unfolding of what Hayek was later to refer to as the 'original idea' (Kresge and Wenar 1994: 134).

5 Alfred Schütz uses William James's distinction between the nucleus of concept and the fringes where the nucleus is attached to the situation of the thinker, and relates this to Husserl on daily thought propositions as 'occasional propositions', in order to substantiate his distinction between practical and cognitive thought (Schütz 1943: 133, 139–40).

6 For Schütz, Henri Bergson's intuitionist linguistics (notably the concepts of 'duree' and prereflective consciousness), as well as Max Weber's sociological method and his concept of rationalization as a process of disenchantment, were important steps in the right direction; but both lacked an adequate philosophical foundation. Consequently, Schütz was attracted to Edmund Husserl's account of transcendental phenomenology, although he became dissatisfied with the way Husserl's quest for certainty ensured that the concept of the transcendental ego lost touch with the wide-awake world of everyday experience. Burke Thomason's *Making Sense of Reification* provides a useful account of this uneasy tension within Schütz's concerns, representing a compromise between the 'profound respect for [detached] reason and science and a deep and abiding fascination with the modes of thought of ordinary social action' (Thomason 1982: 130).

7 Points of contact between Hayek and Popper existed before, such as Popper's address to the Hayek–Robbins seminar at the LSE in 1935, and a footnote

252 Notes to Chapter 4

reference to the paper on 'The Poverty of Historicism' made in Hayek's 'Economics and Knowledge' in 1937. In addition, Hayek played a crucial role in securing Popper's post-war publication by Routledge, and in obtaining a post in philosophy for Popper at the LSE in the mid-1940s.

8   It is interesting to consider Hayek's and Popper's positions on objectivist and subjectivist accounts of social science and, in particular, how Hayek uses Popper to raise questions about the truth claims of natural science. Hayek utilizes Popper's arguments to raise doubts about the celebration of natural science in Western civilization. However, in 'Degrees of Explanation' he supports Popper's claim that:

> the theoretical sciences are all essentially deductive, that there can be no logical procedure as 'induction' which leads with necessity from the observation of facts to the formulation of general rules, and that the latter are products of creative acts of the mind which cannot be formalised.
> (Hayek 1967: 3)

He clearly remains wedded to the conception of the objects of natural science being closed systems and those of social science being open systems. In significant respects, this position is close to that of Peter Winch's *The Idea of a Social Science and its Relation to Philosophy* (1958). However, while Wittgenstein was a cousin of Hayek, their brief encounters on trains and a more substantial discussion at Cambridge provides a thin basis for suggesting any intellectual connections.

9   On this issue, Hayek states that 'There is clearly no merit in being born into a particular community' (Hayek 1960: 100). There are remarkable parallels between these conclusions and the correspondence between Alfred Schütz and Herbert Spiegelberg in 1943 on the concept of equality. Schütz's comments on the draft of Spiegelberg's 'A defense of human equality' explicitly called for the recognition of difference between two levels, the level of scientific detachment and that of actual lived experience where individuals are engaged in unequal relations (see Wagner 1983: 174–5). Whether Hayek was aware of these arguments is yet to be documented more concretely; nevertheless, the similarity of approach remains a remarkable coincidence. This is further reinforced by the paper by Schütz on 'Equality and the Social Meaning Structure' (Schütz 1957).

10 Hayek provides some provocative remarks for considering recent debates on equal opportunities and gender discrimination. Hayek does accept 'special rules' which are relevant to women, for instance, subject to the proviso that a majority both of the group concerned and of everyone else agree. Otherwise, he argues if 'only those inside the group favour it, it is privilege, while if only those outside the group favour it, it is discrimination' (Hayek 1960: 154). Parallels can be seen in Schütz's brief comments on the subjective and objective moments of racial discrimination in the USA (Schütz 1957). In vol. III of *Law, Legislation and Liberty*, Hayek relates the same argument to considerations of poverty and what he terms the nonsense word of 'under-privilege'. Here, he argues that benevolent discrimination to assist the less fortunate breaches the central principle of equality before the law in the name of charity and 'opened the floodgates to arbitrariness' (Hayek 1979: 103).

11 On this, Hayek's account is at odds with the trajectory of Popper's 'critical rationalism' and, in particular, with the concept of the 'objective third world' of knowledge in Popper's paper on 'Epistemology Without a Knowing

Subject' (Popper 1969). Hayek acknowledges Popper's contribution to anti-rationalist insights in the natural sciences; however, when dealing with social objects Hayek's position is closer to that of Schütz in his critique of the standpoint of scientific detachment (that second-order constructs, if they are to serve as adequate accounts of social life, should directly relate to the first-order constructs of everyday life).

5 Capitalism, the state and societalization

1 The conception of power as a 'variable-sum game', in Parsons' account of the political institutions, whereby power expands and contracts along the lines of bank credit (as the lubrication of the political machine), is criticized for its inaccuracy. For Jessop, this does not breach the zero-sum condition, for money is the symbolic medium of exchange. Therefore, if money expands without a corresponding increase in productivity, its value declines to the point where all participants are in the same condition. Even where some productivity increases, this is a contingent matter and it does not ensure that all participants will benefit (raising the role of the centre and the periphery). The treatment of power as a collective resource by Parsons, Jessop suggests, reduces the number of participants to one. Jessop particularly criticizes Parsons' excessive concentration on the abstract operation of functional subsystems, to the neglect of the concrete relations between groups where exploitative exchange relations take place. In this case, he explicitly cites Dahl's early formulation of power against the position of Parsons (Jessop 1969: 425–8).

2 The theoretical framework developed by Jessop reflects Parsons' grand theory of the social system and its subsystems (devised to address the functional prerequisites of adaptation, goal attainment, integration and pattern maintenance or latency). Although the specific content of the relations has been altered, the four forms of power identified by Jessop correspond to the fulfilment of these four functions and the maintenance of the balance between the subsystems. Jessop is concerned to establish an adequate account of both the internal structure of each subsystem or substratum and the interrelationships between them (Jessop 1972: 16). In particular, he integrates the account of social strains developed by Neil Smelser (Smelser 1962) in accounting for how these four functions – namely facility strain, mobilization strain, normative strain and value strain – remain unfulfilled. Of particular importance is the functionalist insight that oppositional movements can emerge in response to mismatches and/or conflicts within and between the substrata of society. Hence, the specific outcomes of such events depend upon the structural features of the concrete social order in question, and the operation of subsystem-specific exchange relations (money, power, influence and the activation of commitments) which (through the operation of sanctions) act as symbolic modes of constraint (ibid.: 15–26, 43–53).

3 At this stage in Jessop's intellectual development, Marxism is incorporated as a branch of constraint theory, and is seen as in need of considerable revision if it is to perform the analytically useful task of generating effective explanations of contemporary capitalism. Nevertheless, he develops an account of the key dynamic principles of the capitalist mode of production (notably the contradiction between the technical forces of production and the division of labour or

relations of production) as well as the possibility of revolutionary change in a specific period of capitalist development. Jessop views class conflict through Dahrendorf's revisionist conceptual spectacles, and considers Marx's theory of revolution as a historically-specific manifestation of Smelser's account of the mobilization of collective behaviour. He sees Dahrendorf not as making a distinctive theoretical contribution, but instead as merely empirically refocusing class analysis. In addition, Jessop introduces the Gramscian reformulation of Marxism for the first time, following the publication of *The Modern Prince and Other Essays* in 1969 (Gramsci 1971). Jessop only touches on the 'class character of the state' identified by Marx, Engels and Lenin in their treatment of the state as an epiphenomenon of class struggle, and identifies Gramsci's account of state autonomy and hegemony (as the mobilization of consent) as a useful neo-Marxist treatment of the 'normative order'. In particular, he begins to reformulate the base–superstructure relationship to account for the mobilization of consent by the institutions of civil society (religious, educational, trades union, political party, media and familial institutions) as a component of the 'war of position' between dominant and subordinate classes. While the parallels between these insights and his general theory of consensus, conflict and change can be identified, these are taken as a reinforcement of his theoretical framework, rather than as throwing it into question.

4 Blau raises the existence of four types of value which have different roles to perform in the constitution of social exchange: *particularistic values* facilitating integration and social solidarity by transferring the loyalties of individuals onto the collective order; *universalistic values* acting as yardsticks against which it is possible to compare the acts of exchange with individuals beyond personal circles; *legitimation values* serving to facilitate authoritative leadership; and *opposition values* which facilitate the legitimation of criticism and the emergence of social movements beyond interpersonal social networks (which, in turn, ensure reform and stability) (Blau 1964, *passim*).

5 Jessop distinguishes three types of social order:

1 Where all members possess equal power and the output of secondary resources is optimal which, in combination, means that fair shares are sustained and disorder is a product of the disruption of equality of power.

2 Where hierarchies of power are combined with reciprocity (possibly benefaction) in exchange (that the peripheral desires are rewarded and the power of the centre is reassured) and disorder follows from changes in exchange relations with the replacement of reciprocity with exploitation.

3 Where a hierarchy of power and exploitation of the periphery by the centre are normal features combined with strong central control over the expectations and value commitments of the periphery; so that exploitation is not subjectively experienced, and disorder follows from the loss of control over the cultural system and from the ineffectiveness of the system in meeting institutional expectations.

In Type 1 societies (such as the Kachin Hills people of Burma) or in Type 2 societies (such as African chiefdoms and the Indian caste system), consensus formation takes place through a shared culture and an equitable distribution of rewards. However, in Type 3 societies (the advanced capitalist societies) the hierarchical relations of power and the structural differentiation of institutional life mean that conflict and disorder depend more upon institutional integration (Jessop 1972: 78, 91–143).

6 At this level the nominal definition of concepts corresponds to the theoretical identification of relations. However, Willer identifies the inadequacies of this framework for assuming the existence of singularly-defined manifest interests, and proposes a 'more complex symbolic construction', with the proviso that the integration of such complexity may mean that the model loses the capacity to retain the mechanism in Dahrendorf's model and any degree of isomorphism (Willer 1967: 52–63).

7 Jessop's empirical method in the study of political culture also demonstrates the neo-Kantian assumptions within his early work. He combines existing secondary data sources (from polls and psephological studies) with his own primary sources involving questionnaire and interview data collected in 1968 and 1972. In the secondary-source evidence he identifies a number of themes which are pertinent to this investigation: political culture combining a respect for symbolic traditional institutions in general terms with strong criticisms of specific aspects; a similar pattern of general consensus on the importance of central values but a populist indictment of the dominant order; existing theories of deference and traditionalism which fail to convey these complexities; and marginal evidence of consistent co-variations in attitudes towards different dominant institutions. Together, Jessop suggests, these raise the need for a reformulation of deference and civility. The sampling frame included three constituencies in North East London in the summer of 1968 (Stepney, Wood Green, Wanstead and Woodford), to facilitate a comparison of socio-economic classes, and two regional constituencies in 1972 (Isle of Ely and Easington) to introduce an agrarian and an industrial electorate to the sample. The surveys involved postal questionnaires followed by interviews on a smaller scale, partly to ensure a higher response rate. The questionnaire included a range of questions designed to indicate political and social values and beliefs, deference, traditionalism, status and class consciousness, and verbal commitment to civic culture. The intention of the study was to accommodate the complex interactive process of opinion formation and voting behaviour. The data facilitated statistical causal modelling along the lines established by Blalock (1964) for non-experimental research.

8 Jessop contends that an adequate account of deference which could address the complexities of voting behaviour in concrete historical and social conditions would be able to explain the existence of middle-class deference (already empirically identified by Butler and Stokes (1974) and by Parkin (1972)). Parkin's account had a tangible impact on Jessop, for its contention that, given the ideological pre-eminence of conservative values, voting for the Labour Party by a member of any social class is a deviant act. Both Parkin and Jessop raise the importance of ideology and the structural location of working-class communities (characterized by homogeneity, immobility and proximity), although Parkin neglects the non-deferential working-class conservatives. In addition, Jessop finds little evidence empirically to support the existence of a working-class counter-culture based upon socialist values in opposition to the central value system.

9 Jessop identifies the important contribution of Marxist legal theory for initiating the debates on the form and function of the state in relation to capital

accumulation, particularly (the work of the Soviet theorist) Evegny Pashukanis and of Burkhard Tuschling. Pashukanis sought to establish the role of bourgeois law as a moment in the circuit of capital, on the grounds that exchange of commodities (as the bearer of value) can only take place through the activities of legal subjects. Hence, any account of the realization of surplus value should account for the close connection between the juridical and commodity dimensions of capital accumulation. Pashukanis also identified the emergence of legal subjects as a necessary feature of the circulation of commodities. In turn, this facilitated the existence of legal subjects as abstract bearers of rights, extending the principle of formal equality from the economic to the political sphere, with the establishment of the state as an abstract collective subject underwriting legal relations (so that the *Rechtsstaat* as an impersonal public power, separate from the private sphere, is the necessary basis of a bourgeois market order). Jessop argues that the focus on the abstract universal legal subject does not adequately consider and account for the distinct effects of different legal subjects, and their relations with non-legal subjects. Nevertheless, Jessop indicates the way in which Pashukanis highlights the historical and contradictory constitution of the unity of public and private law.

Tuschling extends this analysis by situating the legal system in terms of the interrelations of production, distribution and exchange. In particular, he demonstrates that, with the emergence of the legal subject, a specialized legal institutional apparatus and the consolidation of law as an organizational principle, the systematization and regulation of generalized commodity relations between capital and labour became possible. Hence, the formal autonomy of the legal system is a significant factor in the mediation of the contradiction between the formal equality and actual substantive socio-economic inequalities of the class-divided social formations. The autonomy of law from the capital–labour relation and from individual capitals ensures the continuation of capitalist appropriation of surplus value, and the concentration and centralization of capital on the grounds of efficiency. Tuschling also raises the way in which the mediation of capitalist economic imperatives through legal forms involves a degree of indeterminacy in terms of policies and their effects. For Jessop, the contribution of Marxist legal theory was to highlight the ways in which the functions of the state and the law are overdetermined by the commodification of labour power, and in which formal legal equality and freedom are substantively inverted in the economy and in politics (Jessop 1980d: 339–68; 1982: 84–7, 122–3).

10 Jessop isolates three forms of crisis: the *fiscal crisis of the state* where the revenues necessary for the maintenance of the political preconditions of accumulation undermine the process of capital accumulation (O'Connor 1973; Offe 1984); the *crisis of administrative rationality* whereby the state's administrative organization according to predetermined rules for policy implementation becomes inefficient in delivering policy goals, and encounters opposition from individual capitals when policies threaten their interests (Habermas 1973; Keane 1984; Offe 1975); and *crises of legitimacy or mass loyalty* whereby conflicts within the economy are increasingly manifested in the state, and also disrupt the balance of forces which sustains the implementation of policies for the continued accumulation of capital (Habermas 1973; Keane 1984; Offe 1984).

11 Jessop identifies thirteen points which should be addressed in state theory:

1   The state is a specific institutional ensemble with multiple boundaries, no institutional fixity and no pre-given unity in both formal and substantive terms.
2   The formal unity of the capitalist state is possible around certain formal norms such as law, money, space (territory) and time.
3   Formal unity is always related to the substantive unity of the state.
4   Any substantive unity within a state system derives from the struggles and projects which impose unity and coherence on the system through a global political project.
5   There are a range of possible state systems within specific but variable institutional limits.
6   Structural selectivity implies that the state is never neutral, although the precise form of selectivity (in gender or class terms) is a contingent matter.
7   Non-neutrality is a problem for the logic of representation.
8   The class character of the state depends on its implications for class strategies rather than being inscribed in the state form.
9   As a social relation, the state is the crystallization of past strategies in addition to the privileges it ascribes to some projects and strategies.
10 The operation of the complex dialectic of structures and strategies means that interests are only specifiable within the political system.
11 Interests and forces extend beyond class interests and forces.
12 The specification of interests can only take place through the consideration of definite alternatives within specific horizons of action.
13 State power is a relational property and can only be understood in terms of the institutional liabilities and capacities of the state system in relation to the forces operating within and through the state (including state managers, class forces, intellectual groupings and new social movements) (Jessop 1990d: 267–70).

12 This enables Jessop to restate the relevance of Nicos Poulantzas' account of the state as a 'complex form-determined social relation', a condensation of the balance of social forces, in a manner analogous to the account developed by John Hoffman (1988). Hoffman identifies the state's role in maintaining the illusion of a community with a common interest, in the face of competing and conflicting particular interests in civil society. This is introduced to pinpoint the ways in which Poulantzas connects these concerns to the materialization of such power relations in the institutional ensemble of the state itself. In addition, Jessop suggests, Poulantzas identifies the role of the state as the strategically selective terrain through which social forces operate, with its consequent implications for asymmetry in the organization of power (Jessop 1990d: 303).
13 An autopoietic system is defined, along the lines established by Luhmann, Varela, Maturana and Zeleny, as a complex unity consisting of a system of definite components existing in time and space which are delimited by the relations between the components of the system. An autopoietic system is defined in theoretical terms as a closed, self-referential, self-(re-)producing and self-maintaining organization. In such a system, through the interaction of the constituent parts and their products, reproduction is ensured through the generation of the same organization of processes and the emergence of a topological boundary between the system and the external environment. Jessop highlights the distinction between the organization of the autopoietic system and the contingent structure of the system. Together, these define the limits and possibilities for the reconstitution and

258 *Notes to Chapter 5*

recombination of the component parts, through which the forms of organization can vary without systemic degeneration and crisis. In addition, these features determine the ways in which the system in question responds to the environmental changes (perturbation) which trigger structural transformation. On the relations between autopoietic systems within a broader social system, these accounts identify forms of 'structural coupling' through which each system interacts with the environment (composed of other systems and their interactions) and through which the perturbations are produced. In turn, these interactions and the systems so identified (with varying forms of openness and closure) may constitute a composite autopoietic system, if the relations between the components operate in a way which ensures compensable perturbation between disruptive tendencies. While Luhmann is unwilling to commit himself to definite outcomes in the process of evolutionary change in such systems, Jessop argues that it is feasible to specify historically-specific systemic properties and structural constraints in conjunction with the balance of social forces in a given conjuncture in order to identify pathways in social change, so that the limits and possibilities for social change are path-dependent (Jessop 1987d; 1990d). Jessop's recent work on the path dependency of forms of post-Socialist Eastern European development is an empirical application of these assumptions (Hausner, Jessop and Nielsen 1995).

6 Metatheorizing the state

1 Retroduction and retrodiction, whereby the 'real-concrete' becomes the 'concrete-in-thought', have been usefully elaborated by Bob Jessop's theoretical formulation of 'contingent-necessity'. This describes the way in which a combination of different causal mechanisms produce a necessary outcome, but it remains contingent whether the causal powers and liabilities of the object in question are activated under specific conditions (the configuration of other objects with their own causal powers and liabilities) to produce a significant effect (Jessop 1982: 212). Such contingency means that the same causal mechanisms can produce quite different results (depending upon the conditions) and/or, alternatively, that the operation of two or more different causal mechanisms can have the same effect or, through cancelling each other out, have no effect at all at the level of concrete and complex events. This situation is said to be 'overdetermined', implying its 'underdetermination' at more abstract and simple levels of analysis (Sayer 1992: 85–117). Jessop summarizes this approach as:

> the retroductive specification of a hierarchy of conditions of possibility – the more abstract levels being compatible with more possible outcomes, at the same time as being indeterminate with reference to the actual result, the more concrete levels defining progressively more restrictive limits on the actual result as they overdetermine the more abstract conditions of possibility.
>
> (Jessop 1982: 218)

At the highest level of abstraction, it is possible to isolate simple, necessary relationships which can be developed by building theoretical models and postulating structures and mechanisms which, if they exist and operate in the way so defined, would account for the social phenomena in question. At the lower levels of abstraction, the more concrete relationships must be seen at best as contingent, and they can only be established through empirical analysis of the partial conditions or one-sided aspects of the object of analysis.

There are, of course, certain dangers within this form of analysis. First, one must present theory in a manner which avoids the use of 'chaotic conceptions', the arbitrary division of the indivisible and/or the lumping together of the unrelated, carving up the object of analysis with little regard for its real structure of concrete manifestations. Instead, one must aim to establish 'rational abstractions' which isolate significant aspects of social life with their own autonomous force or unity (Marx 1857: 100; Sayer 1992: 138–43). Second, the formation of hypotheses should be dealt with very carefully, to ensure that a sound hypothesis exhausts the *explanandum* under consideration, specifying the conditions which account for the existence of the *explanandum* at the level of abstraction and the degree of complexity at which it is defined. In addition, the hypothesis should be capable of moving to lower levels of abstraction and greater degrees of complexity without losing its logical consistence. The goal of realist analysis is to reduce the extent of our ignorance of the 'intransitive', either through the further specification of causal mechanisms involved, or by replacing current theories with more determinate ones. For as Jessop states, 'Theoretical analysis is a continuing process, involving the ever renewed transformation of existing theories, concepts, techniques and evidence' (Jessop 1982: 220). Hence, it is important not to become too attached to specific abstract concepts, and constantly to cross-check them against empirically acquired knowledge (comparative and historical analyses). Bad abstraction must be jettisoned when it is found wanting and when better alternatives exist.

Bibliography

Note: Bob Jessop's chosen style of reference is as R. D. Jessop prior to 1974, and as B. Jessop thereafter. This convention has been followed here.

Aglietta, M. (1979) *A Theory of Capitalist Regulation: The US Experience*, London, Verso.
Almond, G. A. and Verba, S. (1963) *The Civic Culture*, Princeton, Princeton University Press.
Althusser, L. (1971) *Lenin and Philosophy and Other Essays*, London, NLB.
—— (1977[1965]) 'Contradiction and Overdetermination', in *For Marx*, London, NLB: 87–128.
Althusser, L. and Balibar, E. (1970[1968]) *Reading Capital*, London, NLB.
Altvater, E. (1973) 'Notes on Some Problems of State Interventionism', *Kapitalistate* 1: 96–108 and 2: 76–83.
Arato, A. (1974) 'The Neo-Idealist Defence of Subjectivity', *Telos* 21: 108–61.
Archibugi, D. and Held, D. (eds) (1995) *Cosmopolitan Democracy: An Agenda for a New World Order*, Cambridge, Polity.
Avinieri, S. (1968) *The Social and Political Thought of Karl Marx*, Cambridge, Cambridge University Press.
Bachrach, P. and Baratz, M. (1962) 'Two Faces of Power', *American Political Science Review* 56: 947–52.
—— (1963) 'Decisions and Nondecisions: An Analytical Framework', *American Political Science Review* 57: 632–42.
—— (1970) *Power and Poverty: Theory and Practice*, Oxford, Oxford University Press.
Bakhtin, M. M. (1981) *The Dialogic Imagination: Four Essays*, Austin, Texas, University of Austin Press.
Ball, T. (1975) 'Models of Power: Past and Present', *Journal of the History of the Behavioral Sciences* (July) 211–22.
—— (1978b) 'Two Concepts of Coercion', *Theory and Society* 5: 97–112.
—— (1988) *Transforming Political Discourse: Political Theory and Critical Conceptual History*, Oxford, Blackwell.
Beer, S. (1982) *Britain against Itself: The Political Contradictions of Collectivism*, London, Faber and Faber.
Bell, D. (1960) *The End of Ideology*, Glencoe, Free Press.
Bentley, A. (1967) *The Process of Government*, Chicago, University of Chicago Press.
Benton, T. (1981a) '"Objective" Interests and the Sociology of Power', *Sociology* 15 (2): 161–84.
—— (1981b) 'Realism and Social Science: Some Comments on Roy Bhaskar's *The*

Possibility of Naturalism', *Radical Philosophy* 27: 13–21.
Berlin, I. (1969) 'Two Concepts of Liberty', in *Four Essays on Liberty*, Oxford, Oxford University Press: 118–72.
Bertramsen, R., Thomsen, J. and Torfing, J. (1991) *State, Economy and Society*, London, Unwin Hyman.
Bhaskar, R. (1978) *A Realist Theory of Science*, 2nd edn, Hemel Hempstead, Harvester Wheatsheaf.
—— (1979) *The Possibility of Naturalism: A Philosophical Critique of the Contemporary Human Sciences*, Hemel Hempstead, Harvester Wheatsheaf.
—— (1983) 'Beef, Structure and Place: Notes from a Critical Naturalist Perspective', *Journal for the Theory of Social Behaviour* 1: 81–95.
—— (1986) *Scientific Realism and Human Emancipation*, London, Verso.
—— (1989a) *The Possibility of Naturalism*, 2nd edn, Hemel Hempstead, Harvester Wheatsheaf.
—— (1989b) *Reclaiming Reality*, London, Verso.
—— (1991) *Philosophy and the Idea of Freedom*, Oxford, Blackwell.
Blaikie, N. (1993) *Approaches to Social Enquiry*, Cambridge, Polity.
Blalock, H. (1964) *Causal Inferences in Non-Experimental Research*, Chapel Hill, N. C., University of North Carolina Press.
Blanke, B., Juergens, U. and Kastendiek, H. (1976) 'The Relationship Between the Political and the Economic as a Point of Departure for a Materialistic Analysis of the Bourgeois State', *International Journal of Sociology* 6 (3): 414–44.
—— (1978) 'On the Current Marxist Discussion on the Analysis of Form and Function of the Bourgeois State', in Holloway, J. and Picciotto, S. (eds) *State and Capital: A Marxist Debate*, London, Edward Arnold: 108–47.
Blau, P. (1964) *Exchange and Power in Social Life*, New York, Wiley.
Blowers, A. (1983) 'Master of Fate or Victim of Circumstance – The Exercise of Corporate Power in Environmental Policy-Making', *Policy and Politics* 11: 393–415.
Boddy, J. and Crotty, R. (1974) 'Class Conflict, Keynesian Policy and the Business Cycle', Monthly Review 26 (October): 1–17.
—— (1975) 'Class Conflict and Macro-Policy: The Political Business Cycle', *Review of Radical Political Economy* 7 (1): 1–19.
Bonefeld, W. and Holloway, J. (eds) (1991) *Post-Fordism and Social Form: A Marxist Debate on the Post-Fordist State*, Basingstoke, Conference of Socialist Economists/Macmillan.
Bourdieu, P. (1986) *Distinction: A Social Critique of the Judgement of Taste*, Cambridge Mass., Harvard University Press.
Bowles, S. and Edwards, R. (1985) *Understanding Capitalism; Competition, Command and Change in the US Economy*, New York, Holt Reinhart.
Brown, V. (1994) *Adam Smith's Discourse: Canonicity, Commerce and Conscience*, London, Routledge.
Bryant, C. G. A. (1985) *Positivism in Social Theory and Research*, Basingstoke, Macmillan.
Burczak, T. (1994a) 'The Postmodern Moments of F. A. Hayek's Economics', *Economics and Philosophy* 10: 31–58.
—— (1994b) 'Reply to Bruce Caldwell: Can Subjectivism be Non-Hermeneutic?', *Economics and Philosophy* 10: 315–17.
Burrow, J. W. (1981) *A Liberal Descent: Victorian Historians and the English Past*, Cambridge, Cambridge University Press.
—— (1987) 'The History of Ideas in Theory and Practice', *The John Coffin Memorial Lecture*, 12/2/87, London, University of London.

Butler, D. E. and Stokes, D. (1974) *Political Change in Britain*, London, Macmillan.
Caldwell, B. J. (1988a) 'Hayek's Transformation', *History of Political Economy* 20(4): 513–41.
—— (1988b) 'Hayek's Trend of Economic Thinking', *Review of Austrian Economics* 2: 175–8.
—— (1992) 'Hayek the Falsificationist: A Refutation', *Research in the History of Economic Thought and Methodology* 10: 1–15.
—— (1994) 'Hayek's Scientific Subjectivism', *Economics and Philosophy* 10: 305–13.
Cantril, H. (1965) *The Pattern of Human Concerns*, New Brunswick, Rutgers University Press.
Carver, E. (1986) 'The Emigration of the Austrian Economists', *History of Political Economy* 18(1): 1–32.
Caton, H. P. (1976) 'Politics and Political Science', *Politics* 11: 149–55.
Caygill, H. (1995) *A Kant Dictionary*, Oxford, Blackwell.
Chalmers, A. (1988) 'Is Bhaskar's Realism Realistic', *Radical Philosophy* 49: 18–23.
Clarke, S. (ed.) (1991) *The State Debate*, Basingstoke, Conference of Socialist Economists /Macmillan.
Clegg, S. (1989) *Frameworks of Power*, London, Sage.
Collini, S. (1991) *Public Moralists: Political Thought and Intellectual Life in Britain 1850–1930*, Oxford, Oxford University Press.
Crenson, M. (1971) *The Un-Politics of Air Pollution: A Study of Non-Decision Making in the Cities*, Baltimore, Johns Hopkins Press.
Crosland, A. (1956) *The Future of Socialism*, London, Cape.
Dahl, R. A. (1956) *A Preface to Democratic Theory*, Chicago, University of Chicago Press.
—— (1957) 'The Concept of Power', *Behavioral Science* 2: 201–5.
—— (1958) 'A Critique of the Ruling Elite Model', *American Political Science Review* 52: 463–9.
—— (1961a) 'The Behavioral Approach in Political Science: Epitaph for a Monument to a Successful Protest', *American Political Science Review* 58.
—— (1961b) *Who Governs?: Democracy and Power in an American City*, New Haven, Yale University Press.
—— (1966a) 'Further Reflections on "The Elitist Theory of Democracy"', *American Political Science Review* 60: 296–305.
—— (ed.) (1966b) *Political Oppositions in Western Democracies*, New Haven, Yale University Press.
—— (1970) *After the Revolution?* New Haven, Yale University Press.
—— (1971) *Polyarchy: Participation and Opposition*, New Haven, Yale University Press.
—— (1982) *Dilemmas of Pluralist Democracy: Autonomy versus Control*, New Haven, Yale University Press.
—— (1984[1963]) *Modern Political Analysis*, 4th edn, Engelwood Cliffs, N. J., Prentice-Hall.
—— (1985) *A Preface to Economic Democracy*, Cambridge, Polity.
—— (1986a) *Democracy, Liberty and Equality*, Oslo, Norwegian University Press.
—— (1986b) 'Power as the Control of Behaviour', in S. Lukes (ed.), *Power*, Oxford, Blackwell (originally published as 'Power' in *International Encyclopaedia of the Social Sciences* (1968), ed. D. L. Sills, vol. 12: 405–15, London, Macmillan).
—— (1989) *Democracy and its Critics*, New Haven, Yale University Press.
Dahl, R. and Lindblom, C. (1953) *Politics, Economics and Welfare*, New York, Harper (2nd edn 1976).

Dahl, R and Tufte, E. (1974) *Size and Democracy*, London, Oxford University Press.
Dahrendorf, R. (1959) *Class and Class Conflict in Industrial Society*, London, Routledge.
—— (1968) *Essays in the Theory of Society*, London, Routledge.
Dancy, J. (1985) *Introduction to Contemporary Epistemology*, Oxford, Blackwell.
Dilthey, W. (1883) 'Introduction to Human Sciences', in *Wilhelm Dilthey: Selected Writings*, ed. H. P. Rickman, Cambridge, Cambridge University Press.
Dunleavy, P. and O'Leary, B. (1987) *Theories of the State: The Politics of Liberal Democracy*, Basingstoke, Macmillan.
Easton, D. (1965) *A Framework for Political Analysis*, Englewood Cliffs, N. J., Prentice-Hall.
—— (1967) *A Systems Analysis of Political Life*, London, Wiley.
Engels, F. (1884) *On the Origins of the Family, Private Property, and the State*, London, Lawrence and Wishart.
Esser, J. and Hirsch, J. (1989) 'The Crisis of Fordism and the Dimensions of a "Post-Fordist" Regional and Urban Structure', *International Journal of Urban and Regional Research* 13 (3): 417–37.
Feyerabend, P. (1975) *Against Method*, London, Verso.
—— (1978) *Science in a Free Society*, London, New Left Books.
Fine, B. and Harris, L. (1979) *Rereading Capital*, Basingstoke, Macmillan.
Fleetwood, S. (1993) 'Is Hayek a Transcendental Realist?', mimeo, paper given at the Nordic Workshop on Economic Methodology, University of Helsinki, 3–5 June.
Frey, F. W. (1971) 'Comment: "On Issues and Non-Issues in the Study of Power"', *American Political Science Review* 65: 1081–101.
Gallie, W. B. (1955/6) 'Essentially Contested Concepts', *Proceedings of the Aristotelian Society* 56: 167–98.
Gaventa, J. P. (1980) *Power and Powerlessness: Quiescence and Rebellion in an Appalachian Valley*, Urbana, University of Illinois Press.
Gellner, E. (1979) *Spectacles and Predicaments: Essays in Social Theory*, Cambridge, Cambridge University Press.
Giddens, A. (1976) *New Rules of Sociological Method: A Positive Critique of Interpretative Sociologies*, London, Hutchinson.
—— (1979) *Central Problems in Social Theory: Action, Structure and Contradiction in Social Analysis*, Basingstoke, Macmillan.
—— (1982) *Profiles and Critiques in Social Theory*, Basingstoke, Macmillan.
—— (1984) *The Constitution of Society*, Cambridge, Polity.
Gilroy, P. (1982) *There Ain't No Black in the Union Jack*, London, Unwin Hyman.
Glyn, J. and Sutcliffe, B. (1972) *British Capitalism, Workers and the Profits Squeeze*, Harmondsworth, Penguin.
Gough, I. (1975) 'State Expenditure in Advanced Capitalism', *New Left Review* 92: 53–92.
—— (1979) *The Political Economy of the Welfare State*, Basingstoke, Macmillan.
Gould, S. J. (1977) *Ever Since Darwin: Reflections in Natural History*, London, Penguin.
—— (1989) *This Wonderful Life: The Burgess Shale and the Nature of History*, New York, Norton.
Gramsci, A. (1971) *Selections From Prison Notebooks*, London, Lawrence and Wishart.
Gray, J. (1986) *Hayek and Liberty*, 2nd edn, Oxford, Blackwell.
Green, D. (1987) *The New Right: the Counter Revolution in Political, Economic and Social Thought*, Brighton, Harvester.
Greenstein, F. I. (1969) *Personality and Politics*, Chicago, Markham.

Habermas, J. (1973) *Legitimation Crisis*, London, Heinemann.
—— (1989) *The Structural Transformation of the Public Sphere*, Cambridge, Polity.
—— (1992) *Faktizat und Geltung*, Frankfurt, Suhrkamp.
Hacking, I. (1983) *Representing and Intervening: Introductory Topics in the Philosophy of Natural Science*, Cambridge, Cambridge University Press.
Hall, J. A. (1987) *Liberalism: Politics, Ideology and the Market*, London, Paladin.
Hall, S. (1980) 'Popular-Democratic vs. Authoritarian Populism: Two Ways of Taking Democracy Seriously', in Hunt, A. (ed.) *Marxism and Democracy*, London, Lawrence and Wishart: 157–85.
—— (1983a) 'The Great Moving Right Show', in Hall, S. and Jacques, M. (eds) *The Politics of Thatcherism*, London, Lawrence and Wishart: 19–39.
—— (1983b) 'The Little Caesars of Social Democracy', in Hall, S. and Jacques, M. (eds) *The Politics of Thatcherism*, London, Lawrence and Wishart: 309–21.
Hall, S., Critcher, C., Jefferson, T., Clarke, J. and Roberts, B. (1978) *Policing the Crisis: Mugging, The State and Law and Order*, Basingstoke, Macmillan.
Ham, C. J. (1985) *Health Policy in Britain*, 2nd edn, Basingstoke, Macmillan.
Hanson, N. (1958) *Patterns of Discovery*, Cambridge, Cambridge University Press.
—— (1969) *Perception and Discovery: An Introduction to Scientific Inquiry*, San Francisco, Copper.
Harré, R. (1979) *Social Being*, Oxford, Blackwell.
—— (1986) *Varieties of Realism: A Rationale for the Natural Sciences*, Oxford, Blackwell.
Harré, R. and Madden, E. (1975) *Causal Powers*, Oxford, Blackwell.
Harré, R. and Secord, P. F. (1973) *The Explanation of Social Behaviour*, Oxford, Blackwell.
Hartwell, R. M. (1995) *A History of the Mont Pèlerin Society*, Indianapolis, Liberty Fund.
Hausner, J., Jessop, B. and Nielsen, K. (1995) *Strategic Choice and Path Dependency in Post-Socialism: Institutional Dynamics in the Transformation Process*, London, Elgar.
Hayek, F. A. (1928) 'Intertemporal Price Equilibrium and Movements in the Value of Money', in *Weltwirtschaftliches Archiv* 2: 33–76 (reprinted in Hayek 1984).
—— (1937) 'Economics and Knowledge', *Economica* 13 (2): 33–54 (reprinted in Hayek 1949).
—— (1939) 'The Economic Conditions of Inter-State Federation', *New Common-wealth Quarterly* 5 (2): 131–49.
—— (1941) *The Pure Theory of Capital*, London, Routledge.
—— (1944) *The Road to Serfdom*, London, Routledge.
—— (1945) 'The Use of Knowledge in Society', *American Economic Review* 55 (4): 519–30 (reprinted in Hayek 1949).
—— (1949) *Individualism and the Economic Order*, London, Routledge.
—— (1951) *John Stuart Mill and Harriet Taylor: Their Friendship and Subsequent Marriage*, London, Routledge.
—— (1960) *The Constitution of Liberty*, London, Routledge.
—— (1967) *Studies in Philosophy, Politics and Economics*, London, Routledge.
—— (1973) *Rules and Order: Law, Legislation and Liberty* vol. I., London, Routledge.
—— (1976) *The Mirage of Social Justice: Law, Legislation and Liberty*, vol. II., London, Routledge.
—— (1978) *New Studies in Philosophy, Politics, Economics and the History of Ideas*, London, Routledge.
—— (1979[1952]) *The Counter-Revolution of Science: Studies on the Abuse of Reason*, Indianapolis, Liberty Press.

—— (1979) *The Political Order of a Free People: Law, Legislation and Liberty* vol. III., London, Routledge.
—— (1982) 'Consolidated Preface To The One-Volume Edition', in *Law, Legislation and Liberty: A New Statement of the Liberal Principles of Justice and Political Economy*, London, Routledge.
—— (1984) *Money, Capital and Fluctuations: Early Essays*, London, Routledge.
—— (1988) *The Fatal Conceit: The Errors of Socialism, Collected Works of F. A. Hayek* vol. I, ed. W. W. Bartley III, London, Routledge.
—— (1991) *The Trend of Economic Thinking: Essays on Political Economists and Economic History, Collected Works of F. A. Hayek* vol. III, ed. W. W. Bartley III and S. Kresge, London, Routledge.
—— (1992) *The Fortunes of Liberalism: Essays on Austrian Economics and the Ideal of Freedom, Collected Works of F. A. Hayek vol. IV*, ed. P. G. Klein, London, Routledge.
Hayek, F. A., Pierson, N. G., von Mises, L., Halm, G. and Barone, E. (eds) (1935) *Collectivist Economic Planning: Critical Studies on the Possibility of Socialism*, London, Routledge.
Held, D. (1987) *Models of Democracy*, Cambridge, Polity.
—— (ed.) (1993) *Prospects for Democracy: North, South, East and West*, Cambridge, Polity.
Hempel, C. G. (1965) *Aspects of Scientific Explanation*, New York, Free Press.
Hirsch, J. (1978) 'State Apparatus and Social Reproduction', in Holloway, J. and Picciotto, S. (eds) *State and Capital: A Marxist Debate*, London, Edward Arnold: 57–107.
—— (1983) 'The Fordist Security State and New Social Movements', *Kapitalistate* 10/11: 75–84.
—— (1984) 'Notes Towards A Reformulation of State Theory', in Hänninen, S. and Paldán, L. (eds) *Rethinking Marx*, Berlin, Argument-Verlag/New York, International General/IMMRC: 155–60.
—— (1991) 'From the Fordist to the Post-Fordist State', in Jessop, B., Kastendiek, H., Nielsen, K. and Pedersen, O. (eds) *The Politics of Flexibility: Restructuring State and Industry in Britain, Germany and Scandinavia*, London, Elgar: 67–81.
Hoffman, J. (1988) *State, Authority, Democracy*, Brighton, Wheatsheaf.
Holloway, J. and Picciotto, S. (eds) (1978) *State and Capital: A Marxist Debate*, London, Edward Arnold.
Holmwood, J. and Stewart, A. (1991) *Explanation and Social Theory*, Basingstoke, Macmillan.
Humboldt, W. von, (1854[1791]) *The Sphere and Duty of Government*, London, Edwards.
Hunter, F. (1953) *Community Power Structure: A Study of Decision Makers*, Chapel Hill, N. C., University of North Carolina Press.
Husserl, E. (1931) *Ideas: General Introduction to Pure Phenomenology*, London, Allen and Unwin.
—— (1960) *Cartesian Meditations: An Introduction to Phenomenology*, trans. D. Cairns, The Hague, Martinus Nijhoff.
—— (1970) *The Crisis of European Sciences and Transcendental Phenomenology: An Introduction to Phenomenological Philosophy*, trans. D. Carr, Evanston. Ill., Northwestern University Press.
Hutchison, T. W. (1981) *The Politics and Philosophy of Economics: Marxians, Keynesians and Austrians*, Oxford, Blackwell.
Isaac, J. (1987a) *Power and Marxist Theory: A Realist View*, Ithaca, Cornell University Press.

—— (1987b) 'Beyond the Three Faces of Power', *Polity* XX (1): 4–30.
—— (1990) 'Realism and Reality: Some Realistic Considerations', *Journal for the Theory of Social Behaviour* 20 (1): 1–32.
Jessop, R. D. (1969) 'Exchange and Power in Structural Analysis', *Sociological Review* 17: 415–31.
—— (1971) 'Civility and Traditionalism in English Political Culture', *British Journal of Political Science* i: 1–24.
—— (1972) *Social Order, Reform and Revolution*, Basingstoke, Macmillan.
(Jessop, B.) (1974) *Traditionalism, Conservatism and British Political Culture*, London, Allen and Unwin.
—— (1977) 'Recent Theories of the Capitalist State', *Cambridge Journal of Economics* 1 (iv): 353–73.
—— (1978a) 'Marx and Engels on the State', in *Politics, Ideology and the State*, ed. S. Hibbins, London, Lawrence and Wishart.
—— (1978b) 'Capitalism and Democracy: The Best Possible Political Shell?', in *Power and the State*, ed. G. Littlejohn, London, Croom Helm.
—— (1979) 'Corporatism, Parliamentarism, and Social Democracy', in Lehmbruch, G. and Schmitter, P. C. (eds), *Trends Towards Corporatist Intermediation*, London, Sage.
—— (1980a) 'The Transformation of the State in Postwar Britain', in Scase, R. (ed.), *The State in Western Europe*, London, Croom Helm.
—— (1980b) 'The Political Indeterminacy of Democracy', in Hunt, A. (ed.), *Marxism and Democracy*, London, Lawrence and Wishart: 55–80.
—— (1980c) 'The Capitalist State and Political Practice: Review of Nicos Poulantzas, *State, Power, Socialism*', *Economy and Society* 9 (i): 108–27.
—— (1980d) 'On Recent Marxist Theories of Law, the State, and Juridico-political Ideology', *International Journal of the Sociology of Law* 8: 339–68.
—— (1980e) 'The Gramsci Debate', *Marxism Today* (February): 23–5.
—— (1982) *The Capitalist State: Marxist Theories and Methods*, Oxford, Blackwell.
—— (1983a) 'Business Organisations and the Rule of Capital', *West European Politics* 10: 139–62.
—— (1983b) 'Accumulation Strategies, State Forms and Hegemonic Projects', *Kapitalistate* 10/11: 89–112.
—— (1983c) 'The Capitalist State and the Rule of Capital: Problems in the Analysis of Business Associations', in Marsh, D. (ed.), *Capital and Politics in Western Europe*, vol. 6, no. 2: 139–62.
—— (1983d) 'The Democratic State and the National Interest', in Coates, D. and Johnston, G. (eds), *Socialist Arguments*, Oxford, Martin Robertson: 83–106.
—— (1985a) *Nicos Poulantzas: Marxist Theory and Political Strategy*, Basingstoke, Macmillan.
—— (1985b) 'The Non-Structuralist Legacy of Nicos Poulantzas', in Appignanesi, L, (ed.), *Ideas From France: the Legacy of French Theory*, London, Institute of Contemporary Arts: 38–41.
—— (1986a) 'The Economy, The State and The Law: Theories of Relative Autonomy and Autopoietic Closure', *EUI Working Papers*, 87/263, Florence, European University Institute.
—— (1986b) 'The Prospects for the Corporatisation of Monetarism in Britain', in Jacobi, O., Jessop, B., Kastendiek, H. and Regini, M. (eds), *Economic Crisis, Trade Unions and the State*: 105–30.

―― (1986c) 'Thatcherism's Mid-Life Crisis', *New Socialist* (March): 11–5.

―― (1986d) 'Economy, State and the Law: Theories of Relative Autonomy and Autopoietic Closure', *EUI Working Papers*, 87/263, Florence: European University Institute.

―― (1987a) 'Power and Strategy in Foucault and Poulantzas', *Ideas and Production* 6: 59–85.

―― (1987b) 'The Economic Theory of the State', in Eatwell, J., Milgate, M. and Newton, P. (eds), *The New Palgrave*, vol. 2, London, Macmillan: 75–7.

―― (1987c) 'Mode of Production', in Eatwell, J., Milgate, M. and Newton, P. (eds), *The New Palgrave*, vol. 3, London, Macmillan: 489–91.

―― (1987d) 'Economy, State and Law in Autopoietic Theory', *Essex Working Papers in Politics and Government*, no. 42, ed. D. Marsh.

―― (1988a) 'Regulation Theory, Post-Fordism, and the State: More Than a Reply to Werner Bonefeld', *Capital and Class* 34: 147–69.

―― (1989a) 'Thatcherism: The British Road to Post-Fordism?', *Essex Papers in Politics and Government*, October.

―― (1989b) 'The Nation-State, Surveillance, and Violence', in Held, D. and Thompson, J. (eds), *Social Theory of Modern Societies: Anthony Giddens and his Critics*, Cambridge, Cambridge University Press.

―― (1989c) 'Neo-Conservative Regimes and the Transition to Post-Fordism' in Gottdiener, M. and Komninos, N. (eds), *Capitalist Development and Crisis Theory: Accumulation, Regulation and Spatial Restructuring*, Basingstoke, Macmillan.

―― (1990a) 'What comes after Thatcherism?', *New Statesman and Society* 23 November: 8–9.

―― (1990b) 'Regulation Theories in Retrospect and Prospect', *Economy and Society* 19 (2): 153–216.

―― (1990c) 'Putting States in their Place: State Systems and State Theory', in Leftwich, A. (ed.) *New Directions in Politics*, London, Elgar: 61–76.

―― (1990d) *State Theory: Putting Capitalist States in Their Place*, Cambridge, Polity.

―― (1991a) 'Polar Bears and Class Struggle; Much Less than a Self Criticism', in Bonefeld, W. and Holloway, J. (eds), *Post-Fordism and Social Form: A Marxist Debate on the Post-Fordist State*, Basingstoke, Macmillan.

―― (1991b) 'The Welfare State in the Transition from Fordism to Post-Fordism', in Jessop, B., Kastendiek, H., Nielsen, K. and Pedersen, O. (eds), *The Politics of Flexibility: Restructuring State and Industry in Britain, Germany and Scandinavia*, London, Elgar: 82–105.

―― (1991c) 'Thatcherism and Flexibility: The White Heat of a Post-Fordist Revolution', in Jessop, B., Kastendiek, H., Nielsen, K. and Pedersen, O. (eds), *The Politics of Flexibility: Restructuring State and Industry in Britain, Germany and Scandinavia*, London, Elgar: 135–61.

―― (1992a) 'From Social Democracy to Thatcherism: Twenty Five Years of British Politics', in Abercrombie, N. and Warde, A. (eds) *Social Change in Contemporary Britain*, Cambridge, Polity: 14–39.

―― (1992b) 'Fordism and Post-Fordism: A Critical Reformulation', in Storper, M. and Scott, A. J. (eds), *Pathways to Industrialisation and Regional Development*, London, Routledge.

―― (1993) 'Towards a Schumpeterian Workfare State? Preliminary Remarks on Post-Fordist Political Economy,' *Studies in Political Economy* 40 (Spring): 7–39.

―― (1994) ' The Transition to Post-Fordism and the Schumpeterian Workfare

State', in Burrows, R. and Loader, B. (eds), *Towards A Post-Fordist Welfare State?*, London, Routledge.
—— (1995) 'The Regulation Approach, Governance and Post-Fordism: Alternative perspectives on Economic and Political Change?' *Economy and Society* 24 (3): 303–33.
—— (1996) 'Interpretive Sociology and the Dialectic of Structure and Agency', *Theory, Culture and Society* 13 (1): 119–28 .
Jessop, B., Bonnett, K. and Bromley, S. (1990) 'Farewell to Thatcherism? Neo-Liberalism vs New Times', *New Left Review* 179: 81–202.
Jessop, B., Bonnett, K., Bromley, S. and Ling, T. (1984) 'Authoritarian Populism, Two Nations and Thatcherism', *New Left Review* 147: 32–60.
—— (1985) 'Thatcherism and the Politics of Hegemony: A Reply to Stuart Hall', *New Left Review* 153: 87–101.
—— (1987) 'Popular Capitalism, Flexible Accumulation and Left Strategy', *New Left Review* 165: 104–22.
—— (1988) *Thatcherism: A Tale of Two Nations*, Cambridge, Polity.
Jessop, B., Jacobi, O. and Kastendiek, H. (1986) 'Corporatist and Liberal Responses to the Crisis of Postwar Capitalism', in Jacobi, O., Jessop, B., Kastendiek, H. and Regini, M. (eds), *Economic Crisis, Trade Unions and the State*: 1–13.
Kant, I. (1987[1787]) *Critique of Pure Reason*, 2nd edn, London, Dent.
Kaufmann, F. (1933) 'On the Subject Matter and Method of Economic Science', *Economica* XIII (Nov.): 381–401.
—— (1944[1936]) *Methodenlehre der Sozialwissenschaften*, translated as *Methodology of the Social Sciences*, London, Oxford University Press.
Keane, J. (1984) 'Introduction', in Offe, C., *Contradictions of the Welfare State*, London, Hutchinson: 11–34.
Keat, R. and Urry, J. (1982) *Social Theory as Science*, 2nd edn, London, Routledge and Kegan Paul.
King, A. (1975) 'Overload: Problems of Governing in the 1970s', *Political Studies* 23: 283–96.
King, D. (1987) *The New Right*, Basingstoke, Macmillan.
Kirzner, I. (1992) *The Meaning of Market Process: Essays in the Development of Modern Austrian Economics*, London, Routledge.
Kornhauser, W. (1959) *The Politics of Mass Society*, London, Routledge.
Kresge, S and Wenar, L. (eds) (1994) *Hayek on Hayek: An Autobiographical Dialogue*, London, Routledge.
Kuhn, T. (1970) *The Structure of Scientific Revolutions*, 2nd edn, Chicago, University of Chicago Press.
—— (1977) *The Essential Tension: Selected Studies in Scientific Thought and Change*, Chicago, University of Chicago Press.
Kukathas, C. (1989) *Hayek and Modern Liberalism*, Oxford, Clarendon Press.
Laclau, E. (1977) *Politics and Ideology in Marxist Theory*, London, Verso.
Laclau, E. and Mouffe, C. (1985) *Hegemony and Socialist Strategy: Towards A Radical Democratic Politics*, London, Verso.
Lakatos, I. (1970) 'Falsification and the Methodology of Scientific Research Programmes', in Lakatos, I. and Musgrave, A. (eds), *Criticism and the Growth of Knowledge*, Cambridge, Cambridge University Press.
Lawson, T. (1994a) 'Realism and Hayek: A Case of Continuous Transformation' in Colonna, M., Hageman, H. and Hamouda, O. (eds), *Capitalism, Socialism and Knowledge: The Economics of F. A. Hayek* vol. II., Aldershot, Elgar.

—— (1994b) 'A Realist Theory for Economics' in Backhouse, R. E. (ed.), *New Directions in Economic Methodology*, London, Routledge: 257–85.

Layder, D. (1985) 'Key Issues in Structuration Theory: Some Critical Remarks', *Current Perspective in Social Theory* 8: 25–46.

Lemert, C. (ed.) (1993) *Social Theory: The Multicultural and Classic Readings*, Oxford, Westview.

Lenin, V. I. (1917) *State and Revolution*, Moscow, Progress.

Lenski, G. E. (1966) *Power and Privilege*, New York, McGraw-Hill.

Lindblom, C. E. (1965) *The Intelligence of Democracy*, New York, Free Press.

—— (1977) *Politics and Markets*, New York, Basic Books.

Ling, T. (1991) 'Review of Jessop, *State Theory* [1990]', *Capital and Class* 44: 129–35.

Lipietz, A. (1983) *The Enchanted World: Inflation, Credit and the World Crisis*, London, Verso.

—— (1987) *Miracles and Mirages: The Crises of Global Fordism*, London, Verso.

Lipset, S. M. (1959) *Political Man*, London, Mercury.

Luhmann, N. (1982) *The Differentiation of Society*, New York, Columbia University Press.

—— (1985a) 'The Unity of the Legal System', in Teubner, G. (ed.), *Autopoietic Law: A New Approach to Law and Society*, Berlin, De Gruyter: 12–35.

—— (1985b) 'Closure and Openness; On Reality in the World of Law', in Teubner, G. (ed.), *Autopoietic Law: A New Approach to Law and Society*, Berlin, De Gruyter: 335–48.

—— (1985c) *A Sociological Theory of Law*, ed. M. Albrow, London, Routledge.

—— (1987) 'The Self-Reproduction of Law and its Limits', in Teubner, G. (ed.), *Dilemmas of Law in the Welfare State*, Berlin, De Gruyter: 111–27.

Lukes, S. (1973) *Individualism*, Oxford, Blackwell.

—— (1974) *Power: A Radical View*, London, Macmillan.

—— (1977) *Essays in Social Theory*, London, Macmillan.

—— (ed.) (1986) *Power*, Oxford, Blackwell.

Machlup, F. (1936) 'Why Bother with Methodology?', *Economica* III (Feb): 39–45.

—— (1942) 'Competition, Pliopoly and Profit', *Economica* IX (Feb/May).

—— (1955) 'The Problem of Verification in Economics', *Southern Economic Journal* 22: 1–22.

—— (1960) 'Operational Concepts and Mental Constructs in Model and Theory Formation', *Giornale degli Economisti* 19: 553–82 (reprinted in Machlup, F., *Methodology of Economics and Other Social Sciences*, New York, Academic Press: 159–88).

—— (1967) 'Theories of the Firm: Marginalist, Behavioral, Managerial', *American Economic Review* 57: 1–33.

MacIntyre, A. (1981) *After Virtue*, Notre Dame, Ind., University of Notre Dame Press.

Madison, J., Hamilton, A. and Jay, J. (1987[1788]) *The Federalist Papers*, ed. I. Kramnick, Harmondsworth, Penguin.

Manicas, P. (1987) *A History and Philosophy of the Social Sciences*, Oxford, Blackwell.

Mann, M. (1970) 'The Social Cohesion of Liberal Democracy', *American Sociological Review* XXX: 423–39.

Margolis, J. (1986) *Pragmatism Without Foundations: Reconciling Realism and Relativism – The Persistence of Reality* vol. I, Oxford, Blackwell.

Marshall, T. H. (1950) *Citizenship and Social Class*, Cambridge, Cambridge University Press.

Marx, K. (1857) *Grundrisse*, ed. M. Nicolaus, Harmondsworth, Penguin.

270 Bibliography

Masterman, M. (1970) 'The Nature of a Paradigm', in Lakatos, I. and Musgrave, A. (eds), *Criticism and the Growth of Knowledge*, Cambridge, Cambridge University Press.

Menger, C. (1981[1871]) *Principles of Economics*, trans. J. Dingwall and B. F. Hoselitz, introduction by F. A. Hayek, New York, New York University Press.

—— (1963[1883]) *Problems of Economics and Sociology*, ed. L. Schneider, Illinois, University of Illinois Press.

Miliband, R. (1969) *The State in Capitalist Society: The Analysis of the Western System of Power*, London, Wiedenfeld and Nicholson.

—— (1970) 'The Capitalist State – Reply to Poulantzas', *New Left Review* 59: 53–60.

Miller, D. (1977) 'Socialism and the Market', *Political Theory* no. 5 (November): 473–89

Mills, C. W. (1956) *The Power Elite*, Oxford, Oxford University Press.

Mises, L. von (1949) *Human Action: A Treatise on Economics*, London, Hodge.

—— (1958) *Theory and History*, London, Cape.

—— (1981) *Epistemological Problems of Economics*, New York, New York University Press.

—— (1990) *Money, Method and the Market Process: Essays by Ludwig von Mises*, selected by Margit von Mises, ed. R. Ebeling, Norwell, Mass., Kluwer Academic.

Mouffe, C. (1979) 'Hegemony and Ideology in Gramsci', in C. Mouffe (ed.), *Gramsci and Marxist Theory*, London, Routledge and Kegan Paul: 168–204.

Nordlinger, E. (1967) *The Working Class Tories*, London, MacGibbon and Kee.

—— (1981) *The Autonomy of the Democratic State*, Cambridge, Mass., Harvard University Press.

O'Connor, J. (1973) *The Fiscal Crisis of the State*, New York, St. Martin's Press.

O'Neill, J. (1989) 'Markets, Socialism, and Information: A Reformulation of a Marxian Objection to the Market' in Paul, E. F., Miller, F. D. Jnr., Paul, J. and Greenberg, D. (eds), *Socialism*, Oxford, Blackwell/Social Philosophy and Policy Center, Bowling Green State University.

Offe, C. (1975) 'The Theory of the Capitalist State and the Problem of Policy Formation' in Lindberg, L. et al. (eds), *Stress and Contradiction in Modern Capitalism*, Lexington, D. C. Heath: 125–44.

—— (1984) *Contradictions of the Welfare State*, London, Hutchinson.

Outhwaite, W. (1975) *Understanding Social Life: The Method Called Verstehen*, London, Allen and Unwin.

—— (1987) *New Philosophies of Social Science: Realism, Hermeneutics and Critical Theory*, Basingstoke, Macmillan.

—— (1994) *Habermas: A Critical Introduction*, Cambridge, Polity.

Pahl, R. and Winkler, J. (1974) 'The Coming Corporatism', *New Society* (October).

—— (1976) 'Corporatism in Britain', in *The Corporate State*, London, CSSP (Centre for Studies in Social Policy).

Parkin, F. (1972) *Class Inequality and Political Order*, London, Paladin.

Parsons, S. (1990) 'The Philosophical Roots of Modern Austrian Economics: Past Problems and Future Prospects', *History of Political Economy* 22(2): 295–319.

Peacock, M. (1993) 'Hayek, Realism and Spontaneous Order', *Journal for the Theory of Social Behaviour* 23(3): 249–64.

Pearce, F. (1989) *The Radical Durkheim*, London, Unwin Hyman.

Platt, J. (1996) *A History of Sociological Research Methods in America 1920–1960* Cambridge, Cambridge University Press.

Polanyi, M. (1951) *The Logic of Liberty*, London, Routledge.

Polsby, N. (1980[1963]) *Community Power and Political Theory: Problems of Evidence and Inference*, 2nd edn, New Haven, Yale University Press.
Popper, K. (1957) *The Poverty of Historicism*, London, Routledge.
—— (1959[1934]) *The Logic of Scientific Discovery*, London, Hutchinson.
—— (1963) *Conjectures and Refutations: The Growth of Scientific Knowledge*, London, Routledge.
—— (1969) 'Epistemology Without a Knowing Subject' in Gill, J. H. (ed.), *Philosophy Today* no. 2, London, Macmillan.
—— (1972) *Objective Knowledge*, Oxford, Clarendon.
Poulantzas, N. (1969) 'The Problem of the Capitalist State', *New Left Review* 58: 67–78.
—— (1973) *Political Power and Social Classes*, London, NLB.
—— (1974) *Fascism and Dictatorship*, London, NLB.
—— (1976) *The Crisis of the Dictatorships*, London, NLB.
—— (1978) *State, Power, Socialism*, London, NLB.
Prendergast, C. (1986) 'Alfred Schutz and the Austrian School of Economics', *American Journal of Sociology* 92(1): 1–26.
Quine, W. V. (1961) *From a Logical Point of View*, New York, Harper and Row.
Rickert, H. (1986[1902]) *The Limits of Concept Formation in Natural Science: A Logical Introduction to the Historical Sciences*, Cambridge, Cambridge University Press.
Ritzer, G. (ed.) (1992) *Metatheorizing: Key Issues in Sociological Theory*, no. 6, London, Sage.
Robbins, L. (1935) *An Essay on the Nature and Significance of Economic Science*, London, Macmillan.
Rose, G. (1981) *Hegel Contra Sociology*, London, Athlone.
Runciman, W. G. (1966) *Relative Deprivation and Social Justice*, London, Routledge and Kegan Paul.
Russell, B. (1912[1959]) *The Problems of Philosophy*, Oxford, Oxford University Press.
Sayer, A. (1985) *Method in Social Science: A Realist Approach*, London, Hutchinson.
—— (1989) 'Postmodernism in Question', *International Journal of Urban and Regional Research* 13 (4): 666–93.
—— (1992) *Method in Social Science: A Realist Approach*, 2nd edn, London, Routledge.
—— (1996) *Radical Political Economy*, Oxford, Blackwell.
Schattschneider, E. E. (1960) *The Semi-Sovereign People: A Realist's View of Democracy in America*, New York, Holt, Rinehart and Winston.
Schmitter, P. (1979) 'Still the Century of Corporatism?', in Lehmbruch, G. and Schmitter, P. C. (eds), *Trends Towards Corporatist Intermediation*, London, Sage: 7–52.
Schütz, A. (1943) 'The Problem of Rationality in the Social World', *Economica* X (May): 130–49.
—— (1944a) 'The Stranger: An Essay in Social Psychology', *American Journal of Sociology* 50 (5): 499–507.
—— (1944b) 'On Multiple Realities', *Philosophy and Phenomenological Research* V: 533–76.
—— (1945a) 'The Homecomer', *American Journal of Sociology*, 50 (5): 369–76.
—— (1945b) 'Some Leading Concepts of Phenomenology', *Social Research* 12 (1): 77–97.
—— (1946) 'The Well-Informed Citizen: An Essay on the Social Distribution of Knowledge', *Social Research* 13 (4): 463–78.
—— (1950) 'Felix Kaufmann: 1895–1949', *Social Research* 17 (1): 1–7.
—— (1951) 'Choosing Among Projects of Action', *Philosophy and Phenomenological Research* XII (2): 161–84.

―― (1953) 'Common-Sense and Scientific Interpretation of Human Action', *Philosophy and Phenomenological Research* XIV (1) 1–38.

―― (1957) 'Equality and the Meaning Structure of the Social World', in Bryson, L., Faust, C. H. and Finkelstein, L. (eds), *Aspects of Human Equality*, New York, Harper.

―― (1958) 'Some Equivocations on the Notion of Responsibility', in Hook, S. (ed.), *Determinism and Freedom*, New York, New York University Press.

―― (1959) 'Husserl's Importance for the Social Sciences', in Breda, H. L. van, *Husserl: 1859–1959*, *Phaenomenologica* vol. IV, The Hague, Martinus Nijhoff (and in Schütz, A., *Collected Papers I: Studies in Phenomenological Philosophy*, ed. M. Natanson, The Hague, Martinus Nijhoff: 140–9.

―― (1964[1957]) 'The Problem of Transcendental Intersubjectivity in Husserl', in Schütz, A. *Collected Papers II: Studies in Social Theory*, ed. Roderon, A., The Hague, Martinus Nijhoff: 51–84 (translation of 'Le Problème de l'Intersubjectivité Transcendentale crez Husserl', in *Husserl: Cahiers de Royaumont, Philosophe no. 3*, Paris, Editions de Minuit, 1959).

―― (1967[1932]) *The Phenomenology of the Social World*, Evanston, Ill., Northwestern University Press (a translation of *Der sinnhafte Aufbau der sozialen Welt*, Vienna, Springer).

Schütz, A. and Luckmann, T. (1973) *The Structures of the Lifeworld: vol. I*, trans. Zaner, R. M. and Engelhardt, H .T. Jnr., Evanston, Ill., Northwestern University Press.

―― (1989) *The Structures of the Lifeworld: vol. II*, trans. Zaner, R. M. and Parent, D. J., Evanston, Ill., Northwestern University Press.

Skinner, Q. (1969) 'Meaning and Understanding in the History of Ideas', *History and Theory* 8: 3–53.

Skocpol, T. (1979) *States and Social Revolutions: A Comparative Analysis of France, Russia and China*, Cambridge, Cambridge University Press.

―― (1985) 'Bringing the State Back In: Strategies of Analysis in Current Research', Evans, P., Rueschemeyer, D. and Skocpol, T. (eds), in *Bringing The State Back In*, Cambridge, Cambridge University Press: 3–37.

Smelser, N. J. (1962) *Theory of Collective Behaviour*, London, Routledge.

Smith, A. (1812[1759]) *The Theory of Moral Sentiments, or, an Essay Towards the Analysis of the Principles by Which Men Naturally Judge Concerning the Conduct and Character, First of Their Neighbours and Then of Themselves*, London, Cadell.

―― (1950[1776]) *An Inquiry into the Nature and Causes of the Wealth of Nations* ed. E. Cannan, London, Methuen.

Smith, M. J. (1998a) *Ecologism: Towards Ecological Citizenship*, Buckingham, Open University Press.

―― (1998b) *Social Science in Question: Towards a Postdisciplinary Framework*, London: Sage.

―― (2000a) *Culture: Reinventing the Social Sciences*, Buckingham: Open University Press.

―― (2000b) *Situating Hayek: Phenomenology and the Neo-Liberal Project*, Routledge Studies in Social and Political Thought 18, London, Routledge.

―― (2001a) *Political Discourses: Rethinking Ideologies and Political Theory*, forthcoming.

―― (2001b) *Risk, Modernization and Citizenship*, Buckingham, Open University Press.

―― (2002) *Governance: State, Economy and Culture*, New State Theory vol. II., forthcoming.

Stonier, A. and Bode, K. (1937) 'A New Approach to the Methodology of the Social Sciences', *Economica* IV (Nov) 406–24.
Taylor, C. (1967) 'Neutrality and Political Science', in Laslett, P. and Runciman, W. G. (eds), *Politics, Philosophy and Society*, Oxford, Blackwell: 25–57.
Taylor, S. (1982) *Durkheim and the Study of Suicide*, London, Macmillan.
Teubner, G. (1985a) 'Introduction to Autopoietic Law', in Teubner, G. (ed.), *Autopoietic Law: A New Approach to Law and Society*, Berlin, De Gruyter: 1–11.
—— (1985b) 'Evolution of Autopoietic Law', in Teubner, G. (ed.), *Autopoietic Law: A New Approach to Law and Society*, Berlin, De Gruyter: 217–41.
—— (1987a) 'The Transformation of Law in the Welfare State', in Teubner, G. (ed.), *Dilemmas of Law in the Welfare State*, Berlin, De Gruyter: 1–10.
—— (1987b) 'After Legal Instrumentalism: Strategic Models of Post-Regulatory Law', in Teubner, G. (ed.), *Dilemmas of Law in the Welfare State*, Berlin, De Gruyter: 301–25.
Thomason, B. (1982) *Making Sense of Reification: Alfred Schütz and Constructionist Theory*, London, Macmillan.
Tocqueville, A. de (1968[1835–40]) *Democracy in America*, ed. J. P. Mayer and M. Lerner, London, Fontana.
Wagner, H. (1963) 'The Displacement of Scope', *American Journal of Sociology* LXIX: 571–84.
—— (1983) *Alfred Schütz: An Intellectual Biography*, Chicago, University of Chicago Press.
Walzer, M. (1983) *Spheres of Justice*, New York, Basic Books.
Whitt, J. A. (1979) 'Towards a Class-Dialectical Model of Power: An Empirical Assessment of Three Competing Models of Political Power', *American Sociological Review* 44: 81–100.
—— (1982) *Urban Elites and Mass Transportation*, Englewood Cliffs, N. J., Princeton University Press.
Wickham, G. (1984) 'Power and Power Analysis: Beyond Foucault?', *Economy and Society* 12 (4): 468–90.
Willer, D. (1967) *Scientific Sociology: Theory and Method*, Englewood Cliffs, N. J., Princeton University Press.
Winch, D. (1996a) *Riches and Poverty: An Intellectual History of Political Economy in Britain 1750–1834*, Cambridge: Cambridge University Press.
—— (1996b) 'Adam Smith's Theory of Economic Development: Our Problems and His', mimeo, paper delivered to the Social and Political Thought Faculty Seminar, University of Sussex, 18 Jan.
Winch, P. (1958) *The Idea of a Social Science and its Relation to Philosophy*, London, Routledge.
Windelband, W. (1894) Geschichte und Naturwissenschaften, Strassburg, Heitz, 2nd edn: transcript of Rectoral Address at the University of Strassburg.
Wolfinger, R. (1971) 'Nondecisions and the Study of Local Politics', *American Political Science Review* 65: 1063–80.

Index

activists 60, 80, 81, 82, 173
Against Method 34
agency 21, 30, 44–7, 51, 65, 71, 210, 2232, 235; *see also* praxis
agenda formation xii, 59, 67, 79, 88, 92, 93, 106, 197, 248n4
Althusser, L. 164, 175, 177, 185, 187, 191, 210, 221
anticipated reactions 67, 68, 79; law of 67
Austria: Viennese intellectual circles 2, 11, 114, 126, 136, 139
authoritarianism 5, 68, 100, 138, 187, 196, 197, 199, 249n5; authoritarian plebiscites 59
autonomy 11, 52, 61, 86–7, 89–90, 91, 94, 95, 96, 98, 102, 105, 106, 159, 176, 187, 189, 192, 198, 199, 215, 219; and control 59–60; local 80; of reason 115; relative 159, 175, 177, 184, 189, 195, 200, 204–9, 219, 220
Avineri, S. 160, 163

Bachrach, P. 6–9, 71
Baden School 24, 25, 113
Bakhtin, M. 3
Baratz, M. 6–9, 71
behaviourism 36, 54, 55–66, 68, 81, 164, 223
belief/belief systems 3, 31, 56, 65, 70, 80–3, 84, 87, 98, 119, 126, 131, 144, 145, 149, 233
Bentley, A. 55
Benton, T. 70–1
Bergson, H. 30, 116, 117, 129

Berlin, I. 62, 86
Between Facts and Norms 73
Bhaskar, R. 18–20, 37–47, 49, 50, 55, 71, 160, 174, 191, 222, 223, 224, 225, 228, 229–30, 232, 234, 235–6, 237–9
Bismarck, Chancellor O. von 23; Bismarckianism 150, 176
Blalock, H. 63, 108, 223, 234
Blua, P. 160, 161, 164–5, 169
Blowers, A. 67–8
Blum, J, 95
Bourdieu, P. 13
Brown, V. 3
Burke, E. 120, 140, 148
Burrow, J. W. 2

Caldwell, B. 144, 226–7
Cantril, H. 79
Capital 180, 185
Capital and Class 182
capitalism 7, 11, 16, 45, 64, 90, 91, 92, 95, 96, 98, 99, 101, 104–5, 119, 137, 158–221, 235, 236, 241, 225n5, 256n9, 256n10, 257n11
Capitalist State, The 174, 178, 181, 190, 195, 200, 234
Carnap, R. 17
Cartesianism 20, 29, 120; *see also* Descartes, R.
Cassierer, E. 24
catallactics 114
catallaxy 7, 11, 52, 110–157, 165, 241, 244
causality/causation 9, 13, 15, 18, 19, 20, 21, 23–4, 38, 40, 42–48, 61–2, 63,

66, 74, 77, 84, 86, 87–8, 108, 113, 157, 160, 164, 169, 170–1, 177, 181, 191, 203, 217, 224–5, 230, 232, 234–5, 238–9, 246n5, 258n1
checks and balances 60, 61, 91, 154–5; external 56; *see also* separation of powers
choice 98, 107, 123, 124, 127, 130, 133, 136, 141, 197; Hobson's 131; moral 69, 71; rational 10, 88, 106, 111, 112, 123, 250n1
civic culture/orientation 80, 92, 96, 97, 169, 171, 173, 186, 233, 241; reorientation 100–7
civic idealism/responsibility 56, 80
civic virtue 56, 100–1, 105
civil society/institutions 215, 55, 65, 80, 170, 175, 178, 180, 183, 190, 196, 199, 205, 206, 212, 213, 214
Chomsky, N. 223
Class and Class Conflict in Industrial Society 168
Clegg, S. 55, 62, 69, 71, 223, 241
closed systems 18, 19, 39, 40, 51, 58, 61, 84, 87, 88, 108, 111, 156, 231, 236
coercion 76, 77, 80, 104, 131–3, 135, 140, 141, 144, 151, 152, 162, 169, 183, 186, 197, 200, 245
Cohen, H. 24
competition: as discovery procedure 126–30; economic 76, 101, 103, 110, 112, 119, 127, 128, 136, 152, 155, 157, 179, 193–4, 196, 201, 212, 213, 214 (*see also* market); political 60, 73–8, 82, 88, 110, 186
Comte, A. 19, 120, 148
conditions for social systems/states xii, xiii, 6, 8, 9, 11, 45, 52–3, 55, 58–61, 63, 64–5, 72–3, 75–83, 89–90, 108–9
consensus 58, 65, 77, 94, 161, 167, 169, 172, 175, 181, 184, 198, 199, 233; manipulated 68; normative 158
consent 7, 56, 57, 182, 183, 184, 189, 195, 197, 198, 200, 201, 245, 254n3, 254n5, 255n7
Constitution of Liberty, The 130, 135, 140, 146, 147, 153

contra-cultural value system 171
conventionalism xiv, 20, 30–7, 38, 39, 71
corporatism 92, 184, 192–6, 198
corpuscularian-mechanical world view 19–20, 229
cost of repression/liberalization 74, 77, 85, 91, 92
Crenson, M. 67–8
Crisis of the Dictatorships, The 185
Critique of Pure Reason 21, 28
Crosland, A. 133, 134
cultural values 6, 24, 26, 171, 172–3
culturology: *see* political culture

Dahl, R. 3, 7, 9, 10, 11, 14, 22, 52, 54–109, 138, 157, 158, 165, 186, 223–233, 240, 241, 244; conditions of democracy 58–9
Dahrendorf, R. 87, 160, 161, 162, 168, 234
deadlock/immobilism, political 57, 85, 155
decision making xii, 55, 57, 62–9, 73, 88, 92, 96, 97, 99, 104, 105, 108, 135–8, 142, 149, 157, 188, 198, 205–6, 218, 245, 248n4, 249n7; in New Haven 64; non-decision making 68
democracy 4, 7, 64–5, 84, 88–90, 92, 99, 102–7, 130–41, 144, 147, 152, 155, 186, 207, 224; conditions of 58–9; Madisonian 55–8, 60; parliamentary 149, 194; participatory 75, 85, 91, 93, 94; pluralist 93, 223–4; populist 55, 57–8; polyarchic: *see* polyarchy; *see also* checks and balances, populism, voting
Democracy and its Critics 106
Democracy in America 64, 77, 91
Derrida, J. 3
Descartes, R. 29, 145
Development of Hermeneutics, The 28
Dewey, J. 30
Der sinnhafte Aufbau der sozialen Welt: *see The Phenomenology of the Social World*
dictatorship 61; military 91, 186
Dilemmas of Pluralist Democracy, The 87, 94
Dilthey, W. 24, 27–8, 115–16

Index

Dunleavy, P. 54, 73
Durkheim, E. 89, 167, 223

Easton, D. 55, 61
Eckstein, H. 82
Ecologism: Towards Ecological Citizenship xiii
Economica 130
education 64, 65, 72, 77, 78, 80, 89, 102, 103, 122, 133, 134, 212; literacy 77
egalitarianism 55, 61, 65, 101, 133, 134, 171
Einstein, A. 33
elections 56, 57, 58–9, 73, 82, 85, 88, 108, 155, 169, 171, 186, 199; *see also* voting
elites 75, 147, 172, 178; elite politics 64; rule by: *see* oligarchy
empiricism xiv, 14–20, 21, 28, 30–1, 38–40, 51, 53, 55–66, 72, 80, 108, 113, 158, 169, 170, 171; *see also* realism
epistemic fallacy 39, 41, 229
equality 77, 78–9, 83, 92, 93, 94–5, 96–9, 100–7, 134, 135, 137, 142, 186
essences 23, 43, 66, 240
exchange: *see* market
Exchange and Power in Social Life 164
Explanation and Social Theory 236

fact/value distinction 5, 85
falsificationism (hypothetico-deductive method) 16, 33, 35–7, 226
Fascism and Dictatorship 185
Fatal Conceit, The 128
Feyerabend, P. 34–5, 36, 71, 239
Fine, B. 179–80, 191, 211
Foucault, M. 3, 158, 160, 202, 208, 239
freedoms 74; of association 74, 98; economic 150; of expression 74, 98; to vote 74, 131; *see also* liberty
Friedrich, C. J. 67
From a Logical Point of View 31
Fromm, E. 132
Future of Socialism, The 133

Gaventa, J. 69–70

Gellner, E. 35
general law 15, 16, 23, 25, 26, 84
German Historical School 23, 24
Gestalt-switch: *see* paradigm shift
Giddens, A. 45–6, 232
Gilroy, P. 223
good polity xii, 5–6
Government, The Sphere and Duty of 150
Gramsci, A. 48, 175, 176, 178, 183–4, 186, 187, 189–90, 195, 196, 198, 200, 209, 210, 216, 220, 221

Habermas, J. 72–3
Hacking, I. 16, 17, 18, 31, 34, 239
Hall, J. 56
Hall, S. 159, 174, 184, 196–8
Ham, C. 69
Harré, R. 223, 224, 240
Harris, L. 179–80, 191, 211
Hayek, F. 2, 3, 7, 9, 10–11, 14, 22, 52, 62, 90, 110–57, 158, 165, 204, 205, 210, 223, 225–33, 240, 241, 244
Heidelberg School: *see* Baden School
hegemony 73, 74, 75, 76, 77, 78–9, 80, 89, 107, 108, 171, 173, 178, 183, 184, 186–90, 194, 195, 196–9, 200–2, 209, 212, 215, 216–20, 221
Hegemony and Socialist Strategy 185, 190
Held, D. 89
Hempel, C. 16
hermeneutics 24, 27–8, 116, 227, 228, 230, 239; hermeneutic circle 28
hierarchies 61, 77, 91, 96, 153, 164, 172, 211
Hildebrand, B. 23
Hirst, P. 159, 174
historical inevitability 16
historicism 23, 26, 118
History of Sociological Research Methods in America 1920–1960, A 2
Hobbes, T. 55, 61, 149
Human Action 115
Hume, D. 15, 20, 21, 55, 61, 62, 66, 169, 223, 224
Hunter, F. 64
Husserl, E. 28–9, 30, 110, 116, 117
hypothetico-deductive method: *see* falsificationism

idealism xiv, 11, 14, 18, 20–22, 37–9, 40, 42–51, 52, 63, 72, 80, 83–4, 87, 93, 108, 113, 130, 158, 161–73, 203, 217, 218, 220, 224, 228, 233, 236, 240; transcendental 37, 38, 63, 72, 83, 84, 88, 157, 225, 229, 230, 238
ideal type 27, 30, 95, 108, 116, 124–5, 142, 167, 225
idiographic thought 25, 26, 84, 87
individualism 10, 69, 71, 101, 106, 120, 229; true and false 137; *see also* methodological individualism
interests 57, 59, 60, 62, 63–4, 66, 67, 68, 69–71, 74, 83, 91, 92, 93, 97, 100, 101–2, 105, 106–8, 141, 161, 168–9, 171, 172, 176, 184, 186, 188–90, 192, 194, 198, 202, 203, 219; of capital and workers 16, 177, 186, 195, 201, 202; common 175, 186, 202, 218; interest groups 55, 72, 89, 93, 168; national 182, 186, 202; rational self-interest 76, 106; self-interest 118, 129, 148, 170
international environment 80, 89, 199, 205, 211, 213, 214; law 154
intersubjectivity: *see* subjectivity
intransitive dimension/domain: *see* transitive dimension
Introduction to the Human Sciences 27
intelligibility determinism 38, 42, 51, 63, 75, 77, 80, 84, 108, 157, 171, 181, 225, 229, 238
Isaac, J. 15, 48, 49, 50, 62, 223–4, 239

James, W. 30
Jefferson, T. 103
Jessop, B. (R. W.) 7, 9, 11, 14, 52, 158–221, 223, 233–6, 241, 242, 244

Kant, I. 20–21, 24, 28, 29, 50, 66, 150, 224
Kantianism/neo-Kantianism 20–2, 59, 66, 73, 106, 110, 115, 140, 150, 229
Kapitalistate 200
Kaufmann, F. 126
Keat, R. 15, 16, 18, 30, 37, 174, 191, 223, 229, 234

Keynesianism 7, 148, 192, 196, 198, 209, 210, 212
Knies, K. 23
Krueger, M. C. 119
Kuhn, T. 4, 31–5, 36, 37, 39, 71, 222

labour 101, 103–4, 135–6, 152, 166, 199, 200, 219, 235; and capital 47, 181, 183, 194, 195; child 57; division of 60, 133, 145, 155, 176, 186, 199, 211, 213, 214; theory of value 159
Laclau, E. 158, 159, 160, 174, 178, 184, 185, 189–90, 194, 195, 196–7, 209, 216, 217, 221, 233
Lakatos, I. 35–7
law 64, 100, 104, 128, 132, 138, 139, 140, 149, 151, 155, 156, 197, 204, 207, 217; equality before 134, 137; rule of 117, 119, 141–7, 148, 152–3, 154
Law, Legislation and Liberty 118, 120, 128, 140, 144, 145–6, 147, 153
Lawson, T. 11, 116, 223, 227–8, 229, 230–3, 237–8
Layder, D. 71
legislature 56, 60, 85, 107, 150, 154–6, 187, 194; *see also* parliaments
Lemert, C. 1
liberalism 4, 17, 55–7, 69, 77, 94, 95, 101, 110, 111, 117–18, 120, 125, 126, 133–4, 137–8, 139, 139–44, 147–50, 178, 186, 207, 224, 241; neo-liberalism 7, 10, 110, 133, 140, 148, 192, 196, 197, 199, 242, 243, 244
libertarianism 150, 151
liberty 36, 86, 89, 95, 106, 107, 118, 120, 125, 130–41, 142, 144, 146, 147, 148–9, 152; civil 73, 75; individual 117, 141; positive and negative 86, 148; as power 131; *see also* freedom
Limits of Natural Scientific Concept Formation in Natural Science, The 25
Lindblom, C. 92–3, 97
Lipietz, A. 160, 210, 212, 235, 236
Lippmann, W. 140
literacy 77
Locke, J. 21, 55, 56, 104, 120, 148

Logic of Liberty, The 143
Logic of Scientific Discovery, The 226
Luhmann, N. 158, 160, 203, 204, 206–7, 216, 219, 221, 233, 236
Lukes, S. 62, 67–71

McCarthy, Senator J. 65
Mackenzie, F. 145
Machlup, F. 116, 126–7, 140
Madison, J. 55, 56, 57–9, 103; *see also* democracy, Madisonian
majoritarianism 57, 94, 137
Manicas, P. 15, 48, 239
Marburg School 24, 113
market/exchange relations 11, 52, 76, 79, 91, 92, 97, 98, 100, 101–5, 110–18, 119–25, 126–30, 132, 135–6, 143, 145–8, 150–3, 155, 161–73, 179, 182, 196, 198–9, 210, 214, 232, 241; global 215
Marx, K. 52, 160, 163, 168, 176, 180, 185, 191, 211, 218, 219, 223
Marxism 7, 16, 52, 64, 70, 90, 101, 158, 159, 160, 163, 167, 173, 174–5, 176–9, 183–5, 189, 190–1, 210, 216, 219, 235; neo-Marxism 7, 11, 52, 158–221, 224, 233, 235, 240, 244
mass media 65, 72, 73, 80
Masterman, M. 34
Menger, C. 23–4, 27, 113, 140
Merriam, C. E. 119
metatheory 1–12, 14, 25, 50–3, 108, 222–45; first/second/third order 4
Methodenstreit 23, 24
methodological individualism 24, 45, 55, 62, 68, 69, 106
methodological nominalism 66
methodological pluralism 35
Miliband, R. 178
Mill, J. S. 120, 148
Miller, D. 100
Mises, L. von 112–16, 117, 126, 140, 145, 226, 233
Mondragon Co-operative Movement 99, 100
Montesquieu, C. de S. 55
Mont Pèlerin Society 120, 139, 140
Morgenstern, O. 116

Mouffe, C. 158, 185, 189–90, 197, 209, 216, 217, 221, 233
Mumford, L. 145

National Experience, The 97
Natorp, P. 24
naturalism/anti-nautralism 15, 22, 24, 35, 42, 44, 116, 231
Neutrality in Political Science 236
Newtonian science 19, 32–3
Nicos Poulantzas: Marxist Theory and Political Strategy 200
nomothetic thought 25, 26, 84, 87, 113, 115, 173; *see also* general laws
norms/normative dimension 8, 10, 18, 30, 49, 51, 52, 54, 59, 65, 72–3, 85–92, 88, 89, 97, 101, 106, 108, 111, 112, 114, 115, 117, 133, 138, 139, 145, 148, 158, 160, 161, 162, 164, 167, 177, 181, 212, 214, 225, 231, 239, 241, 244; eight norms of polyarchy 60, 61

Offe, C. 160, 182–3, 193
O'Leary, B. 54, 73
oligarchy 58, 59, 61, 65, 73, 75, 76, 82, 97; iron rule of 90
open systems 20, 39, 40, 43, 49, 50, 118, 225, 231, 232, 234, 236, 238
Outhwaite, W. 29, 49, 53, 73
ownership 77, 92, 96, 99, 100, 103, 104, 105, 199

paradigm 4, 19, 36, 39, 83, 212, 229; shift 32–3, 222
parliaments 72, 76, 148, 154, 186, 197, 207; parliamentarianism 192–4, 196, 198; *see also* legislature
Parsons, S. 26, 115, 222
Parsons, T. 121, 161, 177
party system 85, 105, 108, 155, 172, 197, 212, 218
Peacock, M. 223, 227, 231–2
phenomenological reduction 29
phenomenology 11, 22, 29–30, 37, 110, 111–19, 125, 126, 130–41, 149, 156–7, 165
Phenomenology of the Social World, The 29, 116

Planned Society 145
Platt, J. 2
pluralism 7, 10, 11, 36, 51, 55, 61, 62–3, 64, 66–8, 71, 178, 224; methodological pluralism 35; neo-pluralism 73, 240–1, 244
Polanyi, M. 143
political culture 82–3, 89, 90, 103170, 171–3, 233; culturology 165
political science 6, 61, 62, 66, 83, 106, 148, 223; in 1950s and 1960s 51, 61, 62; *Neutrality in Political Science* 236
Political Order of a Free People, The 147
Politics and Philosophy of Economics, The 225
Politics, Economics and Welfare 93
Polsby, N. 62, 64, 66, 68, 69
polyarchy 10, 72–3, 186, 223, 224, 225, 241, 244; polyarchic civility 3, 7, 54–109, 165; polyarchic democracy 56, 58, 59, 75, 79, 80, 82, 85, 89, 90, 107, 109, 178; eight norms of 60, 61
Polyarchy: Participation and Opposition 73, 83, 91
Popper, K. 16–17, 33–7, 49, 64, 126, 144, 226, 227
populism 55, 57–8, 173, 195, 196–9, 202, 233; *see also* tyranny of a majority
positivism xiv, 17, 19, 22, 33, 34, 35, 140, 227–8, 239
Possibility of Naturalism, The 235
Poulantzas, N. 158, 160, 176, 178, 179, 182, 184–91, 193, 196, 198, 201, 202, 208, 212, 221
Poverty of Historicism, The 226
power 45–6, 56, 62–3, 66–72, 87, 95, 119, 131, 137–8, 149, 156, 161–74, 176, 183, 194, 202, 207, 220, 223; bloc 183, 184, 186, 188–9, 194, 197, 198–9, 201–2, 215
Power and Marxist Theory 223
Power and Powerlessness: Quiescence and Rebellion in an Appalachian Valley 70
praxis 44, 45, 46, 88, 118; *see also* agency
Preface to Democratic Theory, A 55
Preface to Economic Democracy, A 97

Principles of Economics 113
Prison Notebooks 183
Prison Writings 196
Problems of Economics and Sociology 23

Quine, W. van O. 31

rational action 123
rational choice 10, 88, 106, 111, 112, 123, 250n1
rationalism 21, 25, 48, 110, 114, 115, 120, 125, 143, 144–5, 148, 157; false 149
Reading Capital 185, 191
Reaganomics 7
realism xiv, 11, 12, 15, 18–20, 36, 38, 39–51, 52, 53, 71, 72, 85, 86, 88, 131, 157, 159–61, 170, 174, 178, 191, 204, 211, 214–16; empirical 19, 20, 38, 44, 55–66, 72, 85, 86, 88, 157, 170, 220, 225, 228, 229–30, 237–8
Realist Theory of Science, A 18
regularity determinism 18, 42, 51, 63, 66, 108, 169, 224, 225, 229, 234
relevance: principle of 124; value 25, 26, 234
resources: 7, 119, 136, 162, 166–7, 206; cognitive 50; economic 76, 126; political 45, 60–1, 64, 67, 78, 79, 92, 94–7, 98, 102–3, 105, 108, 154
retrodiction 49–50, 230, 236
retroduction 49–50, 236
Rickert, H. 24
Ritzer, G. 3–4
Road to Serfdom, The 119
Rorty, R. 3
Roscher, W. 23
Rousseau, J.-J. 79, 101, 107, 120
Rudolf Meidner Plan 99
rule of capital 186
rule of law 117, 119, 128, 132, 134, 140, 141–7, 150–1, 152–3
rules: (non-)constitutional 60, 61–2, 109, 132, 140–1, 142, 149, 152; of conduct 111, 117, 122, 129, 135, 138, 139, 140, 144–5, 148, 151, 154, 155, 156–7, 165, 204, 241; of the game 65, 67, 75, 80; general

134, 141, 142, 143, 148, 150, 152, 152, 154, 156; of participation and competition 82, 92, 101
Runciman, W. G. 79
Russell, B. 22, 62

Sayer, A. 49, 191, 211, 214, 223
Schattschneider, E. 67
Science in a Free Society 35
Scientific Sociology 167
Schütz, A. 11, 110, 116–17, 120–7, 129–31, 134, 139–40, 142, 145, 146, 148, 149, 156, 231–2
separation of powers 56, 60, 90, 95, 153–4; *see also* checks and balances
Shils, E. 57
Skinner, Q. 2
Smith, A. 120, 148, 149, 150
sociality of politics 11, 55, 73, 91, 245
Social Science in Question xiii, 1
Social Theory as Science 174
Social Theory: The Multicultural and Classic Readings 1
societalization 7, 53, 158, 160, 203, 208, 210, 214–5, 220
society effects 3, 158, 203, 206, 208, 242, 244
sovereignty 55, 149; dispersed 156; of law 154; of parliament 154; popular 55, 57–8, 60, 94, 137–8; *see also* rule of law, rules
Sphere and Duty of Government, The 150
Spheres of Justice 107
State, Power, Socialism 187, 188, 196
structuralism 4, 175, 177, 189, 192, 235; post-structuralism 4, 159, 191, 216, 217, 233
structuration theory 45, 208
structure 20, 39–42, 43–4, 45–52, 69, 71, 161, 168, 169, 209–11, 224, 231, 236, 237, 239; and agency/action 45, 46, 51, 172; and conduct/regulation 111, 117, 118; duality of 45, 46; and emergence of states 200, 203–4, 208, 213, 215, 219–20; and experience/knowledge/meaning 38, 117, 157, 177, 227, 229, 231, 238; structural conditions for pluralism 90; structural determinism 71; language 45; of science 17, 31social/state 48, 66, 68, 79, 85, 86–7, 92, 97, 100, 101, 103, 104, 109, 147, 148, 164, 165, 166, 170–1, 176, 179, 180–2, 187–9, 195, 196, 224, 230, 244
Structure of Scientific Revolutions, The 34
Structure of Social Actions, The 121
Studies in Philosophy, Politics and Economics 130
subcultural pluralism 79–80
subjectivism 10, 112, 114, 117, 118, 125, 226, 227
subjectivity 20, 25, 28–9, 51, 111–19, 138, 142; intersubjectivity 30, 110, 116, 117, 125, 127, 132, 138, 152, 190, 231; in science 30, 31–2

Thatcherism 7, 175, 184, 192, 196, 197, 198, 199, 202, 210, 221
Theory and History 113
Theory of Moral Sentiments, The 148
There Ain't No Black in the Union Jack 223
Tocqueville, A. de 55, 64, 76, 77, 89, 91, 103, 105, 120, 138
Traditionalism, Conservatism and British Political Culture 169
transcendental 21, 24, 25, 28, 37–8, 39, 40, 50, 52, 57, 63, 72, 85, 84, 88, 110, 157, 158, 220, 224, 225, 22–33, 237–8
transcendental epoche 29
transitive dimension/domain 18, 20, 38, 39, 40, 42, 49, 50, 52, 191, 216, 229, 230, 239; objects 42, 230
trust 75, 76, 79, 81, 82, 84, 92, 129, 151, 152, 153, 170, 180
tyranny of a majority 55, 56, 57, 60, 138

ubiquity determinism 42, 51, 52, 66, 181, 224, 230
unions, trade 65, 74, 89, 103, 171, 172, 215
Un-Politics of Air Pollution, The 67
Urry, J. 15, 16, 18, 30, 37, 174, 191, 223, 229, 234

voluntarism 55, 71, 101, 195

voting 57, 58–9, 60, 61, 64, 88, 102, 172–3, 234; blocks 85, 94; deferential/class deviant 165, 169–71, 172; equality 92, 93, 104, 105; *see also* elections

Yugoslavia 97, 100
Walter Lippmann Colloquium 140
Walzer, M. 107
Watson, J. N. 62
Wealth of Nations, An Inquiry into the Nature and Causes of 148
Weber, M. 26–7, 30, 116, 158, 161, 167, 168, 205, 224, 234
welfare state/social welfare 23, 75, 78, 96, 102, 107, 133, 178, 183, 186, 192, 196, 198, 199, 205, 207. 208, 209, 212, 217
Werturteilstreit 23, 25, 27
Whitt, J. A. 69–70
Who Governs? 64, 65
Willer, D. 158, 160, 161, 167–8, 190
Winch, D. 2, 148
Windelband, W. 24
Wolfinger, R. 64, 68
Wundt, W. 28